ELECTORAL BEHAVIOR IN
UNREFORMED ENGLAND

Electoral Behavior in Unreformed England

PLUMPERS, SPLITTERS, AND STRAIGHTS

John A. Phillips

Princeton University Press
Princeton, New Jersey

Copyright © 1982 by Princeton University Press
Published by Princeton University Press, 41 William Street,
Princeton, New Jersey
In the United Kingdom: Princeton University Press, Guildford, Surrey

All Rights Reserved
Library of Congress Cataloging in Publication Data will be
found on the last printed page of this book

Publication of this book has been aided by a grant from the Paul Mellon
Fund of Princeton University Press

This book has been composed in Linotron Baskerville
Clothbound editions of Princeton University Press books
are printed on acid-free paper, and binding materials are
chosen for strength and durability

Printed in the United States of America by Princeton
University Press, Princeton, New Jersey

For Bill who said it shouldn't be done,
And Don who said it should.
For Alex who said it couldn't be done,
And Roy who said it could.

But most of all for Jennifer, whose Daddy lived
in the palace.

CONTENTS

TABLES, FIGURES, AND MAP

TABLES

FIGURES

MAP

PREFACE

S TUDENTS OF LATER eighteenth- and early nineteenth-
century English politics have focused much attention
on both the members of the unreformed House of Commons and the constituencies for which they sat. Recent
demonstrations of the increasing importance of the parliamentary political parties in the last two decades of the eighteenth century have forced considerable revisions in standard interpretations of politics before the Great Reform Act.
However, this improved picture of the English political
system has all but omitted the unreformed electorate. The
nature of electoral politics has been accorded only cursory
treatment, and the electorate itself has been denigrated or
ignored even though substantial numbers of voters participated in the political process at general elections after 1761.
The need for an accurate assessment of the electorate has
been recognized by J. H. Plumb and others, but the sheer
size of the electorate posed an almost insurmountable obstacle to further research. A study of several large constituencies at a single general election would strain the capabilities of traditional historical methods, and a study over
time that linked the records of individual voters for longitudinal analysis simply could not be accomplished without
major assistance from computers. By relying on sophisticated computer hardware and software, this study of electoral behavior combines available data concerning more
than 15,000 individual electors in four English boroughs
at the eight general elections between 1761 and 1802. These
voters in Norwich, Maidstone, Northampton, and Lewes
provide a nonrandom, but sufficiently representative basis
for generalizations about the most active and most important portion of the unreformed electorate contained in the
relatively large and reasonably "open" borough constitu-

encies. By conducting both cross-sectional and longitudinal analyses of behavioral patterns in these boroughs during this transitional period in English politics and society, this study addresses a series of hitherto unanswered yet fundamental questions concerning the structure of the electoral system, the nature of the electorate, the level and extent of electoral participation, the consistency of participation and partisan choice, the development of partisan behavior, and the social parameters of partisanship.

The discussion begins with a brief account of party systems and political development, a description of the constituencies to be examined, and a delineation of the hypotheses to be tested with both quantitative and traditional evidence. By focusing broadly, the second chapter clarifies several aspects of the electoral system (specifically patronage, participation, and corruption) that had a serious bearing on the development of party politics across the country. These same topics, reduced to the level of individual constituencies, are considered in the subsequent chapter, which discusses the local impact of participation and the significance of the varying opportunities for participation. After this establishment of structural reasons for expecting different levels of partisan development in the several boroughs, the traditional evidence of partisan activity in each of the towns is examined, as are the several bases for political conflict suggested by election literature produced in conjunction with these electoral contests. This close look at the four boroughs also sets the stage for an analysis of voting patterns, but such an analysis is delayed by the fifth chapter's examination of the voters. The four electorates are compared at specific elections and across time, both among themselves and within themselves, to answer questions about the nature of the electorate such as those asked by Plumb and John Brewer. In the succeeding chapter, voting patterns finally become the primary focus, as individual-level and aggregate analyses are employed to measure turnover, straight and split voting, consistent party voting, and the "floating" vote. Comparisons of voting patterns in the several boroughs allow an assessment of contextual effects as well as the varying impact of the parliamentary political parties. A comparative analysis also forms the basis for the last substantive chapter. The marked rise in partisan voting that is apparent after 1780 in some constituencies posed the need to measure the impact of socio-economic variables on partisan choices. The results of this measurement are surprising; the developing partisan alliances of the late eighteenth century seem to have been influenced less by socio-economic variations among voters than by their religious, and perhaps even patently ideological differences. Thus it seems that political cleavages in this society preceded rather than stemmed from the new economic and social cleavages brought about by industrialization.

By addressing issues such as these and by shifting the discussion of electoral politics to a more empirical base, this book is not concerned with unreformed politics so much as with late eighteenth-century society as it was reflected in one aspect of the political process, the act of voting.

■

Seldom has anyone encountered so much kindness and willing assistance while pursuing historical data. The following assessment of the behavior of thousands of Englishmen toward the end of the eighteenth century owes much to many, but one individual and two institutions stand above the rest. Any longitudinal assessment of large numbers of cases must be able to link the records for specific individuals across time and across space. Without the peerless programming skills of Roy Weaver, then of the University of London Computer Centre, and his Dunkirk spirit when programming problems seemed insurmountable, the innumerable obstacles to this goal posed by these data and the demands of historical research would have proven fatal. The nominal-record-linkage system that created the data base on which this research rests could not have been constructed without his sheer genius, and the system has proven so effective that it is currently providing the basis for a study of electoral behavior in the era of the Great Reform Act.

Next in importance are two institutions: the University of London and the University of California. The University of London Computer Centre made freely available to me one of the best computing facilities in the world, and the Institute of Historical Research of the University of London made it possible for me to take advantage of the Computer Centre as well as providing assistance of other kinds at every turn. In addition, the Regents of the University of California and the Research Committee of the Academic Senate of the University of California, Riverside provided major funding for this research. Dean David Warren and Vice-Chancellor Michael Reagan of UCR also lent critical support to this enterprise through their encouragement of the Laboratory for Historical Research, and I am particularly grateful for their generous assistance.

Of the many other individuals who contributed to this work, I would like to single out for particular thanks Professor Donald Ginter of Concordia University, Montreal. His comments on a draft of this book may have set the world's record for detail. He has prevented countless errors and has greatly improved my argument at many points, though there are remaining deficiencies that he unsuccessfully attempted to eliminate. I would also like to thank my mentors, Henry Horwitz, William O. Aydelotte and Donald McCrone of the University of Iowa, and I would like to express my appreciation to Richard Davis and Derek Hirst of Washington University, Henry Snyder of LSU, R. A. Smith of Emory University, and Van Perkins of UC Riverside. Each of these individuals has lent insights and occasioned alterations that have strengthened my work; they are not responsible, of course, for the errors that remain. My other colleagues at UCR have proven to be a constant source of stimulation and inspiration, and I am grateful for their friendship. I am also indebted to Elisabeth Sichel Tobey and to my wife, Ginny Ettinger, for their careful editorial assistance with the manuscript.

Parts of Chapter 1 appeared in the *Journal of Modern History* 52 (1980), and an earlier version of Chapter 2 was published in the *Journal of British Studies* 19 (1979). I wish to thank these journals for permission to reprint material from my articles.

I have benefited greatly from the cooperation of the staffs of the Norwich and Norfolk Record Office, the Kent Record Office, the London Guildhall Library, the Northamptonshire Record Office, the East Sussex Record Office, the Society of Genealogists, Dr. William's Library, the Friend's Library, Quality Court (Chancery Lane), the British Library, and the Public Record Offices in Chancery Lane and Portugal Street. I am grateful to Connie Young for using her artistic abilities in copying the Norwich election cartoon of 1768 and for preparing most of the tables in the book. And finally, breaking with tradition and hopefully signifying an inroad into outmoded forms of communication, I would like to thank not a hard-pressed secretary nor an equally coerced wife, but myself for typing the manuscript of this book.

Riverside, California
October 1981

ABBREVIATIONS

AHR   *American Historical Review*
APSR   *American Political Science Review*
BJPS   *British Journal of Political Science*
BIHR   *Bulletin of the Institute of Historical Research*
BL   British Library
CJ   *Journals of the House of Commons*
EHR   *English Historical Review*
ESRO   East Sussex Record Office
HMN   *Historical Methods Newsletter*
JBS   *Journal of British Studies*
JIH   *Journal of Interdisciplinary History*
JMH   *Journal of Modern History*
KRO   Kent Record Office
NNRO   Norwich and Norfolk Record Office
NRO   Northamptonshire Record Office
PRO   Public Record Office, Chancery Lane
PROP   Public Record Office, Portugal Street
TRHS   *Transactions of the Royal Historical Society*

ELECTORAL BEHAVIOR IN
UNREFORMED ENGLAND

"Pray God lend the electors more sense and the elected more honesty, or may God put an end to English parliaments or English parliaments will soon put an end to the little sense and honesty remaining among us."

JOHN UPTON to LORD ROMNEY
March 15, 1754

"In the hour of danger, freemen will decide upon public principles and determine their choice of men according to the complexion of the time."

ISAAC PRESTON, *Appeal to the Electors of Great Britain*
London, 1784

CHAPTER ONE

The Unreformed Political System

O N JULY 5, 1802, Thomas Ward arrived in Norwich's market square where the hustings had been erected for the election of two members to represent the city in parliament. On mounting the steps to the platform, Ward met the town clerk and responded to a series of questions that his name was Thomas Ward, that he lived in the parish of St. Lawrence, that he was a cordwainer by trade and a freeman of Norwich.[1] He then took the oath of loyalty to the Crown, swore another oath that he was indeed a free-man and had held his freedom for at least twelve months,

[1] The exact procedure involved in the balloting process varied from constituency to constituency and from time to time. John Vincent is unclear on the procedure followed most commonly after the Reform Act, but the general pattern before the first Reform Act in freeman boroughs is mirrored in the Norwich procedures. Other constituency types adopted balloting methods that apparently did not differ radically from the general process in Norwich. At Northumberland elections, for example, the same oaths were used, but some electors did not swear all of the relevant oaths. Specifically, the bribery oath was demanded rather infrequently, and the freeholder's oath seems to have been waived for some Nottingham voters. Various political wards within constituencies also adopted variant practices on occasion. Even the number of polling platforms remained in a state of flux. Maidstone, for example, erected a single platform at which all votes were recorded until the election of 1830. Beginning in 1830, the manuscript pollbooks reveal two polling stations, one for voters with surnames A through L and another for the remaining letters of the alphabet. At Lewes, too, one polling booth sufficed until 1830. John Vincent, *Pollbooks: How Victorians Voted*, Cambridge, 1967, pp. 3-5; *Narrative of the Contested Election*, Norwich, 1780; *An Exact List of the Burgesses and Freeholders . . . Who Polled*, Nottingham, 1774; "The Poll for Members of Parliament," manuscript pollbook, Election papers VII, Maidstone Municipal Records, KRO, Maidstone; W. B. Hills, *The Parliamentary History of Lewes*, Lewes, 1908, p. 37.

and finally affirmed that he had received no bribes of any kind in return for his votes. The clerk thereupon asked for whom he wished to vote, and Ward answered with the names of the "Blue-and-White" candidates, William Smith and John Frere.[2] Before the poll closed, 2,360 other Norwich freemen declared their choices in similar fashion for either the Blue-and-White candidates or their rivals, the Orange-and-Purples.

During the same Norwich election, Robert Starkey, gentleman, of St. Augustine parish appeared at the hustings and went through a somewhat different procedure. Starkey and 500 other Norwich electors were qualified to vote on the basis of their property holdings rather than as freemen, since Norwich held political status as both borough and "county."[3] As a county, Norwich contained this relatively small contingent of men who had not been admitted as freemen of the city, but who qualified to vote as a result of their freeholds worth forty shillings or more annually. In addition to their names, addresses, and occupations, these freeholders were questioned about the nature and location of their respective freeholds. The second oath required them to confirm their actual possession of the described property. After answering the clerk's questions and swearing the requisite oaths, Starkey cast his two votes for the Orange-and-Purple candidates, William Windham and Robert Fellowes. Of the more than 2,800 electors who turned out to vote in this Norwich election, more than 2,600 (93 percent) cast both of their votes for one of the competing slates of candidates proposed with as much political fervor as possible by the two local partisan organi-

[2] More complete descriptions of the Norwich elections of 1802 and 1761 are contained in Chapter 4. The election of 1802 is also considered by C. B. Jewson, *Jacobin City*, Glasgow, 1975, and Richard W. Davis, *Dissent in Politics, 1780-1832*, London, 1970.

[3] Fuller accounts of England's diverse franchise requirements are contained in Sir Lewis B. Namier and John Brooke, *The House of Commons, 1754-1790*, 3 vols., London, 1964, 1:2-35.

zations.[4] The remaining 200 voters either split their votes between the two slates of candidates or chose to use only one of their two votes, thus "plumping" for a single candidate. The massive amount of political propaganda issued in conjunction with the Norwich election seems to have polarized the electorate effectively.

Despite every effort by the Orange-and-Purples, Windham and his running mate were defeated by a wave of anti-Administration sentiment within the Norwich electorate, and Windham was forced into the embarrassing position of accepting a "pocket-borough" seat in St. Mawes from the Marquis of Buckingham. Thus Windham was finally delivered from the "eternal hot water" in which the strongly held political opinions of his Norwich constituents had placed him so often. Buckingham expressed some satisfaction at Windham's acquisition of a St. Mawes seat and assured Windham that unlike the "Jacobinical" Norwich voters, his new St. Mawes constituents would bind him only to the belief "that the Pilchard was the best of all possible fish." Buckingham felt that Windham's exchange of seats was a distinct improvement, since "health and money [were] both very idly employed when sacrificed to a popular election."[5] Electors in sixty-six other parliamentary boroughs across the country went to the polls in 1802, and more than 60,000 borough voters were afforded an opportunity to exercise their franchises.[6]

Four decades before, in 1761, the citizens of Norwich had greeted the first general election under the reign of the new King, George III, with much less interest. As in 1802, four men vied for Norwich's two parliamentary seats,

---

[4] A New Election Budget in Five Numbers, Norwich, 1802, and The Poll for Members of Parliament, Norwich, 1802.

[5] William Windham, The Windham Papers, ed. Lord Rosebery, 2 vols., London, 1895, 2:195. St. Mawes was a freehold borough with a total of thirty electors.

[6] John Cannon, Parliamentary Reform, 1640-1832, Cambridge, 1973, pp. 278-89; Namier and Brooke, House of Commons, vol. 1.

7

but this earlier Norwich contest was conducted in the absence of national political issues and with minimal partisan activity on behalf of either the two candidates proposed by the city's Corporation or the two challengers. The Corporation candidates, Edward Bacon, a staunch friend of the Government, and Harbord Harbord, a political independent, swept to an easy victory.[7] The voters in parliamentary boroughs in other parts of the nation were equally unenthusiastic about this general election. Altogether, voters in only forty-one other towns went to the polls during the 1761 general election, and less than 40,000 borough voters were called upon to choose their representatives to parliament.[8] Participation did not increase consistently throughout England between the general elections of 1761 and 1802, but these two elections serve a dual purpose by illustrating the dissimilarity of mid-eighteenth-century and late eighteenth-century politics and by bracketing the elections around which this study revolves. (See Figure 2.1.)

The dramatic changes in England's political system separating the nonpartisan, apolitical Norwich election of April 1761 from the heavily partisan, issue-oriented campaign of July 1802 are the focus of this look at electoral behavior before the Great Reform Act. The changes so apparent in Norwich were not felt uniformly across the island, or even uniformly among England's enfranchised borough inhabitants. Nevertheless, the political complexion of a large portion of England's borough electorate underwent substantial alterations in the later years of the eighteenth century. These alterations resulted in new modes of political behavior long before the official reform of the political system.

---

[7] Edward Bacon captured the votes of 67 percent of the Norwich electors while Harbord Harbord bested him with the support of 77 percent of the voters. Thompson and Harvey won 32 percent and 22 percent respectively. *The Poll for Members of Parliament*, Norwich, 1761.

[8] John Cannon indicated a total of forty-two English borough contests while Namier and Brooke counted forty-one English borough contests and one Welsh borough contest. Cannon, *Parliamentary Reform*, pp. 280-89; Namier and Brooke, *House of Commons*, 1:65.

UNREFORMED ELECTORAL POLITICS

Several recent accounts of English parliamentary politics in the age of the American Revolution begin by pointing to the disfavor into which the traditional "Whig" interpretation of eighteenth-century politics fell after the frontal assault mounted by Sir Lewis Namier and a number of other critics of unreformed politics who applied a new approach, "structural analysis," to the study of the Georgian political system.[9] The traditional view of party politics over the eighteenth century before the Namierite revolution was that of a tide flowing virtually unchecked from the first Whig/Tory disputes arising from the Exclusion Crisis of 1679-1680 to the party struggles of the nineteenth century.[10] The continuity of party names and the apparent similarities between the parties of the late seventeenth and late eighteenth centuries led many to assume a direct relationship and a straightforward political continuity between the two eras. The drastic revision of these traditional views has been chronicled by Sir Herbert Butterfield and is too well known to need more than adumbration.[11] The publication of the Porritts' exposé of popular politics before the first Reform Act began the revision of these earlier glowing accounts of both parliamentary party politics and the power of public opinion in the latter part of the century. Allegations of undue pressure, venality, and every other kind of corruption imaginable soon dominated discussions of unreformed political behavior. The subsequent publi-

[9] F. O'Gorman, *The Whig Party and the French Revolution*, London, 1967; F. O'Gorman, *The Rise of Party in England*, London, 1975; E. A. Smith, *Whig Principles and Party Politics*, Manchester, 1975; John Money, *Experience and Identity: Birmingham and the West Midlands, 1760-1800*, Montreal, 1977.

[10] One of the principal statements of the argument for party continuity was made as late as 1938 by Sir Keith Feiling, *The Second Tory Party*, London, 1938.

[11] Sir Herbert Butterfield, *George III and the Historians*, London, 1957, pp. 193-300. Butterfield, of course, castigated the Namierites for their attempted revision.

9

cation of the private papers of John Robinson (M.P. for Harwich, official election manager for the Government in 1780, and unofficial manager in 1784) further discredited the traditional ascriptions of coherence and meaning to popular politics under George III.[12] Before the revelations of the Robinson papers, historians had viewed the crushing defeat of Charles James Fox and the infamous Coalition in 1784 as an example of the ability of "public opinion, once aroused, [to] override the limitations of the franchise, and make even the unsatisfactory representative system . . . an organ of the nation's wishes," and hailed 1784 as the beginning of party politics in a modern context.[13] Pitt's party was hailed as a nationally based party, "if ever there was a national party."[14] However, in his detailed election reports, Robinson had considered the elections of 1780 and 1784 strictly in terms of influence and corruption. Robinson was certain of a Government victory through manipulation, coercion, and the like in 1784, and his certainty of success persuaded William Pitt to press for an early dissolution of parliament and to stage a premature election. Robinson's prediction of a Government victory at the polls in 1784 proved correct, albeit inaccurate, and if Robinson's papers were taken at face value, "nothing remotely resembling what we now understand by the term public opinion played a decisive role in the election. The results of the general election, like the results of the other elections held

[12] Edward Porritt and A. G. Porritt, *The Unreformed House of Commons*, 2 vols., Cambridge, 1909; W. T. Laprade, *The Parliamentary Papers of John Robinson, Camden Miscellany*, Third Series, 33 (1922); W. T. Laprade, "Public Opinion and the Election of 1784," *EHR* 31(1916):224-37. Two of the more interesting responses to Laprade are: J. H. Rose, "The Route of the Coalition (1784)," *The Nineteenth Century and After* 95(1924):453-54 and E. G. Hawke, "William Pitt and Some Deluded Historians," *The Nineteenth Century and After* 94(1924):531-36.

[13] C. G. Robertson, *England under the Hanoverians*, London, 1930, p. 304. The first edition of Robertson's text appeared in 1911.

[14] G. M. Trevelyan, *British History in the Nineteenth Century*, London, 1922, p. 40.

10

in that period, were due to influences of quite a different character."[15] According to the new interpretation of popular politics in unreformed England, public opinion not only failed to have a decisive effect in elections, it had no effect at all.

These dismissals of eighteenth-century voters as irrelevant and public opinion as a myth were quickly and widely acclaimed. Since Robinson's papers apparently demonstrated the insignificance of the *vox populi* and popular participation in 1780 and 1784 specifically, and in *all* unreformed elections by implication, it seemed clear to some that it would be "contrary to the evidence for any future writer to advance the theory or to offer the statement that Pitt in 1784 was the 'choice of the people' or that the 'nation' elected Pitt in preference to Fox and North."[16] Thus, well before the publication of Sir Lewis Namier's magisterial studies of the structure of politics at the accession of George III, the traditional "Whig" interpretation of the eighteenth century had fallen into disrepute. When Namier extended the attack to parliament itself, the reversal of opinion concerning eighteenth-century politics seemed complete. Namier dismissed party politics as meaningless in the parlia-

[15] Robinson correctly predicted a Pittite victory, but his reckoning of the number of seats to be won and lost by the Government was off rather badly. The accuracy of Robinson's assessment is discussed in: John Cannon, *The Fox-North Coalition*, London, 1969, p. 216; Derek Jarrett, *Britain, 1688-1815*, London, 1965, p. 393; I. R. Christie, *The End of North's Ministry*, New York, 1958, pp. 161-62, 253. The source of the estimate of 160 seats lost by the Coalitionists may have been John Aikin's 1825 account that claimed "upwards of 160 members, almost all of them friends of the Coalition ministers, were rejected." Aikin's statement was then altered slightly by John Holland Rose's account of the election. Rose contended "as many as 160 members of the Opposition were thrown out, and by a very obvious joke they were termed Fox's Martyrs." The next step was the generally accepted version of 160 seats lost by the Foxites. John Aikin, *Annals of the Reign of King George III*, London, 1825, p. 341; J. H. Rose, *William Pitt and National Revival*, London, 1911, p. 169. Actually, 163 members lost their seats, but only 96 of them were Coalitionists.

[16] C. E. Fryer, "The General Election of 1784," *History* 9(1925):223.

ment of 1761, and party all but disappeared from discussions of Georgian politics either within or outside parliament; "factions," "connections," and other descriptive (not to say pejorative) terms took the place of "party" in most discussions.[17] Party terminology did not disappear entirely from accounts of the period, though. Namier himself continued to use partisan adjectives in describing political events even when discussing the parliamentary maneuvering of the 1760s. Nevertheless, "party" as an explanation of events within parliament lost out to "influence" or "personality" while "party" in descriptions of the countryside was replaced by "corruption" and "control." Even nineteenth-century political history was affected by these dismissive allegations concerning the unreformed political system.[18]

Despite the initial success of the Namierite revolution, many historians have since argued forcibly and persuasively the danger of accepting too readily or applying too broadly the stereotypical image of the eighteenth century propounded by the Porritts, Namier, and others. Research into electoral and parliamentary politics well before 1761 has effectively discounted "Namierite" interpretations of the early eighteenth century such as that proposed by Robert Walcott. Discussions of later eighteenth-century politics have also challenged the Namierite image of "interest" politics devoid of meaningful political issues, but less consensus has emerged in opinions concerning the period after the accession of George III.[19] Arguments asserting there was

[17] A very recent example is John Owen, *The Eighteenth Century*, New York, 1974, pp. 94-122. Also see: Lewis Namier, *The Structure of Politics at the Accession of George III*, London, 1929 (2nd ed., 1957); Lewis Namier, *England in the Age of the American Revolution*, London, 1930.

[18] Norman Gash, *Politics in the Age of Peel*, London, 1953; H. J. Hanham ed., *Dod's Electoral Facts*, Brighton, 1972, p. xxiii; W. L. Burn, "Electoral Corruption in the Nineteenth Century," *Parliamentary Affairs* 4(1951):442. Burn felt that "bribery was probably at its height in the middle of the nineteenth century."

[19] Robert Walcott, *English Politics in the Early Eighteenth Century*, Cambridge, Mass., 1956; J. H. Plumb, "The Growth of the Electorate in Eng-

"no party organization outside Parliament, nor ever had been, nor could be until after 1832" are about as common as contradictory assertions that "one could not begin to make sense of the 1784 election if one ignored politics and party."[20] A recent portrayal of the 1784 election even defied Fryer's 1924 dictum against discussions of the election as "the choice of the people." Paul Kelley referred to the 1784 election as "a radical solution to the constitutional debate between Pitt and Fox" and an "appeal to the people," thus reiterating Belsham's contemporary but often discounted comment that "upon no occasion whatever was the sense of the people at large more clearly, strongly, and unequivocally ascertained."[21] Predictably, a position squarely in the middle has emerged as well. Rather than interpreting Pitt's victory solely as the result of Robinson's skillful manipulation of "the old engines of influence and patronage" or as "a triumph of public opinion," John Brooke maintains the general election of 1784 was "both of these things at the same time."[22]

---

land from 1600 to 1715," *Past and Present* 45(1969):90-116; W. A. Speck and W. A. Gray, "Computer Analysis of Pollbooks: An Initial Report," *BIHR* 43(1970):105-12; W. A. Speck et al., "Computer Analysis of Pollbooks: A Further Report," *BIHR* 48(1975):64-90; Richard W. Davis, *Political Change and Continuity*, Newton Abbot, 1972, pp. 43-58; Donald Ginter, *Whig Organization in the General Election of 1790*, Berkeley, 1967, pp. xi-lvi; Richard W. Davis, "Deference and Aristocracy in the Time of the Great Reform Act," *AHR* 81(1976):532-39.

[20] Ivor Bulmer-Thomas, *The Growth of the British Party System*, 2 vols., London, 1965, 1:28; Cannon, *Fox-North Coalition*, pp. 227, 240.

[21] Paul Kelley, "Radicalism and Public Opinion in the General Election of 1784," *BIHR* 45(1972):88; M. D. George, "Fox's Martyrs: The General Election of 1784," *TRHS*, 4th Ser. 21(1939):147; William Belsham, *Memoirs of the Reign of George III*, London, 1805, 3:351. Also see N. C. Phillips, *Yorkshire and English National Politics*, Christchurch, 1961.

[22] Namier and Brooke, *House of Commons*, 1:130. While historians continue to disagree over the nature of later eighteenth-century politics, the Namierite revision has taken firmer hold and created greater consensus among some social scientists. Austin Ranney has rejected the use of the term "party" before 1832. Joseph LaPalombara and Ivor Bulmer-Thomas also have dismissed "party" from their accounts of eighteenth-century

Certainly parliament contained political alliances that might be called parties during the last decades of the eighteenth century. The papers of William Adam, M.P. for Wigton and "on the whole the most important man of business within the Portland and Foxite Oppositions," demonstrate the existence of an "opposition electoral organization [that] showed signs of developing an apparatus like that of a modern political party."[23] From the late 1770s, the labels "Tory" and "Whig" took on renewed meaning in parliament, and, it seems, in the nation as a whole. The alleged transformation of the parliamentary alliances from "personal parties" during the 1770s into more clearly and ideologically defined entities in the 1780s, however, is less important in this discussion than the simple fact of the existence of "party" in the political system.[24] Whatever their parliamentary solidarity and effectiveness, these parties did not limit their activities to parliament. In expanding their interests into the country and often reinforcing or altering local political allegiances, the machinations of Adam and

politics. Austin Ranney, "The Concept of Party," in *Political Research and Political Theory*, ed. Oliver Garceau, Cambridge, 1968, pp. 145-46; Joseph LaPalombara and M. Weiner, eds., *Political Parties and Political Development*, Princeton, 1966, p. 8; Ivor Bulmer-Thomas, *Growth of the British Party System*, London, 1965, 1:28.

[23] Ginter, *Whig Organization*, pp. xxii-xxiv. Much corroborative evidence exists. For example, Earl Temple felt that the Westminster election of 1784 was "indeed a cruel blow upon party." *Royal Commission on Historical Manuscripts Reports*, Rutland MSS., 4 vols., London, 1905, 3:84-85. For other accounts, see E. A. Smith, "The Election Agent in English Politics, 1734-1782," *EHR* 84(1969):12-35, and O'Gorman, *The Whig Party*, p. 233.

[24] Namier and Brooke, *House of Commons*. Hoffman's recent study argued that "Rockingham had never advanced a single step toward promoting any sort of national organization of electors to support Whig candidates." Yet, Butterfield argued that the Rockinghamites were a party, and O'Gorman's discussion of the rise of party concurs. Nevertheless, using Ginter's terminology, it is clear that the Rockinghamites did not constitute a "party system." R.J.S. Hoffman, *The Marquis*, New York, 1973, p. 369; Herbert Butterfield, "George III and the Constitution," *History* 43(1958):28-33; O'Gorman, *Rise of Party*, pp. 187-218, 231-57, 471-77.

the Portland Whigs helped stimulate the development of a "party system" during the 1780s in which political parties competed "not only among themselves but also for the attention and support of the political nation as a whole."[25] The Adam papers alone (and Adam was by no means the only political manager for the Whigs) indicate eighty-three constituencies in which some centrally connected party activity occurred in the course of the 1790 campaign.[26] Individual constituencies were the target of an impressive display of parliamentary political activity even in the previous general election. Aided by greatly improved parliamentary reporting in the press, and the increasing circulation of both London and local newspapers, "the election of 1784 took place amid one of the most extensive publicity campaigns of the eighteenth century." This campaign which decided the fate of the new Pitt ministry differed from its predecessors "in the nature and extent of the publicity that accompanied and preceded it."[27] Election literature of all kinds raised general political issues reminiscent of the bitter disputes during the "rage of party" in the animated elections of Queen Anne's reign. This is not to argue that political parties invariably determined, or even influenced every parliamentary election, far from it. Many elections in the last decades of the eighteenth century were completely unaffected by political parties, parliamentary debates, or issues in any form. Nor were developments continuous or even necessarily connected across England's 245 parliamentary constituencies as the country entered a period of turbulence engendered by events at home, and in

[25] Ginter, *Whig Organization*, p. xvii.

[26] Ibid., pp. xxxviii-xli.

[27] Dora Mae Clark, *British Opinion and the American Revolution*, New Haven, 1930, p. 7. Newspaper circulation increased from 9.5 million in 1760 to over 15 million in 1782. For other discussions of propaganda and the press, see Donald Read, *The English Provinces*, London, 1964; P.D.G. Thomas, "The Beginnings of Parliamentary Reporting in Newspapers, 1768-74," *EHR* 74(1959):623-36; George, "Fox's Martyrs," p. 138.

America, Canada, and France. Politics in these diverse constituencies were nothing if not complex and highly variable, not to say idiosyncratic (as the discussion in Chapter 4 illustrates), but such remarkable diversity did not prevent widespread, occasionally pronounced, and frequently related changes among the most numerous segments of England's large urban electorate.

An abundance of electoral propaganda, much of it of high quality, distinguished not just the election of 1784, but the elections after 1770 generally from their mid-eighteenth-century predecessors and denoted an important new aspect of popular politics.[28] Yet, neither the trappings of these elections nor the publication of mountains of propaganda are as revealing as actual political behavior. The voting patterns of the inhabitants of Norwich, Maidstone, Northampton, and Lewes at the elections held over the forty-one year period between 1761 and 1802 confirm much that later eighteenth-century political propaganda can only imply. A detailed examination of these towns over this extended period reveals the emergence of new political environments conducive to the growth of partisan behavior and points to a new political reality in many large constituencies dominated by parties (both local and national), issues, and principles. A substantial, and to a degree identifiable, portion of the electorate experienced a rapid politicization under the influence of the activities of both parliamentary and local political parties. Parties and issues were not always closely allied, and the kaleidoscope of po-

[28] According to George's catalogue of prints, a new scale emerged in the 1770s and continued to grow over succeeding decades. During the 1760s, an average of fifty-three prints were issued each year. The average reached 126 per year in the 1770s, 199 per year in the 1780s, and 202 per year in the first decade of the new century. M. D. George, *Catalogue of Personal and Political Satires*, London, 1938; M. D. George, *English Political Caricature to 1792*, Oxford, 1959, p. 178. Also see, John Brewer, *Party Ideology and Popular Politics at the Accession of George III*, Cambridge, 1976, pp. 141-56.

litical activity and popular responses changed rapidly from town to town.

Despite the complexity of these elections and the intricate and frequently confusing blend of local concerns, personal loyalties, and national issues, a broad pattern is discernible. John Money has shown "the genesis of a relationship between politics and public opinion more characteristic of nineteenth-century England than of the age of oligarchy" in Birmingham by the 1760s, but Englishmen far beyond the reaches of a single midlands town shared a growing political awareness and were affected by the increasing tensions of the last two decades of the century.[29] The profound ideological issues injected into political life by incidents such as the renewed debate over the penalties imposed on Nonconformists, the struggles caused by the American problem, and the questions raised by the French Revolution hastened the process begun by the furor in the 1760s over John Wilkes and the question of general warrants. These issues, even the vociferous Nonconformist demand for political equality, were not invariably matters of clearly defined partisan dispute; members of the parties emerging in parliament occasionally treated critical issues in a nonpartisan fashion, and often differed among themselves as well as with their ostensible leaders over matters of considerable national import. But be that as it may, reasonable agreement and important consistencies developed with sufficient frequency to help lend definition to political disputes at all levels. The all-important issue of war or peace, for example, divided the parliamentary parties in much the same fashion at both crisis points in the later years of the century. C. J. Fox and the "Whigs" opposed the war against France in the early 1790s just as they had opposed the war against America fifteen years earlier. A firm conviction against war of any description, such as some voters seemed

[29] Money, *Experience and Identity, passim*; John Money, "Taverns, Coffee Houses, and Clubs," *Historical Journal* 14(1971):15-47.

quick to adopt for economic reasons if nothing else, left them almost no choice but support for anti-Administration (Whig) candidates in both instances. Complete agreement never existed, of course, at either parliamentary or local levels, yet pro- or anti-war stances helped shape popular political behavior in Norwich and several other larger towns. Some issues failed to produce complete consensus, most notably religion, but even in the face of dissension within the ranks of the "Whig" party, Dissenters had little recourse but to support the Whigs if they wished to use their votes for the benefit of their various religious denominations.

These new considerations began a transformation of the English political nation. Neither the parties nor the major political issues of the day were invariably crucial elements in structuring the behavior of the electorate, but the parliamentary parties, local variations of the parliamentary parties, completely independent local parties, and, above all, *issues*, played an increasingly critical role in some constituencies, particularly those that contained most of the borough electorate. Given the freedom to vote without undue pressure, i.e., bribery or coercion, many English electors toward the end of the century behaved in a manner quite like the behavior of electors in other situations thought to be dominated by partisan considerations. Impressively high levels of partisan behavior at specific elections and across several elections in the years prior to 1802 measured up to the standards of postreform England. At the same time, the behavior of a growing body of electors in the 1780s and 1790s differed significantly from the behavior of electors during the 1760s and 1770s when party politics played a less prominent role in parliamentary elections. Thus the significance of the behavior of many of England's voters during the 1780s and 1790s is highlighted through comparisons of their behavior with that of electors in preceding *and* succeeding decades. And rather than repeating the twin themes of continuity and change that dominate many accounts of English politics, this examination of English voters as they encountered a new political environment focuses most heavily on change. Englishmen in Norwich, in Maidstone, and to a lesser extent in Northampton and Lewes, adopted new modes of political behavior in the years following the crises of the 1770s, and they behaved in an even more strikingly dissimilar manner following the crises of the subsequent decade.

PARTISAN BEHAVIOR

The impact of parties and issues can be measured most appropriately through popular political behavior, and specifically through voting behavior. To be sure, "ticket voting [party voting] alone does not establish the presence of a self-conscious party in the electorate which is a durable psychic phenomenon," nor is voting behavior necessarily "the single best indicator of public opinion."[30] And unquestionably, England's electoral system contained political corruption in a bewildering variety of forms both before and after the first Reform Act.[31] Just as certainly, some apparently political behavior, whether votes at elections or opinions expressed in other ways, reflected apolitical, or at best quasi-political relationships among individuals in various communities. Nevertheless, voting behavior is the best available measure of popular politics, and when considered within the context of the vagaries of politics in particular boroughs, allows a tangible measure of popular partici-

[30] Joel Silbey and S. McSeveney, *Voters, Parties, and Elections*, Lexington, Mass., 1972, p. 58; R. P. Formisano, "Deferential-Participant Politics," *APSR* 68(1974):482; Lee Benson, "An Approach to the Scientific Study of Past Public Opinion," *Public Opinion Quarterly* 31(1968):560-61; Joel Silbey, *Political Ideology and Voting Behavior in the Age of Jackson*, Englewood Cliffs, N.J., 1973, p. 6. The term "public opinion" originated during the 1760s. Read, *The Provinces*, p. 4.

[31] T. J. Nossiter, *Influence, Opinion, and Political Idioms in Reformed England*, Brighton, 1975; Michael Drake, "The Mid-Victorian Voter," *JIH* 1(1971):473-90; D. G. Wright, "A Radical Borough in Parliamentary Politics: Bradford, 1832-1841," *Northern History* 4(1969):132-66.

pation and popular political awareness. Unfortunately, the eighteenth-century electorate is not an easy group to assay, and the peculiarities of the unreformed system dictate in large part the measurement of their voting behavior.

Unlike many definitions of "partisan voting" and "partisan behavior" in other political systems, a major component of "partisan behavior" in England before reform was nothing more than politically coherent behavior at single elections, because the *two* votes accorded each elector at eighteenth-century contests vastly complicated political behavior and complicate measurements of political behavior. The vast majority of England's parliamentary constituencies, county and borough, sent two members to the House of Commons, and each voter, accordingly, had two votes to cast. The double vote meant that an elector could cast both votes for the two candidates of one party, thus casting a straight party vote, or he could split his votes and support a single candidate of each party. He also could decide to cast only one of his votes and discard the other, a practice called "plumping." If a party proposed a single candidate, plumping was necessary to cast a partisan ballot for that party, but nonpartisan considerations could easily result in single votes even when a party sponsored two candidates. Straight-party voting, splitting, and plumping were common occurrences at unreformed elections, just as they were after the passage of the Great Reform Act. The changes in the number of voters choosing to cast partisan ballots and the corresponding variations in the proportion of the electorate either splitting or casting politically unnecessary plumpers is crucial to this evaluation of electoral behavior.

"Partisan behavior" during the political struggles of this era also implied relatively consistent behavior on the part of individual electors at successive elections. Certainly issues and attitudes could and did change among the various electorates, among the leadership and membership of the national parties, and in the intentions, desires, and memberships of local parties (regardless of their level of asso-

20

ciation with the parliamentary parties), but taking national and local conditions into account, the voters in these boroughs were faced with choices that usually mandated consistent political behavior. For example, the "Blue-and-White" party in Norwich after 1780 asked voters to support a political stance invariably opposed to the Administration, whether over the war in America, the war with France, or less tangible issues like the rights of "freeborn" Englishmen. Such political consistency, also achieved by the independent party in Maidstone, should have provoked consistent voting choices from a committed electorate in these boroughs. The electorates of both Norwich and Maidstone responded appropriately.

A large "floating" vote comprised of individuals who switched parties from election to election is possible in *any* political system dominated by parties. A recent analysis of voting behavior in the reign of Queen Anne actually interpreted a large floating vote as evidence of the "participatory" nature of politics.[32] However, a large floating vote suggests coherent, rational behavior on the part of the electorate *only* if voters are assumed to be weighing the issues and deciding accordingly to vote for different parties at successive elections. If, on the other hand, issues and party positions are relatively constant, as they often were after 1761 in the four constituencies examined here, an assumption of rationality and meaningful participation on the part of the electorate leads to an expectation of straight-party voting at specific elections and consistent party choices at successive contests. Modern electors who change parties between elections are often drawn from the most apathetic and uninformed segment of the electorate, and it seems highly likely that their eighteenth-century counterparts were cast from a similar mold.[33] Splitters, unnecessary plumpers,

[32] Speck, "Computer Analysis: Initial," *passim*; Speck, "Computer Analysis: Further," *passim*.

[33] Jean Blondel, *Voters, Parties, and Leaders*, Harmondsworth, 1963, p. 72.

and inconsistent voters may have been either politically unaware, which would account for their random behavior, or subject to a greater degree of political manipulation than the electors behaving in a partisan, and consistently partisan manner. The emergence of self-consciously partisan voters within local electorates should have prompted increasingly rational political behavior, and reduced, if not eliminated, splitting, unnecessary plumping, and inconsistent voting.[34]

The proportion of the electorate consistently participating in elections also played an important role in determining the nature of electoral politics. Rates of consistent participation play a significant role in many modern elections, and an equally strong case can be made for the importance of repeated participation in late eighteenth- and early nineteenth-century elections. An electoral system containing a high proportion of experienced voters is much more susceptible to the development of partisan attachments than an environment in which each election is conducted with a preponderance of newly recruited electors.[35] Several elections in the reign of Queen Anne illustrate the change. According to W. A. Speck, an extraordinarily large "floating vote" was perhaps the most striking characteristic of Augustan elections. This high proportion of the electorate switching their support from one party to the other at successive elections argues against the development of strong partisan ties among the early eighteenth-century electorate, and it occurred at elections dominated by newly recruited voters. The Hampshire election of 1710 is a case in point. Not quite 31 percent of the 1710 Hampshire electorate participated in the previous Hampshire election of 1705. Fewer than four in ten Hampshire electors at the 1705

[34] Formisano, "Deferential-Participant Politics," p. 482.

[35] G. Di Palma, *Apathy and Participation*, New York, 1970; Michael Steed, "Participation through Western Democratic Institutions," and Dennis Kavanagh, "Political Behavior and Political Participation," in *Participation in Politics*, ed. Parry Geraint, Manchester, 1972.

contest reappeared in 1710 to cast their votes despite the relatively short interval separating the two elections.[36] Similarly, just 54 percent of the electors in Westmorland who had participated in the 1701 Westmorland general election returned to vote during the 1702 Westmorland contest; almost half of the 1701 electorate had disappeared in less than twelve months.[37] Such exaggerated electoral turnover should have been less than conducive to the development of partisan behavior, and voting patterns indicate the accuracy of this expectation. Despite the consistency of party platforms at both elections, approximately one-quarter of the Hampshire electors casting partisan votes in 1705 switched to the other party in 1710. Therefore, demonstrating electoral continuity across elections at the contests of the later eighteenth century is almost as important as the demonstration of increasing partisan continuity from election to election. Both demonstrations form integral parts of this account of the development of partisan ties in the electorate.

PUBLIC OPINION

Whether votes, partisan or nonpartisan, reflected public opinion is an issue that cannot be fully addressed given the scarcity of opinion data from populations so far removed in time. Fortunately, scores of petitions to the Crown between 1768 and 1790 provoked by several of the fundamental political issues beginning with "Wilkes and Liberty" ostensibly reveal the "opinions" of thousands of Englishmen, and the pollbooks from parliamentary elections furnish accounts of the political stances of thousands of elec-

[36] Speck, "Computer Analysis; Initial," p. 107. A clearer discussion of the issue is provided by Richard W. Davis, "The Whigs and the Idea of Electoral Deference," *Durham University Journal* 47(1974):79-91.

[37] Robert Hopkinson, "Elections in Cumberland and Westmorland, 1695-1723," Ph.D. diss., University of Newcastle-upon-Tyne, 1973, pp. 252-53.

tors in many boroughs and a few counties.[38] Disputes over the meaning of these petitions and the significance of the *vox populi* split the ranks of contemporary observers, much as disagreements over the meaning of votes cast at elections divide more recent commentators on the nature of unreformed electoral politics. Lord North expressed the perhaps suspiciously self-serving opinion that the nation was not inflamed over the Wilkes issue in 1769. He contended "the drunken and ignorant have been made dupes to the crafty and factious, signing papers that they have never

[38] The "law of available data" determined the two boroughs used to illustrate the 1768 petitioning, and frequently dictated the boroughs to be used in the other analyses. The behavior of Liverpool electors, for example, could not be examined for 1768 because the pollbook of 1768 has disappeared and the election of 1774 went uncontested. Exeter suffered from the same two problems, and Worcester reversed them. Worcester remained uncontested in 1768 and the pollbook for the 1774 contest has not survived. Therefore, only Coventry and Northumberland could be tested for the electoral choices of the petitioners in 1768. Similarly, the petitions examined in detail in Tables 1.1 and 1.2 were selected "randomly" in an informal sense, on the basis of available electoral and petition data. Frequently, a petition was presented with only the signatures of the officers of the corporation or the leading men of the county. Even populous borough constituencies like Norwich that occasionally submitted petitions signed by massive numbers of citizens (e.g., Norwich parliamentary petition, 1778) could fall into this practice. The two Norwich petitions of 1782 against Fox and the Coalition were signed by Norwich's officeholders alone. Added to the lack of signatures on occasion, the failure of petitions and contested elections to coincide as well as the nonsurvival of pollbooks reduced the number of constituencies that could be examined. The petitions to the Crown used in this analysis are included in the Home Office Papers, 55, Public Record Office, London. Most were contained in H.O. 55, 1/1 through 16/4, with a few others scattered among the remaining H.O. 55 petitions concerning the King's health. The pollbooks cited, with the exception of the manuscript pollbooks for Maidstone, are from the collections at the Institute of Historical Research, University of London, and the Guildhall Library, London. I wish to thank Mr. Geoffrey Langley of the Bristol Central Library for supplying a copy of the Bristol pollbook of 1774. The number of petitions to the Crown over each of these issues is uncertain. Some of the petitions submitted may not have survived.

read and determining questions that they did not know."[39] Horace Walpole, on the other hand, though unsure of the legitimacy of the method by which many addresses were procured, took the petitions quite seriously, contending that even addresses expressing nothing more than loyalty to the Crown at critical periods did as much harm as good since "they inflamed the spirit of contest and party" in the constituencies.[40] Dr. Johnson disparaged the petitioning process, noting that after the presentation of a petition at a public meeting, "those who are sober enough to write add their names and the rest would sign if they could. Of the petition nothing is remembered except that he [the signer] is sure that it is against the government."[41] Dr. Johnson's assessment is a popular one among historians intent on denigrating popular political behavior, and it does reflect the continuing court/country division that affected national political allegiances, but it portrayed at least one aspect of the petitioning process inaccurately; petitioning movements rarely conveyed an overwhelming consensus against the government. Petitions backing the Administration usually offset those condemning it, and in the most frenetic petitioning of the period prompted by C. J. Fox and the infamous Coalition, the overwhelming preponderance of the petitions expressed their absolute support of the Crown and the new Administration.[42]

A test of the general view expressed by Johnson, North,

[39] W. Cobbett, ed., *Parliamentary History of England*, 36 vols., London, 1806-1820, 16:759.

[40] Horace Walpole, *Correspondence*, ed. W. S. Lewis, 39 vols., New Haven, 1967, 2:24; letter to Sir Horace Mann, October 1775, and 2:77-87; Horace Walpole, *Last Journals*, ed. A. F. Steuart, 2 vols., London, 1910, 2:475.

[41] E. C. Black, *The Association*, Cambridge, Mass., 1963; Clark, *British Opinion*, pp. 87-88, 133, 164 for more recent doubts concerning the validity of "opinions" expressed by petitions.

[42] The preponderance of the petitions concerning Wilkes and general warrants attacked the Government, but the petitions prompted by the American crisis were mixed, and those stemming from the King's ouster of the Fox-North Coalition were uniformly favorable to the government.

and others, that petitions were full of sound and fury, signifying nothing, yields interesting results. The relationship between the "opinions" of the petitioners and their behavior at parliamentary elections provides an illuminating perspective on the question of public opinion and voting behavior. Several later eighteenth-century petitions and elections permit rare glimpses of individual political behavior and display a level of consistency, coherence, and rationality that is both striking and illuminating.

The Coventry by-election of 1768 illustrates the remarkably strong relationship connecting opinions expressed through petitions and opinions demonstrated through votes cast at elections. The Administration candidate at this contest, Sir Richard Glyn, won 64 percent of all votes cast, yet those electors who signed the Coventry petition to the king in favor of John Wilkes and against the "tyranny" of the Administration completely reversed the overall pattern. Coventry politics were conducted ordinarily "without much reference to national affairs," yet in an impressive display of solidarity, only 24 percent of the petitioners voted for Glyn; 76 percent cast their ballots for the anti-Administration candidate, Thomas Nash.[43] Glyn, supported by the Administration despite his "opposition" votes in 1764 over general warrants, was the candidate of the anti-Corporation party in Coventry, and this confusion between his local position and his national posture should have resulted in a much greater variance in the behavior of the Coventry electorate. Instead, the votes of Coventry's petitioners were closely and consistently related to their stances on the Wilkes affair.

---

[43] Namier and Brooke, *House of Commons*, 1:401; *Correct Copy of the Poll for Members of Parliament*, Coventry, 1768. All voters did not sign petitions in Coventry or any other borough, nor were all petitioners necessarily electors, although some towns made this claim. However, a sufficient number of voters signed petitions in each of the towns examined to justify using the petitioners as "samples" of enfranchised opinions even though they never constituted a random sample.

Although not limited to two candidates, electoral behavior at the Northumberland contest of 1774 was no less striking. The ballots of the Northumberland electors who had signed the Northumberland petition defending John Wilkes in 1770 again reversed the overall voting pattern of their constituency. Percy and Delaval, the Court candidates, received more than half of all votes cast (53 percent), while less than a third (30 percent) of the total electorate backed the challengers, Middleton and Fenwick. Instead of helping elect the Court candidates, the pro-Wilkes petitioners cast a mere 23 percent of their votes for Percy and Delaval, reserving 67 percent for the challengers who had "attacked the too great influence of the Crown" during the campaign.[44] Of course, the Northumberland election did not revolve solely around the Wilkes issue. The Duke of Northumberland, possibly in celebration of his new dukedom, attempted for the first time in 1774 to suggest two candidates at the parliamentary election, having previously recommended only one man to the gentlemen of the county. One of his candidates, Sir Hussey Delaval, was defeated in the poll while the other (Northumberland's son) was returned. The issue raised by Northumberland's overstepping the bounds of conventional "influence" may have confused the election, as might the Nonconformist connections of the other candidates, Middleton and Fenwick. Nevertheless, despite the opinion of one observer that "political issues do not appear to have entered much into the contest," the relationship between petition signatures and votes is remarkable. Middleton and Fenwick may have insisted that they represented only resistance to the efforts of the Duke to unduly influence the contest, but it seems that the electorate saw more than that, or at the very least, that the court/country split in the county was closely related to

[44] *A Complete Collection of the Papers which Appeared at the Contest for Northumberland*, Alnwick, 1826, p. 139. These vote totals do not equal 100 percent.

the pro-Wilkite sentiment also in evidence among the electorate.

Votes and petition signatures were as closely related during the American crisis of 1775-76. Eight hundred men signed a Bristol petition in September 1775 testifying their abhorrence at "this unnatural rebellion" instigated by the "conduct of a few disappointed men," and pledged their warmest support for any and all measures adopted by the King aimed at "the extirpating of licentiousness." A year later, 1,200 Bristol residents submitted another petition, this time pleading for conciliatory measures in the colonies and imploring the King to avoid a civil war that would ruin England and America.[45] Almost 75 percent of the voters who signed the pro-Administration petition in 1775 had supported the Court candidates at the Bristol election of 1774; less than 10 percent of the enfranchised signers of the anti-Administration petition voted for the Government candidate at the same Bristol election (Table 1.1).[46] The votes of both sets of petitioners differed significantly from the overall voting pattern at that election; the two sets of petitioners were at complete loggerheads politically. Ten times (proportionately) as many Bristol petitioners against the Americans voted for Court candidates as their fellow citizens who took the side of the colonists. The Bristol contest did not hinge exclusively on the American crisis, and most of the propaganda issued in conjunction with this very lively campaign between Edmund Burke and Matthew Brickdale for Bristol's second seat involved the Quebec Act and the dangers of Catholicism. Yet whatever role religion

[45] H.O. 55, 1/9, 11/64, PRO.

[46] Determining political stances on petitions and at elections required linking the data from the two sources and creating a file with the votes and petition stances of those petitioners who also participated at the elections. Many of the petition signers never appeared at the relevant polls and probably were not enfranchised, but approximately half of the petitioners could be traced in the pollbooks. The techniques of nominal record linkage are discussed in Appendix I.

played in the election, at least one simple dichotomy distinguished these candidates. Cruger and Burke were both opposed to the Government's measures against the Americans, while Brickdale supported and was supported by the Government, receiving more than £2,000 in secret-service funds for his campaign. This dichotomy was reflected vividly in the poll, with 2,668 double votes going to Cruger and Burke and more than 1,500 plumper votes cast for Brickdale alone. This same dichotomy appears in the votes of petitioners.

Also revealed in Table 1.1, the voting patterns of petitioners in Newcastle, Nottingham, and Liverpool differed as radically from overall borough voting patterns as the votes of Bristol petitioners, and the pro- and anti-American petitioners in Coventry managed to equal the disparities in Bristol. Although worded less stridently than the Bristol petitions of 1775 and 1776, the Coventry petitions of 1775 voiced decidedly opposing views. The anti-American petition, signed by 124 citizens, "sincerely lamented the fatal effects of the unnatural contest" but resolved "on every occasion to pay due obedience to the legislative authority and to support and defend" the King. Another 516 inhabitants of Coventry expressed their "warmest wishes that such conciliatory measures as necessary" might be adopted to put a speedy end to the "calamitous and destructive differences between Great Britain and the colonies."[47] Just over 8 percent of the petitioners for conciliation voted for Court candidates at the Coventry election of 1774; more than 90 percent of the petitioners against America did so. To note that each statistical variation in Table 1.1 is statistically significant using a variety of measures considerably understates the frequently striking variations among petitioners.[48]

[47] H.O. 55, 12/4, 9/4, PRO.

[48] Using x^2 and a number of other measures, the differences in voting patterns of petitioners and all electors were consistently significant at the .01 level. The strengths of the relationships also were quite strong.

29

Table 1.1: Support for Administration Candidates among Petitioners over America and All Electors

Borough	Petition's Position Toward Administration	Percentage of Petitioners for Court Candidates	Percentage of All Electors for Court Candidates	Date of Election Used for Comparison	N
Bristol	Anti	7.4	27.6	1774	1200
Bristol	Pro	73.9	27.6	1774	800
Coventry	Anti	8.1	47.2	1774	240
Coventry	Pro	93.4	47.2	1774	150
Coventry	Pro?*	92.0	47.2	1774	180
Liverpool	Pro	76.7	55.7	1780	472
Newcastle	Anti	14.7	52.2	1777†	1135
Nottingham	Pro	83.5	53.1	1774	223
Administration Plumps		49.2	15.3		

* This "petition" (H.O. 55, 8/6, Pro) is simply endorsed "America" and may be a list of signatures that have become separated from the former petition (H.O. 11/6).
† By-election.

As might be expected from the overwhelming national sentiment against Charles Fox and the Coalition in 1784, the votes of petitioners and other electors at this famous general election were not separated by such wide gulfs. Almost everyone appearing at the hustings in any constituency voted against Foxite candidates. Nevertheless, differences evident in Chester, Maidstone, and Northampton demonstrate as clearly, if somewhat more subtly, the strength of the opinions of petitioners and electors (Table 1.2). In all three boroughs, a majority of the electorate voted against Foxite candidates, and since the petitioners in each borough also denounced Fox and the Coalition in no uncertain terms, it is less than surprising to find the petitioners voting against Foxites as well. [49] Hence the figures in Table 1.2 cannot equal the striking disparities in Table 1.1. Yet in each case, statistically significant differences distinguish petitioners against Fox from other voters.[50] In spite of the general consensus against Fox and all Coalitionists, the petitioners managed a more dramatic opposition to Foxite candidates, even when the association between Fox and certain candidates was questionable. In challenging the Administration (Pittite) candidates at the Chester election of 1784, for example, John Crewe asserted his opposition to Fox, and at several points in the contest issued statements expressly "declaring that I am no Foxite, as has been insidiously reported." Disregarding Crewe's denials, voters credited the insidious (and undoubtedly accurate) reports, and chants such as "We'll have neither a Crewe nor a Fox," along with the incumbents' previously demonstrated opposition to Fox proved decisive.[51] The Grosvenor interest operating in the borough must have helped defeat Crewe's

[49] See for example, J. Hartley, *A History of the Westminster Election*, London, 1784.

[50] Significant at the .01 level with x^2. Entire voting patterns (Whig, Tory, and split) were considered by these tests.

[51] *Papers and Squibs Relating to the Chester Election of 1784*, Chester, 1784, pp. 30, 43, 49.

independent bid, but the greater degree of Administration support among the petitioners strongly suggests a connection between the issues common to the petition and the race. Crewe finished a poor third in the poll.

Voters and petitioners in Maidstone behaved similarly, but the pro-Administration Maidstone petitioners accorded Administration candidates a larger share of their votes. More impressive, though, is the strength with which petitioners against Fox voted against Foxite candidates in Northampton, normally an apolitical borough. The Northampton electorate divided relatively evenly between the two Administration candidates (Compton and Trotman) and the single Foxite candidate (Charles Bingham). The pro-Administration petitioners, on the other hand, voted for the Administration's candidates overwhelmingly.[52] Of the boroughs examined in Table 1.2, only the votes of the Reading petitioners closely resembled those of the electorate, and this solitary lack of statistical significance is directly attributable to the failure of the general election of 1784 to provoke a contest in Reading. The issues raised at the Reading election of 1780 (the basis of the comparison in Table 1.2) were completely unrelated to the issues addressed in the Reading petition.[53]

In virtually every election described thus far, an alternative set of criteria can be used to assess the contest in question. At Chester in 1784, Crewe's association with the local "independents" against the Grosvenor interest in the borough might have played a role in determining some votes. The Coventry election also may have been influenced by the struggles between the Corporation party and the anti-Corporation coalition that supported Glyn. The Northumberland election pitted the "courtly" element and the influence of the Percy family against the "country" opposition to both Court and the Percys. Even so, the evidence

[52] *A Complete Collection of Papers . . . Northumberland, passim.*
[53] *A Correct List of the Voters . . . Reading,* Reading, 1784; John Man, *Stranger in Reading,* London, 1810.

Table 1.2: Support for Administration Candidates among Petitioners and All Electors in 1784

Borough	Petition's Position toward Administration (i.e., Pitt)	Percentage Petitioners for Administration Candidates	Percentage All Electors for Administration Candidates	Date of Election Used for Comparison	N
Chester	Pro	84.5	72.1*	1784	891
Maidstone	Pro	61.3	52.7*	1784	327
Northampton	Pro	83.4	52.2*	1784	153
Reading	Pro	18.4	20.6	1780	348

* Differences statistically significant at .01 level when entire voting pattern considered.

of conformity among the petitioning electorate on national issues is extraordinarily impressive. Undoubtedly other issues were at work in each of these political battles; political behavior is seldom, if ever, unidimensional. Yet taken as a whole, the electors who signed petitions displayed strikingly congruent political positions in every constituency in which the parliamentary elections were related to the national issues discussed in the petitions.

The political stances of voters expressed through signatures on petitions closely mirrored their political positions at general elections, even in 1784. The disparaging remarks of Lord North and Dr. Johnson notwithstanding, the petitions are solid evidence of political consistency that contradicts cursory dismissals of the opinions, principles, and desires of the electorate. Certainly many petition managers and election managers endeavored to arouse political awareness. Gamaliel Lloyd, one of the men circulating the 1780 Yorkshire petition calling for parliamentary reform, took along with him as he canvassed door to door, "a person that speaks the Leeds dialect in great perfection and who in a concise and intelligent manner explained the nature [of the petition], so that I may trust those who sign the duplicate I hand about do so from conviction and not merely because their neighbors have signed it before them." Citing Lloyd's performance, Ian Christie concluded that despite the possibility of powerful men exerting pressure on their dependents to either sign or not sign, the object of the petitioners "was to gain adherence out of conviction."[54] Even though such lofty aspirations doubtlessly exceeded the capabilities of the political system in many instances, and despite the less than lofty ambitions of some election agents, votes and petitions alike suggest that the petition and election managers often met the goal of obtaining votes and opinions from informed citizens. The "information" at the disposal of the electorate and the public at large

[54] Ian R. Christie, *Wilkes, Wyvill, and Reform*, London, 1962, p. 106.

tended to be less than accurate, and the issues raised by the parties often found expression in language that was both simplistic and unrealistic. Yet, whatever the deficiencies in their acquaintance with the issues, the voting public was asked to make genuine choices at many elections. The exaggerations and deceits of partisan propaganda merely reduced the difficulty encountered by the electorate in making political choices. Members of the political nation responded to the issues as presented, and their responses, however misdirected, are revealing.

POLITICS IN FOUR BOROUGHS

Demonstrating the changes in England's political environment during the reign of George III through an examination of the entire English electorate participating in the general elections between 1761 and 1802 would be both impossible and unnecessary. Looking at one election in a single large constituency involves thousands of records of individual electors, and expanding the focus to two successive elections in a particular constituency more than doubles the task. An assessment of electoral behavior can be conducted most effectively at the level of the individual voter and most revealingly through a study of individual voters over time. Optimally, such a longitudinal study of individual voters can be accomplished by following each elector from election to election, observing his behavior, or his absence, at each contest, thus creating what is usually called a "panel survey."[55] However, the creation of such panels from invariably deficient historical records usually requires a gargantuan effort. Following Robert Starkey of Norwich, for example, through successive Norwich pollbooks and piecing together a comprehensive account of his activities is an arduous task, particularly when additional

[55] A fuller discussion of the creation of panel surveys and their advantages is contained in D. Campbell and J. Stanley, *Experimental and Quasi-Experimental Designs for Research*, Chicago, 1966.

information pertaining to Starkey is sought in other sources, such as land tax rolls, poor rate assessments, Nonconformist registers, and the like.[56] Men with more common names, like Thomas Ward, pose greater dilemmas that are resolved best through computerized nominal record linkage. Unfortunately, programmed nominal record linkage prevents the use of random sampling techniques.[57] The entire electorate at one election must be compared with the entire electorate at the second election if reasonably accurate linkages are to be achieved. Hence, looking at the votes of Norwich electors alone over the first eight general elections of George III's reign involved almost 18,000 voting records that could be combined, with considerable effort, into extended records encapsulating the behavior of 8,454 Norwich voters across forty-one years. Supplementing these voting records with economic and religious data for these Norwich voters added tens of thousands of records to the Norwich file. A similar look at the entire unreformed electorate would involve more than one million individual records.[58]

Fortunately, rather than uniformity, the English electorate presented an extraordinarily varied pattern that substantially reduced the requirements of a quantitatively based analysis. Some of the unreformed voters were little more than nominal electors, and a number of English parliamentary constituencies hardly deserved the name. The county constituencies, though important politically and largest by far of the parliamentary constituencies in terms

[56] John Phillips, "Nominal Record Linkage and the Study of Individual-Level Electoral Behavior," *Laboratory for Political Research*, University of Iowa, 1976, pp. 1-77.

[57] There is a means of avoiding entire populations when computerized nominal record linkage is to be employed, but at the time this research was in progress, the method had not been devised. John Phillips, "Achieving a Critical Mass While Avoiding an Explosion," *JIH* 9(1979):493-508.

[58] More than one million records would be involved if all the relevant data had survived, which, of course, is not the case. Many boroughs could not be examined under any circumstances.

of the proportion of the *nominal* electorate they contained, defied analysis. Popular politics were beyond the ken of much of the county electorate. In some counties, such as Warwickshire, elections allowed popular political participation by the otherwise unenfranchised inhabitants of growing urban areas (Birmingham in this instance), and in some counties, notably Middlesex, political events involved large segments of the populace. Yet of the forty English counties, voters in Hertfordshire alone went to the polls more than three times during the eight general elections following 1761. Electors in only six other counties participated in as many as three contested elections during the period, while fifteen counties never once allowed a poll of their electors. Ten other counties did so a single time in the eight opportunities presented by general elections. Altogether, the unpolled or once-polled counties accounted for almost two-thirds of the total.[59] A few of the unpolled counties felt the brunt of political struggles that never resulted in polls, but behavior in these relatively rare contested, yet unpolled, county constituencies could not be measured. Moreover, even in those rare instances when county electors were politically active, the demands of nominal record linkage prevented analysis. The county electors could not be identified well enough to link voting records with any certainty and the additional data that would have been vital in identifying their social and religious status was unmanageable.

Two of the four major types of borough constituencies also failed to be sufficiently active politically to warrant attention. The "corporation" boroughs in which the right to vote was limited to the few members of the borough's corporation were very infrequently contested, and the

[59] Cannon, *Parliamentary Reform*, pp. 278-79. Herefordshire, Kent, Middlesex, Surrey, Westmorland, and Berkshire were contested three times. All others save Hertfordshire were contested once, twice, or not at all. A major study of Middlesex exists in George Rudé, *Wilkes and Liberty*, Oxford, 1962. Also see John Money, *Experience and Identity*.

"burgage" boroughs, where voting rights adhered to pieces of property (burgages) rather than people, rarely saw a formal poll.[60]

Eliminating the counties, the corporation boroughs, and the burgage boroughs, left 141 English boroughs of two franchise types in which the electorate could be, and often was, politically active. Leading in numbers of constituencies as well as in numbers of voters were the ninety-two boroughs allowing freemen (or freemen and freeholders) to vote. The forty-nine remaining boroughs subscribed to some variant of the "inhabitant householder" franchise and allowed most men of this sort to vote. Yet the "inhabitant" and "freeman" boroughs *alone* contained far too many voters for a comprehensive analysis, and the vagaries of data survival and political activity ruled out any random sample of these relatively active constituencies to determine the specific electorates to be examined. Therefore, four non-random, not strictly typical, but nonetheless revealing boroughs were selected for a detailed, individual-level analysis of the electorate and of electoral behavior before the Reform Act altered England's political geography.

A possibly atypical choice occasionally can be used to better advantage than a randomly selected target, and Norwich seemed to be one of those happy exceptions to the rule.[61] In the face of the utter impossibility of a randomly chosen constituency, a biased selection was the logical alternative, and Norwich, in addition to representing one of the geographical regions identified by Namier as potentially distinctive, was selected as a possibly extreme example of the potential degree of partisanship evident in some

[60] After 1761, fewer than 20 percent of the corporation and burgage boroughs were contested. The implications of this phenomenon are discussed in Chapter 2. For a brief account of the problems of record linkage that eliminated the possibility of examining county electors, see Phillips, "Critical Mass."

[61] William Keech, *The Impact of Negro Voting*, Chicago, 1968, p. 17.

popular political behavior.[62] If party politics played a role in the behavior of *any* English electorate, it should have been evident among Norwich's large electorate. Ample, albeit impressionistic, evidence survives of the activities of partisan organizations in Norwich, and if these impressions are credited, issues and partisan considerations reigned supreme in Norwich's parliamentary elections. Political issues dominated local press coverage of many later eighteenth-century elections, and collections of personal papers attest the keen interest and excitement that accompanied local and national political affairs in Norwich.[63]

Though on the verge of being dwarfed by England's industrial revolution and the concomitant urbanization of the northwest, Norwich could still boast, however unjustifiably, of being England's second city in the mid-eighteenth century. As East Anglia's principal textile manufacturing center, as well as the region's commercial and marketing capital, Norwich's only rivals for provincial preeminence were York and Bristol. By the 1760s, Norwich's population had grown to almost 40,000 souls scattered over no less than thirty-four separate parishes within the city's surviving medieval walls. This large population constituted a microcosm of preindustrial English urban society. Virtually all Norwich manufacturing took place within individual homes; a large proportion of the population lived at the mercy of relatively frequent and occasionally severe economic fluc-

[62] Namier, *England in the American Revolution*, p. 199.

[63] T.H.B. Oldfield, *The History of the Boroughs of Great Britain*, 2 vols., London, 1794, 2:288. Oldfield said of Norwich, "It is entirely free and independent in its representation and is only influenced in the election of its members by integrity, virtue, and abilities. Here the right of delegating this important trust is placed where it ought to be, and where our Constitution, pure and free from alloy, vested it in so large a body of the people, that the dictatorial authority of those who call themselves great has no effect." Though Oldfield certainly overstated the case a bit, his opinions are confirmed in large part by B. D. Hayes, "Politics in Norfolk, 1750-1832," Ph.D. diss., Cambridge University, 1958.

UNREFORMED POLITICAL SYSTEM

tuations; a goodly number of Norwich's residents were unquestionably and hopelessly impoverished, and a substantial part of the town's inhabitants, rich and poor, chose not to conform to the dictates of the Church of England. Led by a prominent Quaker family, the Gurneys, Nonconformity permeated Norwich society.[64] Such a diversity of religious, social, and economic groups within the town furnished potential fuel for economic and social conflict. Determining the relationship, if any, between Norwich's internal diversity and the heated political conflicts that marked Norwich's local and parliamentary elections was a principal objective of this research.

Three other constituencies, Maidstone, Northampton, and Lewes, were chosen more randomly (within the limits of the "law of available data") with the goal of providing some indication of the variations among the electorates in freeman and inhabitant boroughs. The selection of Maidstone continued the consideration of behavior in freeman constituencies. The town itself had not achieved the size or the regional importance of Norwich, and confined its electorate to freemen alone instead of freemen and freeholders. Freeholders in Maidstone qualified for Kentish elections, but the town's franchise could be obtained only through the acquisition of freeman status. Rather than producing an electorate proportionately as well as numerically smaller than Norwich's, however, Maidstone's approximately 700 voters equalled and possibly surpassed the Norwich electorate's share of the adult male population. A private, local

[64] Penelope Corfield, "Social and Economic History of Norwich, 1650-1850," Ph.D. diss., University of London, 1976; J. T. Evans, "The Political Elite in Norwich, 1620-1690," Ph.D. diss., Stanford, 1971; James Campbell, "Norwich," in *The Atlas of Historic Towns*, ed. M. Lobel, 2 vols., London, 1975, 2:1-30; P. Browne, *History of Norwich*, Norwich, 1814; W. Hudson and J. C. Tingey eds., *Records of the City of Norwich*, 2 vols., Norwich, 1910. Norwich merited a rating of four in Rozman's comparative look at English preindustrial towns, one of only seven towns in England with a ranking of four. Gilbert Rozman, *Urban Networks in Russia, 1750-1800*, Princeton, 1976, pp. 220-28.

census of Maidstone in 1782 indicates one in three adult male residents in possession of the freedom of the city and accordingly in possession of the franchise.[65]

Maidstone politics have been described in sharply contrasting terms. Several descriptions of partisan activity in Maidstone were contradicted by allegations of corruption and venality at Maidstone elections.[66] This disagreement concerning the nature of Maidstone politics served as a nice contrast to the supposed incorruptibility of Norwich politics. Also, the consistency of Maidstone's contested elections lent particular value to Maidstone's political data. Uncontested elections plagued England's borough constituencies before the second Reform Act, and each of the three other boroughs in this study left at least one election uncontested. Maidstone's uniquely unbroken string of polls, beginning in 1715 and continuing through the Reform Act, constituted a valuable, uninterrupted data base for this effort to describe and explain changes in behavior over time.[67] Maidstone also represented another of Namier's politically distinct geographical areas, the southeast.

With Norwich and Maidstone representing England's "freeman" boroughs, England's "inhabitant" boroughs found representation in this study through Northampton and Lewes, even though Northampton's franchise differed somewhat from many of the other "inhabitant" borough constituencies. Instead of requiring the payment of "scot and lot" (the local poor rate) in addition to demanding inhabitant householder status as did most inhabitant bor-

[65] J. Howlett, *Observations on the Increased Population in Maidstone*, Maidstone, 1782; W. Rowles, *A General History of Maidstone*, London, 1809.

[66] Namier and Brooke, *House of Commons*, 1:313-14; John Gale Jones, *A Sketch of a Political Tour Through Kent*, London, 1795, p. 79; George Crosby, *Crosby's Parliamentary Record*, Leeds, 1849, p. 227; Oldfield, *Representative History*, 4:76.

[67] Maidstone is the only borough in which a poll occurred at every general election between 1701 and 1832. London was the only other borough coming close to this record. Cannon, *Parliamentary Reform*, pp. 280-89.

41

oughs, Northampton allowed all resident adult males not in receipt of poor relief to vote. As a result of its "potwalloper" franchise, Northampton included a larger share of its adult male population within its electorate. Of a total population of some 7,000, nearly 1,000 men held the franchise in Northampton. Such a large electorate could not be controlled by a single patron, but political issues seem to have contributed very little to most electoral decisions in Northampton. Nor were the Northampton voters given a chance to render a decision, at least not a legitimate decision, on many occasions. In addition to the three uncontested elections between 1761 and 1802, one of the contested elections (1768) occasioned one of the most outrageous spectacles of wholesale corruption and coercion of the entire eighteenth century. The infamous "election of the three earls" in 1768 hardly lent credit to the political behavior of Northampton's electors, but paradoxically this ruinously expensive contest left in its wake conditions much more amenable to political behavior free from overt and undue pressures.[68]

Northampton's uncontested and sometimes corrupted elections did not generate insurmountable analytical problems, though, and Northampton was particularly well suited in other respects to an assessment of electoral behavior since it represented not just the "inhabitant" boroughs and the midlands (in Namier's political geography), but also, in relation to Norwich, the opposite end of the political spectrum. On the basis of the evidence of traditional sources, partisan behavior on the part of the Northampton electorate seemed an extremely remote possibility. Thus, the voting patterns of Northampton's electors formed an excellent foil for those of the Norwich electorate. Just as partisan behavior should have been evident in Norwich if it occurred anywhere, partisan behavior should have been noticeably

[68] Namier and Brooke, *House of Commons*, 1:345-46; Porritt and Porritt, *Unreformed Commons*, 1:226-27.

missing among Northampton's heterogeneous and broadly based electorate since any signs of a local partisan apparatus were conspicuously absent as late as the 1790s. Northampton's passive, normally issueless elections stood in stark contrast to the issue-oriented, hotly debated, and violently contested elections so common in Norwich.

The fourth borough of the group, Lewes, represented England's "inhabitant" boroughs more accurately than Northampton. Electors qualified to vote in Lewes elections by heading a household *and* by paying "scot and lot." These more stringent requirements created a small, though growing, electorate in this town of approximately 5,000 inhabitants. Less than 190 men turned out to vote at the closely fought Lewes election of 1768, while more than 330 voted at the equally close contest of 1802.[69] The small size of the Lewes electorate did not prevent considerable electoral activity; every general election following 1761 led to a poll. The poll of 1784 closed after a few minutes when it became painfully obvious that one of the three men standing for election was not a viable candidate, but at each contest, several candidates appeared and a formal ballot was taken. Lewes politics were reasonably open after the death of the Duke of Newcastle, and national political issues were not unknown in the Lewes press. The number of politically motivated petitions from the inhabitants of Lewes bespeaks some general awareness of popular political issues as well.[70] However, national political issues vied with local political concerns for the attention of the Lewes voters. The impact of these local concerns, often in direct opposition to na-

[69] At the election of 1768, eighteen votes separated the winner and loser. In 1802, only six votes separated the victor, Henry Shelley, from the vanquished, long-time incumbent, Thomas Kemp.

[70] *The Town Book of Lewes, 1702-1837*, Lewes, 1973, pp. 69-70; William Lee, *History of Lewes*, London, 1795; H.O. 55, 15/32, 17/24, PRO. *CJ*, January 28, 1773; March 12, 1781; March 4, 1790; and February 23, 1791. Lewes also petitioned the Crown over the Fox-North affair and the King's recovery of health.

tional concerns, made Lewes an exceptionally interesting borough in which to examine the interplay of the pressing issues raised in the country at large and the perhaps equally pressing issues unique to Lewes.[71]

Before examining individual electors and political behavior in these four constituencies, several related topics demand attention. In particular, three aspects of the political system as a whole are vital to any account of electoral behavior. Patronage, corruption, and uncontested elections posed serious, and potentially fatal, obstacles to the development of meaningful partisan behavior of any kind; only in the absence of all three could the electorate realize its political potential. The course of patronage over the eighteenth century has not been assessed dynamically, nor has the incidence of contested and uncontested elections attracted sufficient attention. Any discussion of the behavior of the electorate must be postponed until three things are clear: the extent to which patronage and corruption limited the exercise of the franchise among the enfranchised, the frequency with which the electorate was afforded an opportunity to exercise its franchise, and the degree to which electors took advantage of existing opportunities for participation. The following chapter deals with the first two areas; the subsequent chapter considers the third.

[71] As described in some detail in Chapter 4, Lewes's partisan activities were unrelated to national political issues until 1802. The "Coalition" comprised of Henry Pelham and Thomas Kemp campaigned jointly against various "independent" candidates after 1780 even though Kemp was a Pittite and Pelham a Foxite. Ian R. Christie, *The End of North's Ministry*, New York, 1958, p. 329.

CHAPTER TWO

The Structure of Electoral Politics in Unreformed England

DISCUSSIONS of the unreformed English electoral system usually revolve around its three major flaws: the control of borough seats in the Commons by individual patrons, the general lack of opportunities for popular participation, and electoral corruption. The standard examples of Old Sarum (for patronage), the election of 1761 (for the lack of participation), and the Oxfordshire election of 1754 (for corruption), have been cited so often that disparaging bits of information, such as the £20,000 Tory expenditure in Oxfordshire in 1754, are permanently imbedded in the secondary literature and have resulted in the dismissal of eighteenth-century popular politics as unworthy of serious consideration.[1] Instead of using such extreme examples to illustrate the depths to which electoral politics could sink, this more systematic inquiry into the nature of electoral politics enumerates both electoral patronage and electoral participation over the entire eighteenth century, and considers electoral corruption in a necessarily more speculative fashion.[2] From this broader

---

[1] The Tory expenditure was £20,068/1/2, and the total cost of the election probably exceeded £40,000. Robert J. Robson, *The Oxfordshire Election of 1754*, Oxford, 1949, p. 158. A few of the other references to the expensiveness of this election are: James Townsend, *The Oxfordshire Dashwoods*, Oxford, 1922; John B. Owen, *The Eighteenth Century*, New York, 1975, p. 101; J. Steven Watson, *The Reign of George III*, Oxford, 1960, p. 59, and even Lewis Namier and John Brooke, *The House of Commons, 1754-1790*, 3 vols., London, 1964, 1:4.

[2] Possibly the worst offenders in this category are E. Porritt and A. G. Porritt, *The Unreformed House of Commons*, 2 vols., Cambridge, 1909, but the more recent accounts are little different, if less descriptive. See Owen,

perspective, it is clear that the dismissal of popular politics in England before the Reform Act is unwarranted. Electoral politics played an increasingly important role in the political system during the reign of George III, and to neglect its importance is to misinterpret the political environment of unreformed England.[3]

POLITICAL PATRONAGE AND ELECTORAL DEFERENCE

Patronage in the parliamentary boroughs was an undeniable fact, widely recognized and even defended by contemporary observers on the grounds that it served a useful function in protecting controversial or particularly important members of the Commons from the vagaries of electioneering. Patronage has been described as a "remarkably stable" element of the eighteenth-century political system in John Owen's recent account of its status in Hanoverian politics, but the following assessment demonstrates that far from being stable, patronage increased substantially over the century.[4] However, the unmistakable increase in the

---

The Eighteenth Century, p. 101, and Asa Briggs, *The Making of Modern England*, New York, 1959, pp. 100-117. These oft-cited stories of corruption, along with the publication by Laprade in 1922 of John Robinson's papers that considered elections only in terms of influence, led C. E. Fryer to warn historians against ever again speaking of the election of 1784 as the "choice of the people." C. E. Fryer, "The General Election of 1784," *History* 9(1924):223.

[3] For other discussions of the importance of popular politics see J. H. Plumb, "Political Man," in *Man Versus Society in the 18th Century*, ed. J. L. Clifford, New York, 1968, and the works of George Rudé, Ian Christie, and E. C. Black on extra-parliamentary behavior.

[4] John Owen, "Political Patronage in Eighteenth Century England," in *The Triumph of Culture*, ed. Paul Fritz, Toronto, 1972, p. 369. The level of patronage at particular points was assessed by contemporaries and has attracted much attention from historians. See particularly the 1792 "Report of the Society of the Friends of the People" in *The Annual Register*, London, 1793, 35:81-97; T.H.B. Oldfield, *History of the Boroughs of Great Britain*, 2 vols., London, 1794; Romney Sedgwick, *The House of Commons, 1715-1754*, 2 vols., London, 1970; Namier and Brooke, *Commons*; John

number of influenced borough seats did not affect each region of the country uniformly, and the effect of patronage on England's various borough electorates was exceedingly diverse. As a result, increases in both the number of patrons and the number of patron-influenced seats in the Commons had a relatively minor impact on popular participation in parliamentary elections after 1761.

Although the nature of patronage varied as widely as the patrons themselves, broadly speaking, it assumed one of two forms: nomination or influence. Occasionally patrons possessed the absolute authority to "nominate," and thus insure the return of, a member (or perhaps both members) from a parliamentary borough. More commonly, however, a patron's effectiveness was much less certain. Most exerted only an informal and possibly challengeable "influence" over a Commons seat.[5] The distinction is well illustrated by the second Duke of Newcastle's nominative power in Boroughbridge and Aldborough, and his lesser influence in Newark, East Retford, and Lewes. Newcastle's right to select both members for the two Yorkshire towns that he referred to as "my two boroughs" was completely unchallenged. Newcastle owned a majority of the burgages (to which votes were attached) in Boroughbridge and thus had an undeniable right to decide elections.[6] Aldborough was in much the same position although it was a "scot and lot"

Cannon, *Parliamentary Reform*, Cambridge, 1973, p. 50; and Ian R. Christie, *The End of North's Ministry, 1780-82*, New York, 1958.

[5] Namier adopted the distinction maintained by the Society of the Friends of the People between nomination, "that absolute authority in a borough which enables the patron to command the return," and influence, "that degree of weight . . . which accustoms the electors in all vacancies to expect the recommendation by a patron, and induces them, either from fear, from private interests, or from incapacity to oppose, because he so recommended, to adopt him." Lewis B. Namier, *The Structure of Politics at the Accession of George III*, 2nd ed., London, 1957, p. 143. Also, A. Aspinall and E. A. Smith, *English Historical Documents, 1783-1832*, London, 1959, 11:220-21.

[6] Namier and Brooke, *Commons*, pp. 432-34.

borough. Again the Duke's ownership of property in the town enabled him to decide Aldborough's "representatives." In contrast, as lord of the manor in Newark, Newcastle's political interest was strong, yet the town's thousand voters, unwilling to relinquish completely their part in the selection of representatives, contested elections periodically. Newcastle's other interest in Nottinghamshire was equally precarious. The freemen of East Retford, though far fewer than in Newark, were as much influenced by the town's corporation as by the Duke. Even though no contested elections occurred in East Retford between 1741 and the Duke's death in 1768, his weight in the borough was "influence" only, and that over a single seat. Nor was Newcastle able to decide more than one of the representatives for Lewes, Sussex, in spite of his ownership of much of the town.[7] Lewes voters complied with Newcastle's wishes as a rule, but only conditionally, particularly after 1761.

The thin line separating "nomination" from "influence" would be of little consequence since the following evaluation of patronage equates the two types of control. However, the distinction raises the issue of electoral deference, and in doing so helps distinguish patronage from corruption and reveals the relative electoral freedom permitted by most patron "control." Deferential behavior has long been regarded as one of the most characteristic traits of English voters, reformed as well as unreformed.[8] Unfortunately, the term "deference" has been used to cover such a wide range of political behavior, including outright corruption, that the distinction between *truly* deferential be-

---

[7] L. B. Namier, *England in the Age of the American Revolution*, London, 1930, p. 409; Namier, *Structure of Politics*, pp. 9, 137.

[8] Although D. C. Moore suggests "deference communities" ended in the 1860s, deferential behavior remains a topic of considerable interest even in studies of modern Britain. D. C. Moore, *The Politics of Deference*, Hassocks, 1976, pp. 401-15; David Butler and Donald Stokes, *Political Change in Britain*, New York, 1971, pp. 120-27; R. T. McKenzie and A. Silver, *Angels in Marble*, London, 1968; and E. A. Nordlinger, *The Working Class Tories*, London, 1967.

havior and behavior provoked by coercion or some other form of inducement has been blurred to the point of meaninglessness.[9] Truly deferential behavior did not necessarily lessen the political freedom of the electorate. The political "influence" exerted by most patrons allowed a considerable degree of political activity by the public, in contrast to the power of "nomination" possessed by a very few patrons that left the electorate no real choice. Neither "influence" nor "nomination" resembled corruption, where politics was perverted by extraneous factors. "Influenced" borough electorates retained the possibility of rejecting the political leadership provided by a patron, even if the challenge and rejection simply meant the replacement of one patron with another. This potential political power retained by the electorate rendered deferential behavior very unlike what is commonly implied by the term in many descriptions of eighteenth-century politics. It permitted a considerable measure of independence to a politically alert electorate.

As important as the distinction between "nomination" and "influence" is in placing patronage in proper perspective, it cannot be maintained in the following analysis. Almost every borough contained one or more families of particular importance and potential influence in the community, and distinguishing those wielding real power from those without a decisive influence is difficult enough without the added problem of gradations of patronage. Even when major controlling families or individuals can be identified, measurements of their relative impact are much too inexact to allow finer distinctions. "Nomination" and "influence" must be combined into a simpler, inclusive cate-

[9] For a complete discussion of the meaning of deference and its role in the political system, see Richard W. Davis, "The Whigs and the Idea of Electoral Deference," *Durham University Journal* 67(1974):79-91; Richard W. Davis, "Deference and Aristocracy in the Time of the Great Reform Act," *AHR* 81(1976):532-39; J.G.A. Pocock, "The Classical Theory of Deference," *AHR* 81(1976)516-23; David Spring, "Walter Bagehot and Deference," *AHR* 81(1976)524-31.

gory, "patronage," that is the basis of the estimates of patron influence in the following tables and figures.

Norwich provides an excellent example of the problems inherent in determining the strength of a patron's impact on local politics. Norwich politics are among the clearest in all of the parliamentary boroughs, but even there the issue of patron influence is complex. In addition to several important families that periodically vied for power, the Earl of Buckinghamshire mistakenly saw himself as preeminent in Norwich politics after successfully suggesting Harbord Harbord as a member for Norwich in 1756. For the next three decades, the Earl believed that his approval was sufficient to insure a candidate's return, and he was not alone in perceiving his interest as significant, and perhaps even decisive.[10] Before the 1786 by-election at which the Earl's brother, Henry Hobart, stood against Thomas Beevor, Jeremiah Ives wrote the Earl, informing him that his "family interest was at stake in the election," and that "it now must be established or it will receive such a check as will not be easily recovered."[11] Hobart won the election in an apparent triumph of the "family interest," and after the 1786 election was declared void, also won the contest in 1787. Yet the victories of 1786 and 1787 came after Hobart's defeat in 1784 at the hands of a Whig (and worse, a Foxite), William Windham, and one of the telling issues raised against Hobart during that campaign was his "allegiance to a peer."[12] Hobart's victory in 1786 seems to have been in spite of, rather than because of, his "family interest."

Moreover, several contemporary and more recent ac-

[10] Historical Manuscripts Commission, *Report on the Manuscripts of the Marquess of Lothian*, London, 1905, p. 373.

[11] Ibid., pp. 430-31.

[12] *A Narrative of the Contested Election in Norwich*, Norwich, 1785, p. 15. One of the poems stated:

> May its sons ever hold
> Their rights dearer than gold
> Nor bow to the nod of a Peer.
> Mr. Hobart, Adieu, You're allied to a Peer.

50

counts of Norwich politics after 1761 evince Norwich's almost complete freedom from patronage.[13] Oldfield's contemporary evaluation of Norwich politics could not have been more laudatory; he described Norwich as "entirely free and independent in its representation, and . . . only influenced in the election of its members by integrity, virtue and abilities."[14] It is highly unlikely, then, that Buckinghamshire's influence played a significant role in Norwich elections. His influence may have played some part in the early process of candidate selection, but failed to determine the behavior of the bulk of the Norwich electorate. Therefore, neither of Norwich's seats is counted among those "influenced" by patrons, despite the pretensions of the Earl. In other boroughs where patronage *can* be identified, it usually is impossible to determine with any degree of accuracy whether the control was "nominative" or "influential."[15]

Thus reconciled to an unavoidably crude measure and an equally rough measurement, several basic inquiries can proceed with the reminder that most patronage was only "influence" and therefore not completely irreconcilable with considerable electoral freedom of choice. Was patronage a stable phenomenon in eighteenth-century politics? Was it becoming more pervasive? Or, as might be expected from the radical changes in the political climate of England over the century, was patron influence less common both early and late in the century when party battles were being waged in parliament than in mid-century when parliamentary di-

[13] B. D. Hayes, "Politics in Norfolk, 1750-1832," Ph.D. diss., Cambridge University, 1958; C. B. Jewson, *Jacobin City*, Glasgow, 1975.

[14] *History of the Boroughs of Great Britain* 2:288.

[15] The uncertainty in identifying patronage also is illustrated by Hoffman's recent assertion that Rockingham influenced the return of Robert Gregory for Maidstone in 1768, when earlier assessments attributed the decision to the influence of the Earl of Aylesford, and others denied that anyone had enough influence to insure a return. R.J.S. Hoffman, *The Marquis*, New York, 1973, p. 192; Namier and Brooke, *Commons*, 1:313-14.

visions played a minor role, if they existed at all?[16] Of course, patronage and party conflict were not mutually exclusive, but a high degree of party spirit among the electorate at any election or series of elections should have made it more difficult to control a seat through "influence" (if not through "nomination") than at times of relative partisan quiescence. Rather than the general stability recently claimed, or increases limited to the nonpartisan, apolitical years of George II's reign, a comparison of several elections across the century reveals a marked and consistent increase in the number of patron-influenced borough seats.[17] (See Table 2.1.) The substantial expansion of patron influence by individ-

[16] For detailed accounts of the gyrations of English parliamentary and electoral politics over the century, see W. A. Speck, *Tory and Whig*, London, 1969; B. W. Hill, *The Growth of Parliamentary Parties, 1689-1742*, London, 1975; Frank O'Gorman, *The Rise of Party in England*, London, 1975; or more generally if less acceptably, part 1 of Ivor Bulmer-Thomas, *The Growth of the British Party System*, London, 1953.

[17] These estimates of patronage are based on the following assessments: *1690*: J. H. Plumb, "Elections to the House of Commons in the Reign of William III," Ph.D. diss., Cambridge University, 1936. *1734*: Sedgwick, *House of Commons*. This list was compiled from an evaluation of each constituency and each member. *1761*: Namier, *Structure of Politics*. The second edition list is much more complete than the original. *1761, revised*: Namier, *Structure of Politics*; Namier and Brooke, *Commons*; and Cannon, *Reform*, p. 50. *1780*: Christie, *North's Ministry*, p. 53. *1790*: "The Society of the Friends of the People," in C. Wyvill, *Political Papers*, 6 vols., London, 1794-1802, 3:189-251 and the *Annual Register*, London, 1793, 35:81-97.

Since the Society was agitating for parliamentary reform when its list was drawn up, its accuracy might be suspect. However, rather than positively biased, the list seems conservative, if anything. The compiler, George Tierney, disagreed with Oldfield's assessments in many boroughs and listed a total of 309 controlled seats as opposed to Oldfield's total of 359. By eliminating the Welsh and county seats (the latter excluded on principle to conform to Namier's estimates), the number of controlled seats was reduced to 264. Even so, the revised 1761 list is more inclusive than Namier's original estimate and thus more appropriate for comparison to 1790. Ian Christie's estimate of patronage in 1780 supports the general pattern. Applying Namier's standards, Christie counted 221 privately influenced seats, an increase over Namier's 205, and a total of 240, up from Namier's 235. Christie, *North's Ministry*, p. 53.

uals more than compensated for the marginal rise and ultimate decline in the number of seats dominated by governmental interests. The already long list of 153 boroughs influenced by patrons during the parliamentary election of 1690 grew to a majority of all parliamentary borough seats by 1761 (235 by Namier's estimate and 255 by a revised estimate). At the next to last general election of the century, 1790, fully two-thirds of the borough seats in parliament were under some degree of patron influence.[18] Even with as many as 255 seats in parliament filled by patrons' candidates at the general election of 1761, this first election of the new reign was not "the peak of aristocratic power" during the century if electoral patronage is the measure. Nor was there any "tendency on the part of patrons to abandon their boroughs" toward the end of the century.[19]

Table 2.1: Influenced Borough Seats, 1690-1790
(Number and Percentage of All Borough Seats)

	1690	1734	1761	1761 (revised)*	1790
Seats controlled by private patronage alone	133 (32.8%)	184 (45.4%)	205 (50.6%)	224 (55.3%)	264 (65.2%)
Seats controlled by Government alone	20 (4.9)	30 (7.4)	30 (7.4)	31 (7.7)	6 (1.5)
Total controlled seats Government and private	153 (37.8)	214 (52.8)	235 (58.0)	255 (63.0)	270 (66.7)

* See note 17

[18] Discussing patronage from the standpoint of the total amount of patronage is necessary because it is frequently quite difficult to distinguish government control and private control. For example it is not clear whether Hythe was controlled by the Government or by Lord Dorset. An even more troublesome problem is the occasional incidence of patrons selling seats to the Government, such as the case with East and West Looe in 1734. The Government obviously received the benefit of the patronage, but from an electoral perspective, the patron (Sir John Trelawney in this case) was still the key. See Sedgwick, *House of Commons*, pp. 214 and 365-70.

[19] Namier and Brooke, *Commons*, p. 24; Cannon, *Reform*, p. 49.

These figures indicate no "peak" of power, only a steady rise.[20] The pattern of borough politics in Wiltshire reflects the general expansion of patron influence, although the severe loss of electoral freedom in Wiltshire far outstripped the nation generally, and occurred only after a period of considerable freedom from interference early in the century. Wiltshire's uninfluenced borough seats almost equalled the seats under some degree of patron influence at the election of 1690 (fifteen open seats, seventeen closed seats). The number of seats free from patron interference increased in 1734 when patrons determined only nine of the thirty-two seats in the county. Before the election of 1761, however, a major reversal left twenty-one seats in the hands of patrons, overshadowing the eleven remaining open. By the election of 1790, twenty-eight borough seats were in the hands of patrons, leaving only four in which elections could be conducted with complete freedom by the respective borough elecotrates.[21] Whether measured generally or specifically, assertions of stability in the eighteenth century are seriously misleading from the perspective of electoral patronage. Even if the two estimates that present the fewest problems of comparability, 1734 and 1761-revised, are con-

[20] Besides the general acceptance of the Society list by both Namier and Cannon, and its moderation in comparison to Oldfield, its general credibility is enhanced by a specific comparison with Mary Ransome's figures for Wiltshire. Citing Robinson's contemporary assessment of the extent of patronage in Wiltshire, Ransome drew up a list of influenced boroughs that differs from the Society list in four instances: Chippenham, Devizes, Hindon, and Wooton Bassett. Surprisingly, the History of Parliament Trust volumes support the Society assessments unquestionably in three of the four constituencies, and in the fourth (Devizes), there is too little evidence for a resolution of the difference. Mary Ransome, "Parliamentary History," *Victoria County History of Wiltshire*, ed. R. Pugh, 10 vols., London, 1954, 5:20-30; *Annual Register*, 35:81-97; Namier and Brooke, *Commons*, pp. 408-22.

[21] Ransome, "Parliamentary History," p. 209.

sidered in isolation, an argument for stability remains untenable.[22] Almost a tenth of the 405 parliamentary borough seats fell to patrons over this thirty-year span alone.

This expanded control stemmed from the increasing ranks of borough patrons rather than from the acquisition of more control by existing patrons. Namier noted that borough "mongers" were "rather small fry" in 1761, and his description accurately portrays any decade in the century. The Duke of Newcastle led the borough mongers by a wide margin in 1734 with eleven seats under some degree of influence. Only two other peers influenced as many as six seats, and the remainder of the patrons (both noble and non-noble) determined one or two seats at most (Table 2.2).[23] Newcastle continued to lead the pack in 1761, although his total had dropped to seven seats, followed by Lords Falmouth and Edgcumbe with five seats each. Seven seats also marked the greatest extent of individual influence

[22] The lists of patron-influenced seats for 1734 and 1761-revised were drawn from the wealth of information in the History of Parliament Trust volumes for the respective periods, and the standards used to determine patronage were applied uniformly. The other estimates of patronage should be relatively comparable, but the fact that each was compiled at a different time for a different reason creates a problem of comparability largely overcome by the consistency of the figures for 1734 and 1761-revised. See note 17. The number of peers fluctuated within a narrow range, but for the pupotes of these comparisons, the following estimates of the number of peers in specific years seemed adequate. The approximately 160 peers in 1690 had grown to 178 in 1735. By 1761 their numbers had shrunk slightly to 174. (John Cannon counted 172 in 1759 and 171 in 1714.) The Pitt peerages increased the ranks of the aristocracy to 206 by 1790. See A. S. Turberville, *The House of Lords in the Reign of William III*, London, 1913; *The House of Lords in the Eighteenth Century*, London, 1927; and *The House of Lords in the Age of Reform, 1784-1837*, London, 1958. Also see Cannon, *Reform*, p. 50.

[23] The same sources used to produce the lists of patron-influenced seats were used to draw up the lists of patrons. In the case of the 1790 estimate, the original Society figures of seventy-one peers and ninety-one commoners were reduced to sixty-seven and eighty-three respectively by the elimination of the Welsh and county seats. See note 17.

55

in 1790, the Earl of Lonsdale having succeeded Newcastle as principal borough monger.[24]

The burgeoning numbers of patrons and patron-influenced seats clearly indicate the instability of the eighteenth-century political system; continued success by borough mongers, on the other hand, could have led to a remarkably "stable" electoral system if the patrons had accomplished their collective goal of eliminating the *vox populi* in the selection of members of parliament. But the existence of a growing body of patrons does not support the usual dismissals of electoral politics as unimportant. Paradoxically, the image emerging from the preceding demonstration of increasing patron control exercised by a growing number of patrons is both accurate and deceptive. To be sure, patronage was a genuine flaw in the political system; it undoubtedly reduced or eliminated popular political participation in some constituencies, and seemed to do so with increasing frequency over the century. From a parliamentary perspective, these gains are extremely important since increasing patron influence could have a major impact on

Table 2.2: Peerage/Commoner Patronage

	1690	1734	1761	1790
Percentage of English peerage exercising patronage	20	29	33	36
Percentage of controlled seats influenced by peerage	53	54	54	45
Average no. of seats/peer	2.3	2	2	2.3
Average no. of seats/commoner	1.2	1.4	1.7	1.5

[24] Peerages were not a prerequisite for successful patronage. Although peers tended to be slightly more successful in acquiring seats, the peerage and gentry shared the boroughs fairly equally among themselves. Patronage did produce peerages, but only rarely. A successful, though base, borough monger could cling to the hope of a reward commensurate with his often great effort, and occasionally, as in the case of Sir James Lowther (created Earl of Lonsdale) and Edward Eliot (created Baron Eliot), such hopes were rewarded.

the composition of the Commons. Nevertheless, the figures in Table 2.1 do not accurately portray the impact of patronage in terms of either the parliamentary boroughs or the borough electorate. The overall rise obscures extreme variations within the country that are critical to an adequate measurement of the general effect of patronage on the political system. A more detailed analysis of private patronage drastically alters the conclusions that might be drawn from the rising number of influenced seats seen in isolation. Regional variations in the number of borough seats influenced by patrons allowed relative freedom in the areas of the country with the largest proportions of the electorate (Table 2.3). Moreover, the inability of patrons to control boroughs completely (i.e., both seats), as well as their failure to control them consistently (Table 2.5), allowed the survival of a meaningful element of popular participation even in boroughs affected by patronage. The role of electoral politics was not diminished by the fall of more borough seats into the hands of individual patrons (or families); rather everything points to a substantial resurgence of popular political participation after 1761 with a corresponding increase in its importance.[25]

Even though some erosion of electoral freedom occurred in every part of the country as a result of the increased incidence of patron influence, the impact of patronage varied markedly across the country as a result of the considerable variation in the concentration of parliamentary boroughs, franchise types, and borough electorates. The deterioration of electoral freedom in Wiltshire, for example, was much more serious than that experienced by Norfolk or the country in general. Almost 90 percent of the borough seats in Wiltshire had been lost to "borough mongers" by 1790, while only 30 percent of the seats in Norfolk

[25] For a more complete discussion of the increasing importance of electoral politics after 1768, see E. C. Black, *The Association*, Cambridge, Mass., 1963, and Cannon, *Reform*.

fell to patrons.[26] The general increase so apparent in the
national figures (Table 2.1) is evident in each of the four
distinct political regions identified by Namier, but the variations between the regions are extreme and indicate the
exercise of much more freedom of choice among the borough electorates of the southeast and, conversely, an almost
total submission to patron control by the electorates of the
southwest (Table 2.3).[27] Namier's four regions may have
no identifiable social or economic importance, but they do
provide a convenient shorthand for examining the geo-
graphic diversity of patronage. The "southwest," as precisely defined, may be little more than a figment of Namier's
fertile and versatile imagination, yet as this analysis demonstrates, the number of influenced seats in the Commons
was unevenly distributed areally, and as a result, the potentially negative impact of patronage on popular political
participation was not realized uniformly across the country.
Most of the increase in the number of patron-influenced
seats affected a single area; for the entire century, two-
thirds of the increase in patronage occurred in the boroughs of the southwest alone. Between 1761 and 1790, fully
80 percent of the increase occurred there, and the simple
fact that the relatively underpopulated southwest absorbed
most of the increase in the number of seats influenced by
patrons is extremely important to an assessment of the

[26] Ransome, "Parliamentary History," p. 209. According to the "Society
of the Friends of the People Report," one of Thetford's seats and the two
Castle Rising seats were controlled in Norfolk in 1790, leaving seven other
borough seats free. *Annual Register*, 35:81-97.

[27] Namier, *England in the Age of the American Revolution*, p. 199. The
regions were: (1) the southeast: Middlesex, Hertfordshire, Essex, Kent,
Surrey, Sussex, and Suffolk; (2) the southwest: Hants, Berkshire, Wilt-
shire, Dorset, Somerset, Devon, Cornwall, Gloucestershire, Worcester-
shire, Herefordshire, and Monmouth; (3) the midlands: Lancashire,
Cheshire, Salop, Staffordshire, Derbyshire, Warwickshire, Leicestershire,
Northamptonshire, Oxfordshire, Buckinghamshire, and Bedfordshire;
(4) the northeast: Norfolk, Cambridgeshire, Huntingtonshire, Rutland,
Lincolnshire, Nottinghamshire, Yorkshire, Durham, Northumberland,
Cumberland, and Westmorland.

national impact of patronage.[28] The three other areas of England matched neither numerically nor proportionately the tripling of the already large number of influenced borough seats in the southwest between 1690 and 1790. The number did not quite double in the southeast, and only increased by about half in the northeast and midlands. The northeast actually reversed the trend toward more patron influence at the end of the century, and many of the increases were minimal. The national increase in patron control, therefore, affected electoral participation far less disastrously than the overall numbers suggest. Many boroughs were politically besieged by prospective patrons during the eighteenth century, but a single region (the southwest) absorbed the greatest damage leaving one region (the southeast) relatively open, and the two remaining regions (the midlands and the northeast) with at least reasonable opportunities for electoral choice.

These regional variations have particular significance for the electoral system generally because of the unequal proportion of the borough electorate in each region. The submissive electorates in the multitude of small southwestern

Table 2.3: Borough Seats under Private Patronage

Region (Total number of Borough seats in Region)	Number of Seats Influenced (Percentage of that Region's Total Borough Representation)				
	1690	1734	1761	1761 revised	1790
Southeast (84)	18 (21.4%)	22 (26.2%)	28 (33.3%)	30 (35.7%)	35 (41.7%)
Northeast (72)	31 (43.1)	51 (70.8)	41 (57.9)	46 (63.9)	44 (61.1)
Southwest (183)	59 (32.2)	79 (43.2)	110 (60.1)	115 (62.8)	146 (79.8)
Midlands (66)	25 (37.9)	32 (48.5)	26 (39.4)	33 (50.0)	39 (59.1)

[28] Thirty-one of the thirty-nine additional seats influenced in 1790 were in the southwest (comparing the revised 1761 figure to 1790).

59

boroughs involved barely a quarter of the borough electorate even though almost half of the parliamentary boroughs were located in the southwest. On the other hand, the most open region, although containing less than 20 percent of the parliamentary boroughs, included almost a third of the total borough electorate, and along with the other two relatively open regions, accounted for no less than three-quarters of the borough electorate in spite of their relatively small numbers of parliamentary boroughs.[29] Thus, the expected impact on electoral freedom of choice as a result of the relatively large number of borough seats falling into private hands was substantially less than it might have been, and far less, in fact, than it seems if patronage is measured by the number of influenced borough seats as in Table 2.1.

This disparity in the regional proportions of parliamentary boroughs and borough electorates influenced by patronage stemmed from a combination of the differences in borough populations and the exceedingly diverse and unevenly distributed franchise requirements of the boroughs scattered among the four regions. Rather than a uniform franchise, as in the counties where a forty-shilling freehold entitled the owner to a vote, the franchise requirements of the boroughs were sometimes very broad, occasionally very narrow, and often neither broad nor narrow. As a result, borough electorates ranged in size from Westminster's 12,000, to Old Sarum's infamous seven, and Gatton's less well known but equally ridiculous two.[30] This extreme range

[29] The regional proportions of borough seats and borough electorates were:

	Southeast	Southwest	Midlands	Northeast
Percentage of Borough Seats	20.7	45.2	16.3	17.8
Percentage of Borough Electorate	31.4	25.4	21.0	22.2

[30] There were no lists of qualified voters in any of the boroughs. Therefore, the electorate can be gauged accurately in the corporation and bur-

is reflected in the regional proportions of patronage. The concentration of small, limited electorates in the southwest explains the relatively small proportion of the borough electorate contained in its lion's share of the parliamentary boroughs.

The specific franchise qualifications found in the parliamentary boroughs can, with some oversimplification, be grouped into four major categories. First, and smallest generally, were the twenty-seven corporation boroughs; their restriction of the franchise to members of the corporation resulted in an average electorate of only thirty.[31] Second, and larger by far, were the twenty-nine boroughs in which the franchise was tied to the ownership of particular pieces of property (burgages), and the six in which the burgage franchise had been slightly altered to include freeholders generally. The electorates in the burgage or freehold boroughs (both referred to as burgage boroughs in the following discussion) averaged just over 130 in 1761. Third in terms of size, with an average of about 600 voters each, although most open in terms of their franchise requirements, were the forty-nine "inhabitant" boroughs, that included twelve boroughs allowing all inhabitant householders not in receipt of poor relief or charity to vote (the potwalloper franchise) and thirty-seven towns restricting

gage boroughs, but in the inhabitant and freeman boroughs the number of electors is only an estimate based on the number actually voting. Those constituencies without contests at all pose a serious problem; nothing more than a guess is possible.

[31] These figures are based on the borough franchises of 1761. The franchise qualifications were not stable over the century, particularly among the burgage boroughs. Speck lists forty-one burgage boroughs in Anne's reign and this number shrank to thirty burgages in 1734 along with six freehold franchises, which for all intents and purposes can be considered in the same category as burgage boroughs. Those changing (and their new franchises) were: Aldborough (scot and lot), Castle Rising (freeman), Corfe Castle (scot and lot), Droitwich (corporation), Lichfield (freeman), Newton (corporation), Saltash (corporation), and Malton (freeman). After 1734, Malton reverted to its original status, and Honiton and Newport, Cornwall became burgage boroughs. Speck, *Tory and Whig*, pp. 126-31. Also Sedgwick, *House of Commons*, and Namier and Brooke, *Commons*.

the franchise somewhat by permitting only those inhabitant householders paying "scot and lot" to vote.

Fourth, and largest, ninety-two constituencies extended the franchise to borough freemen. Once made a freeman, an individual was entitled to vote in all ensuing elections, regardless of actual residency, and this lack of a residency requirement often resulted in the participation of large numbers of nonresident voters at contested elections. The freeman boroughs constituted the largest single group of boroughs, and with an average of more than 750 voters in each constituency, contained an overwhelming majority of the entire borough electorate.[32]

Most susceptible to patronage were the burgage boroughs. The disadvantages posed by their relatively large electorates (in comparison to the corporation boroughs) were more than offset by the simple fact that an individual could gain absolute control of a burgage borough through the purchase of property. Even the tiny electorates in the corporation boroughs could prove obstreperous, but pieces of property could hardly mount an effective resistance to patron control. Therefore, the unequal distribution (both numerically and proportionately) of burgage boroughs among the regions is partially responsible for the regional variations already indicated. Almost a third of the boroughs in the northeast contained burgage franchises, yet less than 3 percent of the midlands boroughs tied votes to property.[33] Excluding the burgage boroughs from consideration sub-

[32] Using the Namier and Brooke estimates of the electorates, the freeman boroughs included approximately 71,070 voters.

[33] The regional proportions (%) of franchise types in 1761 were:

Borough Types	Southeast	Southwest	Midlands	Northeast
Freeman	46.3	38.0	52.9	58.3
Inhabitant	29.3	28.3	32.4	8.3
Corporation	7.3	15.2	11.8	5.6
Burgage	17.1	18.5	2.9	27.8
	N = 41	92	34	36

stantially alters the regional patterns evident in Table 2.3, and strengthens the argument for the existence of electoral freedom in much of the country (Table 2.4). Instead of increasing markedly in every region, patronage gained ground only very slightly in the southeastern nonburgage boroughs over the century and lost ground in the northeast where the greatest concentrations of burgage boroughs led to the least overall resistance. While a number of nonburgage seats in the midlands fell to patrons in the general attack on the boroughs, patronage really succeeded only in the southwest, where two-thirds of the nonburgage boroughs came under some patron influence by 1790. Electoral patronage failed most strikingly in the southeast, but popular participation outside of burgage boroughs remained relatively common in the midlands and northeast as well. At least half of the nonburgage boroughs in the midlands and the northeast remained open in 1790, and the impact of the relative openness in nonburgage constituencies outside of the southwest was much greater than the impact of patronage in the southwest, since 75 percent of the electorate lived outside the region of marked patron control, and fully 95 percent of all borough electors resided in nonburgage boroughs.

Shifting the focus of the analysis from control at one election to control over time, and from parliamentary seats

Table 2.4: Percentages of Borough Seats Influenced by All Patronage, Excluding Burgage Boroughs*

Region	1690	1734	1761 revised	1790
Southeast	21.4	19.1	20.2	27.6
Northeast	41.7	45.8	30.6	33.3
Southwest	31.1	37.2	53.0	65.6
Midlands	37.9	45.5	37.9	50.0

* The number of burgage boroughs changed over the eighteenth century. These calculations are based on those that allowed burgage franchises at each election.

to parliamentary boroughs (Table 2.5), further qualifies the conclusions that might otherwise be drawn from the overall increase in the number of patron-influenced borough seats. A considerable, indeed a remarkable, degree of electoral freedom existed in spite of the often successful efforts of patrons. In the first place, patronage seldom succeeded over the long run, thus leaving boroughs free at least occasionally. In the second place, relatively few constituencies were even partially influenced (i.e., one of the two borough seats in the hands of a patron) at each of the four elections examined, and far fewer were completely controlled at each point (Table 2.5). Restricting the focus to the three eighteenth-century elections increases the number controlled at each election only slightly. Patronage affected less than a quarter of England's parliamentary boroughs at each of the general elections considered, and patrons consistently influenced only a little over a third of the boroughs after 1734. What is more, in both cases patrons completely controlled even fewer; the voters in thirty-four of the fifty boroughs marred by patronage consistently after 1690 had a voice in selecting one of their two members to represent the borough, and of the sixty-eight controlled after 1734, twenty-eight allowed the patron to fill only one seat. Even the burgage boroughs retained a measure of freedom of choice.

Table 2.5: Consistently Influenced Borough Constituencies

	1690-1790		1734-1790	
	One Seat Controlled	Both Seats Controlled	One Seat Controlled	Both Seats Controlled
Nonburgage Boroughs	23	9	23	22
Burgage Boroughs	11	7	5	18
Totals	50		68	
	(25% of all boroughs)		(34% of all boroughs)	

ELECTORAL PARTICIPATION

The ultimate failure of patronage to end electoral participation and reduce parliament to an appointive body is
strikingly illustrated by its inability to eliminate the electoral
process even in those boroughs where patrons wielded influence. An impressive amount of electoral activity emerged
in the later decades of the century in spite of patronage.
In order to demonstrate the magnitude of electoral activity
in the parliamentary boroughs, electoral participation must
be measured from three distinct perspectives. Initially, the
total number of contested boroughs at each general election
during the century is examined (Figure 2.1). The pattern
that emerges is surprising in light of the continuing increase
in the amount of electoral patronage being exercised in the
boroughs.[34] The second measurement compares the number of contests in boroughs with "small," "intermediate,"
and "large" electorates and demonstrates the frequency of
electoral activity in the populous boroughs that contained
most of England's voters (Figure 2.2). Finally, the differences in the frequency of elections among the four franchise types show the same result; the boroughs with the
broader franchises that contained the overwhelming majority of the electorate were the ones being contested (Figure 2.3). All three comparisons lead to a single conclusion:
in spite of the efforts of patrons, much of the borough
electorate was politically active, and often regularly active,
in the closing decades of the eighteenth century.

If each of the English parliamentary boroughs had been
represented by a single member in the Commons, a rise in
the level of patron-influenced seats should have been accompanied by a decline in the number of contested elections across England. Single-member constituencies, however, were rare until after the redistribution of parliamentary

[34] Figure 1 is based on John Cannon's list of contested elections in
Reform, pp. 278-89, and Henry Horwitz's list for 1690. Henry Horwitz,
"The General Election of 1690," *JBS* 11(1971):90.

65

seats in 1885. With the exception of five single-member boroughs and two that elected four members, the unreformed parliamentary boroughs each sent two members to the Commons.[35] This peculiarity of the electoral system meant that elections could be contested in boroughs even when a patron controlled one of the two seats, the electoral battle being waged over the uninfluenced seat. The Duke of Newcastle's influence over the selection of one of the members to represent Lewes, for example, did not prevent a contest there in 1768 to decide their other representative. Similarly, some of the most common electoral contests were fought over a single seat, the other remaining in the hands of a patron. Fourteen of the most frequently contested boroughs in the reign of George III were partially influenced at either or both of the general elections of 1761 and 1790.[36] The loss of a seat to a patron was not the same as the loss of a borough to patronage, and the loss of an entire borough to patronage was as rare as the loss of a single seat was common. Borough electorates could be as active, and borough elections could be contested as frequently, in the presence as in the absence of a patron, providing of course that one of the seats was not controlled.[37]

Instead of an invariably inverse relationship between contested boroughs and patron-influenced seats, Figure 2.1 indicates a significant increase in the number of contested elections after 1761. The steady decline in the total number of contested constituencies that marked the general elec-

[35] The exceptions were London and Weymouth/Melcombe Regis returning four members each and the single-member constituencies of Abingdon, Banbury, Bewdley, Higham Ferrers, and Monmouth.

[36] The fourteen frequently contested yet controlled at some point were: Bedford, Boston, Bridgewater, Cirencester, Dorchester, Dover, Evesham, Great Marlow, Honiton, Ilchester, Leominster, Lewes, Okehampton, and Shaftesbury.

[37] The official electoral manager for the government, John Robinson, estimated at least 116 "open" boroughs in the 1780 elections. W. T. Laprade, ed., *The Parliamentary Papers of John Robinson, Camden Miscellany*, 3rd ser., London, 1922, pp. 71-82.

66

tions after 1722 was halted in 1761, justifying in a sense Cannon's characterization of 1761 as the peak of aristocratic power. During the general election of 1761 only 21 percent of the 203 boroughs were contested, and after 1761, the number of contested boroughs increased generally, if sporadically, with a jump to 31 percent in 1768 and another jump to 35 percent in 1774. Increasing patron influence did not prevent greatly increased electoral participation after the election of 1761 at which fewer boroughs were contested than at any other point in the century.

The general increase in the number of contested borough elections following the 1761 election was unequally distributed among Namier's four regions. Not surprisingly, contested elections were fought most frequently in the regions with the fewest small and restricted-franchise boroughs. However, the regional differences are only a reflection of the more important variations in the number of contested elections among boroughs of different sizes and franchise qualifications. Size and franchise type often were closely related borough characteristics (the larger boroughs invariably were "freemen" or "inhabitant" constituencies),[38] and while it is difficult to distinguish the independent role played by size in determining the frequency of contested elections, it is clear nonetheless from Figure 2.2 that size was a significant determinant of the frequency of contested elections. The most politically active boroughs over the entire century were the thirty-three large boroughs that included fully two-thirds of the borough electorate.[39] Surprisingly, the election with the smallest number of contests among the large boroughs, as well as those with intermediate electorates of between 200 and 1,000, was 1747 rather than 1761, yet in *both* a substantial shift also occurred in

[38] Of the thirty-three large boroughs (greater than 1,000 electors), all but Northampton (potwalloper), and Southwark, Newark, and Westminster (all scot and lot) had freeman franchises.

[39] The thirty-three large boroughs contained approximately 70,200 electors in the 1760s. Estimated from Namier and Brooke, *Commons*, vol. 1.

FIGURE 2.1 *Percentages of Contested Borough Elections and Patron-Influenced Seats, 1690-1802*

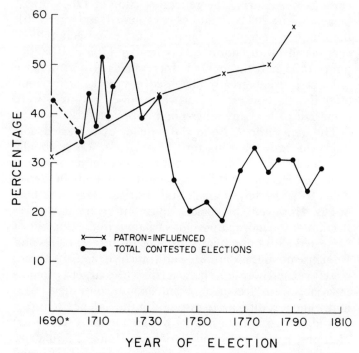

* Election of 1690 for comparison. Continuous measurement beginning with election of 1701.

1761. More than 50 percent of the boroughs with large electorates were contested at each election after 1761, and the level of contests in those boroughs with somewhat smaller electorates increased from approximately 26 percent to an average of over 41 percent after the same election. Only in the small boroughs were contests unlikely in 1761 and almost equally unlikely in subsequent decades.

A similar picture emerges from a comparison of contested elections in boroughs of different franchise types (Figure 2.3). The restricted nature of their franchises and

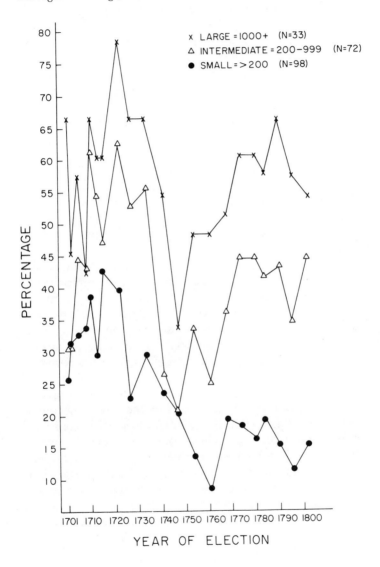

FIGURE 2.2 *Proportions of Contested Elections among Parliamentary Boroughs with Large, Intermediate, and Small Electorates, 1701-1802*

their greater susceptibility to manipulation or control led to far fewer contests in the burgage and corporation boroughs than in the other two types. During the first sixty years of the century, however, the percentage of burgage and corporation borough contests was usually much closer to that of the "inhabitant" and freeman boroughs than during the last forty years. After 1768, the proportion of contested burgage and corporation boroughs fell to less than 10 percent while the proportion of contested freeman and inhabitant boroughs climbed to over 40 percent. Following the twin lows of just over 25 percent in 1747 and again in 1761, the level of contests rose to a peak of 51 percent among the inhabitant boroughs (in 1774) and 45 percent among the freeman boroughs (in 1784). Thus the increase in the overall level of electoral contests evident in Figure 2.1 is due solely to the dramatic increase in the number of contests in the "inhabitant," freeman, "large," and "intermediate" boroughs.

As with the regional variations in patron control, the patterns in Figures 2.2 and 2.3 derive their significance not from the number of boroughs contested, but from the number of electors involved. The most frequently contested boroughs contained almost all of the borough electors. Curiously enough, the proportional shares of the borough electorate were almost identical whether the boroughs are distinguished by franchise-type or by size. The freeman boroughs contained just over 71,000 voters (two-thirds of the entire borough electorate) while the "large" boroughs (which were almost all freeman constituencies) contained more than 70,000.[40] Similarly the 99,000 electors in the freeman and "inhabitant" boroughs were matched by the 98,000 included in the "large" and "intermediate" boroughs. In sharp contrast, the twenty-seven corporation boroughs contained altogether only a few more than 800 electors, and the thirty-five burgage boroughs could barely

[40] See notes 32 and 39.

FIGURE 2.3 *Proportions of Contested Borough Elections by Franchise Type, 1701-1802*

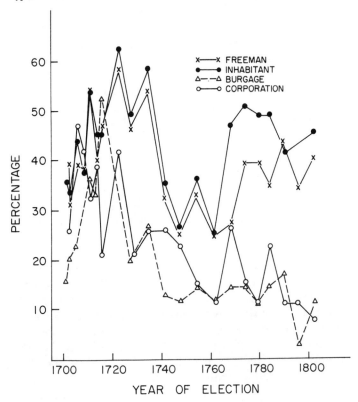

muster 4,600 voters, just as the total electorate in the "small" boroughs was under 6,500. Although the combined corporation and burgage boroughs constituted 31 percent of the parliamentary boroughs, and the ninety-two boroughs with "small" electorates accounted for almost half of all borough constituencies, each of their combined electorates amounted to less than 6 percent of the borough electorate. Therefore, an impressive 66 percent of the borough electorate (the total in the "large" boroughs) participated in

71

elections more often than not after 1761. This proportion can be expanded to 94 percent of the borough electorate (the total of either freeman and inhabitant or large and intermediate boroughs) living in boroughs that frequently allowed electors to exercise their franchises formally. Clearly, the opportunities for formal participation in the political system by the entire borough electorate (Figure 2.1) were much greater than would be expected from the sharp rise in the level of patronage and were even more common in the very boroughs where the impact of participation could be greatest, those with large and open electorates (Figures 2.2 and 2.3).

The level of popular political participation in England's boroughs actually may be considerably understated in these three figures since they include only those elections contested to the point of an actual poll, while contests frequently were fought up to, yet short of, a poll.[41] Full-scale electioneering might be followed by a "canvass" of the electorate in which as many voters as possible were asked pointedly how they intended to vote if given the opportunity. The results of the canvass could then be used to decide whether or not the contest was worth pursuing. Canvasses often forced one or two of the candidates to withdraw, leaving the borough officially uncontested in spite of the contest that actually occurred. Surviving canvass books attest the completeness and accuracy of many canvasses, and in many respects, participation in an election contested in this fashion was almost indistinguishable from participation in a contest resulting in a poll.[42] The number of canvasses before each of the eight general elections in question has not been, and probably cannot be, measured accurately.

[41] For a discussion of contested but unpolled elections, see Robert W. Smith, "Political Organization and Canvassing: Yorkshire Elections Before the Reform Bill," *AHR* 74(1969):1548, and M. D. George, "Fox's Martyrs: The General Election of 1784," *TRHS*, 4th ser., 21(1939):135-36.

[42] For example, see the description of Northampton in 1780. Namier and Brooke, *Commons*, p. 346.

Therefore, the possibility that this demonstrated increase in polled elections coincided with a decline in the number of canvassed, but unpolled contests cannot be ruled out. If the rise in the number of polled elections took place only in those places that had previously decided elections on the basis of canvasses, there may have been no net increase in popular participation measured broadly.[43] Nevertheless, there is no reason to believe that any such correlation exists. The use of canvasses seldom completely eliminated the possibility of a poll, and the growing number of polled elections could just as easily have been complimented by a burgeoning contingent of canvassed constituencies, whether polled or unpolled. At any rate, for the purposes of this discussion of electoral behavior, the frequency of the act of voting itself, not the relative frequency of canvassing, is vital. The incidence of canvassing, while important to an overall evaluation of popular participation, holds less significance.

CORRUPTION

Electoral corruption is at the same time more concrete and less tangible than electoral patronage. Parliamentary elections could not be declared void on the basis of patronage per se, but election returns were invalidated occasionally after unsuccessful candidates substantiated charges of electoral corruption that may or may not have involved patronage.[44] And despite its relative concreteness, corruption cannot be measured quantitatively. An examination of several common charges of corruption can only illustrate the danger in accepting allegations of this kind of illegal po-

[43] For a discussion of parliament's role in the changing franchise requirements, occasionally on the grounds of undue control (i.e., patronage), see J. H. Plumb, "The Growth of the Electorate in England from 1600-1715," *Past and Present* 45(1969):90-116.

[44] Norwich is an excellent example. See *A Correct Copy of the Evidence on the Norwich Petition by Which the Election of Henry Hobart Was Declared Void*, Norwich, 1787.

litical activity too readily. Although outright corruption is as undeniable a fact as electoral patronage, an examination of several allegations of electoral corruption suggests that the common interpretation of an "open" vote as simply the "corrupt agreement between one rogue and another" is unwarranted.[45] England was not just a "nation of buyers and sellers." The well-publicized campaign practices of the eighteenth and nineteenth centuries sometimes lend themselves to such an interpretation, it is true, but eighteenth-century electioneering involved much more than "canvassing the respectable and corrupting the rest."[46]

A common allegation of improper practices before or during a contested election concerns politically motivated corporate manipulation of the electorate in freeman boroughs.[47] The authors of the *Municipal Corporations Report* levelled a serious accusation against the freeman boroughs generally in 1835, arguing that the corporations were guilty of tampering with the size and composition of their electorates by wholesale creations of freemen and "honorary" freemen prior to elections.[48] The report's table of the numbers of freemen created annually after 1801 in several freemen boroughs appeared to substantiate this claim. Notable

---

[45] T. J. Nossiter, *Influence, Opinion and Political Idioms in Reformed England*, Brighton, 1975, recto of dedication page. Lord John Russell, the source of the quote, disagreed with this view in 1857, as does Nossiter in his arguments concerning the reformed electorate.

[46] J. R. Pole, *Political Representation in England and the Origins of the American Republic*, London, 1966, p. 459. T. J. Nossiter, "Elections and Political Behavior in County Durham and Newcastle, 1832-74," Ph.D. diss., Oxford University, 1968, p. 369.

[47] House of Commons Sessional Papers, *Report of the Commission on Municipal Corporations*, vol. 26, London, 1835, p. 2710. Citations to Parliamentary Papers are confusing at best. These references to the *Municipal Corporations Report* are to actual printed page numbers in the 1835 Sessional Papers. See P. Ford and G. Ford, *A Guide to Parliamentary Papers*, Shannon, 1972, pp. 71-74. Also see *Mirror of Parliament*, 2 vols., London, 1835, 2:1747. Repeated in J. L. Hammond and B. Hammond, *The Village Laborer*, London, 1912, p. 12 and Porritt and Porritt, *Unreformed Commons*, p. 66.

[48] *Report of the Commission on Municipal Corporations*, vol. 23, p. 35.

74

increases in the frequency of admissions to the freedom of the borough were evident in many constituencies in the years immediately preceding general elections, and the authors of the report accepted these increases as prima facie evidence of corporate corruption, as have some historians subsequently. The preelection increases in the numbers of new freemen admitted in many boroughs during the early nineteenth century are undeniable, and even more striking examples can be found in the eighteenth century. No less than 2,080 citizens of Bristol, for example, became freemen in the month prior to the election of 1774.[49] Yet, mass creations of freemen, even on the scale of Bristol, are unconvincing examples of electoral corruption or successful electoral manipulation. Similar demonstrations of marked increases in voter registration preceding elections should be possible in virtually any political system if (1) a relatively wide segment of the population is allowed to vote, and (2) if the responsibility for claiming the right to vote is left up to the individual citizen. An impending election is a motivating influence that can be expected to expand an electorate, if it can be expanded; corruption or manipulation need not be involved. Even if corruption and/or manipulation do account for at least a portion of the increased size of the electorate, the political impact of such increases may well be negligible. The party choices of newly admitted freemen in Liverpool, Colchester, Norwich, and Maidstone at elections in the last decades of the eighteenth and early decades of the nineteenth centuries lend support to such a conclusion.[50] Both (or all) parties benefited relatively equally from preelection increases in the size of the voting public.

[49] "The Bristol Pollbook," p. 8, Central Library, Bristol. This massive increase in the number of electors actually established a precedent for allowing votes from freemen "whose copies were taken after the test of the writ."

[50] E. M. Menzies, "The Freeman Voter in Liverpool 1802-1935," *Historical Society of Lancashire and Cheshire Transactions*, 124(1973):85 and M. E. Speight, "Politics in the Borough of Colchester, 1812-47," Ph.D. diss., University of London, 1969, p. 144. See also, Nossiter, "Elections and Political Behavior," pp. 6-11.

Thus, the tables of the *Municipal Corporations Report* may indicate electoral mobilization, but they cannot be used to argue that the voters were "entirely under the influence of the corporations" in the freeman boroughs. Nor do they support the contention that the power to create freemen was the single "most important electoral device at the disposal of any party."[51] In some instances, specific charges of this kind of corporate misconduct are demonstrably erroneous. For example, the Porritts maintained that on the eve of the 1774 election in Northampton, 396 freemen were created by the corporation in an effort to sway the election, yet the register of freemen in Northampton reveals only 23 additions in 1772, 6 in 1773, and 10 in 1774.[52] Actually, since Northampton was not a freeman borough and allowed all inhabitant householders to vote, additions to the ranks of Northampton's freemen were politically unimportant in any event. Nor could any irregularities be found in several other constituencies, including Norwich and Maidstone.[53] This is not to deny that manipulation of this sort was attempted in some boroughs occasionally, but the general incidence of these efforts may have been exaggerated. It simply cannot be assumed that such tactics were

[51] Hammond and Hammond, *The Village Laborer*, p. 12. Also see, John H. Moses, "Elections and Electioneering in the Constituencies of Nottinghamshire: 1702-1832," Ph.D. diss., Nottingham University, 1965, pp. 412-13. For a contradictory argument, see Peter Jupp, *English and Irish Elections*, London, 1973, p. 90.

[52] Porritt and Porritt, *Unreformed Commons*, pp. 64-65. "Northampton Register of Freemen: 1730-1802," Northampton City Recorder's Office, Northampton.

[53] There are a series of suspicious entries in the Norwich Freeman Admissions Book during 1773 and 1778. Usually each page contained three names, but during those years, several pages (18 and 17 respectively) were either left blank or only contained one entry. Names could have been added later, but never were. NNRO, Case 17, Shelf c, Rep. 135, volumes 1-4. Also there was an increase in the number of admissions in 1783 to 292, following a ten-year average of 83. In the ten years after 1783, an average of 82 freemen per year were admitted.

76

effective in substantially reducing the electorate's freedom of choice.

Another frequently encountered charge of corruption stems from the common practice of "treating" before (and sometime during) the poll. Reports of excesses in the dispensation of food and drink are common, such as the report from the Seaford election of 1796 that "the gluttonies performed . . . have already dispatched two of the Electors, who died on Friday of repletion," or the frequently recounted episode of the 1768 Northampton contest.[54] Yet even carried to its greatest lengths, treating did not necessarily impede freedom of choice in elections; it may well have been an effective means of rewarding loyal support, and mobilizing and reinforcing favorable opinion, rather than a means of altering election results by subverting the electorate. Even Ivor Jennings, a harsh critic of the unreformed system, admitted that treating could not "affect the vote unless it was omitted."[55]

Charges of bribery also are common, but bribery does not seem to have been a widespread practice in spite of some accounts to the contrary. In fact, the incidence of bribery actually may have increased after the Reform Act. When Greville asked for an assessment of the new (post-1832) constituency in Maidstone, he was told that the electors were "worse than the old" because they were universally corrupt.[56] The *Municipal Corporations Report* reached essentially the same conclusion concerning Norwich, noting

[54] *Kentish Chronicle or Canterbury Journal*, Friday, May 27, 1796. At the 1768 Northampton contest, the Earl of Halifax exhausted his store of matured port and turned in desperation to his choicest claret, whereupon the "rabble" deserted his side and joined the forces of the Earl of Northampton, "turning up their noses and vying 'never to vote in the interest of a man who gave them sour port to drink.' " Turberville, *The House of Lords in the Eighteenth Century*, p. 467 and Joseph Grego, *Parliamentary Elections*, London, 1892, p. 227.

[55] Sir William Ivor Jennings, *Party Politics*, 3 vols., Cambridge, 1960-1962, 1:83.

[56] Norman Gash, *Politics in the Age of Peel*, London, 1953, p. 125.

that the widespread use of money in Norwich parliamentary elections had been unknown until the election of 1832.[57] The conclusion of the report is amply supported by other evidence. Perhaps most revealing was the successful petition that voided the Norwich election of 1786. Of 262 voters challenged by the petitioners, only 33 were charged with bribery, an unimpressive number given the more than 2,600 electors voting in that contest.[58] A number of *other* violations invalidated the election, including sixty-one freemen declared ineligible to vote as a result of receiving poor relief in the twelve months preceding the election. Fraud, deception, and simple errors notwithstanding, bribery in Norwich was not widespread before the passage of the Reform Act. It is difficult to distinguish fact from fiction in Norwich, as it is in most other boroughs, since the evidence is so often open to interpretation, but even though no one would deny that Norwich elections were expensive affairs, the behavior of the Norwich electorate cannot be explained by money in the form of bribery or treating.

While the cost of elections varied considerably in Norwich, expenses usually were in excess of £1,000. The two Norwich parties (the Blue-and-Whites and the Orange-and-Purples) often underwrote much of the cost, and the combined outlay of the party and an individual candidate (or pair of candidates) could run as high as £13,000 for a single election.[59] However, the fixed costs of campaigning, such as the often considerable expense of bringing in out-voters (in a freeman borough like Norwich), treating, and printing propaganda were high in a borough with close to 3,000

[57] *Report of the Commission on Municipal Corporations*, vol. 26, p. 2486.

[58] *A Correct Copy of the Evidence for the Norwich Petition*, pp. 1-29.

[59] Windham Papers, British Library Additional Manuscripts (hereafter, BL Add. MS.) 37908, ff. 15. Windham agreed to pay £2,500 of the election expenses if victorious and £1,500 if he lost. £8,000 was spent by Windham and Frere in 1802, and probably over £5,000 by the Free Blues. Windham Papers, BL Add. MS. 37885, ff. 10-11. By-elections could be as expensive as general elections. The scrutiny of the Norwich 1786 contest revealed an expenditure of almost £8,000.

electors, and these fixed costs accounted for much of the expenditure. The fixed costs alone usually smacked of bribery since out-voters often received more than just travel compensation for making the journey to cast their votes. Printers, runners, ribbon manufacturers, and a host of other perfectly legitimate, though clearly "corrupted" individuals, benefited materially from contested elections, and these kinds of subtle yet important "bribes" were an inevitable and an expensive ingredient of local campaigns. However, remuneration in any form was conspicuously absent in many Norwich elections, and its absence had little visible effect on the voters. Several Norwich elections were fought with tiny sums by Norwich standards without consequence, and occasionally, as in Thomas Beevor's campaign of 1768, one side spent virtually nothing with no noticeable effect. Beevor ran a strong, if unsuccessful, race against Harbord Harbord and Edward Bacon (the incumbents) and won a more than respectable 41.7 percent of the vote, finishing 461 votes behind Bacon, even though his total costs were only £50 plus the expenses of the election day itself.[60] Bartlett Gurney refused to mount an expensive campaign in 1796, yet won a majority of the resident vote, only to lose at the hands of the out-voters.[61] Furthermore, there are examples of individual rejections of bribery, either with money or with places. William Windham, for example, absolutely spurned bribery as a means of acquiring support although he was willing to spend thousands of pounds honestly during a campaign.[62] There seems to be little justification, then, for the Porritts' characterization of Norwich elections as "squalid electioneering," and this is true of many other borough constituencies as well.[63]

[60] Hayes, "Politics in Norwich," p. 432.
[61] Windham Papers, BL Add. MS. 37908, ff. 213.
[62] Windham Papers, BL Add. MS. 37908, ff. 259 and 305 are excellent examples. Also see *The Windham Papers*, ed. Lord Rosebery, 2 vols., London, 1895, 2:192-93.
[63] Porritt and Porritt, *Unreformed Commons*, p. 71.

Colchester provides an even better indication of the exaggerations common in allegations of bribery and corruption in later eighteenth-century elections. Having described Norwich politics in such favorable terms, Oldfield accused Colchester voters of corruption sufficient to "cause a blush even on the face of political profligacy."[64] A recent study of early nineteenth-century elections in Colchester, however, concluded that despite a high proportion of nonresident voters (a group particularly susceptible to bribery), the charges levelled by Oldfield and others appear to be "largely unjustified"; elections could not be won with bribery alone even there.[65]

Undoubtedly, corruption existed in a variety of forms in the unreformed political system, but much of the electorate seems to have heeded the propagandist's warning that:

> 'Tis said indeed Gold will engage
> Some folks but let them fear,
> That in their avaricious rage
> They buy that Gold too dear.[66]

ELECTORAL POLITICS

The three potentially serious flaws in the English electoral system failed to affect the unreformed electorate on the scale commonly alleged. Popular political participation suffered somewhat from the effects of patronage, but substantial electoral activity occurred during general elections both early in the eighteenth century and again after a lull in the 1750s and 1760s. Borough voters were not excluded from participation by the occasionally intensive efforts to eliminate the electorate from the political process. Nor was

[64] T.H.B. Oldfield, *Representative History of Great Britain and Ireland*, 6 vols., London, 1816, 3:457.
[65] Speight, "Politics in the Borough of Colchester, 1812-1847," p. 164. Also see an excellent contemporary account of bribery in John Man, *Stranger in Reading*, London, 1810, pp. 176-78.
[66] *Kentish Gazette*, September 9, 1780, "Ode on the General Election."

the damage inflicted on the system by guineas as severe as many accounts of the unreformed political system indicate; the evidence of corruption is sketchy at best and often equivocal. In short, the examples with which this chapter began are atypical. The Oxfordshire election of 1754 occurred during the relatively brief period of unusual political inactivity that ended with the election of 1761 and a marked resurgence in popular political activity that continued through the century. The seven electors who made up Old Sarum's electorate (or the two in Gatton) may have posed no problems for electoral patrons, but the vast majority of the borough electorate lived in boroughs far removed from the likes of Old Sarum and seem to have been relatively free from the effects of either patronage or corruption. The electorate, particularly that portion of it contained in freeman and inhabitant boroughs, was a significant element in the eighteenth-century political system. Moreover, the boroughs examined in subsequent chapters represent a reasonable cross-section of the politically active English parliamentary constituencies. Specific patterns of behavior in Norwich and Maidstone may not lead to direct generalizations concerning the entire "freeman" electorate, just as evidence from Northampton and Lewes cannot be expected to reveal completely the nature of electoral behavior in England's "inhabitant" boroughs. Nevertheless, when described in the full context of local political developments, political behavior in the four boroughs chosen for a closer examination should point at least generally to the broader parameters of unreformed electoral behavior.

CHAPTER THREE

The Structure of Borough Politics: Participation and Politicization

M OVING FROM an examination of the structure of politics in the freeman and inhabitant boroughs generally to an examination of political activity in four specific boroughs again raises the related questions of patronage, corruption, and participation. The specific charges of patronage levelled against the "freemen" voters in Norwich and Maidstone and the "potwalloper" voters in Northampton are no more convincing after 1768 than were the general allegations of patronage in the "open" boroughs across the country. Prior to the general election of 1768, however, patronage played a substantial role in the selection of M.P.'s from Northampton, and it may have loomed larger and lasted longer in Lewes. Patronage in Northampton determined much, perhaps all, in the middle decades of the century. Yet, the result of the infamous "election of the three earls" in 1768 owed more to outright corruption than patron influence.[1] And, curiously enough, this major instance of corruption virtually eliminated patronage in Northampton. The 1768 contest severely undermined the finances of two of the aristocratic families involved, reducing, if not eliminating, their role in subsequent elections. Lords Northampton and Halifax, after jointly determining Northampton's representation for more than two decades, proposed two men in 1768 who were challenged by one Thomas Howe, sponsored by the Earl Spencer. Amidst riots of serious proportions, the poll was conducted over fourteen days at an expense to those involved of more than

[1] Chapter 2 includes a brief assessment of the accuracy of the charges levelled against Norwich, Maidstone, and Northampton.

£160,000. At the end of this Rabelaisian spectacle, Sir George
Rodney and Sir George Osborne, the Northampton and
Halifax candidates, had carried the poll against Howe with
the blatant and patently illegal assistance of the returning
officers, only to lose one of their seats to Howe as a result
of a threat of legal action by Earl Spencer. A coin toss
determined which of the two erstwhile "victors" sat with
Howe. Nearly bankrupt as a result of the contest, Lord
Northampton sought permanent exile in Switzerland. Lord
Halifax, also ruined and broken by the election, withdrew
from Northampton politics until his death three years later.
Despite the presence of a Compton (Northampton) candidate in 1784 and 1790, and a Spencer candidate at most
elections after 1768, aristocratic domination of Northampton politics certainly ended in 1768. The one unbroken
peer, Spencer, usually refrained from taking an active part
in parliamentary elections, particularly after the disap-
pointing defeat of his Foxite hopeful in 1784.[2]

The Duke of Newcastle possessed an unquestioned "interest" in Lewes until his death in 1768 reduced the influence of the Pelham family and helped free the town from
aristocratic domination. A Pelham candidate stood for each
election between 1774 and 1796, and actually topped the
poll each time after an initial loss in 1774, but the Lewes
electorate was freer from any controlling interest than the
success of the Pelham family suggests. Rather than family
influence, Henry Pelham's three successive victories after
1774 may have stemmed as much from the formation of
a "Coalition" with Thomas Kemp in 1780. The Pelham
family's influence continued to be felt, undoubtedly, but it
was substantially diminished by Newcastle's death, and the
Pelhams cannot be said to have overwhelmed local politics.
Instead, the "Coalition" seems to have taken pride of place

[2] J. C. Cox, ed., *The Records of the Borough of Northampton*, 2 vols., Northampton, 2:508-12; V. A. Hatley, "Some Aspects of Northampton's History," *Northamptonshire Past and Present*, 3(1966):240-49.

until its defeat in 1802.[3] Nor can patronage be taken seriously in Norwich or Maidstone. Lords Romney and Aylesford ranked in the forefront of Maidstone society and politics, as did the entire Finch family. And in addition to the Earl of Buckinghamshire, the Ives, the Gurneys, and the Harveys exercised some political power in Norwich. Nevertheless, to talk of patronage in either borough would completely misrepresent the nature of parliamentary or local politics. No family was sufficiently important to dominate, or even threaten to dominate, political affairs. The sheer size of the Norwich electorate defied control, and Maidstone's smaller electorate refused the lead of both patrons and the corporation.[4]

Electoral corruption is as elusive in specific boroughs as it is nationally. Few charges were levelled against any of these boroughs particularly, and with the exception of Northampton in 1768, they appear to have suffered very little from corruption. The behavior of the three earls in Northampton requires no further discussion; the scandal acquired considerable infamy as the tremendous expenses of the contest became known. An outlay of so many guineas in such an overtly corrupt fashion was generally held to be disgraceful then and since.[5] The only other specific alle-

[3] Windham Papers, BL Add MS. 37908, ff. 232, 257, 259, 81, 267, 194. Prior to the Lewes election of 1790, an advertisement appeared in the Lewes press for the sale of forty-two freehold houses, each entitling the owner to a vote. The ad noted that the purchaser "will command a very extensive interest in the borough." Three months later, the press noted with relief that the houses had not been sold to one person, thus "tending to increase the independence of the borough." *Lewes Journal*, February 22, March 1, May 24, 1790. According to Oldfield, Lewes did not become altogether independent until 1806, but he phrased his argument in such a way that he seemed to assume Lewes's greater independence when he noted that the town was "*formerly* under the absolute control of the late Duke of Newcastle." T.H.B. Oldfield, *History of the Boroughs of Great Britain*, 2 vols., London, 1794, 1:150.

[4] Norwich and Maidstone are considered in more detail in Chapter 4.

[5] Cox, *Records of Northampton*, 2:502-507; Joseph Grego, *A History of Parliamentary Elections*, London, 1892, pp. 226-27. Not surprisingly, the *Northampton Mercury* took no notice of the contest, corrupt or not.

gation of bribery at any of the more than two dozen contests in these four boroughs is of questionable veracity and remains completely unsubstantiated. Two nineteenth-century election reports (one probably stemming from the other) accused Christopher Hull of bribery at the Maidstone election of 1796, alleging an expenditure by Hull and the Whigs of over £3,000 in a blatant effort to buy a seat. None of the surviving evidence corroborates these charges; much argues against them.[6] Even if such a sum were credible for an extended campaign in so small a constituency, Hull became the Whig candidate only a day before the contest, and it is unlikely that he could have accumulated such a war chest overnight and then dispersed it in a matter of hours.[7] Moreover, most of Hull's supporters in 1796 had been Whig voters in the Maidstone election of 1790.[8] Their consistent behavior, much in accord with developments among the Norwich electorate, tells strongly against the accusations. Northampton's voters alone appear guilty of the Porritts' general charge of "squalid electioneering" at

[6] Grego, *History of Parliamentary Elections*, p. 300. Also in Henry Stooks-Smith, *Register of Parliamentary Contested Elections*, London, 1842, pp. 113-14. This charge was repeated in George Crosby, *Crosby's Parliamentary Record*, Leeds, 1849, p. 227. After Hull's defeat, an unsuccessful election petition was attempted against General Delancey's victory on the clearly valid grounds that as Barracks-Master General, Delancey was specifically prohibited from sitting in the House by 6 Anne, c. 7 and by 25 George III, c. 45. Delancey did hold this office with a salary of £1,500 per annum, but the House refused the petition nevertheless and allowed Delancey to sit. If Hull was guilty of the corruption as charged, it seems hardly likely that he would have attempted such a petition. George Tierney, one of the leading figures in the Society of the Friends of the People, was Hull's counsel. *CJ*, October 20, November 9, and December 31, 1796; March 6, April 21, May 9, and May 15, 1797.

[7] The Whig incumbent, Clement Taylor, did not decide finally against standing for the seat he had occupied for so long until the very last minute. His financial dilemma, which finally forced his retirement to Ireland, seems the only explanation for his action.

[8] Of the eighty-eight returning Whig voters in 1796, forty-seven (53 percent) cast single votes for Hull and only eight voted for the two Tory candidates. Only three of the one hundred seven returning Tory voters cast Whig singles for Hull. Ninety-two (86 percent) cast Tory double votes.

parliamentary elections, and then only once.[9] Their corrupt behavior was reformed drastically from necessity, if nothing else, after the catastrophically expensive 1768 election. No one was left in a position to buy their votes.

The increase in popular participation at elections in the larger and broader franchise boroughs after the general election of 1761 (Figures 2.1 and 2.2) suggests much about the political system, but participation in individual boroughs is equally revealing. The nature of borough politics hinged largely on each borough's political structure, and participation was its most important aspect. Measured cross-sectionally (at one election) or longitudinally (at successive elections), electoral participation was exceptionally high by any standard in all four boroughs. The voters took advantage of each opportunity given them to exercise their franchises at parliamentary elections. While precise measurements of voter "turnout" at particular elections are impossible in prereform, or more pertinently, preregistration England, all evidence points to the participation of an overwhelming majority of the qualified voters at each contested election.[10] Certainly it appears at least on occasion that great

[9] Edward Porritt and A. G. Porritt, *The Unreformed House of Commons*, 2 vols., Cambridge, 1909, 1:71.

[10] Contemporaries were well aware of the problem of identifying electors, and some suggested that in the counties, land tax registers could be used to identify qualified voters. The Durham Act of 1763 attempted to transform the tax registers into informal electoral registers, and the statute of 28 George III, c. 36 (1788) actually called for formal electoral lists to be drawn up from the land tax registers. The second act was repealed in the following session as unworkable and prohibitively expensive, and voter qualification in the counties remained a haphazard, hopelessly muddled affair. Tracing individuals between parishes and townships was virtually impossible, just as it is now. A fuller discussion of these early attempts to devise accurate lists of voters is contained in John Prest, *Politics in the Age of Cobden*, London, 1979. Also see Ivor Jennings, *Parliament*, Cambridge, 1961, p. 67, and Robert W. Smith, "Political Organization and Canvassing; Yorkshire Elections Before the Reform Bill," *AHR* 74(1969):1538-600. In addition to the wardens for the poor, borough officers were instrumental in identifying qualified borough voters. Even so, the accuracy of the de-

pains insured a high turnout. A report from the 1786 Norwich by-election noted that "both parties were active all night hunting after those freemen who had either been kidnapped or who had not polled."[11] At the time of the closing of the poll in Chester at the 1784 contest, "there were on a modest computation not less than 69 freemen unpolled, all of whom had declared in favor of Messrs. G[rosvenor] and B[ootle]."[12] In light of the nearly 1,000 voters who had recorded their choices, the sixty-nine unpolled electors attest to the thoroughness of electoral mobilization in Chester. More substantial evidence bespeaks a very high turnout indeed. Pollbooks for six separate elections at Maidstone and Lewes listed the qualified, yet unpolled, electors as well as the political choices of the voters.

cisions made by the returning officers in each town may have been no more reliable than decisions made by returning officers in the counties, where the task was even more complicated.

An effort was made early in the course of this research to compile electoral lists for the four boroughs involved. Such a list obviously was impossible for Northampton since it would have amounted to a census of the town's male inhabitants not in receipt of poor relief. Norwich and Maidstone, on the other hand, seemed to pose less insurmountable obstacles to the formulation of such a list. In fact, the obstacles were just as formidable and proved as insurmountable as in Northampton. The Norwich freeman rolls were not sufficiently descriptive to allow nominal record linkage involving the Norwich pollbooks. As explained in Appendix I, links were made across elections when a sufficient number of identifiers (i.e., occupations, addresses, etc.) made such links justifiable. The freeman admission rolls could not be employed in this kind of linkage, and a gargantuan effort would have produced a hopelessly flawed list of "qualified" Norwich electors. Maidstone posed the same problem; a list of qualified "freemen" could have been attempted from the freeman admission rolls, but its accuracy would have been sufficiently suspect to prevent any subsequent conclusions from being any more persuasive than the undoubtedly flawed but possibly reliable estimates contained in the pollbooks themselves. The returning officers for Maidstone seemed infinitely more reliable than an observer with extremely limited data some two centuries later.

[11] *The Norwich and Bury Post*, September 19, 1786; *A Correct Copy of the Evidence on the Norwich Election Petition*, Norwich, 1787.

[12] *An Alphabetical List of the . . . Freemen Who Polled*, Chester, 1784.

In the absence of electoral registers (a deficiency the government tried to remedy unsuccessfully on several occasions) such lists of nonvoters could be compiled only from previous pollbooks, freemen rolls, and ratebooks, and therefore must have overlooked some qualified nonvoters. Nevertheless, a considerable effort was expended in their compilation, even to the point of occasionally recording the reasons some voters failed to attend at the hustings.[13]

These lists make a persuasive argument for heavy, and perhaps even increasing, voter turnout over the entire period. More than 86 percent of the electorate participated in the Maidstone election of 1768, and by 1780, the proportion approached 90 percent.[14] The increase in participation was more pronounced in Lewes, and the resulting turnout was impressively complete. Seventy-four percent of the Lewes electors voted in 1774 while 93 percent turned out in 1790. The elections of 1796 and 1802 boasted turnouts of 95 percent and 97 percent respectively.[15] An independently conducted census of Lewes in 1790 supports these impressive figures. Two hundred nineteen of the 243 male householders listed in the census (90 percent) voted in the 1790 Lewes election.[16] Such pollbook lists of non-

[13] Lists of Maidstone's nonvoters are appended to the pollbooks of 1768 and 1780. The Lewes pollbook of 1774 also contains a list of qualified nonvoters. To the Nottingham poll of 1774 was appended a list of "such voters as did not Poll, as far as could be procured." Nottingham residents accounted for 75 nonvoters, but they were outnumbered by the 128 men from London and the countryside listed as not voting. The Maidstone list, as well as several others, gave such reasons as "out of the country" and "infirm" as excuses for nonvoting. See note 10. *An Exact List of the Burgesses and Freeholders . . . Who Polled*, Nottingham, 1774; *The Poll*, Lewes, 1774; *The Poll for Electing Two Burgesses*, Maidstone, 1774.

[14] *The Poll for Electing Two Burgesses*, Maidstone, 1768 and 1780.

[15] Data for Lewes elections obtained from the printed Lewes pollbooks of 1774, 1790, 1796, 1802.

[16] "A Survey of the Borough of Lewes in Sussex . . . Taken in the year 1790," Woolgar MS., Spicilegia . . . Lewensis, pp. 525-44, ESRO. Lewes contained six parishes, of which only four (All Saints, St. Michael, part of St. John Sub-Castro and part of St. Anne's) were within the legal

voters are fairly uncommon; the tedious and often complicated process of verifying electoral rights discouraged efforts to list qualified nonparticipants. However, reports from other boroughs mirror the pattern evident in Lewes and Maidstone. Almost certainly fewer than 10 percent of the voters in Nottingham (1774) and Chester (1784) failed to cast their ballots.[17] Resident Nottingham voters displayed still greater determination to vote; nonresident freemen contributed the majority of the already small number of nonvoters.[18] In comparison, immediately pre- and post-reform participation rates in Maidstone were relatively low. At the five Maidstone elections between 1826 and 1835, turnout averaged less than 80 percent; the participation rate of these later voters in Maidstone only once (1831) exceeded the participation rates at either of the eighteenth-century Maidstone elections for which estimates can be made.[19] Postreform participation rates at Cambridge also underscore the high turnout at prereform elections in Maidstone and Lewes. The participation rates of voters at Cambridge elections between the first and second Reform Acts fell in the same range as those of their unreformed

---

boundaries of the parliamentary borough. The census of the town's house-holders was conducted without regard to the parliamentary boundaries of the borough, but fortunately included street names in its description of Lewes's inhabitants, thus making it possible to compare Lewes's population within the parliamentary boundaries with the residents of Lewes who voted in the election of 1790. J. H. Philbin provides an excellent description of Lewes's political structure before its incorporation in 1831. J. H. Philbin, *Parliamentary Representation, 1832*, New Haven, 1965, pp. 193-94; House of Commons Sessional Papers, *Report of the Commission on Municipal Corporations*, vol. 23, London, 1835, p. 116.

[17] *Burgesses and Freeholders Who Polled*, Nottingham, 1774; *Freemen Who Polled*, Chester, 1784.

[18] One hundred twenty-eight (63 percent) of the 203 nonvoters listed on the Nottingham pollbook lived outside Nottingham.

[19] The turnout rates for later Maidstone elections were: 1826, 75.6 percent, 1830, 84 percent, 1831, 92.4 percent, and 1835, 73.5 percent. Only the 1831 turnout of 92 percent exceeded the proportions of 1768 and 1780. Crosby, *Parliamentary Record*, pp. 225-29.

counterparts. Turnout for the reformed electorate in Cambridge consistently failed to exceed 90 percent and ranged as low as 82 percent.[20]

The more reliably measured rates of consistent participation at successive elections in these boroughs reinforce the evidence of high turnouts at specific contests. The members of an electorate identified at one election and followed over time naturally and inevitably disappear over a period of years from mortality, infirmity, and residential mobility. Of these and other factors reducing the original electorate, mortality alone can be estimated, and then only roughly.[21]

[20] Calculated from figures in Jeremy Mitchell and James Cornford, "The Political Demography of Cambridge, 1832-1868," *Albion* 9(1977):266, 270-71.

[21] Age distributions for the total population are known only after the census of 1821, and age- and sex-specific death rates have not been calculated for the population before 1838. As late as the 1840s and 50s, when infant mortality rates had almost certainly declined from former levels, Armstrong has shown that population death rates are reduced by 20 percent or more if infant deaths are excluded. Therefore, the effects of infant mortality must be considered in any attempt to estimate the likely survival rates of members of an electorate from time$_1$ at an election at time$_2$. Although we are forced to rely on unsuitable rates in attempting to compensate for the effects of infant mortality, T. H. Marshall's classic study estimated later eighteenth-century age distributions and make it possible to use early nineteenth-century calculations with less reservation. Also, a few contemporary estimates of mortality rates in Maidstone and several other towns in the late eighteenth century lend substance to the calculations. Therefore, using Marshall's adequate, albeit possibly flawed, estimate of approximately 29.3 percent of the population falling into the twenty to forty-year-old group, and 46.3 percent falling into the 20- to 60-year-old portion of the population, the 1821 age distributions can be adjusted roughly to correspond to the later eighteenth-century population. Thus, the adjusted age distribution for these eighteenth-century borough populations would be on the order of 33.6 percent, 26.4 percent, 18.9 percent, 13.4 percent, 4.5 percent, and 3.2 percent for each generation between twenty and eighty years of age. These distributions permit the calculation of the adult male death rate for an "average" urban population. Instead of 37.4/1,000 which seems to have been standard for later eighteenth-century borough populations, the death rate for the adult male electorate was probably in the vicinity of 29.9/1,000. If anything, this figure

Lacking age-specific or regional mortality rates and in the absence of adequate demographic data for later eighteenth-century populations, an estimated adult mortality rate, or in this case, adult male survival rate, must be crude, but certainly not much more than 88.6 percent of an electorate could have survived an election hiatus of four years.[22] The

may *underestimate* the true adult death rates prevailing in most towns, thus weakening the argument possible from Table 3.1. Therefore, these figures are most impressive. Howlett observed the differential average annual mortality rates in a variety of English towns during the 1780s, ranging from 1 in 41 at Chester to 1 in 21 at Gravesend. If we assume the average of these towns (about 33/1,000) to be fairly indicative, the estimate of 29.9 may approximate the adult male death rate reasonably closely. At any rate, the margin of error seems acceptably small given the nature of the estimations to be attempted with this information.

Using these figures, rough as they are, an adjusted consistent participation rate can be derived for these electorates that reveals more adequately the rates at which voters turned out at successive elections. Calculating the likely effects of mortality on an electorate frozen at time$_1$ as it is examined at various points over time, the continually diminishing size of the original membership of the cohort must be taken into account. Changes in the size of the original electorate after one or two years would have little impact, but a long-range estimate could badly exaggerate the number of deaths likely to occur over a span of years if natural shrinkage is not built into the calculation. For this study, the effect of the diminishing size of the original electorate was adjusted with a calculation suggested by John Kolp of the Laboratory for Political Research at the University of Iowa:

$$P_2 = IRP_1 - \tfrac{1}{2}(I^2R^2P_1 - IR^2P_1).$$

P_1 is the number of electors at time$_1$, P_2 is the number of those electors alive at time$_2$, I is the interval between elections (in years), and R is the mortality rate. T. H. Marshall, "The Population Problem During the Industrial Revolution," in *Population in History*, ed. D. V. Glass, Chicago, 1965; J. Howlett, *Observations on the Increased Population, Healthiness, and Care in the Town of Maidstone*, Maidstone, 1782; David Baker, "Inhabitants of Cardington, 1782," *Publication of the Bedfordshire Historical Record Society*, London, 52(1973):27-100. Daniel Scott Smith, "The Estimates of Early American Historical Geographers," *Historical Methods*, 1212(1979):24-38.

[22] Rather than using the actual number of electors at time$_1$, applying the formula with P_1 as 100 percent provides general estimates for the proportionate size of the membership of an electorate from time$_1$ returning to participate at an election at time$_2$.

proportion fell to less than 75 percent after ten years. If anything, these estimates understate the impact of mortality, and therefore understate the natural diminution of the electorate over time. Mobility may have had an even greater effect on borough electorates, though it reduced the electorates in Maidstone and Norwich less than in many other constituencies since freeman voters (and freeholders in Norwich) leaving town had the right to return and participate in all elections. Peter Laslett found that two-thirds of the residents of an eighteenth-century rural parish could not be traced over a relatively short period. Of the 61 percent who were no longer in the parish after twelve years, only one-third had died; migration accounted for fully two-thirds of the loss.[23]

In measuring consistent participation, both irregular intervals between contested general elections and uncontested elections in particular boroughs must be taken into account. Of the four boroughs being considered, Maidstone voters alone contested every parliamentary general election from 1761 to 1802. No contest was held at Norwich during the 1774 general election, creating a gap of twelve years during which the Norwich electors had no opportunity to select representatives to parliament, and lapses almost as long occurred frequently in Northampton and Lewes. Three elections went completely uncontested in

[23] Thus, while we are substracting 3 percent annually, more or less, for mortality, these data suggest that perhaps as much as another 6 percent annually should be subtracted from the original population for the effects of mobility. However, the consistent participation rate was so high without adjustments for mobility that it seems reasonable to assume that these electors were more stable than the rural population. Certainly, though, mobility reduced the returning electorate to some degree, and the return rates in Table 3.1 would be somewhat higher if they measured consistent participation solely for those physically able to participate. Peter Laslett, "Le Brassage de la Population en France et en Angleterre," *Annales de Démographie Historique* [Paris] (1969):99-109. Also see, R. S. Schofield, "Age Specific Mobility in an Eighteenth Century Rural English Parish," *Annales de Démographie Historique* [Paris] (1971):261-74.

Northampton, and one lacked a contest in Lewes, along with a second (1784) called off to the chagrin of Sir Henry Blackman after an embarrassingly abbreviated poll. Without adjusting electorates for mortality, consistent participation was extraordinarily high (Table 3.1). In Norwich, Lewes, and Northampton, consistent participation rates never fell below 50 percent for any election separated by an ordinary interval of time (i.e., consecutive elections not separated by uncontested general elections), and on the two occasions in Maidstone when rates fell below 50 percent, voters from previous elections still turned up in large numbers (about 48 percent both times). After adjusting electorates roughly for the effects of mortality, with the full realization that other factors, if measurable, would lower the maximum expected return rate considerably, the uniform persistence shown by the voters in all four boroughs is nothing short of remarkable. The return rate for all contested elections separated by ordinary intervals in all four boroughs invariably remained above 60 percent and occasionally topped 75 percent (Table 3.1).[24] The only notable characteristic other than the overall tenacity of the voters was the somewhat higher return rate in Lewes, possibly as a result of its smaller, and thus more easily mobilized, electorate. There were no tendencies toward higher participation rates over the period, just generally high rates of consistent participation in all boroughs at all elections.

Due to the extreme difficulty inherent in tracing electors across time, comparable return rates for English voters in other eras are rare.[25] Using the few available figures, the

[24] Norwich remained uncontested in 1774 because the dissolution came as such a surprise that Edward Bacon's opponents, though considerable in number, were unable to muster an adequate offensive against his return. The elections of 1761, 1780, and 1802 passed without a poll in Northampton. Lewes voters were not asked for a formal selection in 1761, but experienced a campaign of some kind at each subsequent general election. See Appendix II. Also, Hook MS. 16133, ESRO.

[25] For an indication of the problems of this procedure and a method for overcoming some of them, see John Phillips, "Nominal Record Link-

93

Table 3.1: Consistent Participation (Percentage of Electorate from Previous Election Participating in the Subsequent Election)

	1761-68	1768-74	1774-80	1780-84	1784-90	1790-96	1796-1802
Norwich	61.5	40.6		67.3	52.4	53.4	60.6
Maidstone	50.5	47.8	56.2	58.9	53.9	48.4	55.1
Northampton		50.7			62.0	57.0	
Lewes		58.7	64.0	46.5		63.3	61.3
				53.6			

Consistent Participation
(Compensating for the Estimated Diminution of the Electorate by Death)

	1761-68	1768-74	1774-80	1780-84	1784-90	1790-96	1796-1802
Norwich	76.0	58.0		75.6	62.8	64.0	72.7
Maidstone	71.6	57.9	67.4	66.5	64.6	58.0	66.1
Northampton		60.8			74.3	60.3	
Lewes		70.4	76.7	62.8		75.9	73.5
				72.3			

consistent participation rates of these unreformed electors compare quite favorably with the supposedly partisan electors of the first decades of the eighteenth century and with voters in the later decades of the nineteenth. In fact, consistent participation in these four boroughs exceeded by a comfortable margin the rates in several constituencies for which figures are available during the party struggles of Queen Anne's reign. Even though the intervals between the Westmorland county elections of 1700, 1701, and 1702 were each less than twelve months, only 63 percent of the original electorate returned in 1701 and less than 41 percent reappeared in 1702. Equally low rates marked the Hampshire election of 1710. Less than 42 percent of the 3,517 electors who cast ballots in the election of 1705 returned to vote in the subsequent contest. Adjusted for the effects of mortality, the real rate of return could not have been higher than 50 percent.[26] Unreformed participation also bettered slightly the return rates at Cambridge between the Reform Acts, and essentially equalled return rates in

---

age and the Study of Individual Level Voting Behavior," *Laboratory for Political Research*, University of Iowa (1976):1-17. A method of reducing the task through sampling is considered in John Phillips, "Achieving a Critical Mass While Avoiding an Explosion," *JIH* 9(1979):493-508.

[26] Rather than a function of the respective political systems, the lower return rates noted in the Augustan period may be due at least partially to the fact that rates calculated to date usually refer to county elections. Participation was often a more difficult process for the county electorate since polling places frequently were located at considerable distances. Also, the lower consistent participation rates may be explained in part by the nominal record linkage programs used in tracing voters across elections, and the inherently greater difficulty in identifying county electors when occupations were not recorded in the pollbooks. With fewer "identifiers" available to merge the records of these earlier voters, it may not have been possible to link as high a proportion of the "truly linked pairs." Gloria Guth, "Surname Spellings and Computerized Record Linkage," *Historical Methods* 10(1976):10-19. Robert Hopkinson, "Elections in Cumberland and Westmorland," Ph.D. diss., University of Newcastle-upon-Tyne, 1973, pp. 252-55; W. A. Speck et al., "Computer Analysis of Pollbooks: A Further Report," *BIHR* 48(1975):110.

Ashford more than fifty years after the election of 1802.[27] Only 59 percent of the Cambridge electors created by the Reform Bill returned in 1839, and an even smaller percentage of subsequent recruits to the electorate participated in elections more than five years from the time of their original ballot. As late as 1859, new voters in Cambridge returned to participate in subsequent elections less consistently than their unreformed predecessors in Norwich and Maidstone.[28] The Ashford voters entering the electorate after 1850, alone among those examined, matched the persistence shown by their predecessors in Norwich and elsewhere. After a seven-year interval, 64 percent of the experienced Ashford voters participated in the 1863 general election. Compensating for probable adult mortality rates, this return of nearly 70 percent approximated the rate common in the post-1761 elections.[29]

Of greater structural importance to the political system than the frequency with which electors returned to the polls at subsequent elections, however, were the relative proportions of these experienced voters in subsequent electorates. The lack of experienced voters was one of the most striking aspects of the electoral system in the early years of the century, and the degree of experience, or inexperience, could have drastically influenced an election. A mere 31 percent of the voters casting ballots in the 1710 Hampshire election had participated in the preceding (1705) election; over two-thirds of the electors were newly added.[30] In stark contrast, less than 20 percent of the voters at each Cambridge election between 1832 and 1868 were new additions

[27] Mitchell and Cornford, "Political Demography," pp. 266-67; Michael Drake, "The Mid-Victorian Voter," *JIH* 1(1971):473-90.

[28] Mitchell and Cornford, "Political Demography," pp. 266-67.

[29] Drake, "Mid-Victorian Voter," pp. 481-85. The Ashford return rate calculated from Drake's figures assumes the adult male death rate suggested by Alan Armstrong, *Stability and Change in an English Country Town*, Cambridge, 1974, p. 139.

[30] Calculated from figures in Speck, "Computer Analysis," p. 110.

to the electorate.[31] The proportions at later eighteenth-century elections (Table 3.2) appear to fall midway between these extremes. Actually, despite the apparent differences between the rate in Norwich, Northampton, Maidstone, and Lewes that in ordinary years hovered around 60 percent, and the 80 percent average in postreform Cambridge, the patterns in the four unreformed borough electorates closely resemble that of reformed Cambridge voters. The rapid succession of elections in the newly expanded Cambridge constituency after the Reform Act caused the higher proportion of experienced voters at Cambridge elections. The sixteen contests in Cambridge before 1866, an average of one every two years, severely limited the number of new voters possible at any single election. Another postreform borough, Ashford, points more accurately to the relationship between the proportion of experienced voters in pre- and post-reform constituencies by providing a more temporally appropriate comparison. In those elections not affected by gaps caused by uncontested elections, the "old" electors in Norwich and the other three towns never comprised less than approximately 50 percent of the total electorate, and in one instance made up almost 65 percent of the voters, while in four Ashford elections, the experienced electors usually constituted about 61 percent of the total number of voters.[32] If longer periods had separated the Cambridge elections, a similar pattern would have existed there too. For example, only 59 percent of the Cambridge

---

[31] Calculated from figures in Mitchell and Cornford, "Political Demography," p. 266.

[32] These consistent participation rates, according to the raw figures contained in Drake, "Mid-Victorian Voter," p. 481 were:

Election Year	Consistent Participation	Experienced Voters (%)
1857	76.4	65.7
1863	63.6	59.5
1865	93.5	73.0
1868	85.0	43.9

voters in 1847 would have been "experienced" had the election of 1840 not been followed by three other elections at which new voters could be introduced to the electoral process.[33] With up to twelve years separating later eighteenth-century elections, the percentage of experienced voters remained consistently and notably high. Old electors made up almost 50 percent of the total electorate even in the Norwich (1780) and Northampton (1784) contests that were preceded by uncontested elections. The proportion of experienced voters in the unreformed electorates fell well under 50 percent just once when, at the Lewes election of 1790, the effects of an uncontested election in combination with a substantial overall increase in the size of the electorate led to an unusually large number of new voters.[34]

Many participants in Norwich and Maidstone elections, and to a lesser extent the Lewes and Northampton elections, were seasoned veterans of the electoral process, having voted in at least two previous parliamentary elections (Table 3.3). With the exception of the 1780 figures, which

Table 3.2: Electoral Composition (Percentage of Electorate at an Election Participating in Previous Election)

	1768	1774	1780	1784	1790	1796	1802
Norwich	51.3	NC	45.6	64.6	54.3	56.8	48.7
Maidstone	61.0	64.6	51.1	65.1	54.0	53.0	51.9
Northampton	NA	63.2	NC	49.4	61.8	59.8	NC
Lewes	NA	56.3	82.0	NC	36.6	51.3	54.6

NA = not applicable
NC = no contest

[33] In other words, only 960 of the 1,622 voters casting ballots in 1840 reappeared in 1847, but in the meantime a total of 405 new voters had been added to the electorate at the elections of 1841, 1843, and 1845. Thus, 87 percent of the 1847 electorate had voted in at least one prior election.

[34] In addition to the ten-year interval preceding the election of 1790, the Lewes electorate increased by 49.3 percent. See Chapter 5, Table 5.5.

reflected the impact of the uncontested Norwich election of 1774, Norwich and Maidstone elections involved much the same proportion of experienced voters. Roughly four of every ten voters at the 1790 election in both boroughs were participating in their third consecutive election, and normally the proportion was one in three. Such a solid core of experienced electors must have affected the conduct of parliamentary campaigns, since this long-term participation, coupled with the consistent majority of experienced voters at each election, created the real possibility of an electorate with long standing loyalties and definite political predilections, particularly when faced with candidates who also tended to appear at election after election. The Lewes and Northampton electorates, on the other hand, contained fewer experienced voters at elections held during the 1790s. Three-time voters contributed almost 30 percent of the total in the Northampton elections of 1784 and 1790, but less than 20 percent in 1796. The proportion of returning voters at Lewes elections twice approached or surpassed levels normal in Norwich and Maidstone, yet experienced voters also twice accounted for 22 percent or less of the total.

The discrepancies between the two freeman and two "inhabitant" boroughs are magnified and clarified by a more inclusive measure of experience. Table 3.4 compares general levels of experience among all electors in the four boroughs. More than half the voters in Maidstone and Nor-

Table 3.3: Electors at Three Consecutive Parliamentary General Elections (Percentage)

Election	Norwich	Maidstone	Northampton*	Lewes*
1780	27.1	36.7	—	34.0
1784	31.9	30.1	29.8	—
1790	38.9	41.7	28.6	21.8
1796	35.3	33.2	19.4	22.0
1802	31.1	32.6	—	30.9

* Uncontested elections reduce the number of possible comparisons.

wich participated in more than one election, and quite a
few (9 percent in Norwich and 7 percent in Maidstone)
took part in no less than six elections over the forty-year
period. This sort of long-term participation was much less
common in Northampton and Lewes. Northampton voters
could not have participated in six elections between 1761
and 1802; only five general elections provoked contests to
the point of actual polls. And although participation in
Lewes was possible over a longer period, just 2 percent of
Lewes's voters cast ballots in six elections. Reducing the
number of contests to four, a number at least theoretically
possible in each borough, the differences remain substantial, ranging from almost a quarter of the voters in Norwich
to precisely 10 percent in Lewes. A majority of the electorate in Lewes and Northampton voted in a solitary parliamentary election. Hence, despite the uniformly impressive turnouts at single elections in all four boroughs, levels
of political experience within the various electorates differed markedly. Given the opportunity, electors participated eagerly, but the number of opportunities varied widely
from borough to borough, regulating the degree to which
long-term participation was possible.

It might be argued that a measurement of "experience"
based on those voters actually going to the polls (Table 3.4)

Table 3.4: Percentage of Electorates Participating Repeatedly

	Norwich 7 contests (N = 500)	Maidstone 8 contests (N = 575)	Northampton 5 contests (N = 500)	Lewes 6 contests (N = 300)
Only 1 Election	42.4	44.4	52.6	54.3
2 or more	57.6	55.6	47.4	45.7
3 or more	33.4	33.2	26.1	28.1
4 or more	24.3	19.0	15.1	10.0
5 or more	14.0	12.6	6.3	6.5
6 or more	8.9	6.9		2.0
7 or more	5.5	4.2		
All eight		1.5		

NOTE: N = Random samples of entire electorates.

ignores the fact that some political experience could be acquired in a variety of ways in the unreformed political system. Canvassing, voluntary abstention, and involuntary abstention remain unmeasured with this definition of political experience. Certainly an electorate could be heavily involved in the political process, yet never cast ballots at the hustings. The Yorkshire electorate, for example, engaged in an active campaign in 1784 that never resulted in a poll, and political experience gained through such a heated but unpolled contest could well have helped politicize the electorate involved. The electors in these four boroughs, however, were not subjected to heated, unpolled political disputes. And in the effort to explain the apparent divergence in the voting habits of these various electorates, the failure of the voters in Northampton and Lewes to gain actual parliamentary political experience by casting ballots seems relatively significant. The rapid rise of partisan behavior in Norwich and Maidstone cannot be explained by experience alone, but voting experience in parliamentary elections, or lack of it, was a notable difference in the political lives of the electors in these towns.

MUNICIPAL ELECTIONS

Moreover, the structure of municipal government in each of these boroughs further reduced the similarities so much in evidence in Tables 3.1 and 3.2. Municipal governments, rather than the Crown, largely determined the frequency with which voters went to the hustings. As a result of the Septennial Act (1716), intervals between parliamentary general elections frequently exceeded six years, and at best, more than four years separated parliamentary general elections in this period. Uncontested general elections, common in Northampton and Lewes, often increased the gap drastically, as did the single uncontested election in Norwich. Hence, municipal contests possessed a considerable *potential* importance that was realized by the boroughs in

101

varying degrees. Municipal contests effectively supplemented the parliamentary elections in Norwich and Maidstone, and to a lesser extent, Lewes. Conversely, by the reign of George III the Northampton corporation had been closed to outside participation for more than a century.[35] There, decisions over parliamentary representation alone permitted any activity by the Northampton electorate, and precious few of those decisions were left to the voters. Thus the structure of municipal governments, not the national political system, regulated the amount of electoral activity possible in these boroughs, and to a certain extent, determined the political climate in each town.[36]

Although control of the Norwich corporation usually remained in the hands of a readily identifiable elite, control was precarious at best and constantly under attack at the municipal elections held annually in each of the four "great" wards. The freemen of each Norwich ward chose from their ranks six alderman-for-life and a set number of common councilmen for one year. Elections for some of the other city offices, such as sheriff, required a poll of all city electors.[37] Therefore, every year was marked by at least

[35] J. Freeman, *History of the Town of Northampton*, Northampton, 1817, pp. 28-30; N. Birdsall, *History of Northampton and Vicinity*, Northampton, 1821, pp. 18-20.

[36] Derek Hirst, in describing the political realities of seventeenth-century England, noted that "municipal politics . . . provided a real training ground for many people." Interestingly enough, Daniel Defoe suggested the corollary argument in his discussion of politics in the boroughs during his visits in 1705 and 1707. Pointing to the relative "quiet" at Leeds, Wakefield, and Sheffield (nonparliamentary boroughs), he argued that it was the frequent parliamentary elections that served to "divide the people" even in municipal elections. Derek Hirst, *The Representative of the People?*, Cambridge, 1975, p. 109; Geoffrey Holmes and W. A. Speck, *The Divided Society*, London, 1967, pp. 45-46.

[37] The four "great" Norwich wards (and their component wards) were Mancroft (Giles, Mancroft, and Stephen), Northern (Coslany, Colegate, and Feybridge), Conisford (Ber Street, North Conisford, and South Conisford), and Wymer (West Wymer, Middle Wymer, and East Wymer). Mancroft was represented by sixteen councilmen, Northern and Conis-

one opportunity for the freemen (and freeholders) to exercise their franchises, and frequently the voters went to the polls on several occasions in a single year. The Norwich electorate was not given a chance to vote in the parliamentary general election of 1774, the suddenness of the dissolution preventing an effective opposition to the incumbents of long standing, Sir Harbord Harbord and Edward Bacon.[38] Yet rather than being effectively disenfranchised by the uncontested return of the incumbents, during 1774 each Norwich elector was called upon to vote in two or three elections. Norwich voters filled five vacant aldermanic seats in 1774, scattered over all four wards, and were called upon to participate in the regular common council and shrieval elections as well.[39] In addition to these municipal contests, parliamentary by-elections increased the number of electoral opportunities in Norwich in the later years of the century. Hotly contested by-elections in 1786, 1787, 1794, and 1799 resulted in voter turnouts generally as heavy as in general elections. Indeed, a record turnout accompanied the contest between Henry Hobart and Sir Thomas Beevor for the seat vacated by the death of Sir Harbord Harbord in 1786. More than 2,800 voters, including some not actually qualified to vote, cast ballots in that election, a total not exceeded until the equally vituperative election of 1802 at which William Windham and the Administration party lost to the Whig Nonconformist, William Smith.[40]

---

ford by twelve, and Wymer by twenty. Each of the four wards returned six aldermen to sit on the Corporation.

[38] The 1774 election caught the nation by surprise, as it caught Norwich by surprise since it occurred "six months before its natural death, and without the design being known but the Tuesday before, and that by few persons." Horace Walpole to Sir Horace Mann, October 6, 1774, in Horace Walpole, *Horace Walpole's Correspondence*, ed. W. S. Lewis, 39 vols., New Haven, 1967, 24:44.

[39] During 1774, two aldermen were elected from Coslany Ward and one each from the other three great wards. Norwich Corporation Assembly Books, CS16, vol. 10, NNRO.

[40] See Appendix III.

Municipal elections occurred somewhat less frequently in Maidstone. Freemen could not vote in aldermanic elections and the forty common councilmen, although selected from and by the freemen, held their posts for life. As a result, only vacancies resulting from death or resignation forced elections, and usually several vacancies had occurred before the mayor called for a vote.[41] Nevertheless, council elections were relatively frequent, particularly after the legal victory of the freemen over the Corporation in 1774. Following an especially difficult borough election in 1764, at which the controlling party lost four common council seats, the mayor (Thomas Pope) and the other aldermen attempted to alter the borough charter of 1747 to completely exclude freemen from participation at local elections. An extensive and expensive legal battle in King's Bench, led by George Prentis, saved the voting rights of Maidstone's freemen. The freemen achieved victory through a court decision in which Lord Mansfield remarked that the aldermen "would overturn the constitution itself if it were in their power."[42] This lasting victory was followed by at least twelve municipal elections before 1802, making a minimum of twenty-four elections in the borough during the period after 1761. Because borough contests usually happened during years other than general election years, Maidstone electors went to the polls every other year on average and often participated even more frequently. Sixteen municipal elections can be identified positively from surviving pollbooks for municipal contests, and other elections may well have occurred for which no pollbooks have survived.[43] And since a single parish (and a single ward)

[41] J. M. Russell, *History of Maidstone*, Maidstone, 1881, p. 210 and *passim*; House of Commons Sessional Papers, *Report of the Commission on Municipal Corporations*, vol. 24., London, 1835, pp. 749-70; *Kentish Gazette*, December 12, 1772.

[42] William Roberts James, *The Charters and Other Documents of Maidstone*, London, 1825, pp. xxv, xxvii-xix.

[43] See Table 3.5. The list of municipal elections is derived from the surviving manuscript pollbooks. Other elections for municipal offices may have taken place without leaving a record through a surviving pollbook.

encompassed Maidstone, all elections to the common council involved the entire electorate. Clearly, local political activity could overshadow parliamentary political activity even in a borough like Maidstone where parliamentary general elections always provoked contests. The lives of Maidstone electors seem, in fact, to have been affected much more by municipal contests than by parliamentary elections.

The town of Lewes was not governed by a corporation. Instead, the administration of the town was accomplished officially, if rather informally, through a jury of the court leet. Each year residents elected two constables and two headboroughs on "law day," and town meetings, apparently attended by all householders wishing to vote, decided other issues such as town rates. The frequency of these town meetings, or "law days" increased during the 1780s until 1789, when the calling of *the* town meeting, as the town book described it, gave way to the calling of simply *a* town meeting, of which there were usually several during the year.[44] Since Lewes possessed no charter, Lewes town meetings were extralegal affairs, and the exact number of residents taking part is uncertain, but clearly, the town government was reasonably open and participation was relatively frequent and undoubtedly important enough to warrant large attendances. If Lewes politics lacked the structure and formality lent by a corporation and a municipal government of some complexity, as in Norwich and Maidstone, the conduct of ordinary affairs at least exposed Lewes residents to some "political" activity annually.[45]

Unlike the other boroughs, Northampton was governed by a corporation strictly and unchallengeably in the hands

[44] Verena Smith, ed., *The Town Book of Lewes, 1702-1837*, Lewes, 1972, p. 75. Although there were occasional entries of "a law day" as early as 1786, the change to several "law days" each year was made permanent after 1789.

[45] For example, of the signatories to the tax resolution of 1772, 85 percent were also listed in the pollbooks at the contested parliamentary election of 1774. For a description of the development of the town of Lewes, see L. F. Salzman, ed., *The Victoria County History of Sussex*, 9 vols., London, 1940, 7:7-44.

of the municipal officeholders. The twenty Northampton aldermen were selected by and from the common councilmen, and, in turn, the aldermen chose new common councilmen. Nor were any other city offices filled by the electorate, leaving parliamentary elections as the only opportunity for Northampton voters to exercise their franchises.[46] To make matters worse, three parliamentary general elections lacked contests altogether, and not a single by-election disturbed Northampton's electoral torpor.

Another activity involving the electorate, canvassing, partially compensated for both the lack of municipal elections and the infrequency of parliamentary contests. For instance, while no poll was taken at the election of 1780, a thorough canvass of Northampton's electors preceded the day scheduled for the poll, and the outcome of the canvass foreclosed the possibility of a poll. Canvassers secured promises of 555 double votes and 21 plumps for Lords Althorp and Compton. With only 381 electors either uncanvassed or expressly opposed to the joint candidacy of the two lords, a poll would have served no purpose.[47] However, canvassing was equally common in the three other boroughs; canvasses either preceded or replaced polls in virtually every other election in Norwich, Maidstone, and Lewes.[48] Thus, Northampton stood alone in affording its voters so few opportunities for participation, canvassing notwithstanding.

Canvassing itself deserves closer attention, given its tremendous potential impact on the electorate. The importance of canvassing for mobilizing the electorate has been demonstrated in modern elections, but the nature of the canvass and its probable role in these early contests hardly

[46] *Report of the Commission on Municipal Corporations*, vol. 25, pp. 557-76. Before 1836, Northampton was governed by a common council with only nominal powers. The real power lay with the twenty aldermen.
[47] Namier and Brooke, *House of Commons*, 1:346.
[48] Smith, "Political Organization," pp. 1546-50.

resembled modern canvasses.[49] With two exceptions, England's borough constituencies contained relatively small electorates, and a candidate could accomplish much of the canvass personally, even in a "larger" borough like Norwich.[50] An elector could hardly remain unaware of an election if his vote was actively solicited by the candidate himself. Also, the canvass in effect doubled the number of opportunities for electoral participation. A voter's intention as stated in a canvass usually corresponded closely to his actual vote, and the added opportunity of expressing his choice (often in the presence of one of the candidates) should have aided the process of politicization. Fully 80 percent of the promises given by Lewes electors to canvassers before the 1774 election translated into votes at the hustings, and half of the remainder failed to keep their promises by failing to vote; very few actually switched sides.[51] Such consistency was not uncommon.

Although canvasses did not compensate for the serious deficiency of electoral opportunities in Northampton, the contrast between Northampton and the other three boroughs can be maintained only if the voters in Norwich, Maidstone, and Lewes took advantage of the opportunities

[49] See bibliography in Robert E. Kraut and J. B. McConahay, "How Being Interviewed Affects Voting; An Experiment," *Public Opinion Quarterly* 37(1973):400; J. M. Bochel and P. T. Denver, "Canvassing, Turnout, and Party Support: An Experiment," *BJPS* 1(1971):257-69; W. J. Crotty, "Party Effort and Its Impact on the Vote," *APSR* 65(1971):439-51.

[50] The only exceptions were London, with some 7,000 voters and Westminster with approximately 12,000.

[51] A comparison of the canvass in Lewes before the election of 1774 and the actual voting results reveals only twenty-one electors who were canvassed but failed to vote, or who polled without being canvassed. Of the 184 canvassed voters, the canvass accurately predicted the behavior of 81.5 percent. Glynde Palace Archives, Trevor MS. 793, ESRO. Also see Karl von den Steinen, "The Fabric of Interest in the County," *Albion* 4(1972)206-18. Of 20,000 voters in Yorkshire, 14,000 were canvassed before the election of 1784 by the Association, and another large number was involved in the Fitzwilliam canvass. Robert W. Smith, "Political Organization and Canvassing," *AHR* 74(1969):1546-47.

provided by the municipal contests. Apparently they did, in contrast to modern municipal voters.[52] The relatively sketchy evidence of participation at local elections in Norwich and Lewes suggests heavy turnouts, and the solid evidence of Maidstone elections confirms this impression. Participation rates at Lewes town meetings cannot be gauged accurately without knowing how many were qualified to participate. Nevertheless, many individuals who appeared in the general election pollbooks signed resolutions passed at meetings concerning taxes and other matters. These signatures may have been limited to the supporters of specific resolutions rather than all participants, yet over 60 percent of the individuals who voted in the 1774 parliamentary election had signed the 1772 town meeting resolution concerning a local tax levy.[53] Admittedly, with such limited evidence it is impossible to conclude that all eligible voters participated in local "elections," but more concrete figures for the Norwich sheriff's election of 1781 and the aldermanic race held in Mancroft ward five days later provide substantial supporting evidence. Contemporary assertions of massive participation in local Norwich contests are borne out by voting totals. If either of these Norwich contests was typical, turnout in Norwich municipal contests paralleled the massive turnout at parliamentary elections. More Norwich electors voted in the sheriff's race (2,748) than at any parliamentary election until 1802, and approximately 83 percent of the voters in Mancroft ward at the parliamentary election of 1780 returned to vote in the aldermanic election the following year. The tremendous turnout at both closely fought races verifies the contemporary observation that "never was there so great a struggle for Parliament men as

[52] Howard Hamilton, "The Municipal Voter: Voting and Non-voting in City Elections," *APSR* 65(1971):1135-141.

[53] Smith, ed., *Town Book of Lewes*, pp. 61-62; *A Copy of the Poll*, Lewes, 1774.

on this occasion."[54] Similar direct evidence from other Norwich municipal elections has not survived, but subsequently, contemporaries and a parliamentary investigatory committee agreed that Norwich municipal elections served either as preludes to parliamentary contests or as continuations of previous ones.[55]

More precisely measurable turnouts at Maidstone municipal elections confirm the pattern suggested in Norwich and Lewes. In contrast to modern municipal elections where it often seems that candidates outnumber the voters, participation in Maidstone common council elections rivalled, and even surpassed, the high turnout normal at Maidstone parliamentary elections. The expense of bringing in non-resident freemen from London and other towns prevented local elections from always achieving the sheer size of the total vote at parliamentary elections, but compared to the number of resident electors at parliamentary contests, local elections were impressively well attended (Table 3.5). Indeed, local contests in 1771 and 1788 matched parliamentary vote totals. Even with the occasionally staggering expense, out-voters sometimes were brought in to vote for men to fill common council seats. Surprisingly, no direct correlation existed between the number of common council seats being filled and the number of electors showing up to be counted. The 1768 election attracted less than 400 voters to fill seven seats, while almost 600 decided the single seat available in 1795. The magnitude of the contest did

[54] The 1781 aldermanic race in Mancroft ward immediately followed the sheriff's race between John Patteson and Thomas Colman and the candidates remained the same. Colman won the office of sheriff, but Patteson was elected to the Court of Aldermen. *A Copy of the Poll for Alderman*, Norwich, 1781. Patteson won the aldermanic race with 1,502 votes to Colman's 1,246. The Common Council Assembly Book contains a record of some of the municipal elections after 1782, and turnout seems to have been impressively complete.

[55] *Report of the Commission on Municipal Corporations*, vol. 25, pp. 1963-983; Oldfield, *Representative History, passim*.

not determine the size of the electorate. Strong ties bound these local elections to the Maidstone parliamentary contests. Little enough propaganda has survived from the parliamentary elections, and none at all from the municipal contests, but the manuscript pollbooks for Maidstone common council elections reveal slates of candidates clearly comprised of the same political opponents that vied for control of Maidstone's parliamentary seats. Moreover, the political choices of Maidstone's voters at municipal elections after 1774 closely mirrored their choices at parliamentary

Table 3.5: Turnout at Maidstone Parliamentary and Municipal Contests

	Parliamentary Elections			Number of Common
	All Voters	Resident Only	Municipal Elections	Council Seats Open
1761	782	495		
1764			574	5
1768	643	460	364	7
1771 (2)			632	3
1772 (2)			426	3
1774	642	474	589	2
1775			401	1
1780	706	492		
1782			174	2
1784	639	442		
1786			484	9
1788 (2)			660	4
1790	639	428		
1791			313	7
1793			522	6
1794			234	1
1795			568	1
1796	583	399		
1799			489	6
1801			446	4
1802	619	405		
X̄	669	449	436	

110

elections.[56] Apparently Maidstone's voters turned out in such large numbers at city elections for very good reasons.

PARTICIPATORY POLITICS AND PARTISAN BEHAVIOR

All in all, then, electors in Norwich, Maidstone, and to a lesser extent Lewes had many more opportunities to exercise their franchises than voters in Northampton, and voters in these boroughs consistently took advantage of their opportunities. Municipal elections generated much political activity, occasionally more than parliamentary contests, and electoral experience gained through local contests was just as valuable as experience gained through parliamentary elections. In fact, it could be argued, as it has been for newly developing nations, that before the national parties gained complete acceptance among the electorate, local elections may have had greater salience among the voters. The issues raised and the decisions reached in local contests were more tangible and less remote than most issues debated in parliamentary elections.

The greater number of electoral opportunities in Norwich and Maidstone, combined with the electoral interest evident in local elections, distinguish politics in these two boroughs from politics in Lewes, and even more from politics in Northampton. Political activity in Norwich and Maidstone provided a setting within which partisan behavior seems a logical outgrowth of the development of local parties with parliamentary ties and the injection of political

[56] For example, 72 percent of the electors in Maidstone voting for Brattle and Giles during the municipal contest of 1774 voted Tory in the parliamentary election of 1774. Conversely, 74 percent of those voting for Giles and Hill at the same municipal election voted Whig at the parliamentary election. Even as early as 1768, strong correlations linked voting patterns at municipal and parliamentary contests. Maidstone Municipal Records, Election Papers VII, KRO. *The Poll for Electing Two Burgesses*, Maidstone, 1768; *The Poll for Electing Two Burgesses*, Maidstone, 1774.

issues of considerable magnitude into national elections. A durable partisan organization seemed as likely a development in Norwich where the frequency of contested elections provided a raison d'être for partisan activity as it seemed unlikely in a borough like Northampton where partisans, however dedicated or determined, could have been active once or twice each decade at best. The structure of the Maidstone and Norwich electorates, unlike the two non-freeman boroughs, also contributed to the likelihood of the development of partisan activities. Nonresident freemen (and freeholders in Norwich) contributed substantially to the electorates of both boroughs and were a vitally important element in the vote, occasionally deciding elections in direct opposition to the desires of the resident voters. On average, nonresidents cast 20 percent of the total vote in Norwich and a full third of the Maidstone vote. The difficulty and expense inherent in mobilizing so many nonresident voters greatly enhanced the potential value of some kind of electoral organization. With nonresident voters required even in local elections at times, such an organization would have been particularly useful annually in Norwich and perhaps biennially in Maidstone. Thus, Norwich and Maidstone were thrice blessed. Each had a fully developed municipal government that stimulated the election process, both municipal governments were relatively open, and both possessed a large body of nonresident voters that demanded considerable organization and expense to maximize. Lewes may have possessed one of these critical characteristics, relatively frequent, albeit unstructured, elections. Northampton alone lacked all three.

If, as in Northampton, the act of voting was an isolated event in the lives of electors (in fact, a unique event for the majority), then less political awareness and also less partisan behavior would be expected among voters than if voting was a regular and frequent activity as in Norwich and Maidstone. This is not to say that continual participation led directly or inevitably to partisan electoral behavior since partisanship could not have developed in the absence of parties and/or issues. However, modern evidence suggests that frequent participation, in conjunction with parties and clearly defined issues, often leads to a politicization of the electorate. The political structures of Norwich and Maidstone after 1768 (and perhaps Lewes after 1780) certainly encouraged frequent participation, but the presence of parties and issues must be demonstrated before looking for evidence of politicization.

CHAPTER FOUR

The Substance of Borough Politics: Variations on Three Themes

S TUDENTS OF MODERN electoral behavior often take for granted or choose to ignore "political events and issue predispositions" of particular political systems, albeit at some risk. Frequently, the resulting examinations of electoral behavior take on a strangely apolitical quality.[1] A study of later eighteenth-century English voters must be quite different; virtually nothing can be assumed or ignored.[2] The behavior of voters in unreformed England can be divorced from neither the political climate in the country nor specific political events in each constituency. Indeed, a detailed consideration of the specific characteristics of each constituency is a prerequisite to accurate interpretations of voting behavior at any contested election. The discussion of na-

[1] Richard Rose, *Electoral Behavior: A Comparative Handbook*, London, 1975, pp. 8-10. The Nuffield studies of twentieth-century British elections, and those studies produced under Nuffield's influence, have avoided omissions of this kind, but only at the expense of overemphasizing political minutiae. Rather than being exemplary, these studies have not been as useful as the occasionally apolitical analyses of Rose, Benny, and others. An excellent example of the apolitical approach is: David Reynolds, "A Spatial Model for Analyzing Voting Behavior," *Acta Sociologica* 12(1969):122-31.

[2] Dunbabin suggests that summary statistics cannot be applied to analyses of English politics until after the second Reform Act, if then. To a certain extent, Dunbabin's caution is justified, but used cautiously, some summary statistics can be applied successfully much earlier. For example, Nossiter has been able to deal with "swings" well in advance of 1868. J. Dunbabin, "Parliamentary Elections in Great Britain, 1868-1900: A Psephological Note," *EHR* 71(1966):89; T. J. Nossiter, "Aspects of Electoral Behavior in English Constituencies," in *Mass Politics*, ed. E. Allardt and S. Rokkan, New York, 1970.

tional party developments with which this study began illustrated the increasingly partisan and issue-oriented nature of the political system, and the two preceding chapters demonstrated the greater incidence of electoral participation in the "open" parliamentary boroughs after the nadir reached during the general election of 1761, as well as the consistently high levels of electoral participation in Norwich, Northampton, Maidstone, and Lewes when voters were allowed to vote. However, the extreme variety of borough political structures, ranging from the openness and vitality of Norwich politics to the closed, virtually inert Northampton town government drastically affected opportunities for electoral participation and were critically important in defining the political behavior of borough voters. The existence of party organizations at the national level after the general election of 1784 may no longer be in doubt, but both the extent and the degree to which national political developments affected particular boroughs remains much in question.

Local partisan organizations were at best loosely tied to the flexible and variable parliamentary parties.[3] The "profound" political issues reintroduced nationally beginning with the unrest over John Wilkes and English "liberty" were profound only when recognized, and the connection between these issues, the parliamentary parties, and the electors in specific boroughs is as complicated as it is fundamental to an understanding of electoral behavior.[4] The disparity in the potential for electoral participation in various boroughs has already indicated a much closer link

[3] Donald E. Ginter, *Whig Organization in the General Election of 1790*, Berkeley, 1967; John Owen, "Political Patronage in Eighteenth Century England," in *The Triumph of Culture*, ed. Paul Fritz, New York, 1972; John Owen, *The Eighteenth Century*, New York, 1975; Frank O'Gorman, *The Rise of Party in England*, London, 1975, p. 21; Ernest A. Smith, *Whig Principles and Party Politics*, Manchester, 1975; B. W. Hill, "Fox and Burke: The Whig Party and the Question of Principle," *EHR* 89(1974):1.

[4] John Cannon, *Parliamentary Reform*, Cambridge, 1973, p. 61.

115

tying national to local political developments in Norwich and Maidstone than in Lewes, and Northampton voters seem to have avoided such a link almost completely. Certainly Norwich and Maidstone possessed structural incentives for local party organizations that were largely absent in both Lewes and Northampton. An assessment of the effectiveness of these incentives and the varieties of local partisan developments forms the substance of this chapter.

Political conditions varied widely across time in each borough as well as varying widely from borough to borough. Forty-one years separated the first and last elections considered in Maidstone and Norwich, and the Northampton elections examined herein encompassed almost thirty years. Some change would be expected in virtually any political system over four decades, and England's dynamic national political environment enhanced the potential for change. Two wars, three revolutions abroad, political unrest at home, religious discontent (including rioting), and a host of other crises, large and small, disturbed England's domestic tranquility. Thus, the uncertainty resulting from the potentially diverse political characteristics in each borough at any one election, combined with the changes inevitable in each constituency over an extended period, precludes an isolated, apolitical analysis of voting patterns. Unreformed voting behavior can be understood *only* in the context of local partisan activity, if any, along with the political issues raised by local and national parties or by individuals in the course of electoral campaigns. These basic aspects of local political affairs lend substance to the structure of borough politics described in the second chapter and meaning to the activities of borough voters analyzed in the subsequent discussion.

LOCAL PARTISAN ACTIVITY AND ORGANIZATION

Electors and candidates in all four boroughs shared a common aversion to the old party labels, "Tory" and "Whig,"

116

just as many politically aware Englishmen over the entire country voiced strong objections to the time-worn party names.[5] Despite the increasing importance of the national parties, nascent national party organizations, and a tendency among the Opposition to embrace the term "Whig," Gibbon denounced as late as 1790 the customary party labels as "foolish and obsolete odious words."[6] Three years earlier, Lord Holland relied on the term "Opposition" rather than referring to "Whigs" in his *Short Review of the Political State of Great Britain.*[7] Similarly, a summary of England's political climate in 1794 argued that the "tide of party" compelled every writer to draw "his pen decisively on the side of the Ministry or Opposition," yet eschewed other names for the two parties.[8] More notably, the most exhaustive contemporary study of electoral politics (Oldfield's *Representative History*) uniformly avoided traditional party labels, and with good reason.[9] The growing acceptance of "party" as an integral, if regrettable, component of constitutional government did not extend to a defense of party labels left over from another era. "Whig" was a more acceptable word because of Rockingham, Portland, and others, but "Tory" remained what it was originally, a term of political abuse. The new political groupings in parliament and elsewhere were neither a continuation nor a resurgence of the political cleavages delineated by the labels used so commonly earlier in the century.[10]

[5] An indication of the resistance to the party labels is provided by J.A.W. Gunn, ed., *Factions No More*, London, 1971. Also see Charles Piggott, *A Political Dictionary*, London, 1795.

[6] Keith Feiling, *The Second Tory Party*, London, 1938, p. 2.

[7] Nathaniel W. Wraxall, *A Short Review of the Political State of Great Britain*, London, 1787, pp. 37, 45.

[8] R. R. Legge Willis, "A Glimpse Through the Gloom," London, 1794, p. 1.

[9] T.H.B. Oldfield, *Representative History of Great Britain and Ireland*, 6 vols., London, 1816.

[10] Actually, Feiling's much-maligned study, *The Second Tory Party*, never argued an unbroken continuity.

117

The national reluctance to call politicians "Whigs" or "Tories" helps explain the relative scarcity of such references in local contests, even when political battles followed national party lines. The propaganda of the post-1802 elections in Norwich, for example, frequently employed traditional party labels, but neither term had gained much popularity among Norwich voters before the turn of the nineteenth century. The extensive propaganda generated by later eighteenth-century Norwich campaigns rarely mentioned either.[11] Norwich political alignments were often very closely related to national political issues, and the parliamentary parties frequently played important roles in structuring the political disputes that led to so many heated contests in Norwich. However, partisanship in Norwich and in the other parliamentary boroughs must be understood in much broader terms. The scarcity of "Whig" and "Tory" references can be explained only partially by the widespread national resistance to these terms. Norwich politics can be described very generally in "Whig-Tory" terminology if "Tory" is understood to mean "Ministerial" and "Whig" is taken as its antithesis, "anti-Ministerial." Both locally and nationally, the Norwich "independent" party, the Blues-and-Whites, opposed the established powers after the late 1770s, and "anti-Ministerial" nationally almost always translated into "anti-Corporation" locally. Talk of "party" of any description remained unusual in Norwich until the 1780 election.[12] A handbill distributed at that election urged voters to cast their two votes for Sir Harbord Harbord and William Windham together instead of committing the "extreme folly" of giving one vote to each party (i.e., split-

[11] For examples, see *The Election Budget*, Norwich, 1818 and MS. 4338, NNRO.

[12] A report to Charles Jenkinson from Norwich in 1780 noted the civility of the public meetings there, "even in party matters" and discussed the merits of the candidates of "both of the parties." Liverpool Papers, BL Add. MS. 38213, ff. 139. Also, *A Letter to a Country Gentleman*, Norwich, 1780 speaks of "both the parties" in Norwich.

ting).[13] This undisguised plea for straight-party voting well illustrates the degree of politicization that was affecting Norwich voters by 1780, but the contrast was drawn between the "Ministerialist" and "anti-Ministerialist" candidates, not between Tory and Whig. The stances adopted by Harbord and Windham over issues as important as general warrants and the American War helped define their political principles, as did the sympathies voiced by their opponents in 1780. Nevertheless, neither chose to be closely allied to a parliamentary party. When threatened by his connection with Fox in 1784, Windham identified himself as a "friend to the principles of the Rockingham party" rather than as a "Whig" or a "Foxite." Significantly, partisan references were customarily limited to the local parties.[14] Windham's political stances in the late 1770s and 1780s placed him tentatively and never quite comfortably in the parliamentary Whig camp, yet his opinions firmly secured his position as "Blue-and-White" in Norwich. Sir Harbord Harbord also failed to qualify precisely for "Whig" status in parliament since he followed such an unfailingly independent line in the Commons, yet after his rejection by the city elite in 1780, he could not have been more solidly imbedded, along with Windham, in the ranks of the Norwich Free Blues.

Colors most commonly identified political groups in Norwich. The Norwich "Free Blues" or "Blue-and-Whites" consistently opposed the "Orange-and-Purples" after 1780, and references to Norwich parties by their colors portrayed Norwich political groupings as accurately as any other terminology. Contemporaries recognized colors as adequate

---

[13] *A Narrative of the Contested Election*, Norwich, 1780, p. 56.

[14] *The Election Magazine*, Norwich, 1784, p. 17. Many Norwich residents knew better. A poem after the election noted:

> Clear intellectsom voters bless,
> Wise and consistent we find them:
> First one and all 'gainst Fox address,
> Then elect his PUPIL, WINDHAM.

indicators of political preferences. In the midst of a campaign going badly in 1802, Windham and his running mate, Robert Frere, issued a warning to the Norwich electors not to let the "madness of party and the color of a ribbon" beguile them into allowing the destruction of their Church and King.[15] Charles Fox's adoption of the "buff and blue" (perhaps as a result of the American War) failed to establish a uniform color scheme across the country, but colors continued to serve as important electioneering devices well into the postreform era.[16] In response to a question concerning his political affiliations just prior to the 1841 general election, a Darlington shopkeeper responded, "Sir, I am green. I am green and white to the backbone."[17] Whether the Norwich supporters of Harbord and Windham in 1784 thought of themselves as "Whig," "anti-Ministerialist," or "Blue-and-White" was less important than their ability to identify the political alternatives at the election through any kind of political shorthand. However, "support" and "opposition" terminology was particularly appropriate for an analysis of Norwich politics since "anti-Ministerial" or "Opposition" labels often applied equally well to national and local administrations. In fact, except for the brief period of the Portland administration, an "Opposition" candidate in Norwich, Maidstone, and even Northampton meant someone opposed not only to the national government, but also to the local municipal government. Thus, the terms "Ministerial" and "anti-Ministerial," or "Administration opponent" and "Administration supporter" took on added significance and frequently reflected political differences

[15] In 1787, Windham referred to his supporters as the Free Blues. See Cecilia A. Baring, ed., *The Diary of William Windham*, London, 1866, p. 109; *A New Election Budget in Five Numbers*, Norwich, 1802, p. 36.

[16] For a more complete discussion, see *Notes and Queries*, 6th ser. 1(1880):355-82 and 2(1881).

[17] George Holman, *Some Lewes Men of Note*, London, 1927, p. 63; T. J. Nossiter, "Elections and Political Behavior in County Durham and Newcastle," Ph.D. diss., Oxford University, 1968, p. 416.

more comprehensively than "Whig" or "Tory" ever could have, although the terms often appeared interchangeable in the context of particular contested elections. Oldfield's exclusive use of "Ministerial" to indicate the groups that might as easily have been called "Tory" corroborates what was often true in the boroughs; except for the brief Fox-North ministry, "Toryism" implied support for the King's government (and later Pitt's government).[18]

Election propaganda from Maidstone contests, never collected into volumes and published as in Norwich, has not survived as well. References in the local press to "parties" suggest an early development of local partisan sentiment in Maidstone, perhaps with national associations. No clear-cut evidence of sustained partisan activity marked Maidstone elections until the 1780 contest. A letter from Lord Rockingham to the Duke of Newcastle mentioned the value of Newcastle's introduction of a new candidate to the "Whig interests" in Maidstone before the election of 1768, but such a reference, common in the correspondence of Rockingham and Newcastle, did not necessarily suggest the existence of a well-defined or even recognizable "party" in Maidstone.[19] Patronage seems to have played a substantial role in the nomination of Maidstone's candidates in 1768 and 1774, yet both political and religious issues prompted considerable "independent" activity in 1774, as well as a widespread determination among Maidstone's residents to oppose the efforts of any and all patrons who tried to exert undue influence over Maidstone elections.[20] Rose Fuller recognized full well Maidstone's openness as early as 1761 and the inability of patron influence or coercion of any kind to guarantee Fuller's victory. Addresses in the *Kentish Gazette* during 1774 mentioned more than enough topics for an issue-oriented campaign that year. The local press

[18] T.H.B. Oldfield, *The History of the Boroughs of Great Britain*, 2 vols., London, 1794, *passim*.
[19] Newcastle Papers, BL Add. MS. 32989, ff. 163.
[20] Romney MSS., U1007, c. 42-46, KRO.

considered matters as diverse as the "refusal of liberty to Protestant Dissenters," the Quebec Bill, and the ideas on representation contained in Burke's speech to his Bristol constituents.[21] The renewal of city elections in 1772 at a cost of £900 to Maidstone's freemen also added political vitality to the 1774 parliamentary campaign.[22] The activities of the independents notwithstanding, Heneage Finch won the seat along with Sir Horace Mann.

By 1780, "independents" hailed the nomination and subsequent election of Clement Taylor as their first unmistakable victory, and Oldfield's description of Maidstone politics in 1790 continued the customary "Ministerialist/ /Opposition" terminology even though Oldfield undoubtedly was aware of the close link between the Maidstone independents and the Portland/Fox Whigs. Fox had no firmer supporter in the Commons than Maidstone's "independent," Clement Taylor.[23] Traditional party names did not appear in Maidstone until the extremely important 1786 municipal contest that determined the leadership of the Corporation. At this city election, a contemporary observed that the "Tories," led by Mayor Thomas Pope, elected their own candidates to the vacant Jurat seats, but vainly "exerted every nerve to gain pre-eminence" in the common council elections where the "Whigs" swept the race.[24] Maidstone political controversies were not again described with Whig-Tory labels until the *Kentish Chronicle* reported John Durrand's 1802 candidacy as "on the Whig interest." And since Maidstone local parties did not use their colors (Blue for the opposition and Purple for the Ministerialists) as

[21] Newcastle, BL Add. MS. 32920, ff. 121-22, and *Kentish Gazette*, October 15, 1774.

[22] William Roberts James, *The Charters and Documents of Maidstone*, London, 1825, pp. xxvii-xix; *A Short Treatise on the Institution of the Corporation by a Freeman*, Maidstone, 1786, *passim*.

[23] *Kentish Gazette*, September 9, 1780. Also see J. M. Russell, *History of Maidstone*, London, 1881, pp. 211-12 and *Canterbury Journal*, September 13, 1780. Oldfield, *Representative History*, 4:254.

[24] James, *Charters of Maidstone*, pp. xviii-xxix.

effectively as their Norwich counterparts, Maidstone politics customarily assumed an independent/Corporation, Ministerialist/anti-Ministerialist vocabulary that served reasonably well for identifying political interests until well into the nineteenth century.[25]

"Whig" and "Tory" were completely missing from the political vocabularies of candidates in Lewes and Northampton over these four decades. Actually, very few partisan references of any kind appeared in Northampton elections; except for one mention of a "Ministerialist" candidate in the election of 1790, and a note concerning the "Ministerialist party" in a 1796 election report, Northampton elections concentrated almost exclusively on individuals, not parties.[26] Even the election of the future prime minister, Spencer Perceval, in 1796 failed to elicit party terminology in Northampton. The first references to the Northampton "Tories" appeared in print in 1822, followed by newspaper accounts of "Whig" election tactics in 1827.[27] Therefore, rather than examining local party politics in any of these boroughs within the constraints imposed by terms usually shunned locally and often ignored nationally, local parties (where they existed) can be described most adequately in their own terms, and have been described accordingly whether "anti-Ministerialist," "Opposition," "independent," "Ministerialist," or, as in the case of Norwich, simply through party colors.

Electoral organizations in these four boroughs differed more dramatically. These variations in partisan development, ranging from relative sophistication to virtual nonexistence, corresponded closely with the expectations raised by the varying levels of political activity identified in Chap-

[25] Kentish Chronicle, July 9, 1802; Henry Stooks-Smith, The Register of Parliamentary Contested Elections, London, 1842, pp. 113-14.

[26] J. C. Cox, ed., The Records of the Borough of Northampton, 2 vols., Northampton, 1898, 2:508.

[27] V. A. Hatley, "Some Aspects of Northampton History," Northamptonshire Past and Present 3(1966):240-49.

ter 3. By the 1780s, the two most politically active boroughs (Norwich and Maidstone) contained well-established, de-personalized, issue-oriented electoral organizations. Such sophisticated and continuous partisan activity may not have taken place in Lewes, yet certain evidence of partisan activity accompanied the Lewes election of 1780.[28] Northampton, on the other hand, exhibited few signs of political activity. There, "friends" acting for single candidates conducted elections of a different nature.[29] In fact, these four boroughs shared only two political activities, canvassing and petitioning. Canvassing occurred in each borough prior to virtually every election, and all four petitioned the Crown in 1784 to express their support for the King and their appreciation of his ouster of Fox, North, and the rest of the Portland administration. Yet even a shared activity like petitioning distinguished Norwich and Maidstone from the two other towns; petitions from both Norwich and Maidstone were as common as petitions from Northampton and Lewes were rare. Norwich petitioned the Commons incessantly on matters as diverse as the American War, triennial parliaments, the slave trade, the war with France, and the price of corn.[30] Maidstone also petitioned against the slave trade and addressed the Commons on assorted other topics including smuggling and poor relief.[31] Conversely, other than the election petition occasioned by the 1768 struggle

[28] The Lewes election of 1784 was contested for only a few hours. Sir Henry Blackman withdrew after losing the support of the independents. See William Lee, *Ancient and Modern History of Lewes*, London, 1795. *Lewes Journal*, October 10 and October 24, 1774.

[29] Despite the similarity of political stances sometimes apparent in candidates for Northampton, joint campaigns were judiciously avoided. Under the circumstances, a partisan vote was cast only with some difficulty. See the description of Northampton politics that follows.

[30] *CJ*, January 25, 1775; February 17, 1778; March 4, 1779; February 7, 1783; March 21, 1785; February 22, 1786; January 26, 1787; February 15, 1787; March 3, 1788; May 6, 1793; and February 17, 1795.

[31] *CJ*, March 11, 1779; February 7, 1780; February 7, 1788; February 22, 1791; October 26, 1796; and June 17, 1799.

of the three earls over Northampton's representation, Northampton never petitioned the Commons.[32] Lewes petitioned on three occasions concerning matters of less than universal political interest. Lewes citizens complained once about the hardship suffered by innkeepers forced to quarter troops, expressed the need to collect small debts, and asked permission to enlarge their marketplace.[33]

In other respects, politics in Norwich and Maidstone achieved a level of development not matched by politics in Lewes or Northampton. Most importantly, party structure attained greater complexity and commensurately greater visibility in both freeman boroughs. From the election of 1780 onward, managers directed Norwich party activity, with members of party hierarchies often providing capable leadership through several elections. As critically, Norwich and Maidstone proved capable of accomplishing changes of party leadership very smoothly, thus accommodating fluctuations in the political careers of certain individuals as well as the occasional problems caused by major political realignments that led to conflicts between personal loyalties and partisan ties. Neither Sir Harbord Harbord's shift to the Norwich anti-Ministerialists in 1780 nor William Windham's more dramatic switch to Administration ranks in 1794 after more than a decade's alliance to the Rockingham and Foxite Whigs greatly disturbed either of Norwich's party organizations.[34] The prominence of the local politicians involved in both parties and the similarity of local and national political cleavages aided party stability during such crises, and the addition of long-standing family ties also reinforced partisan alignments. The Gurneys, the most

---

[32] *CJ*, November 10, 1768.

[33] *CJ*, January 28, 1773; March 12, 1781; March 4, 1790; February 23, 1791.

[34] The lack of a disturbance in the second instance was more remarkable than in the first. The parties took both incidents with aplomb, but the electorate, unfazed by the first change, was somewhat taken aback by Windham's shift. See Figure 6.1.

125

prominent Quaker family in Norwich if not in all Norfolk, supplied financial and moral support, and occasionally supplied candidates for the Norwich Free Blues, while the Ives and the Harveys (not to mention the extensive connections of the Earl of Buckinghamshire) helped provide a core of support for the Orange-and-Purple party.[35]

Thus, the sitting members for Norwich and/or the candidates at particular elections often assumed only titular positions at the head of their local parties; rather than personal loyalties and friendships, the Norwich parties relied heavily on extensive connections and long-term leaders in addition to the support provided by the candidates themselves. Beginning with the campaign of 1780, the Norwich Free Blues recruited candidates on the basis of their political principles, to the virtual exclusion of other considerations. William Windham's candidacy in 1780, for example, stemmed directly from his efforts two years earlier to rally support for the Norwich petition against the American War.[36] The Free Blue decision to support Sir Harbord Harbord also during that campaign recognized his opposition to general warrants specifically and his obstructionist tactics against Lord North's administration generally. Harbord's backing from the Blues came after he had been dropped by the city government as Edward Bacon's running mate in favor of Alderman John Thurlow, the brother of the lord chancellor.[37] The Free Blues failed twice to draft a leading citizen to stand against their one-time champion, Windham, at the by-election of 1794 brought on by Windham's "traitorous" acceptance of the Ministry of War un-

[35] These same families were important in Norwich well into the nineteenth century. H. J. Hanham, ed., *Dod's Electoral Facts*, Brighton, 1972.

[36] Windham Papers, BL Add. MS. 37908, ff. 7-17 and Thomas Amyot, *Some Account of the Life of William Windham*, London, 1812, p. 11. John Crewe, Elias Norgate, and William Barnard were the most important individuals in the Whig party leadership.

[37] *A Narrative of the Contested Election*, pp. 12-31.

der Pitt.[38] The Blues finally ran a respectable, though fruit-
less, race in the absence and without even the knowledge
and consent of a third, desperation choice, the Foxite bar-
rister, James Mingay. Even though the difficulty in finding
a candidate prevented a canvass before the actual poll, Mingay garnered almost 40 percent of the votes cast.[39] When
the same difficulty of finding a suitable candidate impeded
preparations for the regular election in 1796, the Free Blues
ran Bartlett Gurney in absentia and actually won a majority
of the resident vote. Gurney finished with a city-wide majority of twelve votes, only to lose at the hands of the London voters brought in by the Corporation to support Windham and his equally pro-Administration running mate,
Henry Hobart. Aided by these nonresident voters, Windham squeaked by with a majority of less than 90 votes of
more than 2,500 cast.[40]

Maidstone parties proved capable of the same impersonal, independent activity that diminished the personal
influence of specific candidates. For over a decade, the
Opposition party possessed a candidate and a leader in the
person of Clement Taylor, a prominent paper manufacturer in Maidstone. Yet the party managed to conduct the
election of 1796 in the face of Taylor's withdrawal from
the race just a day before the scheduled poll, probably as
a result of his impending bankruptcy.[41] The independents
replaced Taylor with Christopher Hull and waged a vigorous fight in the twenty-four hours available. Taylor's decision not to stand hurt the party, to be sure, and the independents lost the election, but the overnight candidate,
Hull, gathered a substantial number of votes, including

[38] *Norfolk Chronicle*, July 12, 1794.
[39] Amyot, *Life of William Windham*, p. 35.
[40] *The Poll for Members of Parliament*, Norwich, 1796. The pattern is
evident even without a computer-assisted analysis.
[41] Taylor went bankrupt in 1797 and it was duly registered. Register of
Bankrupts, B6, 9:206 (October 17, 1798), PRO.

most of Taylor's former staunch supporters.[42] This strong
electoral holdover from the 1790 election demonstrated
the strength and solidarity of the Opposition party in the
face of adversity. Hull's extremist political stance may have
contributed more to his loss than the brevity of his candidacy. The government press labelled him "Citizen Hull,"
and his radicalism possibly proved too great for the rank
and file in Maidstone despite their willingness to support a
relatively radical anti-Ministerialist candidate like Clement
Taylor in the previous election.[43] Until the appearance of
Matthew Bloxham in 1788, the Maidstone "Ministerialists"
lacked a consistent candidate. As early as the 1780 election,
John Brenchley, a noncandidate, successfully managed the
party.[44] Brenchley continued as party leader until his death
in 1793 when another noncandidate, George Bishop, assumed control.[45] Under the leadership of Brenchley and
Bishop, the party proposed two candidates for each parliamentary election between 1780 and 1802, invariably opposing a single independent candidate, and in one election
accomplished the return of both of their nominees (1796).

In addition to party managers, both parties in Norwich
and Maidstone employed party headquarters during each
election after 1780, coordinating party activities from a
tavern, or several taverns if required by the campaign. Given
the common practice of "treating electors," taverns were
particularly appropriate locations for the conduct of party
activities. Political meetings of some import took place in
Norwich inns as early as 1768, and the activities of the
"Coalition" or "Juncture" of Harbord Harbord and Edward Bacon during the 1768 election resembled the work-
ings of a party in many respects. However, the first clear

[42] See Chapter 6. Of the 281 votes cast for Hull, 140 were plumps and
of the 88 plumpers for Taylor in the previous election, 75 voted for Hull.
[43] *Morning Chronicle*, May 27, 1796.
[44] Lewis Namier and John Brooke, *The House of Commons, 1754-1790*,
3 vols., London, 1964, 1:314.
[45] Maidstone Municipal Records, Parliamentary Elections, KRO.

indication of the organizational significance of party inns emerged in the 1780 campaign between the strongly anti-Ministerial Free Blue candidates and their equally committed Orange-and-Purple opponents. William Windham, apparently still leery of the label "party," asserted in his own defense that "what is party at the Shakespeare [the main Ministerial inn] may be principle at the Swan [Free Blue headquarters for the election]." Of the several inns occasionally drafted into party service in Norwich, the Pope's Head and the White Swan emerged as the chief centers of the Free Blues. Almost as invariably, the Orange-and-Purples organized their electioneering efforts from the King's Head and the Shakespeare.[46]

While the dearth of surviving propaganda prevents equal detail concerning the permanency and utility of party inns in Maidstone, evidence from several elections points to the Castle Inn as the major "independent" establishment. The creation of the "Maidstone Union Club" headquartered at the Castle enhanced its function as party headquarters.[47] The Maidstone Minsterialists, under the guidance of John Brenchley, generally directed their campaigns jointly from the Star and the Mitre.[48] It seems to have been this tavern organization that created the confusion leading to the Municipal Corporations Commission's allegation, many years after the fact, that the Maidstone municipal election of 1795 pitted rival breweries against each other instead of rival parties. Actually, the 1795 contest, another in a long series of hotly contested partisan battles for control of the Corporation, simply took on an additional economic dimension

---

[46] *Miscellaneous Pieces in Prose and Verse Relative to the Contested Election*, Norwich, 1768, pp. vi, 15-16. *Election Magazine*, p. 33. In addition to these inns, the White Lion and the Bull were "Blue-and-White" inns and the Currier Arms and Rampant Horse were "Orange-and-Purple."

[47] *Maidstone Journal*, June 29, 1802. John Gale Jones, *A Sketch of a Political Tour Through Rockingham, Chatham, Maidstone, and Gravesend*, London, 1796, pp. 79-80.

[48] *Kentish Gazette*, May 31, 1796; *Maidstone Journal*, May 24, 1796.

as George Bishop (a brewer and manager of the Ministerialists) simultaneously attempted to gain a seat on the common council and control over several other Maidstone public houses. Bishop, though successful in gaining a seat on the council, failed to expand the number of inns in his spirits empire.[49]

The Norwich Free Blues profited from the efforts of extraparty organizations ten years before the Maidstone "Whigs" benefited from the formation of the "Union Club." The Norwich Independent Club, founded in 1780, foundered in the subsequent decade, to be replaced by an even more useful organization for the Free Blues, the Norwich Revolution Society.[50] Assisted by the London Corresponding Society, the Norwich Revolution Society exerted some force in Norwich elections until, falling into disrepute as a result of the war with France, it was replaced by yet another organization helpful to Free Blue political efforts, the Norwich Patriotic Society. The membership of the Patriotic Society approached 600 in 1795, and its members actively campaigned in municipal as well as parliamentary elections, consistently advancing the cause of Free Blue candidates.[51] The leaders of all three "radical" societies often ranked among the hierarchy of the anti-Ministerial party. William Barnard, president of the Revolution Society, acted prominently in Norwich elections on behalf of the anti-Ministerialists long before his affiliations with either the Revolution or Patriotic Societies. Thomas Goff and John Cousins of the Revolution Society helped direct three successive Free Blue campaigns after 1790. "Citizen Cousins,"

[49] House of Commons Sessional Papers, *Report of the Commission on Municipal Corporations*, vol. 24, London, 1835, pp. 96-97. Also see Maidstone Municipal Records, Parliamentary Elections, KRO.

[50] *Norwich and Norfolk Mercury*, March 16, 1782 and November 8, 1788. C. B. Jewson, *Jacobin City*, Glasgow, 1975, pp. 27-29, and B. D. Hayes, "Politics in Norfolk 1750-1832," Ph.D. diss., Cambridge University, 1958, pp. 241-51.

[51] See Jewson, Hayes and BL Add. MS. 27815, ff. 122.

as a hostile press described John Cousins, brought John Thelwall to Norwich in 1796 to speak for the Opposition candidate Bartlett Gurney.[52] And Peter Wilson, plumber, and Richard Dinmore, saddler, who were respectively the president and secretary of the Patriotic Society, played major roles in the Free Blue campaigns of 1796 (for parliamentary seats and municipal offices). This overlap in leadership guaranteed Free Blue support from the societies.[53] The Orange-and-Purples responded to the anti-Administration organizations by forming the Gregorian Club in 1790 and the Castle Corporation Club in 1793, both of which aided the Ministerialists in local and national elections.[54] Yet even though each of these organizations in Norwich claimed substantial support in the community at various times, the anti-Ministerialists benefited most from societal support. The Orange-and-Purple party could, and did, draw freely on the resources of the city administration; the Free Blues had few channels of support other than those offered by these voluntary associations.

The parties in Maidstone and Norwich also drew upon individual talent outside their own ranks and mobilized assistance from prominent individuals as well as national organizations. During the agitation accompanying the election of 1796, nationally affiliated speakers appeared in both towns to assist Opposition candidates. John Thelwall "endeavored to sharpen the contest [in Norwich] by his popular harangues in the market place against Mr. Windham and the war system of the Pitt administration."[55] During the same campaign, John Gale Jones of the London Corresponding Society visited Maidstone at the request of the Maidstone independents. Jones spoke on several occasions against Pitt and in favor of Maidstone's Foxite incumbent,

[52] *Election Budget, 1799*, Norwich, 1799, p. 6.

[53] Jewson, *Jacobin City*, p. 29 and BL Add. MS. 27815, ff. 163.

[54] *Norfolk Chronicle*, July 10, 1790, and January 10, 1793.

[55] Amyot, *Some Account of the Life of William Windham*, p. 40 and John Thelwall, *An Appeal to Popular Opinion*, Norwich, 1796.

131

Clement Taylor, who "had been uniform in his principles" and deserved to be returned accordingly.[56]

Although politics in Maidstone closely resembled Norwich in many respects, the use of printed election propaganda by the Norwich parties was unparalleled; enough broadsheets, squibs, pamphlets, songs, poems, plays, and political cartoons appeared in connection with each parliamentary election to fill a small volume.[57] With the fairly high literacy rate in these boroughs (probably better than 70 percent), these efforts were not for nothing.[58] Newspaper coverage of Maidstone elections was sparse, and printed propaganda, though occasionally distributed, seems to have been limited to a few handbills. On the other hand, any press coverage of Maidstone elections represented a step forward; before the contest of 1780, the local press ignored elections. And significantly, the initial newspaper coverage of elections in Maidstone appeared along with the first sustained party activity. Besides, the paucity of printed propaganda may have been more a function of Maidstone's size than level of political sophistication. Norwich contained approximately 40,000 inhabitants and far more than 2,000 resident electors after 1780, distributed over thirty-four parishes. Twelve political wards and four "great" wards within the city as well as hundreds of nonresident voters

[56] Jones, *A Sketch of a Political Tour*, pp. 79-83.

[57] For most of the post-1761 Norwich elections, the election propaganda *was* published as a single volume.

[58] Brewer has summarized much of the evidence of high literacy rates in the later eighteenth century, and specific evidence can be mustered very easily. Hatley has shown that more than 70 percent of the bridegrooms in Northampton were able to sign the marriage register. The petitions to the Crown cited in Chapter 1 also attested to the high literacy rate found in England's boroughs, at least in the sense that the ability to sign one's name is a measure of literacy. The number of X's with names appended on these petitions (H.O. 55, PRO) never totalled more than 10 percent and often accounted for fewer than 5 percent of the signatures. John Brewer, *Party Ideology and Popular Politics at the Accession of George III*, Cambridge, 1976, p. 142; V. A. Hatley, "Literacy at Northampton, 1761-1790," *Northamptonshire Past and Present* 5(1976).

further complicated Norwich political communication.[59] In sharp contrast, a single parish (and a single ward) encompassed Maidstone's population of slightly more than 7,000. Nonresident voters aside, contacting the approximately 500 resident electors in Maidstone presented a much less formidable task than reaching Norwich's 2,000.[60] Undoubtedly, the mountain of printed material issued at Norwich elections reflects the complexity and organization behind Norwich politics, but the relative lack of printed material issued in conjunction with Maidstone elections should not be misinterpreted.[61] Political campaigns in such a compact borough might have been conducted as effectively, perhaps even more effectively, through canvassing as through the printing press. A more personal campaign also reduced the expenses entailed by reams of published propaganda.

Partisan activities in Lewes are less distinct in retrospect, and were muddled by the continuing, though severely reduced, influence of the Pelham family. After the victory of Henry Pelham and Thomas Kemp in 1780, these two incumbents jointly contested each succeeding election in spite

[59] W. Hudson, *Leet Jurisdiction of the City of Norwich*, Norwich, 1891; James Campbell, "Norwich," in *The Atlas of Historic Towns*, ed. M. Lobel, 2 vols., London, 1975, 2:15.

[60] The proportion of the nonresident vote in Norwich and Maidstone changed frequently, and sometimes radically, over these elections.

				Election Year				
	1761	1768	1774	1780	1784	1790	1796	1802
Norwich(%)	6.5	17.4	—	15.8	18.7	15.0	19.8	31.4
Maidstone(%)	36.7	38.1	26.2	30.3	30.8	33.0	31.6	34.6

[61] Enough printed material from Maidstone elections has survived to suggest that possibly the Maidstone contests were not devoid of published propaganda even if the Maidstone parties did not match the standard set by the Norwich partisan organizations. For example, see a printed handbill from George Byng to the "Independent Freemen of Maidstone" of July 10, 1788, Maidstone Municipal Records, Election Papers VII, KRO, and a pamphlet by John Hampden reprinting *Two Letters on the Test Act printed in the Gazetteer*, Maidstone, 1790.

133

of their consistently different political principles. The local "independents" may have been responsible for the opposition mounted against the "Coalition" (as the Pelham-Kemp link was called) at each election after 1784, but to assail simultaneously the Pittite Kemp, and his Foxite running mate, Pelham, forced the independents to ignore national political alignments even though the Lewes press actively discussed the very issues the Coalition expected the voters to ignore.[62] Not until John Pelham replaced Henry Pelham did the Coalition represent a united front on national issues. Thus, the pattern of local and national opposition identifiable in Norwich and Maidstone did not apply to political events in Lewes until 1796. Considerable partisan activity seems to have been common in Lewes elections after 1780, including the distribution of printed handbills, yet neither the extent of these partisan efforts nor their political bases are clear.[63]

An electoral organization worthy of the name never materialized in Northampton in the later years of the century. The "friends" of respective candidates conducted individualized and generally apolitical campaigns, if they can be called campaigns. On several occasions, two candidates clearly holding the same political principles opposed a third with radically divergent views, yet equally invariably, each candidate conducted his affairs completely separately. The efforts of Lords Northampton and Halifax against Earl Spencer rather than "party" organization led to the single joint campaign. The "juncture" of Sir George Bridges Rodney and Sir George Osborne at that infamous contest of 1768

---

[62] The *History of Parliament* incorrectly described Kemp as a "considerable man in the Corporation"; Lewes remained unincorporated until 1831. J. H. Philbin, *Parliamentary Representation, 1832*, New Haven, 1965, pp. 193-94; Lee, *History of Lewes*, p. 123.

[63] Shiffner MSS. 303, 305, 2994; Hook MSS. 16-33, ESRO. Also see, *Lewes Journal*, October 24, 1774; April 15, 1784; February 15, 1790; June 14, 1790; May 30, 1796; May 23, 1796.

134

amounted to something less than a coalition of principle.[64] During the close contest of 1796, Spencer Perceval roundly condemned the practice of asking a voter to pledge more than one of his votes and publicly disavowed any association with such "nefarious" activities. Nor would Perceval ask for "plumpers," a course of action he repudiated as "most directly and plainly interfering with the election of another candidate." He adopted this stance even though one of the other candidates (who lost) joined him in supporting the Administration while the other (incumbent and victor) counted himself among the Government's most ardent enemies.[65]

The development of party organizations in these four boroughs corresponded closely to their widely varying opportunities for electoral participation. Party activity in Norwich, where municipal and parliamentary elections required incessant electoral participation, far outstripped Lewes and Northampton. Frequent popular participation in local and national elections also marked Maidstone's political structure, and the activities of the Maidstone parties rivalled those of Norwich in every respect except published electoral propaganda. Maidstone politics underwent substantial alterations in the last two decades of the century; partisan activity, barely apparent in the 1760s and 1770s, emerged considerably strengthened in the years after the victory of the freemen over the Corporation in 1774. Lewes, with relatively frequent if somewhat informal electoral participation, experienced some partisan activity beginning in 1780, but it was limited in scope and preoccupied with local concerns. And Northampton, where the chances for electors to express their opinions or their political choices were rare, lacked party organizations altogether. A stronger re-

---

[64] There are a variety of accounts of this well-known election, but the most revealing is Cox, *Records of Northampton*, 2:500-507.

[65] Perceval Papers, BL Add. MS. 49179, ff. 39-42 and BL Add. MS. 49184, ff. 38.

lationship between participation and partisan development is difficult to imagine.[66]

POLITICAL ISSUES

A solid foundation of explicitly political issues sustained the partisan activity so much in evidence at Norwich and Maidstone elections. The ability of modern voters to grasp political abstractions has been almost entirely discredited by behavioral analyses of American and Western European electorates, and to argue that eighteenth-century voters were politically aware and politically informed may seem singularly indefensible, if not perverse. However, evidence from elections after 1761 suggests that voting behavior in Norwich and Maidstone, if not in Lewes and Northampton, was more than the uninformed choice of the mob or the directed choice of the subservient.[67] Undoubtedly, coercion and political manipulation in a variety of forms produced some votes even in open constituencies like Norwich and

[66] Chapter 3 includes a more detailed discussion of the varying rate of popular political participation in these boroughs. Clearly this relationship has not been demonstrated as generally true for all of England's parliamentary boroughs, and some borough electorates may have developed highly politicized and politically active partisan organizations in the absence of frequent electoral participation. Nevertheless, politicization in the face of electoral inactivity should have been a much more difficult, and thus considerably rarer, occurrence. See for example, E. C. Black, *The Association*, Cambridge, Mass., 1963, and the related studies of popular political activity in places such as York and Yorkshire where political zeal was common and polls were uncommon. N. C. Phillips, *Yorkshire and English National Politics*, Christchurch, 1961.

[67] A full discussion of this conclusion is the major thrust of Chapter 6. Actually, the classic voting studies such as Angus Campbell et al., *The American Voter*, New York, 1964, have undergone a considerable challenge recently. The image of modern voters as apolitical, apathetic, unaware, and ridiculously idiosyncratic has been substantially altered as the classic studies have proven to be too time-bound for generalizations. See particularly, Norman Nie et al., *The Changing American Voter*, New York, 1979; John Pierce, ed., *The Electorate Reconsidered*, Beverly Hills, 1980; Joel Silbey et al., eds. *History of American Electoral Behavior*, Princeton, 1978.

THREE THEMES

Maidstone, and some votes reflected apolitical, or at best quasi-political relationships among individual electors. Moreover, the fundamental political issues confronting English electors beginning in the mid-1760s may have been imperfectly understood by most of the voters. Nevertheless, whatever the deficiencies in their understanding of the issues, it seems certain that thousands of electors recognized and acted upon the issues raised at the elections of the 1780s and 1790s.

A number of studies have argued against issues, ideas, and opinions in popular or parliamentary eighteenth-century politics for several decades, dismissing voting behavior and any other form of popular political expression as the product of a corrupt political system. Namier himself, however, conscientiously warned against broader generalizations from his conclusions concerning a brief period centered on a single election, a warning usually ignored.[68] And as it turns out, Namier's caveat was well advised; the political atypicality of the year he examined in such detail (1761) more than justified his caution. A new king occupied the throne, fewer contests occurred during the general election in 1761 than at any other time over the entire century, and the major issues that proved so disturbing to many ordinary citizens as well as the social and political elite had not yet appeared. Recent research into voting patterns and modes of behavior early in the century in addition to several accounts of the period after 1761 has challenged Namierite assumptions. J. H. Plumb hinted at the openness of the electorate early in the century, and the intensive work of W. A. Speck, Geoffrey Holmes, and others has confirmed much that Plumb suspected, demolishing in the process Robert Walcott's Namierite arguments concerning Augustine politics. Others, including R. W. Davis, Donald Ginter, and Frank O'Gorman have shown new modes

[68] Lewis Namier, *The Structure of Politics at the Accession of George III*, 2nd ed., London, 1957, pp. ix-xiv, 62-160.

of behavior emerging in England during the decades just after 1761, long before any official reform of the political system.[69]

With a few exceptions like the 1784 Norwich debate over virtual or actual representation, basic political choices, not vague, intangible abstractions confronted voters in the early decades of George III's reign. Instead of recondite reasoning, politically involved Englishmen were presented with uncomplicated, easily understood, black-and-white categories defined in the starkest possible terminology, regardless of the actual complexity of the issue being considered. Advocates of John Wilkes in 1768, for example, posed the question of slavery versus freedom, while Wilkes opponents cajoled potential voters with equally categorical language to support the rights of the King and prevent the threat to established order posed by Wilkes and the other proponents of mob rule.[70] The issue of war and peace in America was slightly more complicated, and it may not have provoked public fervor so easily, yet it required no great sophistication to choose sides.[71] And again in 1784, a simple, albeit misleading choice faced the politically "informed." "The people" could support political mendacity, administrative immorality, and worse, in the shape of Charles Fox, Lord North, and all Coalitionists, or they could defend their King and their Constitution from this unprecedented

[69] W. A. Speck, *Tory and Whig*, London, 1969; Geoffrey Holmes and W. A. Speck, *The Divided Society*, London, 1967; Richard W. Davis, *Political Change and Continuity*, Newton Abbot, 1972; Donald Ginter, *Whig Organization in the General Election of 1790*, Berkeley, 1967; Frank O'Gorman, *The Rise of Party in England*.

[70] A fuller discussion of the Wilkes phenomenon and its impact is included in Chapter 1. Also see, George Rudé, *Wilkes and Liberty*, London, 1962.

[71] The evidence of the petitions to the Crown and to parliament attests the ease with which support was aroused for this more complicated issue. The most recent account is Colin Bonwick, *English Radicals and the American Revolution*, Chapel Hill, 1977.

138

attack.[72] The overwhelming support for the King and Pitt at the polls in the 1784 election is hardly surprising given this framework, nor does it seem incredible that the issue, stated in moral absolutes, could be comprehended fairly widely by petitioners and voters alike. It matters little that few electors possessed the political sophistication necessary to resist the exaggerations of the Government and to weigh more carefully the matter of Fox's India Bill or his infamous alliance with Lord North. Pitt asked the public to make a very simple choice, and those who were actually allowed to express an opinion chose as he wished.

Certainly the parties in Norwich provided enough locally printed arguments setting forth the respective positions of the candidates, not to mention the vast literature produced for national consumption that has been described recently by John Brewer. Electors also could become acquainted with candidates' views at public meetings that were often held in larger parliamentary boroughs to consider pressing political issues.[73] Augmenting public meetings, canvassers and candidates alike conducted highly personalized campaigns, and the general excitement and tension accompanying many of the elections rendered political contests difficult to ignore. Evidence of individual political awareness among the Norwich voters illustrated the clearly defined and well-informed interests in elections, candidates, and issues harbored by some electors. Letters to William Windham in 1794 and again in 1796 expressed in no uncertain terms the precisely defined and strongly held political opinions of some of his Norwich constituents. After a long period of support for Windham as an opponent of the national Administration and the local Corporation, Robert Paul voiced his deep regret in "no longer being able to act with a gentleman whose political character I formerly approved." Similarly, Edward Astley withdrew his backing of

[72] M. D. George, "Fox's Martyrs," *TRHS*, 4th ser. 21(1939):133-68; J. Hartley, *A History of the Westminster Election*, London, 1784.

[73] Brewer, *Party Ideology and Popular Politics*, p. 141.

Windham in 1796 because he could not "yet conceive this war [with France] as just and necessary." The same contest led to Samuel Cooper's endorsement of Windham after Cooper had opposed him over Fox and "the measures which you [Windham] then approved" which were not "reconcilable with the principles of the constitution," in 1784 and again in 1790. More than a few politically aware voters, however, remained loyal to Windham after his party switch in 1794 despite irreconcilable political differences. They were no less aware of issues than their fellows who left or joined Windham's camp; they simply viewed matters differently. Robert White remained confident in Windham's abilities as an M.P., believing "that whatever change your political sentiments may have undergone, the same unbiased principles have been the rule of your conduct." White promised Windham his vote in subsequent elections, though he refused to actively endorse Windham's campaign. John Buckle also expressed concern at Windham's acceptance of the Ministry of War, and refused to again take any "active part in elections" for Windham as a result, yet he too promised to continue voting for Windham because of his "personal knowledge" of Windham's qualities as an M.P.[74] The political sophistication revealed by these comments could not have been reflected in the entire Norwich electorate, or any other borough electorate for that matter, but the expression of such concerns implies a remarkably widespread awareness of political matters among Norwich's rank-and-file voters. Although these men were unusual in expressing their concerns to Windham in writing, they were ordinary Norwich electors in every other respect. The typicality of such clearcut political stances is the concern of Chapters 6 and 7; of concern here are the issues that mattered to those electors who *were* politically aware, whatever their numbers. The general pattern of the issues debated during the Norwich parliamentary battles, a pattern made

[74] Windham Papers, BL Add. MS. 37908, ff. 84.

so much clearer than elsewhere by the survival of election propaganda, is informative, particularly when supplemented by less complete indications of issues raised in other boroughs.

In sharp contrast to the 1761 election that elicited neither issues nor propaganda, the 1768 Norwich election campaign began in November 1767 with political announcements by all three candidates and a "juncture" of the two incumbents, Harbord Harbord and Edward Bacon against the challenger, Thomas Beevor. Beevor responded to the alliance against him by immediately sounding the clarion calls of "liberty" and "no unconstitutional measures." The juncture and the availability of the issues prompted by the question of general warrants and the expulsion of John Wilkes from the Commons caused the consideration of "fundamental and profound" issues in Norwich, as in much of the rest of the nation, for the first time in decades.[75] Norwich newspapers published the parliamentary voting record on the question of general warrants and carried the full text of John Wilkes's March address to the Middlesex electors.[76] Frequent letters debating the merits of the Wilkes affair printed by the Norwich *Chronicle* were supplemented by no less than twenty-five separate arguments for or against general warrants issued in connection with the Norfolk county election that appeared at the same time and in the same places as the city election literature.[77] Although the Norwich incumbents benefited from the powerful assistance of the city Administration, many Norwich electors took the position recommended by Beevor's propaganda:

> I'd vote for the Deaf
> I'd vote for the Dumb
> I'd vote for a crazy Knight Errant;

[75] Cannon, *Parliamentary Reform*, p. 61.

[76] *Norwich Mercury*, December 12, 1767, and March 19, 1768.

[77] *The Contest: or A Collection of Papers Published During the Contest in Norfolk in 1767 and 1768*, Norwich, 1768, pp. 1-65.

Or I'd be more civil
And vote for the Devil,
As soon as a General Warrant.[78]

Of the more than 1,100 electors who cast votes for Beevor at the polls on March 18, 1768, an unprecedented 825 plumped (cast single votes) for Beevor, discarding their second ballot. Two hundred twenty-six others voted for both opponents of general warrants, Harbord and Beevor. Less than 3 percent (70 voters), paired Beevor and his political antithesis, Edward Bacon.

Each of the other boroughs experienced contests in 1768, but only the Maidstone election allowed even the remotest possibility for political issues to play a part. The Northampton race pitted the forces of patronage and corruption against each other as three earls either virtually or literally bankrupted themselves in a struggle for supremacy. Political issues would have been equally hard-pressed to find expression in the Lewes election where three men with indistinguishable political principles stood for parliament.[79] Patronage, personalities, and friendships almost certainly contributed more than anything else to the contest. Maidstone voters alone might have considered political issues in casting their ballots. Two men, Charles Marsham and Robert Gregory (the victors) stood more or less independently, but each stood unmistakably opposed to the Administration while Arthur Annesley represented a political alternative. Annesley's alternative proved in the end to be unattractive, however; he lost to Marsham by a landslide and finished a hundred votes behind Gregory.

During the following general election (1774), Norwich returned its two incumbents, Harbord (now Sir Harbord

[78] *Miscellaneous Pieces*, pp. 1-65.

[79] Clearly, Thomas Hampden, Thomas Hay, and Thomas Miller were, in the vernacular, Whigs. Their political principles, to use the term loosely, differed about as much as their given names. John Brooke, *The Chatham Administration*, London, 1956, pp. 344-47.

142

Harbord, second baronet) and Bacon, without opposition. Discontented Norwich citizens booed Bacon, the Ministerialist, in the marketplace the day of the uncontested return, but no formal opposition appeared, possibly because the premature dissolution came as such a surprise; parliament should have lasted another six months.[80] Had the election been contested, however, the issue of America almost certainly would have supplemented, if not supplanted, any remaining contention over "Wilkes and Liberty" and related issues. Though Norwich's trade had never relied extensively on the colonies, the town's voters presented their first petition to the Commons warning of the disastrous consequences necessarily resulting from a stoppage of trade with North America only a few months after the general election. Norwich interest in American affairs subsequently mounted to a peak in 1778 when thousands of Norwich citizens assumed a determinedly anti-Administration stance in another petition to the House of Commons.[81]

The new concern over the conduct of affairs in the colonies had not completely extinguished the flame kindled among some of Maidstone's voters by cries of "Wilkes and

[80] Gurney MSS., 2/322, October 12, 1774, Library of the Society of Friends, London. Cannon stated that 1784 was the "first political as opposed to statutory dissolution since 1714." Ivor Bulmer-Thomas maintained the same position. John Cannon, *The Fox-North Coalition*, London, 1969, p. 224; Ivor Bulmer-Thomas, *The Growth of the British Party System*, 2 vols., London, 1953, 1:21. Both assertions are incorrect; in addition to the comments in the *Annual Register* for 1774, see W. B. Donne, ed., *Correspondence of George III to Lord North*, 2 vols., London, 1867, 1:201. A letter from Sir Horace Mann to Lord Romney noted receiving "the news of the sudden dissolution of the Parliament . . ." Romney MSS., U1300, c4/4, KRO.

[81] Three hundred men were unemployed in Norwich as a direct result of the Stamp Act according to the *London Magazine*. The Norwich petition over the American crisis was rejected by parliament on the grounds that it had been printed before submission. Actually, Norwich began to show concern over America as early as 1768. *London Magazine*, March 5, 1766; *CJ*, February 17, 1778.

Liberty." An announcement in the *Kentish Gazette* noted the desire of "the most respectable body of freemen" to oppose the candidacy of "a man . . . who had voted in favor of all the . . . iniquitous measures of an infamous administration." However, the selection of Robert Gregory, one of the leading champions of the American cause, by Maidstone's independent faction in 1774 pointed to their concern over events in America.[82] The 1774 general election prompted no electoral contest in Northampton, and no references to the American problem emerged in the Lewes election that year, though the many promises by candidates to protect civil liberties demonstrated the continued salience of the national issues of 1768, due in part perhaps to John Wilkes's 1770 visit to Lewes.[83] These promises included the protection of religious liberty as well, hinting at the potential significance of Nonconformity at Lewes contests. After the radical independent, William Kemp, placed last in the Lewes election with a mere forty votes, the Lewes *Journal* noted (with reference to the infamous number forty-five of Wilkes's *North Briton*) how fortunate it was that Kemp's total did not reach forty-five since "the fame and disgrace of the number would have been equal" had he found five more supporters.[84]

Vigorous partisan activity again permeated the Norwich parliamentary contest of 1780 in the general election that also followed an unexpected dissolution of parliament. And again, national issues dominated electoral propaganda, although the city elite's ouster of Sir Harbord Harbord for the more compatible Ministerial candidate, John Thurlow, interjected an additional major local consideration. The city fathers removed Sir Harbord as quietly as possible in an effort to prevent a contest, but the Free Blues had no intention of letting this election pass uncontested, and capi-

[82] *Kentish Gazette*, October 15, 1774.
[83] L. F. Salzman, ed., *The Victoria County History of Sussex*, 9 vols., London, 1940, 7:19.
[84] *Lewes Journal*, October 24, 1774.

talized on the blatant attempt by the Corporation and the
Orange-and-Purple party to assure the quick return of Bacon and Thurlow. Hence, alongside invocations of the current national political issues and reminders of the general
warrants controversy of the 1768 election, broadsides praised
the principles of the anti-Corporation candidates and hailed
all freemen who scorned "to drink the venal toast/Of SLAV-
ERY and BACON."[85] The personalities of the candidates
also attracted attention, with Bacon singled out for the brunt
of most of the attacks, since, as the Free Blues claimed,
"None in the Senate ever more firmly stood,/Opposing all
things meant for public good."[86] With such a perfect focal
point for a campaign based strictly on personalities, the
Free Blues might have done well to limit the election to an
effort to unseat Bacon as an unfit member of parliament.
However, the American conflict rather than Bacon's character soon became the most frequently mentioned concern
in the campaign, and understandably so. The Free Blues
had chosen William Windham to stand with their newly
acquired candidate, Harbord, on the basis of his leadership
in the petitioning drive against the American War in 1778.
The issue could hardly be dropped. During the campaign,
Windham and the Free Blues denounced the war as abhor-
rent in principle and disastrous in practice, particularly
economically. The fervor that produced 5,000 signatures
on the 1778 petition reemerged as the election progressed.
Citing a 1775 visit to Norwich by Thomas Hutchinson, Ian
Christie and Benjamin Labaree have argued recently that
since Norwich trade largely bypassed the American market,
Norwich opposed any concessions to the colonists. Actually,
Norwich's inhabitants could not have demonstrated much
greater concern, or more willingness to grant the Americans any concession necessary to bring hostilities to a speedy
termination. This willingness to placate the colonists seems

[85] *Narrative of the Contested Election*, pp. 1-26.
[86] Ibid., p. 12.

145

to have been based not on ideological grounds, but simply on the desire for peace and most of all for peaceful trade. In 1778, Norwich had rested "the last Hopes of a deserving, but, we fear, an injured, deceived, and endangered people" on the Commons. Few men in Norwich seemed to have changed their minds by 1780.[87] Other matters raised by election literature included the problem of the "too great and increasing" influence of the Crown (Dunning's famous resolution of April 1780 was printed in full) and the necessity for financial reform, but the war itself commanded most attention from the press and in the widely circulated election handbills.[88] Surprisingly, the issue of war or peace failed to secure Windham's return; the incumbents, Harbord and Bacon, though now representing diametrically opposed political philosophies, returned to parliament once again. The Norwich municipal contests held in the following year also considered the issues raised at the general election. Indeed, local elections after 1780 usually, if not invariably, followed national party lines. The city-wide shrieval race and the election of an alderman for Mancroft ward in 1781 happened to involve the same candidates, and in both instances, the issues of the preceding parliamentary contest fueled the political rhetoric of the campaigns. The Free Blues again cited the American War, heavy taxation, and ruined trade, while the Orange-and-Purples "sneered their defiance to the clamor of the Mob, as they were pleased to call the people." The ensuing struggles for

[87] Christie and Labaree cite the lack of interest in the American question in Norwich, where manufacturing "catered to the Baltic markets and had little concern with American trade." It is difficult to reconcile this position with the Norwich petition of 1778, signed by 5,000 men, condemning the Government's policies in America. Ian R. Christie and Benjamin Labaree, *Empire or Independence*, London, 1976, p. 216; *CJ*, February 17, 1778. Also, *Historical Manuscripts Commission Reports*, Dartmouth MSS., Eleventh Report, part 5, London, 1895, p. 419; and Horace Walpole, *Last Journals*, ed. A. F. Steuart, 2 vols., London, 1910, pp. ii, 119.

[88] *Norfolk Chronicle*, September 5, 1784.

these city offices engendered "as much vehemence as if they [the candidates] had been Ministers of State."[89]

This preoccupation with national issues that began as early as 1768 in Norwich and probably by 1774 in Maidstone somewhat dulls the luster acquired by the celebrated general election of 1784 after so many years of historical commentary. The political issues raised in 1784 may well have attracted more attention in the country generally than the issues and controversies invoked during the course of the three prior parliamentary elections. Nevertheless, of these four boroughs, Northampton alone seems to have been unusually affected by the Fox-North dispute, and then only in the sense that the issues sparked by the infamous Coalition of Fox and North achieved some currency in a borough unaccustomed to issues of any kind. After several elections with no mention of issues or parties, all three Northampton candidates in 1784 clearly identified their respective political positions. Charles Compton and Fiennes Trotman promised they would "zealously maintain the Honour and Prerogatives of the Crown," while Charles Bingham, an incumbent, defended his record in the Commons and tried in vain to avoid a Foxite label. Unfortunately for Bingham, his support of Fox's India Bill could not be denied, and whether or not he was correct in defending his actions as upholding "the ancient, undoubted, and necessary controlling powers of the House of Commons against the united attempts of the other two Branches of the Legislature," his connection with Fox proved fatal.[90] Despite his social rank and the remaining Spencer interest in the borough, Bingham (Lord Lucan) received not many more than half the votes of his equally aristocratic Pittite opponent, Lord Compton, and lost to the other Pittite, Trotman, by a narrower yet still embarrassing margin.

[89] A Copy of the Poll for Alderman, Norwich, 1781, p. 17; BL Add. MS. 27815, ff. 122, and Report of the Commission on Municipal Corporations, vol. 26, pp. 2457-509.

[90] Northampton Mercury, April 5 and April 12, 1784.

147

To be sure, the Fox-North issue overrode other concerns in the Norwich and Maidstone elections of 1784, but in both towns, the concern over issues in 1784 continued trends begun much earlier. However, the publisher of the collected propaganda issued in connection with the Norwich election felt that a new level of political awareness had dominated the campaign. "The state of public affairs seemed to affect the minds of the people. Local attachments now gave way to sentiments of patriotism, and men thought themselves absolved from any engagement not properly founded on principles of public faith." Matters other than the Coalition also gained some salience in Norwich during the election. William Windham ran on his record (his non-parliamentary record) of defending religious toleration for Nonconformists and Papists, as well as his adherence to Foxite principles. He also resurrected the controversy over the American War and the more recent topic of economic reform, reminding the electors of his opposition to the former and his support of the latter.[91]

The question of the correct form of parliamentary representation emerged in the course of the 1784 Norwich election as a topic of considerable and, in this instance, sustained interest. The proper relationship between members of parliament and their constituents was a long-standing question by the 1780s. The defense of virtual representation delineated in Edmund Burke's famous speech to his Bristol constituents, certainly one of the more widely publicized of several opinions current at the end of the century, was not shared by many electors in the four boroughs. Following a well-established custom and exercising the "undoubted right of all constituents to instruct their representatives in Parliament from time to time," the Norwich freemen had submitted a list of twelve instructions to Harbord and Bacon after the 1768 election covering a wide range of topics, among them the need for triennial parlia-

[91] *The Election Magazine*, p. 17.

ments and the desirability of excluding sons of peers from the Commons.[92] The Norwich Blues also sent William Windham periodic reviews of his political conduct during the 1780s, and Windham took considerable care to reply, though he never acknowledged any obligation to abide by the wishes of his constituents.[93] Pledges of conduct from candidates, relatively familiar political ploys in elections for Westminster and Middlesex, were not uncommon in Lewes or Maidstone although resisted to the end by Windham in Norwich. In the 1780 Lewes election, for example, the "independent" candidate, Thomas Kemp, pledged not to accept a place or a pension from the Administration if returned.[94] Prior to the 1788 by-election in Maidstone occasioned by the resignation of one of the incumbents, Matthew Bloxham was forced to pledge himself "a sure friend of Mr. Pitt" before being returned at the conclusion of a short contest with the Foxite, George Byng.[95]

Representation became an actual campaign issue in Norwich alone, perhaps because Windham so adamantly refused to compromise his independence. The Norwich *Mercury* announced on March 19, 1784 that "it is now pretty generally the opinion that a test will be offered to each candidate at the next General Election throughout the Kingdom, declaratory of his [each candidate's] intent to follow such instructions as his constituents may legally think proper to give him." Following this announcement, Windham boldly and unequivocally declared his intention to follow his own course in parliament if elected. His opponent, Hobart, on the other hand, voiced his eagerness "at

[92] *Norwich Mercury*, March 19, 1784. John Stacy, *Topographical and Historical Account of Norwich*, London, 1819, p. 9.

[93] Baring, ed., *Diary of William Windham*, p. 109.

[94] Edward Porritt and A. G. Porritt, *The Unreformed House of Commons*, 2 vols., Cambridge, 1909, 1:271, and Oldfield, *Representative History*, 5:15.

[95] *Kentish Gazette*, July 11, 1788. Bloxham was elected in the place of Gerard Edwards who resigned to take a seat for Rutland. Byng subsequently won a place in the Commons for Newport, Isle of Wight.

all times to obey the instructions of the constituent body." A letter appeared immediately in the press denying that Windham "could be a proper representative of any body of men" because "in the nature of things, it becomes the representative to comply with the wishes of the majority of his constituents." The Free Blues countered this attack as best they could by arguing that while Hobart spoke of the "Dignity of the Crown," he remained "silent as the grave on the Majesty of the People." Alderman Elias Norgate, one of the most prominent Blue leaders, argued convincingly that Sir Harbord Harbord had "opposed the American war in spite of the wishes of most Norwich voters" (a point not necessarily borne out by the facts, but effective nevertheless), and that Windham simply intended to pursue an equally beneficial, independent course in the future. Shortly afterwards, a political satirist wrote a letter to the *Mercury* in which he offered his own candidacy for a parliamentary seat, promising to fight for "either Pitt or Fox [as directed]." He aptly signed his offer, "Your devoted slave." A postscript to his letter rounded off the point he was making with a flourish by proposing a joint candidacy with anyone interested while adding in the same breath, "but curse all coalitions." Such a pointed barb, probably the work of "Free Blue" Alderman Charles Baggs, could not have argued Windham's case more eloquently, and it may have helped Windham, though later (1802) the Free Blues would wield the same charge of insularity against Windham that they tried to counter in 1784. After his desertion of the party in 1794, the Free Blues used even more damning evidence to accuse Windham of ignoring the wishes of the residents of Norwich, and finally managed to unseat him after their third major effort (1802).[96]

Oddly enough, the political fever pitch reached in the nation during the 1784 debates over Fox or Pitt, demon-

[96] *Election Magazine*, pp. 9, 22-23, 26, 35, 46; *Norwich Mercury*, April 3, 1784.

strated by the levels of propaganda at the elections and the number of petitions addressed to the King (including at least one from each of the four boroughs), seems to have abated by 1790. After several elections marked by massive propaganda efforts, the Norwich election of 1790 provoked very little publishing, despite the great issues raised by the Regency Crisis of 1788-89.[97] Indeed, save for a few letters in the press, the Norwich election passed almost unnoticed as Henry Hobart and William Windham, political opposites, humiliated Sir Thomas Beevor at the hustings. The 1790 general election was in many ways a straightforward contest between Pitt's government and the Portland opposition, yet the Norwich electorate seemed unwilling to take a firm stand for one side or the other. Beevor's humiliating defeat may have indicated the anti-Foxite sentiments of many Norwich voters, but the reelection of Windham maintained the political split in Norwich's parliamentary delegation. Norwich had yet to experience the powerful sermons of men like the Reverend Mark Wilkes who preached that "Jesus was a revolutionist," and who later threatened that the King would "not live a month" if he signed the Sedition Bills. Nor had John Thelwall made his contribution to political unrest and polarization in Norwich.[98]

Equally low-key activity dominated the other towns as voters in two of them also chose political opposites. The races in all four boroughs produced the most lopsided results of the entire period. Unsuccessful candidates in each contest averaged just 30 percent of the vote; by comparison, losing candidates in the three contested elections of 1784 won 49.1 percent of the vote on average, slightly more than

[97] The only other Norwich election for which this seems to be true is 1761, and even during the 1761 election some propaganda was distributed. *HMC*, Lothian MSS., London, 1905, pp. 242-43.

[98] Charles Cestre, *John Thelwall*, Paris, 1906, p. 128; Sarah Wilkes, *Memoirs of the Reverend Mark Wilkes*, London, 1821, pp. vii-xiii; Jewson, *Jacobin City*, p. 69.

the 1796 four-contest average of 47.1 percent. Lewes residents welcomed French emigrés in 1790, yet no political references appeared in any local press reports before or after the election. In fact, the establishment of the "Society for the Protection of Liberty and Property against Republicans and Levellers" at Lewes in 1793 seems to have been Lewes's only nationally oriented political activity during the decade.[99] The real stir in Lewes followed the completion of the polling and involved the "respectability" of the men voting for the Coalition of Henry Pelham and Thomas Kemp rather than political principles.[100] The allied incumbents were returned with little protest, just as the incumbents in Maidstone experienced token opposition. Two members of parliament could hardly have resembled each other less than the independent, Foxite Clement Taylor, who sat for Maidstone continuously after 1780 and his colleague, the ardent Pittite, Matthew Bloxham, who entered the Commons in the 1788 by-election. Yet the other Ministerialist candidate at the election, Robert Parker, posed no threat to Taylor. A mere 158 of Maidstone's 643 voters (25 percent) in 1790 cast ballots for Parker, far fewer than the number willing to vote for a wild-eyed radical in the subsequent election.

By 1796, political temperatures had risen considerably all over England. If overstating the case perhaps, the *Annual Register* caught the mood of the nation by noting that "the interest of the public seems so deeply at stake [in the elections] that individuals not only of the decent, but of the most vulgar professions, gave up a considerable portion of their time and occupations in attending the numerous

[99] Perceval Lucas, "The Verrall Family of Lewes," *Sussex Archeological Collections* 58(1920):91-131. Also, W. K. Rector, "Lewes Quakers in the Seventeenth and Eighteenth Centuries," *Sussex Archeological Collections* 116(1978):31-40. "Constitutional Club," *Sussex Notes and Queries* 13(1950):318-21.

[100] A published poll was demanded of the *Lewes Journal*, and the request was granted. *Lewes Journal*, May 30, June 21, and June 28, 1790.

meetings that were called in each part of the Kingdom."[101] The Englishman's addiction to politics again took hold as the exceptionally divisive political issues growing out of the revolution in France split the electorate into opposing camps.[102] The division in Norwich prompted near riots among "political inebriates," as the *Monthly Magazine* called them, over toasts like "Our Sovereign, the King; the Majesty of the people" or "Curse the Five Hundred," and "Damn the Directory."[103] Norwich had suffered through a particularly vituperative by-election two years earlier when the "factious and democratic" Free Blues, upset by Windham's betrayal of their cause, ran James Mingay, the radical lawyer, in his stead. With this tumultuous background, and encouraged now by the religious harangues of Reverend Mark Wilkes and his fellows, as well as the political tirades of professional agitators like John Thelwall, the issues in the 1796 Norwich election should have been as clear as they were fundamental. Norwich also had a circulating library after 1785 with a small annual subscription of eight shillings. The overwhelming majority of Norwich's residents could not afford the annual subscription or the entry fee of 2½ guineas, but the 500 subscribers, supplemented by members of several other book clubs and smaller circulating libraries should have helped clarify the uncomplicated choices facing the Norwich voters at the elections of the 1790s.[104]

Both the Free Blues and Windham had more time to prepare before the 1796 contest than in 1794, and the Free Blue candidate, Bartlett Gurney, also seemed more generally acceptable than James Mingay had been in 1794. Members of the Gurney family had served Norwich in many capacities during their long association with the Norwich anti-Ministerialists, and 1796 saw the first Gurney parlia-

153

mentary candidate. Rallying around their new champion, the Free Blues focused their efforts on the several issues related to the war with France. To point out the inconsistency of Windham's new advocacy of war, his opponents demonstrated their long political memories and their political astuteness by circulating a broadsheet with the full text of Windham's rousing 1778 speech against the American War. They entitled the piece, "Consistency." The Blues also stressed the ruination of trade, the unjust principles behind the war, and resurrected the issue of Windham's disregard for public opinion. Windham obliged by providing new evidence of his disregard of the electorate, not that his behavior in previous elections left much to doubt. Early in the campaign, Windham argued that he was "not aware of any political opinion at present subsisting on which I have the misfortune to differ from the sentiments of the general body of my constituents."[105] Windham's sentiments corresponded poorly with the petition signed by more than 6,000 Norwich residents regretting the "grievous calamities of the war" and denouncing the government's attempt to "interfere with the internal affairs of France."[106] Having treated Norwich's petition "with opposition and contempt" in the first place, Windham now insulted the petitioners further by ignoring its existence. Neither of Norwich's earlier broadly supported petitions (one favoring parliamentary reform in 1793, and one against the American War in 1778) had attracted as many signatures, and the Whig propagandists enjoyed a field day ridiculing the absurdity of Windham's claim to virtually unanimous public support for his role in the war.[107] Supporting their single candidate,

[105] Windham Papers, BL Add. MS. 37908, ff. 202.; *Miscellaneous Verses and Squibs on the Norwich Elections*, Colman Library, Norwich.

[106] *CJ*, February 5, 1795, and *Miscellaneous Verses*.

[107] A. D. Baynes, *A Complete History of Norwich*, London, 1869, p. 284. There were 3,741 signatures on the petition presented by Hobart. It was not accepted by the House because it had been printed prior to presentation. Walpole, *Last Journals*, 2:118 and *HMC*, Dartmouth MSS., Eleventh Report, Part 5, p. 419.

Gurney, the Blues concentrated their attacks on Windham and allowed the other Ministerialist, Henry Hobart, to win a seat virtually unchallenged. Hobart topped the poll accordingly. Windham, on the other hand, lost to Gurney among the resident voters in Norwich, yet squeezed out a victory with the votes of nonresident voters (mostly Londoners) brought in to bolster his total. For the second time in a row, Windham succeeded in "crushing the democratical spirit" which was "manifest in that Ancient City."[108]

Maidstone also experienced an extremely divisive campaign in 1796. Exacerbated by the activities of the Pittite Corporation that included a series of Loyalist pamphlets published in 1792 and 1793 by the mayor, partisan spirits in Maidstone paralleled the notable zeal apparent in Norwich.[109] John Gale Jones, the member of the London Corresponding Society sent out to assist Clement Taylor, found party spirit so high "that many of the neighbors would not traffic with those who were of opposite opinions." According to Jones, the Administration had threatened to put Taylor "to considerable trouble and expense," and Taylor's deteriorating financial condition, culminating later in bankruptcy, induced him to stand down in favor of Christopher Hull.[110] With one day to organize his support, Hull finished a mere forty-seven votes behind the Pittite, Bloxham. However, Hull's loss meant that for the first time in sixteen years Maidstone sent two Ministerialists to the House of Commons.

The 1796 Northampton election, the last contest for almost twenty-two years, followed a different model. The Northampton contest resembled those in Norwich and Maidstone only in the sense that all three involved the casting of votes. Otherwise, Northampton stood completely apart, as Spencer Perceval's successful campaign in 1796

[108] Letter from Samuel Shepperton to William Windham, October 7, 1794. Windham Papers, BL Add. MS. 37908, ff. 91.

[109] The mayor of Maidstone published 7,100 loyalist pamphlets. Austin Mitchell, "The Association Movement, 1792-3," *Historical Journal* 4(1961):72.

[110] Jones, *Sketch of a Political Tour*, pp. 79-81.

avoided political issues almost totally. Edward Bouverie, the other winner, dared not raise political issues since his Foxite principles had become so unpopular nationally and locally. Perceval's electoral address a month prior to the poll served merely as a vehicle for fulsome praise of the mayor and aldermen, and his victory address immediately after the poll discussed the results exclusively in terms of "true friends," "fair weather friends," and "unreliable men" (those who had promised Perceval a vote and then plumped for another candidate).[111] Northampton's electors again returned a split delegation with Perceval topping the poll and Edward Bouverie placing a distant second.

While failing to reproduce the political fervor common to Norwich and Maidstone, Lewes avoided the completely apolitical atmosphere of Northampton and at least managed to achieve harmony between local and national political concerns, although their achievement apparently had more to do with shifting personalities than with rational political choices. John Pelham replaced Henry Pelham in 1796, creating for the first time a Coalition united behind Pitt's government. The Pelham family, including John Pelham, had been Foxites, but followed Windham into Pitt's camp. The continued success of the "Coalition" meant that Lewes's M.P.'s were no longer divided over national issues. Political issues were broached in the Lewes press before the poll, but in sharp contrast to Norwich, where most voters obviously cared more for parties and issues than personalities by the late 1790s, personality still carried the greatest weight in the Lewes electorate. William Green, the challenger in 1796, though representing Whiggish interests somewhat indifferently, at least allowed Lewes voters to integrate national concerns and local interests at long last, albeit almost completely accidentally.[112]

[111] Perceval Papers, BL Add. MS. 49719, pp. 39-42; BL Add. MS. 49184, p. 38.
[112] Apparently, W. H. Green possessed indifferent, if Whiggish, political principles.

Norwich maintained and even increased the frenetic pitch of the 1796 contest at the 1802 election, and the political climate in Maidstone was correspondingly heated. Once again, French affairs assumed paramount importance in both boroughs; the 1802 contest in Norwich marked the fourth successive contest in which the French war was the most frequently mentioned question in the published propaganda. Apparently improving with practice, Whig writers in 1802 bitterly attacked Windham's continued pursuit of the "noble occupation of KILLING MEN AND BURNING TOWNS," and placed advertisements in the press for an auction at which Windham was to sell 100,000 pounds of human hair and 10,000 hogsheads of human teeth.[113] His encouragement of the "sport" of bull-baiting, his denunciation of the Methodists, and the anonymity of his running mate, John Frere, also served as rallying points for the supporters of the Free Blues, but the war retained its preeminence.[114] Windham's rejection of the Peace of Amiens infuriated those opposed to the war for whatever reason, and his explanations of his position failed to mollify Norwich's voters.

Administration propagandists attacked the Whig candidates in Norwich with comparable strength, though reserving their best shots for the Nonconformist ex-Sudbury M.P., William Smith, whose widely known Whig principles led to his selection by the Free Blues. The Administration press immediately labelled him "King-Killer" Smith, and the sobriquet persisted throughout the campaign.[115] The Ministerialists also denigrated the other Whig, Robert Fellowes (unsuccessful candidate at the 1799 by-election), and chose to hold him up to public ridicule as unworthy of the post instead of dwelling on his specific political complexion.

[113] *A New Election Budget, 1802*, p. 4; *Norwich Mercury*, July 3, 1802.

[114] *The New Election Budget, 1802*, p. 12.

[115] Richard W. Davis, *Dissent in Politics, 1780-1832: The Political Life of William Smith, M.P.*, London, 1971, pp. 53-150 and *A New Election Budget, 1802*.

157

The Tories saw no need to examine his politics minutely; as a Free Blue candidate, Fellowes obviously was guilty of espousing "hot anarchy and cold reform," Jacobinical political ideas, regicide, and the subversion of the Church. Of the two Whigs, Smith was by far the more vulnerable to specific charges of treason since he had been examined during the Stone treason trial in 1796. When the Free Blues published an extraordinarily clever diatribe against Windham's war efforts that alleged:

> Ah! See the victim, hark the groan
> Horrid yells and dismal moan,
> Piercing cries that rend the air,
> Torture, agony, and despair
> While carnage reigns as blythe as May
> Carnage is Windham's holiday,

the Orange-and-Purples responded with:

> Haste sans-culottes, your hour is nigh
> The hour of Rebel Anarchy,
> 'Tis Smith who calls, your Patron Friend,
> The Rights of Traitors to defend.
> The Church, the Throne, shall fall on Prey
> For this is Treason's holiday.

The Orange-and-Purples pulled out all the stops in a desperate effort to undercut Smith's support and reelect Windham; the running mates on both sides were less important. Not wishing to miss any bases, the Tories also accused Fellowes of misconduct in the management of local hospital funds.[116] Certainly the behavior of the two party organizations justified the contemporary observation that "a deeper and more lasting discordancy" could not exist between two parties and that never was "a more indelible line of division drawn betwixt men."[117] In the event, the cries of treason

[116] *A New Election Budget, 1802,* pp. 5-12, 19-36.
[117] *Vindication of the Political Conduct of William Windham,* London, 1802, p. 53.

failed to offset the cries of "war maker," and Windham lost the election. Finally he was forced to trade the "eternal hot water" of Norwich politics for the less pressing problems of St. Mawes, where thirty electors were hardly likely to cause him much trouble as long as the Marquis of Buckingham supported his cause.[118] Fellowes easily topped the poll, and Frere finished last in a curious reversal of the election three years earlier when Fellowes lost to Frere hands down.[119]

The dividing line "betwixt men" seems to have been drawn less distinctly in Maidstone in 1802 and assumed an altogether different character in Lewes, for even though serious contests divided both boroughs, the issues in the former were not completely clear, and those in the latter illustrated Lewes's preoccupation with local concerns. John Durrand, the Whig candidate in Maidstone, appealed successfully to the independents after their rejection of "Citizen Hull" in the 1796 election, and Maidstone restored the customary Opposition-Administration split between its representatives after the brief unity of 1796 when two Ministerialists won. While Maidstone's normal pattern reemerged, the state of affairs normal in Lewes since 1780 ended with the defeat of the Coalition. Thomas Kemp lost the seat he had held for twenty years to a challenger with similar, if not identical, national political principles.[120]

RELIGIOUS ISSUES

Each of these towns contained a sufficiently large Dissenting population to insure a response to religion as an election issue. The actual strength of Dissent in each borough cannot be determined precisely, but Maidstone probably possessed the highest proportion of Nonconformists. Rowles

[118] William Windham, *The Windham Papers*, ed. Lord Rosebery, 2 vols., London, 1895, 2:195.
[119] *Election Budget for 1799*.
[120] W. B. Hills, *Parliamentary History of Lewes*, Lewes, 1908, p. 33.

159

reckoned Dissenters made up approximately half of Maidstone's 1808 population of just over 10,000. Northampton Dissenters also numbered in the thousands, and though they may have contributed a slightly smaller proportion of the population, Northampton has been called the "Mecca of English Nonconformity." Lewes's Dissenters formed a "numerous and respectable congregation"; their exact numbers or their effective strength cannot be measured. Norwich's Nonconformist population, estimated as at least 15 percent of the total in the second decade of the nineteenth century (excluding Methodists), may have ranked last, even if the Dissenting population some twenty years earlier comprised a larger share of Norwich's population.[121]

Political activity in Norwich and Maidstone best reveals the relationship between Nonconformity and the developing political parties and political loyalties in the boroughs, because few specific political references to religion survive from Lewes elections, and Mecca or not, no direct evidence links religion and politics in Northampton. Given its pro-Administration and almost completely Anglican Corporation, religion may have helped shape Northampton politics, but the relationship defies examination.[122] Conversely, religious issues were broached time and again at elections in Maidstone and Norwich, and if election propaganda is any indication, few issues achieved as much importance in either community, among the general populace or among the elite. With the single exception of the 1784 Norwich election which was recognized at the time as a deviation, political spokesmen of both parties assumed a

[121] W. T. Rowles, *History of Maidstone*, London, 1809, p. 5. William Page, ed., *Victoria County History of Northamptonshire*, 4 vols., London, 1902, 3:12. There were at least three meeting houses in Northampton, two Independent and one Baptist. *Report of the Commission on Municipal Corporations*, vol. 25, pp. 749-70. J. Chambers, *A General History of the County of Norfolk*, Norwich, 1829, 2:27-65. The total number was estimated as 4,700.

[122] Namier and Brooke, *House of Commons*, 1:27, 37; Lee, *A History of Lewes*, p. 349.

close connection between Dissent and "independent" or "Opposition" political stances. Townspeople in Norwich and Maidstone perceived their Ministerial parties as staunch supporters of the established Church. Ministerialist election literature never hesitated to emphasize the association and to stress the joint danger to Church and State posed by the notorious alliance of Dissent and Opposition. In turn, the "Whigs" seemed quite willing to accept this identification with the Nonconformist community, playing it to their best advantage at every opportunity. Thus a pronounced and definite relationship between religious convictions and political stances was assumed by this propaganda.

More than any other single issue except corruption, accounts of later eighteenth-century politics have stressed religion, agreeing almost invariably that Nonconformity closely paralleled political independence. Recently, however, the standard interpretation has been questioned, and an effort made to demonstrate the failure of the most commonly cited evidence to establish any connection between Whigs and Dissenters. At best, most sources point to a connection, if it existed, only among the Dissenting elite, not the rank and file.[123] Although Bradley was correct in noting the failure of traditional accounts to make a convincing case for a tie linking religious and political dissent, evidence from Norwich and Maidstone argues strongly in favor of such a connection, and the actual voting patterns of both electorates described in the seventh chapter render concrete the assumptions of many contemporaries.

Some articulation of religious issues preceded the definite beginning of sustained partisan activity in Maidstone. The "independent" party was not well established until at least 1774 and possibly not until their 1780 victory against the Ministerialists, yet religious references preceded the 1761 election. Sir Lewis Namier argued that Maidstone

[123] James E. Bradley, "Whigs and Nonconformists: 'Slumbering Radicalism' in English Politics, 1739-1789," *Eighteenth Century Studies*, 9, 1(1975):1-27.

politics in 1761 illustrated the "religious background" of parties "insofar as parties existed among the rank and file," and religion again received attention in 1768.[124] A letter from Lord Rockingham to the Duke of Newcastle prior to that election proposed Robert Gregory as a candidate and asked Newcastle's assistance in recommending Gregory "among the Dissenters" and other "Whig gentlemen" who might be inclined to support such a man.[125] This bond linking religious and partisan preferences became even more apparent in the subsequent election. The same Robert Gregory for whom Rockingham had requested assistance in 1768 (an incumbent in 1780), received absolutely no encouragement or aid from his erstwhile patron, Lord Aylesford, and took care as a result to be elected as a member for Rochester even before Maidstone electors went to the polls. Disregarding his victory in Rochester, a group of "friends of liberty and independence" in Maidstone "determined to return him again, to give him double honor on account of his truly patriotic conduct, and to testify their sovereign contempt for a man [Heneage Finch, ex-member for Castle Rising and proposed candidate for Maidstone] who had voted against the toleration of our fellow Protestants."[126] Even with such ardent backing, Gregory's chances were never good, and he lost to Finch by a large margin. Nevertheless, the support shown his candidacy as a friend of religious liberty, and his ability to win 35 percent of the electorate in the face of all the efforts Lord Aylesford could muster against him signifies the strength of both religion and "independence" at this early stage and, more specifi-

[124] Sir Lewis Namier, *The Structure of Politics at the Accession of George III*, 2nd ed., London, 1957, pp. 113-18.

[125] Newcastle, BL Add. MS. 32989, ff. 29.

[126] *Kentish Gazette*, October 15, 1774. The bill for the relief of Protestant Dissenters was introduced by Sir Henry Hoghton and passed the Commons with only nine votes against it, one of which was cast by Finch. It was voted down, as planned, in the Lords, thus avoiding the possibility of antagonizing the Nonconformist electorate so soon before the general elections. See Porritt and Porritt, *The Unreformed Commons*, p. 277.

162

cally, points to the already strong bond connnecting them. While succeeding Maidstone elections do not often vouchsafe such insights, one of the few printed pamphlets issued at the 1790 election dealt with the Test Act, and religion reemerged in the press during the confused 1796 campaign. Moreover, Oldfield's description of Maidstone politics in 1790 closely resembles Namier's appraisal of Maidstone elections thirty years earlier; Oldfield saw religion as the paramount issue in Maidstone political disputes.[127]

Less consensus marks contemporary and more recent assessments of the relationship between religion and politics in Norwich, but the prominent role religion played is clear nonetheless. One detailed study of Norwich politics concluded that little "odium theologicum" divided local or parliamentary politics until the 1790s. A contemporary observer argued an even stronger position: in his view, Norwich residents were "far more tolerant in matters of religion than of politics," and few, if any, thought "ill of their neighbors for worshipping in a different manner than themselves."[128] Similarly, Elias Norgate reassured William Windham in 1782 that the influence of the Church in Norwich politics "was not very formidable."[129] On the other hand, the Norwich *Mercury* carried virulent attacks on Methodists as early as the late 1750s, and reports of religious intolerance and even religiously provoked violence became commonplace in following decades. A near-riot developed in 1764 over an itinerant preacher's visit; a mob ransacked

[127] *Maidstone Journal*, April 6, 1790, and May 31, 1796. Oldfield, *Representative History*, 4:76. The issue of religion was clouded in Maidstone before 1791 because Matthew Bloxham, the Tory candidate and M.P., supported the repeal of the Test Act in 1789 and again favored repeal in 1790. Not until the events in France began to push many Englishmen into reactionary positions in 1791 did Bloxham cease to support repeal (for whatever reasons of his own). The Whig candidate, Taylor, on the other hand, consistently supported repeal.
[128] Hayes, "Politics in Norfolk," p. 75; *Monthly Magazine* 7(1799):279.
[129] Elias Norgate to William Windham, February 19, 1782. Windham Papers, BL Add. MS. 37908, ff. 8.

a Baptist chapel during a service in 1784, breaking down the chapel door and generally wreaking havoc; and mobs burned several Dissenting chapels in 1791.[130] Abundant Norwich election literature reinforces these impressions of religious conflict and demonstrates the yeoman service to which both Free Blues and Orange-and-Purples put the religious issue. Norwich election material also testifies to the accuracy of traditional assumptions of the affinity of the Dissenters and anti-Ministerialists.

Beginning with the first unmistakably "party" election in Norwich (1780), religion served as a rallying cry for the Administration. Curiously, the links between religion and party appeared initially in the form of accusations, and the anti-Ministerialists seemed particularly slow to take advantage of the already widely recognized relationship. As late as the 1790s when the Free Blues freely acknowledged the tie linking anti-Ministerialists and Nonconformists, they exercised great care to avoid jeopardizing their Anglican supporters. After all, the Dissenters swelled anti-Ministerialist ranks and provided needed backing, but acting in isolation, the Dissenting electorate would have been of little use to anyone. The first undeniable reference to religion in Norwich political propaganda appeared during the 1780 parliamentary election. The Ministerialists defended the joint candidacy (still a questionable practice) of Edward Bacon and John Thurlow as a justifiable device to "defeat the duplicity of the Quakers and the cant of the Presbyterians," arguing that the defeat of Sir Harbord Harbord and William Windham would prevent the political ascendance of John Gurney, leader of the Free Blues, and his fellow Quakers. Sir Harbord was singled out for a particularly blunt attack by his one-time friends:

[130] E. A. Goodwyn, *Selections from Norwich Newspapers*, Ipswich, 1972, p. 77. Also see R. B. Barlow, *Citizenship and Conscience*, Philadelphia, 1962, p. 285; *Gentleman's Magazine*, August 1791, and G. S. Veitch, *The Genesis of Parliamentary Reform*, London, 1913, p. 182.

164

For Bacon and Thurlow let's send him away.
If he will not go, he may stay with John Gurney;
But should he prefer some deep kennel rakers,
He'll surely leave them and go to the Quakers.

The shrieval election the following year aggravated religious tensions. The Norwich aldermen disqualified the winner of the sheriff's race, Simon Wilkin, on the grounds of his Nonconformity. Even though Dissenters had been elected to the common council in the past without incident, the Anglican aldermen decided not to risk any further Free Blue incursions and resorted to this hitherto unexercised, but perfectly legal, ploy to prevent Wilkin's victory.[131]

Norwich parties issued equally forceful statements evincing the importance and the natural allegiance of religion and party during the general election of 1784. Virtually every account of the election, whether focusing on national or local events, agreed that during 1784, "Mr. Fox and his party lost much of their popularity . . . particularly among the Dissenters, by whom they had before been warmly supported."[132] The Norwich election propaganda during that famous election took for granted this alienation among non-Anglicans. Although the Whigs hesitated to acknowledge the loss of at least some of their Nonconformist friends, the alliance with Lord North was widely assumed to be more than many Dissenters could bear in good conscience. Most revealing, however, is not the alleged loss of Dissenting favor by Fox and the Whigs, but the underlying assumption that the considerable assistance formerly given had in large measure now been withdrawn. A Norwich election poem entitled "The Trimming Dissenter" illustrates this attitude perhaps better than any other single

---

[131] "Miscellaneous Verses and Squibs on the Norwich Elections," Colman Library, Norwich. Handbill of September 9, 1780. A copy is included in the *Narrative of the Contested Election*, pp. 33, 41. Bacon and Thurlow issued a rejoinder "totally disapproving of such illiberal expressions."

[132] Amyot, *Some Account of the Life of William Windham*, p. 20.

piece of propaganda. After tracing the political proclivities of the Nonconformists since the Glorious Revolution and observing their enthusiasm for the Opposition in past elections, the poem has the Dissenters chanting:

> We all can change and dance about
> In cotillion or jigs, Sir;
> For Tories now we can dance or shout
> Though we should all be Whigs, Sir.
> How late did we, and thought it fit,
> Drink Charles Fox in a Brimmer,
> And now behold, we toast Will Pitt,
> Such change becomes a Trimmer.

Prior to the election of 1784, general consensus tied the rank and file as strongly as the Dissenting elite to Whig politics, and election literature resumed the established pattern very quickly after the defeat of the infamous Coalition. Regardless of the unpalatable combination of Fox and North, the supposed shift in Nonconformist sympathies did not occur as widely as suggested by election propaganda; the Foxite, William Windham, triumphed in 1784 over an avowed Pittite, Henry Hobart, with the help of the Dissenting interest. Actually, Norwich Dissenters voted consistently and overwhelmingly Whig in each election following 1768. Fox's disreputable alliance with North failed to drive them into the opposite political camp. And even in 1784, the alleged link between the Church and the Tories dominated election accounts. In the words of a Free Blue scribe:

> With High Flying Tories
> The Dean and Canons behind him,
> With Bum-bailiff Garthon
> Rich carried the farce on
> Opposing in vain our Wil Windham.[133]

[133] *The Election Magazine*, pp. 57-59. See Chapter 7 for a more complete analysis of the votes of the Norwich and Northampton Dissenters.

166

Oldfield's 1790 assessment of Norwich politics reasserted the old Whig-Dissent affinity, and added that "political opinions are rendered more personal and violent by the mixture of religious differences."[134] Despite the outbreak of the French Revolution and the resulting political shifts among certain sections of the population and the electorate, subsequent Norwich elections saw a strengthening of the bond between Dissent and Opposition. The by-election of 1794 prompted by Windham's joining Pitt's government involved the Church and the overriding issue of peace or war. For the first time in Windham's long association with Norwich politics, the Church and the city Corporation stood behind Windham's campaign, and he continued to be a Church/Corporation candidate at subsequent elections. The entire Dissenting aristocracy, on the other hand—the Gurneys, the Barnards, and the Taylors—deserted Windham during the campaign and voted almost to a man for James Mingay, Windham's opponent in his new role as champion of the establishment.

Religious and political beliefs were linked consistently in Norwich campaigns after 1794. The arguments could be as specific as the 1794 address to the Quakers warning that they "must either desert their principles or Mr. Windham."[135] Or they could be as inclusive as the 1796 Ministerialist appeal to all Churchmen to combat the threat of the Free Blues who were "headed by some notorious Democrats and Presbyterians." According to the Ministerialist propaganda in 1796, the Free Blues were determined to elect Bartlett Gurney "not merely for the avowed purpose of displacing Mr. Windham, but for the· secret and still more desired pleasure of exalting the Dissenting interest and humbling the true Church Party."[136] The French Rev-

[134] Oldfield, *Representative History*, 4:248.

[135] *Cursory Observations on a Speech of Mr. Windham's*, Norwich, 1794. Taken from the *Morning Chronicle*, December 30, 1794.

[136] Windham Papers, BL Add. MS. 37908, ff. 109, broadside from the 1796 general election.

167

olution afforded Windham and his Ministerialist allies a new and powerful propaganda weapon, the charge of treason. A single charge, however, even one as powerful as this, did not satisfy the Orange-and-Purples. Instead, the Ministerialists focused their efforts against the "combination of Jacobinism and Methodism" that was "engaged in an attempt to overturn the Constitution in Church and State." Such virulent and unrelenting equations of Nonconformity and treason prompted a response in 1802. The Free Blues countered that the Ministerialists should cease their efforts to "render some of the best men in the community despised" and stop hurling accusations at the "old Puritans and current Methodists," many of whom had "uniformly manifested their zeal for the Constitution."[137] Not surprisingly, the Windham-Frere supporters continued to criticize, and, fully aware of the difficult straits in which their candidates found themselves, staked their campaign even more firmly to the religious issue, pleading with the Norwich voters not to let "the madness of party" induce them to "abuse the trust placed in you by your country to promote the Cause of Religion and to Defend the King and Constitution." The appeal failed, however, and a Nonconformist radical, William Smith, replaced William Windham. Perhaps the propagandist should have been more precise about which religious "cause" the voters had a duty to promote.

Social Issues

Hidden among the political and religious rhetoric surrounding elections in the boroughs, and largely overshadowed by it, a number of suggestive if infrequent references hinted at the social dimensions of electoral behavior. What might best be called relative "respectability" emerged, more as a point of discussion than a vital issue, in the 1761 Nor-

[137] *A New Election Budget, 1802*, pp. 3-6.

wich election, reappeared in several other Norwich elections, and periodically complicated contests in Lewes and Northampton. A few days before the 1761 Norwich contest in which two relatively unknown local men challenged the Corporation candidates, Sir Harbord Harbord reported to the Earl of Buckinghamshire that "not a gentleman I know of [would] be found upon the poll" in favor of the two anti-Corporation candidates.[138] During the next Norwich parliamentary contest, the opponents of the Corporation candidate, Edward Bacon, branded him a "foe to the poor," while his rival, Thomas Beevor, allegedly received his principal support from "the middle Rank of People, the Tradesmen, and young Folks."[139] References to age-specific political preferences ceased after 1768, but these early references to social and economic groups within the electorate were echoed in the Norwich elections of 1784 and 1790. Similar sentiments marked the 1784 Northampton election. At the close of a hard-fought and possibly politically oriented campaign in Northampton during April 1784, Earl Spencer expressed the sentiments of the Duchess of Devonshire that some "general infatuation . . . especially among the lower sort," had broken old ties. Spencer, particularly upset over the loss of his Foxite candidate, voiced surprise and dismay at the ungratefulness shown by the people whose children he had maintained in school; they "voted against us by dozens."[140]

Social concerns found expression at Lewes elections in the last decade of the century. Immediately following the 1790 poll, letters appeared in the Lewes *Journal* demanding a complete listing of voters and their votes so "that the country may be enabled to form a judgement on the pretensions of the several candidates by a comparative view of the respectability of those by whom they were supported." The editor of the *Journal* agreed and the entire poll graced

---

[138] *HMC*, Lothian MSS. London, 1905, 62:243.
[139] *Miscellaneous Pieces*, pp. xi, 14, 29.
[140] Feiling, *The Second Tory Party*, p. 161.

the subsequent issue of the *Journal*, including, of course, the occupations of the voters.[141] Eighteenth-century poll-books often included the usually self-ascribed occupations of voters, and the publication of the 1790 Lewes poll complete with the occupations of the electors did not depart from what had become standard procedure in many boroughs. However, the circumstances surrounding the publication of the polling list in Lewes point with unusual clarity to the preoccupation with respectability that appeared in many contested elections. In light of the "great temper and moderation" with which the poll was conducted, and the apparent absence of national issues in the campaign, this emphasis on respectability was not particularly surprising; lacking anything else, social status became a point of contention in 1790. "Respectability" emerged again in the 1802 Lewes contest. Thomas Kemp acknowledged his narrow loss in 1802 by demanding a scrutiny and claiming the "greatest majority of individual respectability" among the voters.[142] Respectable support notwithstanding, Kemp missed winning by an even wider margin after the scrutiny and lost the parliamentary seat he had held since 1780.

More than Lewes's rather ordinary concerns, the political rhetoric issued in conjunction with the Norwich contest of 1802 best denotes the occasionally intense social concerns at the local level. In the midst of a campaign that threatened failure, the Ministerial candidates claimed to have the "great majority of property" on their side and expressed deep regret at the Whig strength among the "poorer and more ignorant classes of people." Far from denying his support from those whom Windham, the Ministerialist, called "low and indigent," the principal Whig candidate, William Smith, complimented the "lower order of citizens" for the firmness with which they resisted the Tory attempts at corruption and coercion, and reminded Windham of the "warmest

[141] *Lewes Journal*, June 21 and June 28, 1790.
[142] *Lewes Journal*, July 12, 1802.

praise" he previously bestowed (as a Free Blue candidate before 1796) on the very citizens he now castigated.[143] Norwich was by no means an exceptional constituency in 1802; the *Annual Register* did not include Norwich on its list of boroughs where the "dangerous spirit between high and low, rich and poor, gentleman and mob, was extremely conspicuous."[144] Nor did 1802 stand out as an exceptional year for political struggles (both parliamentary and extraparliamentary) thought to involve social and economic distinctions. Rioting occurred fairly commonly during the 1790s in parliamentary and non-parliamentary boroughs, and latent class hatreds may have been at least part of the cause. Wyvill felt that Thomas Paine had "formed a party based upon wealth [or the lack of it] among the lower classes of people."[145] Ian Christie's account of the Wilkite agitation two decades earlier stressed the "class resentment" fanning the flames in London. Curiously, during the year in which Wyvill claimed a party of the "lower classes" had been formed, Thomas Walker issued a disclaimer in his defense of political reform after the Manchester riots of 1792. Walker insisted that Englishmen desired nothing more than equality of right and accused the Tories of inciting the "respectable classes" against the "swinish multitude" by perversely interpreting calls for equal rights as a clamor for equality of wealth and possessions.[146]

Thus, whatever the reality behind the claims and counterclaims of parties, politicians, and individuals, social considerations emerged in several elections in these boroughs, both before and after the social upheaval stimulated by

[143] *The Poll for Members of Parliament*, Norwich, 1802, pp. xi, xii; *A Vindication of William Windham*, p. 69; V. Griffiths, *The Picture of Parliament*, London, 1803, p. 104.

[144] *Annual Register*, 1802, 44:184.

[145] Christopher Wyvill, *Political Papers*, 6 vols., London, 1794, 5:23-24, 51.

[146] Thomas Walker, *A Review of Some Political Events in Manchester*, London, 1794, pp. 40-48.

events in France. Voters in Norwich, Lewes, and North-ampton were not alone in pondering the relationship linking social status and political choice. Whether voting behavior actually reflected these expressions of social antagonisms, however, requires a detailed analysis that must be postponed briefly by a look at the electors themselves. Who were the respectable, less respectable, and possibly downright scruffy participants in borough politics? The answer lies in pollbooks, tax rolls, and directories.

CHAPTER FIVE

The Borough Voter

THE PERSISTENT FOCUS on parliament and parliamentary politics among students of the unreformed political system has generated much information concerning the members of the House of Commons and the constituencies for which they sat, but the careful documentation of the structure of the Commons has largely ignored the structure of the electorate. J. H. Plumb noted this omission in studies of Augustan politics and posed a series of unanswered questions that are as basic to an understanding of the later eighteenth century as they are to the reigns of William and Anne. "Who constituted this electorate," and "How deeply into the population did the electorate penetrate?"[1] Similarly, J. R. Vincent has criticized the "qualitative, not to say anecdotal" accounts of the reformed electorate that have shed little light on its composition.[2] John Brewer's recent discussion of the later eighteenth-century "political nation" illustrates the general lack of information concerning the electorate. In asking whether political awareness was limited to the "parliamentary classes" (voters) or included "those of much humbler origin who were either literate or politically interested," Brewer's assumption of the less "humble" origins of the parliamentary classes conceals the obscurity of the electorate.[3] As long as the relative status of the electorate itself is unknown for the most part, it is impossible to determine if an extension of

---

[1] J. H. Plumb, "The Growth of the Electorate in England from 1600 to 1715," *Past and Present* 45(1969):111.

[2] J. R. Vincent, *Pollbooks: How Victorians Voted*, Cambridge, 1967, p. 5.

[3] John Brewer, *Party Ideology and Popular Politics at the Accession of George III*, Cambridge, 1976, p. 141.

173

the political nation (Burke's "British public") into the ranks of the nonelectors would include men of much lower social and/or economic status.[4] This deficiency is pervasive; currently, any statement regarding the nature of the electorate before the end of the nineteenth century is hardly more than speculation, and this lack of information is particularly acute for the unreformed electorate.[5] Descriptions of franchise qualifications are commonplace, and the extraordinary variety of the borough franchises before the relative uniformity imposed by the Great Reform Act is well known, but the specifics of franchise requirements in various constituencies do not answer questions such as those posed by Plumb. To provide answers to these questions and thus identify the electors whose behavior is subsequently analyzed, this chapter systematically examines the composition of enfranchised borough populations.

However, as indicated in Chapters 1 and 2, the electorates of corporation and burgage boroughs are demonstrably of little interest due to their severely limited electorates and the relative political inactivity of their electors. On average, the corporation boroughs contained fewer than thirty voters and any occupational analysis would be superfluous given the exclusive qualification limiting the electorate to members of the local governing elite, often the toadies of some local patron. While the electorates of most burgage

[4] Burke described the "British public" as those "of adult age, not declining in life, of tolerable leisure for such [political] discussions, and of some means of information." Edmund Burke, *Works*, 6 vols., Cambridge, 1971, 5:189.

[5] Besides Vincent's study of pollbooks, some excellent work has begun to appear concerning the reformed electorate providing considerable detail for the post-reform electorate. D. G. Wright, "A Radical Borough in Parliamentary Politics: Bradford, 1832-1841," *Northern History* 4(1969):132-66; T. J. Nossiter, *Influence, Opinion, and Political Idioms in Reformed England*, Brighton, 1975; T. J. Nossiter, "Aspects of Electoral Behavior in English Constituencies," in *Mass Politics*, ed. E. Allardt and S. Rokkan, New York, 1970; Jeremy Mitchell and James Cornford, "The Political Demography of Cambridge, 1832-1868," *Albion* 9(1977):242-72.

boroughs ordinarily outnumbered the invariably tiny electorates in the corporation boroughs, normally less than 130 individuals possessed the franchise in towns with burgage or freeholder franchises. The restriction of voting rights to pieces of property instead of to individuals further reduced the utility of an analysis of burgage voters. Moreover, contested elections occurred rarely in either of these borough types. The thirteen members of the Corporation entitled to vote at parliamentary elections in Buckingham would not warrant close attention under the best circumstances, and their failure to contest an election between 1715 and the Reform Act hardly enhanced their electoral significance. By the same token, Bere Alston's handful of burgage owners scarcely deserved to be called voters after neglecting their franchises from the beginning of the eighteenth century until their right to vote was revoked by parliament in 1832. Two-thirds of the burgage boroughs completely lacked polled elections in the last four decades of the eighteenth century, and of the remaining third, few experienced more than two contests. Yet this sorry record of political inactivity in the burgage boroughs bested that of the corporation boroughs. At each of the general elections between 1761 and 1802, voters in less than 10 percent of the corporation boroughs actually went to a poll. Therefore, the following consideration of electors and electorates, though limited generally to parliamentary boroughs with broader franchises and specifically to voters in very few boroughs, represents the entire borough electorate fairly well since the constituencies with broader franchises contained virtually the entire borough electorate and encompassed almost all electoral activity during the general elections. The electors in the ninety-two freeman constitutencies and the voters in the forty-nine boroughs allowing inhabitant householders not on relief to vote (or inhabitant householders paying "scot and lot") comprised well over 90 percent of all borough electors, and these same 141 boroughs also accounted for the overwhelming majority of all contested elections,

175

borough and county. During the general election of 1780, nine of every ten contested elections took place in freeman or "inhabitant" boroughs, and the proportion never fell below 75 percent at the other general elections of the period.[6]

OCCUPATIONAL STRUCTURE

Who were the "parliamentary classes" in England's parliamentary boroughs and how deeply into the citizenry of the boroughs did electorates penetrate? Questions such as these defy simple answers, but any attempt to find answers must rely heavily on the customary unit of measurement in historical analyses of social structure: occupation. Pollbooks, the chief source of information for electors in various boroughs, frequently recorded each voter's occupation and fortunately, the occupations were often, if not always, self-ascribed and occasionally can be supported by other occupational descriptions contained in local censuses and directories.[7] The accessibility and relative completeness of this information enhances its obvious descriptive importance. With this basic measurement at hand, the necessity of larger occupational categories posed a major obstacle to this analysis of borough electorates. Considerations of England's population, or any part of it, either before or after

[6] The degree of political participation in boroughs of various franchise types are considered specifically in Chapter 3. The figures on participation noted here are calculated from the data in John Cannon, *Parliamentary Reform*, Cambridge, 1973, pp. 278-89 and Lewis Namier and John Brooke, *The House of Commons, 1754-1790*, 3 vols., London, 1964, 1:513-20.

[7] The occupations used in these descriptions of the voting public were almost certainly self-ascribed. As described at the beginning of Chapter 1, the polling clerk asked each voter a series of questions, including his occupation. The responses were recorded as stated. Obviously, some constituencies either neglected these questions or pollbook printers decided against including the information, but the procedure in these four boroughs involved self-ascribed occupations. Vincent is unsure about nineteenth-century procedures. Vincent, *Pollbooks*, pp. 3, 51.

the major changes wrought by the Industrial Revolution, have relied almost invariably on completely idiosyncratic methods of describing occupational structure. The diversity of the resulting descriptions substantially reduces their value and usually eliminates their comparability. Historians all too often have adopted wholesale listings of every identifiable occupation and the precise number of people in each, or essentially useless lists of "selected" occupations that combine the worst defects of wholesale listings with the fatal flaw of unspecified, nonrandom selectivity.[8] Rarely have studies of English society attempted concise and comprehensive occupational clusters based on relatively sophisticated distinctions such as Neale's suggested combination of occupational titles with the employment or nonemployment of domestic servants as a means of distinguishing relative ranks within occupational groups.[9] Unfortunately, none of these efforts to overcome the seemingly intractable problems inevitably encountered in grouping occupations, problems that have proven as baffling to census-takers as to historians, resolves the difficulties facing an examination of unreformed electorates.[10] The

[8] For examples of these methods of listing occupations, see W. A. Speck, "Londoners at the Polls under Anne and George I," *Guildhall Studies in London History* 1(1975); J.H.C. Patten, "The Urban Structure of East Anglia in the Sixteenth and Seventeenth Centuries," Ph.D. diss., Cambridge University, 1972, pp. 145-75; Vincent, *Pollbooks, passim*; E. A. Menzies, "The Freeman Voter in Liverpool, 1802-1835," *Historical Society of Lancashire and Cheshire Transactions* 4(1972):83-107; N. L. Tratner, "Population and Social Structure in a Bedfordshire Parish," *Population Studies* 21(1967):261-82. Vincent's use of "selected" occupational categories is particularly unfortunate since his study of Victorian pollbooks is the only existing attempt to examine the entire electoral system in a systematic fashion.

[9] R. S. Neale, *Class and Ideology in the Nineteenth Century*, London, 1972, pp. 30-31.

[10] In addition to the continually changing occupational categories used in the modern British census that can never agree, among other things, on the rank of academics, a revealing account of the trials and tribulations of earlier census-takers is contained in: Charles Booth, "On the Occu-

more ingenious suggestions for combining different indices of social and economic status that might result in realistically complex measurements of each individual's position in society cannot be applied even experimentally with these eighteenth-century communities, since the requisite data never existed or have not survived.[11] The loss of the potentially useful individual income tax assessments of 1798 is particularly unfortunate.[12] Yet any discussion of the occupational composition of the electorate must organize what otherwise becomes an incomprehensible clutter of individual occupational titles, many of which are clearly overlapping or redundant and needlessly confusing.

Voters in Maidstone, Norwich, Northampton, and Lewes claimed well over one hundred separate occupational titles, and recounting the exact number of shoemakers voting in Northampton in 1796 (197), or the number of papermakers in the Maidstone electorate of 1780 (21) would be inappropriate descriptively and virtually useless analytically. Hence, the initial description of several borough electorates is limited to relatively straightforward, albeit unavoidably debatable, groupings of occupations into several functional categories that continue the long tradition of idiosyncracy. These divisions, however, owe much to the occupational groupings adopted in other studies of pre- and post-industrial England, and were particularly influenced by the

pations of the People of the United Kingdom, 1801-1881," *Journal of the Royal Statistical Society* 49(1886):316-415. The census of 1841 listed more than 900 occupations. That of 1861 counted over 1,500.

[11] Michael Katz, "Occupational Classification in History," *JIH* 3(1972):63-88; Michael Katz, "Social Structure in Hamilton, Ontario," in *Nineteenth-Century Cities*, ed. S. Thernstrom and R. Sennett, New Haven, 1969; Michael Katz, *The People of Hamilton, Canada West*, Cambridge, 1975; Theodore Hershberg and R. Dockhorn, "Occupational Classification," *HMN* 9(1976):59-98; W. A. Armstrong, "The Use of Information about Occupations," in *Nineteenth Century Society*, ed. E. A. Wrigley, Cambridge, 1972, pp. 191-310.

[12] PRO, *Guide to the Contents of the Public Record Office*, 2 vols., London, 1963, 1:67-8.

occupational categories adopted in Nossiter's pioneering study of the reformed electorate in England's northeastern counties.[13]

Generally, the acceptability of occupational categories decreases along with reductions in the detail with which individual occupations are described and the amount of supplementary data available for each. Thus the occasional vagueness of the occupational titles listed in pollbooks, along with the limited and incomplete supplementary data concerning the electorate, should create much more serious analytical problems than they do. The occupational descriptions of individual electors contained in the pollbooks are fairly revealing despite their deficiencies. For example, the failure of pollbooks to discriminate between journeymen and masters, or between employers and employees is a serious flaw, yet this pervasive tendency to homogenize occupations is as revealing generally as distinctions within occupations could be specifically. John Vincent has argued that regardless of the sometimes marked gradations among shoemakers, other skilled craftsmen, and workmen of all sorts, "there was nevertheless a feeling that people engaged in making the same kind of thing were the same kind of people."[14] A voter's claim to a specific trade was considered sufficient in the mid-nineteenth century, and however diverse men of that trade might in some ways be, Vincent maintains that his occupational title should be used accordingly. Other than a partial census of Lewes taken privately in 1790, unqualified occupational titles seem to have been as acceptable in the late eighteenth century as in the

[13] Armstrong, "Uses of Occupations," *passim*; Katz, "Occupational Classification," p. 87; R. P. Formisano, "Analyzing American Voting Behavior," *HMN* 2(1969):12; Michael Drake, "The Mid-Victorian Voter," *JIH* 1,3(1971):483; Wright, "Post-Reform Politics," pp. 159-61; Nossiter, *Influence, Opinion, and Political Idioms*, p. 211. Nossiter's categories were: (1) Gentry and Professional, (2) Manufacturing and Merchant, (3) Craft Trades, (4) Retail Trades, (5) Drink, (6) Farming.

[14] Vincent, *Pollbooks*, p. 52.

nineteenth.[15] Thus the failure of the pollbooks to distinguish journeyman shoemakers from master shoemakers prevents an analysis based on a voter's status within his occupation, but if Vincent is correct, the almost complete disregard for these kinds of distinctions in the voting lists and in other sources lessens the need for such an analysis.

Prompted in part by the occupational cohesiveness demonstrated by these butchers, bakers, candlestick-makers, and their fellows, and in part by Michael Katz's warning against confusing stratifications based on rank with stratifications based on function, the seven categories into which the voters from specific occupations were placed initially (Table 5.1) equated different kinds of work and attempted to minimize distinctions within occupations.[16] A separate three-tiered division of occupations was employed subsequently to assess social "rank" among the electors even though the seven functional divisions were roughly hierarchical as well. The functions delineated by these categories reflected differences much more substantial than simply the item being produced. Craftsmen working in leather were not separated from those working with wood, nor were glassblowers distinguished from pewterers. Instead, these seven categories indicated something of the nature of the daily ac-

[15] The local census of Lewes in 1790 distinguished masters and journeymen. Woolgar MSS., Spicilegia . . . Lewensis, pp. 525-44, ESRO.

[16] Katz, "Occupational Classification," p. 66. The percentages given in Table 5.1 and in the other tables where weighted averages are indicated are not exactly weighted percentages but have been described as such to point to their consideration of the total population in question. Each of these tables was constructed from a file containing the *entire* voting population in each of these boroughs over the eight general elections included in the study. The data base created by the nominal record linkage programs yielded a composite file of *all* those casting ballots in any or all of the elections studied. These complete, inclusive files of voting records were then used to construct composite descriptions of the borough electorates. As such, these statistics are actually somewhat more accurate than "weighted" averages would be, although for the descriptive purposes to which these figures are put, neither weighting nor lack of weighting would have been very important.

180

tivities of these men. The relatively educated, leisured lives of "gentlemen" and professional men clearly differed in kind from the activities of small retailers, whose occupations were equally unlike those of journeymen artisans. However, the lack of distinction between master and journeyman in the records raised problems with some occupations since the work of a master cabinetmaker resembled in many respects that of a retailer. Similarly, hosiers or glovers, who were counted here as craftsmen, might have been retailers, just as stonemasons were craftsmen in this schematization although master stonemasons were "among the first rank in Trade."[17] Journeymen bakers, included among the retailers, engaged in retail activities very little, by and large. Nevertheless, the gravity of the problems presented by the occasionally substantial differences between masters and journeymen was diminished considerably by arguments such as Vincent's for occupational unity. At any rate, these categories probably reflect the most significant differences. Relying solely on kinds of activities also overcame many equally intransigent problems encountered if socio-economic distinctions are considered simultaneously or separately. The activities of a cleric, for example, fall squarely in the first category in Table 5.1 (Gentlemen and Professions), yet economically, the most ordinary craftsmen easily surpassed an ordinary cleric. In his 1747 book of occupational advice to parents, Campbell argued that a "journeyman taylor can afford to live and bring up his family with more decency than such a man [a poor cleric]; yet [the cleric] has all the notions of a Gentleman, and there is not a more helpless thing in nature." Besides, "a foolish taylor is not half so contemptible as a poor, ignorant, and perhaps profligate Parson."[18] At the other extreme, enamellers, fine-drawers (menders), watch-finishers, tapestry-weavers, and other craftsmen could command

[17] R. Campbell, *The London Tradesman*, London, 1747, p. 159.
[18] Ibid., pp. 24-37, 190-95, 69-89.

181

incomes in excess of £50 each year and mere journeymen in these trades lived very well indeed, although all of them clearly lacked the "refined" lifestyle of a clergyman or fledgling attorney. For the purposes of this classification scheme, these refinements and other basic differences in lifestyles were of primary importance. Poor clergymen and impoverished attorneys ranked in the first category regardless of their relative economic disadvantages.

The distinction between the second and third categories in Table 5.1 was related to function and to scale of activity, and in some ways was less easily distinguished than the other occupational divisions. The group of men represented in the second category (wholesalers, manufacturers, and entrepreneurs) such as brokers, mercers, woolfactors, and the like, who were either wholesalers or large-scale retailers, had to be distinguished from their counterparts at the other end of the commercial spectrum who were primarily small retailers, yet they could not be described

Table 5.1: Occupational Compositions of Four Unreformed Borough
Electorates: 1761-1802 (Percentage)

| Occupational Category | Borough and Franchise | | | |
	Norwich (freeman)	Maidstone (freeman)	Northampton (potwalloper)	Lewes (scot and lot)
I. Gentlemen, Professions	11.6	9.3	6.3	15.7
II. Merchants, Entrepreneurs	5.1	4.0	4.6	3.6
III. Retailers	16.3	17.9	19.5	18.6
IV. Agriculturalists	3.3	2.9	.7	2.6
V. Craftsmen, Artisans, Skilled Workmen	60.6	52.9	54.9	44.1
VI. Laborers	1.2	8.9	12.2	11.4
VII. Other (unclassifiable)	1.9	4.1	1.8	4.0

NOTE: See note 16. Percentages refer to entire electorates over all elections, not average percentages or "weighted" percentages.

as gentle or professional men by contemporary standards, whatever their pretensions. The fourth category, agriculture, though understandably small in these borough constituencies, made up sufficiently large numbers of the non-resident freemen who were allowed to vote in Norwich and Maidstone to warrant a separate category. The fifth group encompassed craft trades, artisans, and skilled workers not likely to have been retailers. Here the inability to delineate masters and journeymen sometimes presented acute problems, and the more general ambiguity of some entire occupations occasionally caused difficulties, but on the whole, the distinctions were reasonably clear-cut. For example, glovers, hatters, and hosiers were counted as craftsmen on the assumption that the overwhelming preponderance of men following these trades were involved primarily in making goods. Haberdashers, while equally concerned with clothing, sold rather than produced goods, and fell among the retailers in this table. A tailor's position was slightly less definite, yet chances were against an ordinary tailor's common involvement in retail transactions, and tailors were grouped with hatters and glovers accordingly. Almost all "makers" were included in this large category, as well as some "manufacturers," though eighteenth-century voters did not use the term as indiscriminantly to denote wage earners or employers as did their successors in the nineteenth century. "Manufacturer" often meant large-scale producer in the context of these electorates, and clearly large-scale producers were included most appropriately in the second category rather than the fifth.[19] Watchmakers

[19] *The Norwich Directory*, Norwich, 1783; *The Norwich Directory*, Norwich, 1801; *Bailey's British Directory*, London, 1798; Campbell, *London Tradesman*, pp. 250-53. For example, the occupational distributions in Norwich according to the directory for 1783 failed to list most Norwich working men. The number of references to "makers" and "manufacturers" also indicates a change in standard terminology in the town. The Norwich city directory of 1801 relied heavily on the term "manufacturer" while the directory of 1783 hardly mentioned it at all. Therefore, it seems likely that Rudé's warning that a manufacturer could be a wage-earner as well as an em-

were a rare exception to the rule placing "makers" in the fifth category; their place among the retailers stemmed from their failure to make watches. A separate specialized craftsman manufactured each part of a watch from spring to case, and a finisher assembled the parts, leaving the watchmaker, according to Campbell, as production manager and salesman. The other occupations contained in the crafts category generally require no further explanation, with the possible exception of tallow-chandlers. Normally chandlers were counted among the retailers, but descriptions of this occupation tended to agree that men in this trade engaged principally in making the products in question, with retail activities either secondary or nonexistent.

The two final occupational groups seem straightforward enough. Counted as laborers were all those individuals whose occupations required so little skill that to number them among the craftsmen would have cast aspersions on the "mysteries" of the other trades, though admittedly many of the craft trades demanded no great learning. A bookbinder was "chiefly employed in beating the books with a heavy hammer to make the sheets lie close together" and required "few talents, either natural or acquired." Nor did some of the retail trades. The chief "mystery" behind the poultering trade consisted of "buying cheap and selling dear, a secret that might be learned in less than seven years."[20] Soldiering, on the other hand, demanded skills that had to be learned, usually painfully, and these demands were exceeded by the talents requisite for a sailor. Soldiers and sailors cannot be described as craftsmen, nor can they be classified as laborers. A number of other occupations also defied reasonable compromises, and this diverse group from soldiers to land surveyors (a possibly, but not necessarily,

---

ployer is less applicable in these boroughs until after the period under consideration. By the mid-nineteenth century, on the other hand, Nossiter is certain that "manufacturer" meant "operative" almost exclusively. Nossiter, "Aspects of Electoral Behavior," p. 168.

[20] Campbell, *London Tradesman*, pp. 124-36, 275-81.

gentlemanly occupation) made up a final, sparsely populated category.

Applying these functional categories, a comparison of the voters in Norwich, Maidstone, Lewes, and Northampton over all later eighteenth-century elections reveals a borough electorate dominated by craftsmen, artisans, and skilled workmen. Though substantial variations at times distinguished each of the boroughs, the craft trades contributed the largest proportion of the electorate in each of the four constituencies. Oddly, Northampton's minimal franchise requirements (the potwalloper franchise) produced an electorate containing craftsmen and artisans in roughly the same proportions as the freeman boroughs. Northampton's contingent of enfranchised craftsmen also was appreciably higher than in Lewes, where scot and lot payments as well as resident householder status qualified residents to vote. Northampton's extension of the vote to more than 60 percent of its adult male inhabitants may not entirely warrant Namier's characterization of the Northampton franchise as practically "universal," but certainly Northampton allowed a substantially higher proportion of its residents to cast ballots at parliamentary elections than did most boroughs. Yet the Northampton electorate resembled the other borough electorates in many respects. In answer to Plumb's question, when measured occupationally, the electorate was broadly inclusive across the board. The broader Northampton franchise did lead to the largest proportion of laboring men in the electorate, though Lewes and Maidstone lagged not far behind. The ranks of gentle and professional men also fared less well proportionately in Northampton than in the other towns, with the two freeman boroughs falling midway between the extremes set by Northampton's 6 percent and Lewes's 16 percent in Category I.

No great differences marked the proportionate contributions of the wholesalers and manufacturers (and largest merchants) or the smaller retailers to the several borough electorates. Voters from Category II made up between 3 percent and 5 percent of the electorate in each town, and voters from Category III varied roughly between 16 percent and 19 percent. As much variation can be found in the contributions of each group in a single town across several elections (Tables 5.6 and 5.7). Similar analyses of late eighteenth-century Liverpool (freeman) and Reading (scot and lot) reinforce the overall pattern of randomness (Table 5.2). Electorates in "inhabitant" boroughs, if they differed at all from the electorates in the freeman boroughs, exhibited no perceptible pattern. However, electorates of "scot and lot" boroughs seem to have contained fewer craftsmen and considerably higher concentrations of gentle and professional men. Variations in the proportions of larger and smaller merchants, wholesalers, and manufacturers probably reflected local preferences for particular kinds of job descriptions rather than actual differences.

Finally, two other groups merit some attention, although Table 5.1 completely neglects one of the two. Predictably, resident voters in these towns seldom engaged exclusively in agriculture; the relatively large body of farmers in the Norwich and Maidstone electorates simply indicated the presence of large numbers of nonresident voters in both freeman constituencies. While elections in both boroughs brought in nonresident voters from other towns, country residents, who tended to be agriculturalists in larger numbers than resident freemen, turned out en masse on occasion.[21] The other group of some significance in Table 5.1 is subsumed under Categories II and III, those retailers engaged in what might be called the drink trade. Innkeepers and publicans particularly have suffered the brunt of many attacks on corruption both before and after the Great Reform Act. Few occupational groups have been accorded such a distinctive role or have received such abuse in accounts of nineteenth-century politics. On the basis of a close

[21] The occupational differences separating in-voters and out-voters are made clear in Table 5.3.

examination of several northeastern communities in the mid-nineteenth century, T. J. Nossiter argued that "licensees formed about one-tenth of the electorate in most towns."[22] In this respect, at least the unreformed electorate may have differed from the reformed voting public. A mere 1.9 percent of Norwich's voters reckoned themselves in occupations related to alcohol, including liquor and wine merchants that Nossiter counted separately. Lewes and Maidstone contained a stronger drink contingent, with 5.1 percent and 6.7 percent respectively, yet only Northampton approached the levels identified by Nossiter; 9 percent of Northampton's electors engaged in drink-related trades.

With these minor variations, Table 5.1 conveys an overall impression of similarity and relative inclusiveness. Gentle and professional men contributed less than 16 percent of the total in each town (often far less), while craftsmen, artisans, and working men of some description uniformly comprised over 50 percent of each electorate. In fact, the preponderance of Category V is the dominant occupational feature of each borough. This is not to argue, as does E. M. Menzies in a study of Liverpool, that most of these "urban" voters were "lower class," but rather that these electorates seem to have been very broadly based indeed, and that perhaps the electorate reflected the urban occupational range more fully than is usually acknowledged. Although the validity of the assumption evident in John Brewer's recent investigation of the "political nation" that the electorate was less "humble" than the populace at large cannot be assessed without a larger data base and more adequate information concerning the unenfranchised portion of the population, the figures in Table 5.1 do lend it some support. The unreformed electorate was small by modern standards, and though electorates in these constituencies were not "narrow elites" as they often have been characterized, the notable

[22] T. J. Nossiter, "Elections and Political Behavior in County Durham and Newcastle," Ph.D. diss., Oxford University, 1968, p. 185.

absence of voters in Category VI, particularly in Norwich, Liverpool, and Reading, makes it seem unlikely that these electorates reflected the ordinary breakdown of pre-industrial urban occupations (Table 5.2).[23] Even so, again to use Plumb's phrase, the electorate penetrated deeply into the population and included many men of quite "humble" origins. There does seem to have been a distinct disparity between the freeman and potwalloper boroughs on the one hand, and those like Lewes that required resident householders to pay taxes before being allowed to vote. The Lewes electorate contained a substantially larger proportion of gentlemen, as did the Reading electorate, also comprised of "scot and lot" voters. Liverpool's freeman franchise, on the other hand, resulted in the smallest proportion of voters in Category I, and even more craftsmen than Norwich.

The image of considerable inclusiveness in Norwich and Maidstone accurately portrays resident voters. However, all freemen of the town, whether resident or not, voted in freeman boroughs, and occupationally, these nonresident voters, or "out-voters," mirrored the electorates of the scot and lot boroughs rather than the resident freemen voters (Table 5.3). The out-voters in both Norwich and Maidstone numbered in the hundreds and played a vital role in elections when they turned out in sufficient numbers; the Norwich parliamentary return of 1796 would have included a different set of names had the election been decided by the resident voters alone. A larger disparity separated resident and nonresident voters in Norwich than in Maidstone, but the nonresidents were of a rather different mold in both cases. Four times as many Norwich out-voters (proportionately) claimed gentility or professional occupations. Agriculture occupied many nonresident voters and very

[23] W. A. Speck, *Tory and Whig*, London, 1969, p. 16. Speck obviously did not mean to imply that popular participation was not widespread. Far from it; his entire thesis emphasizes the growth of participatory politics under Queen Anne.

188

Table 5.2: Occupational Compositions of Liverpool and Reading
Electorates (Percentage)

Occupational Category	Borough and Franchise	
	Liverpool* (freeman)	Reading† (scot and lot)
I. Gentlemen, Professions	5.4	15.1
II. Merchants, Entrepreneurs	9.4	10.2
III. Retailers	15.8	28.6
IV. Agriculturalists	.1	2.5
V. Craftsmen, Artisans, Skilled Workmen	63.2	38.4
VI. Laborers	4.9	3.0
VII. Other	1.2	2.2

* Samples of 550 Liverpool electors in 1780 and 1790.
† All Reading electors at elections of 1774 and 1780.

few residents, and the proportion of craftsmen and artisans among the nonresidents was less than half that of the electors living in Norwich. Similarly, the gentry were twice as heavily represented among Maidstone's out-voters, and a smaller proportion of craftsmen and artisans living outside Maidstone returned to vote in Maidstone elections. Curiously, the Maidstone nonresident electorate contained a larger share of laboring men. Thus, with the exception of laborers, the overall resemblance of the Norwich, Maidstone, and Liverpool electorates is strengthened if the greater part of their respective voting publics, resident voters, are examined in isolation. Though the out-voters constituted an integral part of these freeman electorates, their numbers tend to obscure the actual occupational range encompassed by the resident electorates of each town.

How closely these electorates reflected the occupational composition of the larger communities cannot be determined precisely. There are no comprehensive descriptions

189

Table 5.3: Occupations of Resident and Nonresident Voters in Norwich and
Maidstone
(Percentage of All Voters at All Elections)

Occupational Category	Norwich		Maidstone	
	Residents	Nonresidents	Residents	Nonresidents
I. Gentlemen, Professions	8.2	29.7	6.8	12.1
II. Merchants, Entrepreneurs	5.4	3.1	5.4	6.1
III. Retailers	19.0	18.2	23.0	17.7
IV. Agriculturalists	.6	14.2	3.1	6.4
V. Craftsmen, Artisans, Skilled Workmen	64.2	30.1	50.9	41.9
VI. Laborers	1.1	2.5	9.8	13.9
VII. Other	1.5	2.2	1.0	1.9

of the populations of any of these towns; surviving city
directories are even less inclusive than the pollbooks. For
example, with fewer than 1,600 entries in each (of whom
more than 10 percent are women), the Norwich city directories of 1783 and 1801 contain approximately half as many
individuals as the pollbooks for the elections of 1784 and
1802. Moreover, the directories usually omitted occupations at the lower end of the spectrum. Worsted weavers,
hoymen, corkcutters, and the like, are as rare in city directories as they are common in pollbooks. Worsted weavers consistently provided a mainstay of the Norwich electorate, making up almost one-third of the entire electorate.
In 1784, 798 weavers cast ballots (with a slight majority for
the Court candidates), yet not a single weaver can be found
in the 1783 city directory. Actually, the only real value of
the city directories lies in their ability to verify some of the
occupational titles claimed by voters.[24]

While the absence of general data concerning all inhab-

[24] Calculated from the *Norwich Directories* of 1783 and 1801.

itants in these towns prevents the degree of electoral penetration into the populace from being determined precisely, an occupational analysis of different aggregations of the populations of Northampton and Lewes reveals something of the inclusiveness of their electorates. The Northamptonshire militia rolls of 1777 should have contained the names of many of the able bodied men residing in Northampton between the ages of eighteen and forty-five. Except for peers, clergymen, articled clerks, apprentices, seamen, and parish constables, who were all exempt, each man of that age group had a duty to serve, and the muster rolls should have been fairly representative of the occupational structure of Northampton. Even the exemption of poor men with three or more children would not lessen the value of the roll appreciably. Unfortunately, anyone selected for militia duty could hire a substitute, and since most men preferred not to serve, those who could afford replacements took advantage of this opportunity to avoid service.[25] Thus, the list is skewed markedly toward the lesser sort. Of almost 12,000 men on the county muster whose occupations are noted, a mere 123 gentle and professional men offset some 2,500 servants and 2,300 laborers. Somewhat smaller disparities characterized the militiamen from Northampton itself. Northampton contributed only 6 percent of the total county muster, yet accounted for almost one-quarter of the "gentlemen" in the Northampton militia. Even so, the Northampton list undoubtedly was severely skewed toward the lesser orders, and given this weighting toward working men, the striking impression derived from a comparison of the 1777 militia roll and the 1774 Northampton electorate is the degree of similarity between the two (Table 5.4). Predictably, a smaller proportion of merchants and entrepreneurs served in the mi-

[25] V. A. Hatley, ed., *The Northamptonshire Militia Lists*, Kettering, 1973. Alan Everitt also has worked with the militia lists with much the same goal in mind. Alan Everitt, *The Pattern of Rural Dissent*, Leicester, 1972, p. 74.

litia, as did fewer retailers of the lesser sort since they could afford to hire stand-ins, and often had little choice if they did not want to run the risk of injuring their businesses. Their absences swelled the ranks of laborers in the militia. Nevertheless, the proportional weights of both the craft trades and the laborers, as well as the gentry, were much closer than might have been expected. Hence, this comparison with the Northampton militia actually reinforces the impression of breadth conveyed by the general occupational structure of the Northampton electorate. Clearly, men further down the social scale were more commonly included among Northampton's voters than was the case in freeman boroughs like Norwich and Maidstone.

The other comparison of electors and residents possible for these four boroughs also appears in Table 5.4. In one sense more complete, yet skewed even more noticeably in the opposite direction, is a partial census taken anonymously in Lewes sometime during 1790. The census-taker's

Table 5.4: Occupations of Voters and Other Inhabitants in Northampton and Lewes (Percentage)

Occupational Category	Northampton Voters 1774 (N = 904)	Northampton Militia 1777 (N = 805)	Lewes Voters 1790 (N = 226)	Lewes Census 1790 (N = 243)
I. Gentlemen, Professions	5.0	3.4	14.5	18.5
II. Merchants, Entrepreneurs	3.9	2.1	5.1	4.5
III. Retailers	19.4	14.0	14.9	24.3
IV. Agriculturalists	1.1	3.1	3.4	2.1
V. Craftsmen, Artisans, Skilled Workmen	56.9	56.3	42.6	32.1
VI. Laborers	11.7	18.6	14.5	8.2
VII. Other	2.2	2.5	5.1	10.3

meticulous concern for detail resulted in a careful identification of each Lewes householder, but herein lies the problem.[26] The census listed *only* householders and their occupations. All other inhabitants were represented by entries of family (household) size. Not surprisingly, then, the Lewes survey resembles the Lewes pollbook; the same individuals, more or less, comprised both lists, and unlike the conclusion drawn from the similarity of the Northampton lists, the correspondence of the Lewes census and the Lewes pollbook evinces an exclusive Lewes electorate, limited by and large to the more "respectable" men of the town. Actually, the Lewes census simply confirms both the occupational titles listed in the Lewes pollbook and the high turnout among the qualified voters which the short pollbook lists of qualified nonvoters indicated. Yet even in Lewes, the electorate showed signs of considerable breadth. Taken together, craftsmen, artisans, and laborers accounted for half of the voters in 1790; these occupations made up just over 40 percent of the census. The electorate also contained a proportionately smaller share of the gentry. The Lewes electorate's exclusiveness did not match what might have been expected from the 1790 census of householders, but was restrictive enough nevertheless.

ELECTORAL RECRUITMENT

As surprising as the breadth of the electorates in three of these boroughs is the stability of the occupational composition evident in all four boroughs over the general elections to 1802. The occupational stability exhibited in Tables 5.6 and 5.7 would be notable under any circumstances, but as indicated in Table 5.5, the borough electorates maintained this relative occupational stability in the face of occasionally

[26] The 1790 Lewes census indicated a population of 2,019, suggesting that Lewes should have had 450 to 500 adult males, yet only 271 were listed as male householders.

193

Table 5.5: Changes in Size of Total Electorates between Elections
(Percentage of previous electorate)

Election Year	Norwich	Maidstone	Northampton	Lewes
1768	+ 19.9	− 5.0	—	—
1774	NC	− 13.6	− 16.0	+ 4.3
1780	− 11.0	+ 10.0	NC	− 21.9
1784	+ 4.2	− 9.5	− 6.4	NC
1790	− 3.4	unchanged	− 1.4	+ 49.3
1796	− 6.0	− 8.8	+ 10.8	+ 23.5
1802	+ 24.5	+ 6.2	NC	+ 12.2

NC = no contest

massive changes in size. While electoral size could, and sometimes did, remain as static as occupational composition, on average successive electorates differed by more than 10 percent, and could expand or contract by 20 percent or more, as in Lewes on three occasions and Norwich twice. Despite size changes as great as the 16 percent drop between 1768 and 1774, and several uncontested elections that resulted in lengthy periods separating elections, the occupational composition of the Northampton electorate remained essentially the same at each of five contested elections (Table 5.6). Such stability seems even more remarkable in the face of the propensity shown by individuals to describe themselves differently over time, and the substantial turnover in the electorate from one election to the next. Very few of the Northampton voters in 1796 had voted in 1768, yet little, if anything, distinguishes the two groups of electors. Similarly, except for an apparent decline in the "gentle" share of the vote, and a slight increase in the use of "merchant" titles, the Lewes electorate of 1802 was occupationally equivalent to the electorate three decades earlier.

Maidstone experienced few minor fluctuations and no appreciable alterations over the eight elections contested there, but the Norwich electorate appears to have under-

Table 5.6: Occupational Compositions of Northampton and Lewes Electorates: 1768-1802 (Percentage)

Occupational Category	1768	1774	1780	1784	1790	1796	1802
Northampton							
I. Gentlemen, Professions	4.9	5.0	NC	7.6	7.2	6.6	NC
II. Merchants, Entrepreneurs	3.8	3.9	NC	4.9	5.2	5.0	NC
III. Retailers	19.4	20.0	NC	20.3	18.5	19.5	NC
IV. Agriculturalists	1.1	.7	NC	.8	.6	.5	NC
V. Craftsmen, Artisans, Skilled Workmen	56.9	56.2	NC	53.4	52.9	55.0	NC
VI. Laborers	11.7	13.0	NC	11.1	13.7	11.3	NC
VII. Other	2.2	1.3	NC	1.8	1.9	2.1	NC
Lewes							
I. Gentlemen, Professions	NA	19.7	19.8	NC	14.5	13.1	11.5
II. Merchants, Entrepreneurs	NA	2.7	1.6	NC	5.1	5.3	3.4
III. Retailers	NA	22.4	19.3	NC	14.9	14.1	22.4
IV. Agriculturalists	NA	3.3	2.1	NC	3.4	2.8	1.6
V. Craftsmen, Artisans, Skilled Workmen	NA	40.4	42.8	NC	42.6	47.3	46.7
VI. Laborers	NA	9.3	10.7	NC	14.5	12.4	10.3
VII. Other	NA	2.2	3.7	NC	5.1	4.9	4.0

NC = no contest
NA = not available—no occupations given

gone substantial alterations before 1802 (Table 5.7). However, fluctuations in the proportionate strength of nonresident voters participating in Norwich elections explain the apparent occupational changes almost entirely. The proportion of the vote cast by nonresidents in Norwich varied widely from election to election and rose fairly steadily from

145 (6.5 percent of all voters) in 1761 to 869 (31 percent of the total) in 1802, and Table 5.7 reflects the increasing influence of the radically different occupational structure of the nonresident voters (Table 5.3). Indeed, the structures of the resident and nonresident portions of the electorate changed very little over these decades; 65 percent of the resident vote came from the craft trades in 1768 compared to over 61 percent in 1796. The 35 percent of the out-voters from the craft trades in 1761 was little changed by 1802 when craftsmen made up 33 percent of the nonresident vote. Fluctuations in the size of the nonresident vote also account for many of the less noticeable variations in the Maidstone electorate over the period.

Continued occupational stability in the face of substantial changes in electoral size should indicate stable recruitment into the borough electorates, and, as illustrated by Norwich, the least stable borough occupationally, newly recruited voters, or at least newly appearing voters, closely resembled politically experienced electors. Some small differences distinguished old and new voters in particular electorates, such as the high concentration of gentle and professional voters among the experienced participants in Lewes and Northampton, and the larger number of merchants (and correspondingly smaller group of craftsmen) among new voters in Norwich. Nevertheless, the overall patterns converge rather closely, and the few noticeable variations are scattered randomly across the four constituencies. Michael Katz has shown that on the nineteenth century Canadian frontier, "when a person left [a] city, someone with similar features entered to take his place."[27] Although not as unusual a phenomenon, replacement in these electorates followed a similar pattern. Allegations of corporate mismanagement and wholesale creations of fraudulent or near fraudulent voters notwithstanding, those entering the electorate for the first time often replaced occupational counterparts from

[27] Katz, *People of Hamilton*, p. 55.

Table 5.7: Occupational Compositions of Norwich and Maidstone Electorates: 1761-1802 (Percentage)

Occupational Category	1761	1768	1774	1780	1784	1790	1796	1802
Norwich								
I. Gentlemen, Professions	8.1	12.0	NC	9.5	9.9	11.9	14.7	15.6
II. Merchants, Entrepreneurs	3.5	5.4	NC	5.2	5.6	4.7	4.8	6.4
III. Retailers	13.7	16.5	NC	17.3	17.0	16.4	16.9	16.4
IV. Agriculturalists	1.1	1.9	NC	3.4	4.9	3.5	3.5	4.6
V. Craftsmen, Artisans, Skilled Workmen	72.2	61.9	NC	59.9	60.2	60.8	56.9	53.1
VI. Laborers	.7	.9	NC	1.4	1.0	1.1	1.2	1.8
VII. Other	.8	1.5	NC	3.4	1.4	1.7	2.0	2.2
Maidstone								
I. Gentlemen, Professions	8.5	12.0	7.5	8.9	9.3	10.8	8.7	8.3
II. Merchants, Entrepreneurs	4.0	5.4	2.8	4.1	4.4	3.3	2.7	5.0
III. Retailers	19.1	18.9	21.2	16,4	17.6	17.3	16.1	16.7
IV. Agriculturalists	6.0	2.5	3.3	1.6	2.0	2.3	2.2	2.9
V. Craftsmen, Artisans, Skilled Workmen	49.7	49.8	54.0	49.7	54.4	52.9	57.8	55.1
VI. Laborers	10.1	7.1	7.5	11.4	8.5	11.5	7.6	8.3
VII. Other	2.5	4.4	3.6	7.9	3.9	2.0	4.9	3.8

NC = no contest

former generations of voters who left the electorate continuously as a result of infirmity, mobility, and death (Table 5.8).

The remarkable occupational consistency of these changing electorates may not have been typical of some other borough constituencies; only one of the four towns examined was much affected by the dramatic alterations in

197

Table 5.8: Electoral Recruitment: Occupations of Experienced and Inexperienced
Voters, 1796 (Percentage)

Occupational Category	Norwich		Maidstone		Northampton		Lewes	
	Inexp.	Exp.	Inexp.	Exp.	Inexp.	Exp.	Inexp.	Exp.
I. Gentlemen, Professions	10.1	9.4	6.8	6.1	5.0	8.9	9.5	15.8
II. Merchants, Entrepreneurs	7.3	3.5	4.8	1.7	4.5	5.3	5.6	5.1
III. Retailers	17.9	16.1	15.1	14.4	22.1	18.2	14.3	13.9
IV. Agriculturalists	1.4	.8	2.1	1.1	.3	.7	3.2	2.5
V. Craftsmen, Artisans, Skilled Workmen	59.9	68.4	62.4	67.4	53.7	55.2	50.8	44.9
VI. Laborers	1.7	.5	7.5	7.7	11.1	10.8	11.9	12.7
VII. Other	1.6	1.3	1.3	1.7	3.4	.9	4.8	5.1

England's economy at the end of the century, and even that one, Northampton, was less affected than many urban, or urbanizing, areas. Norwich, once England's second city, was almost completely bypassed by the Industrial Revolution, as were Maidstone and Lewes, and the stable recruitment into the electorate in these towns may have been typical only in towns with relatively stagnant economies. The electorates in the industrializing and rapidly expanding towns may have been changing rapidly and radically as voters were recruited from fluctuating urban environments.

ECONOMIC STRUCTURE

An economic assessment of these boroughs does not greatly clarify the image of the electorate emerging from the preceding occupational analysis. Based as they are on sometimes small and invariably nonrandom samples, the mean annual rentals of the actual residences of voters and other taxpayers lack precision and do not allow tests of statistical

198

significance.[28] With the crudeness of the measurement, these economic relationships between voters and taxpayers in four towns can do no more than lend some credibility to the impression conveyed by the occupational similarities of

[28] The most consistently available economic records for these voters were annual rentals, since both the poor rate assessments and land tax rolls contained this information for individuals. Unfortunately, but not surprisingly, it was not possible to obtain economic data for all of the electors in Norwich or Maidstone, and virtually impossible to obtain useful data for Lewes and Northampton voters. Thus, it also proved impossible to select random samples with which to test the economic parameters of these populations. In order to link the lists of taxpayers with the lists of voters, three identifiers were used to judge the validity of each individual link. There were sufficient identifiers for taxpayers in all of the Norwich parishes, but the economic data in several parishes were too incomplete or inadequately recorded to be of value. Therefore, economic data were gathered in Norwich only from those parishes with adequate economic records (approximately two-thirds of the total). Instead of using both the land tax and the poor rate, the land tax was used exclusively since it was more complete and it contained annual rentals that were identical to those recorded on the available poor rates. The land tax also gave an account of the value of an individual's stock-in-trade as well as his rental, and differentiated between landlords and owner-occupiers. This final bit of information was critically important since unlike the poor rate, the land tax required residency. Thus, without the notation of occupier/landlord, the land tax lists would have been of little value. In fact, the failure of the land tax lists in some parishes to distinguish owners and occupiers proved to be the principle reason for the exclusion of a parish from detailed consideration. Incomplete names and other inadequacies in particular parish land tax records eliminated relatively few. After gathering and coding the data, computerized linkage programs merged the political and economic data much as they created the extended records of political participation across time. Because of the deficiencies in eighteenth-century record-keeping, omissions caused by the missing parishes, and omissions resulting from mobility, the linkage programs successfully retrieved economic data for approximately 15 percent of the Norwich electorate. These

Occupational Ranks	All Voters 1761	Voters with Econ. Data	All Voters 1790	Voters with Econ. Data
I (Elite)	13.9	14.9	14.1	16.2
II (Middling)	23.7	26.7	22.1	28.1
III (Lesser)	62.4	58.4	63.8	55.7

the boroughs. Voters in open boroughs may not have differed drastically from nonvoting citizens who paid taxes (Table 5.9). The mean rentals of a sample of Maidstone electors (based on poor rate lists of annual rentals) marginally exceeded the mean for the overall taxpaying populace at four points from 1780 to 1796, and the variations in single-point estimates for Northampton and Lewes in 1796 are too small to be taken seriously. Conversely, the higher mean rentals (based on land tax returns) of Norwich electors, along with the substantial mean rentals in both Norwich and Maidstone, hardly suggest electorates that shared the economic conditions of the entire community. The Maidstone figures are particularly impressive since a

---

samples were not random samples by any stretch of the imagination, but there is reason to assume that the samples were representative despite their nonrandomness, as the following comparison of identifiable taxpayers and all voters demonstrates.

Economic data for Maidstone voters were much more complete since Maidstone was a single parish. Maidstone's poor rate assessments were used because they were impressively comprehensive and mirrored the less complete land tax records in recording annual rentals. In Maidstone, as in Norwich, the figures for annual rentals were taken from actual entries under that heading on the tax rolls, not from recreations based on tax assessments. As a result, the rental figures, though still subject to either error or deliberate misstatement in the original records, are more reliable than they might be otherwise. Using a series of linkage programs virtually identical to the set used for the Norwich data, economic data were recovered for almost 50 percent of the Maidstone electorate. Although a substantial portion of the electorate, the Maidstone samples were also nonrandom, but again there were no reasons to assume that the samples were biased in any particular fashion. A comparison of the occupational distributions of the entire electorate and the "samples" of voters for whom economic data could be obtained strengthened the impression that these samples contained a reasonably representative cross-section of the electorate (Table 5.11). Economic data for Lewes and Northampton were less complete and also less interesting given the nature of the political development of both towns. Therefore, the economic samples from each are not very convincing, particularly in light of the occupationally elite Lewes electorate (Table 5.1) which does not correspond at all well to the low mean annual rental obtained from the existing Lewes land tax lists.

larger proportion of the electorate could be identified on Maidstone's rate books, and the parish poor rates that provided these measurements did not involve the serious interpretational problems inherent in the land tax assessments of the late eighteenth century. Certainly electorates were a diverse lot, both economically and occupationally—quite ordinary and sometimes very poor men held the franchise in all four boroughs. Nevertheless, mean annual rentals of almost twenty pounds in Maidstone and more than twenty pounds in Norwich are far too high to indicate electorates that mirrored the economic parameters of each town's populace. Without some means of reconciling these figures with the greater similarities and relatively lower means for both taxpayers and voters in Lewes and Northampton, the evidence remains ambiguous, and seems especially confusing in light of the elite occupational structure of the Lewes electorate. A shift in focus, though, provides an additional measure that helps place the relationships between voters and their communities in proper perspective.

However deeply the electorate penetrated into the economic strata of each borough, the proportion of the adult male population with the vote in each of them compared favorably with the national proportion of adult male voters after the passage of the Great Reform Act. Norman Gash estimated that perhaps 20 percent of the adult male population of England was qualified to vote after 1832, and though the nature of the evidence for both electorates and populations prevents precision, the proportion of the adult male inhabitants with the franchise almost certainly exceeded 20 percent in each of these boroughs.[29] Approximately 22 percent of the adult males resident in Norwich in 1784 and 1802 (the two elections for which estimates can be made) possessed franchises. An equally high proportion of Maidstone's resident adult males voted in 1802, and if the local census of 1782 is nearly correct, an even higher proportion (38 percent) cast ballots in 1784. Nor

[29] Norman Gash, *Politics in the Age of Peel*, London, 1953, p. 89.

201

Table 5.9: Mean Rentals of Voters and All Taxpayers

Source	Town	Date	Mean Rental of Voters	Sample N	Mean Rental of All Taxpayers	N
Land Tax	Norwich*	1780	£27.1‡	211	£15.8	2,080
		1784	27.4	216	16.2	762
		1790	26.6	198	16.7	801
		1796	25.9	277	19.5	623
Poor Rate	Maidstone†	1780	18.0	227	15.7	589
		1784	20.7	229	17.9	559
		1790	20.2	199	17.8	642
		1796	19.6	188	17.9	612
Poor Rate	Northampton	1796	5.4	176	4.7	372
Land Tax	Lewes	1790	7.4	202	7.6	354

* Not a random sample. All voters identifiable on land tax rolls.
† Not a sample, but all taxpayers on rate books.
‡ Decimalized pounds sterling.

do Maidstone and Norwich seem atypical. Lower proportions of all adult males voted in some freeman boroughs such as Liverpool and Shrewsbury, yet in many other constituencies the proportion equalled or exceeded that of Norwich and Maidstone. Nearly 26 percent of the resident males in Colchester, for example, voted in the election of 1796, and the proportions in Exeter, Durham, Gloucester, Hereford, Hertford, and Newcastle-Upon-Tyne, to name only a few, were as high or higher. The proportion of resident adult males with the franchise often mounted even higher in the "inhabitant" boroughs, though the variation was extreme. Potwalloper boroughs such as Cirencester and Honiton seem to have allowed virtually universal male suffrage, while 55 to 60 percent certainly exercised franchises in Northampton.[30] On the other hand, inhabitant boroughs

[30] These estimates are based on a 23 percent average adult male proportion of the population. D. V. Glass has estimated the proportion as 21.5 percent in 1695 and 25.5 percent in 1821, hence 23 percent for the

requiring the payment of scot and lot as well as resident householder status, such as Lewes, fell more closely into line with the freeman boroughs. Something less than 30 percent of Lewes's adult males participated in the 1802 election. All in all, the franchise was as widely, or more widely held in the freeman and inhabitant boroughs before the Reform Act as in the country generally after its passage. This is not to denigrate the effects of the Reform Bill; rather, these figures on proportional participation and the occupational structures of these electorates merely clarify the breadth of the ranks of the enfranchised in the boroughs that accounted for most of the electoral activity of the later years of the century. These electorates may not have reflected the entire population in their respective boroughs, but more than a narrow elite participated in the renewed electoral activity evident in the country after 1761. With only 40 percent of Maidstone's adult males assessed to the poor rate after 1761, and just 60 percent of the adult males in Ipswich rated as late as 1835, the proportion of the population voting in these boroughs seems strikingly high.[31] The exclusion of the very poor in the freeman bor-

---

later eighteenth century should closely approximate the actual distribution of adult males. Population figures for these boroughs were derived from the national census of 1801 and a few local censuses, such as Maidstone's of 1782 and Norwich's of 1786. It should be noted that the proportion of the adult male population voting in Norwich may have been very high for quite some time. Evans felt that the electorate contained 30 percent of Norwich's adult male population as early as 1690. If Hirst is correct, the national proportion may have been this high in the 1640s. D. V. Glass, *Population in History*, Chicago, 1965, pp. 181, 212, 215; J. Howlett, *Observations on the Increased Population . . . of Maidstone*, Maidstone, 1782; *The Norwich Directory*, Norwich, 1801; John T. Evans, "The Political Elite of Norwich, 1620-1690," Ph.D. diss., Stanford University, 1971; Derek Hirst, *The Representative of the People?*, Cambridge, 1975, p. 157.

[31] These figures are based on pollbooks, the census of 1801, and the data in Namier and Brooke, *House of Commons*. The number of rated individuals in Maidstone over the eight points examined ranged from 559 to 623. The 405 resident voters in 1802, for example, compare favorably to the 612 ratepayers that year. In Norwich, approximately 50

oughs, the "scot and lot" boroughs, and to a lesser extent in the "potwalloper" boroughs did not prevent a widely based, albeit relatively prosperous, electorate.

Finally, measured areally, the voters in these boroughs were distributed uniformly and equitably. Even though considerable social, economic, and religious variations can be identified among the parishes and wards of Norwich and Northampton, the proportion of the voters residing in each Norwich ward (and parish) and each Northampton parish corresponded closely to the proportion of the total population contained in that ward or parish. The wealthiest Norwich ward, Mancroft, contributed more than its share of voters to the Norwich electorate (and far more than its share of mayors), but a comparison of population and voters in the wards and parishes of each borough demonstrates the areally equitable distribution of the voters (Table 5.10).[32] Electoral proportions in Northampton's parishes accurately reflected the extreme variations in the concentration of Northampton's population, and the relative strength of Nonconformity in All Saints parish in Northampton and in Norwich's Northern ward had no noticeable impact on voter strength in those sections of the two towns.[33]

---

percent of the freemen were rated in 1834. Maidstone's total even in the second decade of the nineteenth century was not high. Only 33.5 percent of the 2,373 householders were rated in 1825. Maidstone Parish Poor Rate Assessments, vols. 8-12, KRO; William Roberts James, *The Charters and Other Documents of Maidstone*, London, 1825, p. 37; J. L. Hammond and B. Hammond, *The Village Laborer*, London, 1912, p. 15; Penelope Corfield, "Social and Economic History of Norwich, 1650-1850," Ph.D. diss., University of London, 1976, p. 68.

[32] Between 1761 and 1802, Mancroft ward provided over half (51.4 percent) of Norwich's mayors. The other wards split the remainder relatively equally, with 17.1 percent from Wymer, 17.1 percent from Conisford, and 14.4 percent from the Northern ward. Calculated from Basil Cozens-Hardy, *Mayors of Norwich*, Norwich, 1938.

[33] Using the Nonconformist registers deposited in the PRO, Portugal Street, London, the distribution of the identifiable Dissenting voters in Norwich was: Mancroft (ward 1), 3.1 percent; Conisford (ward 2), 16.4 percent; Wymer (ward 3), 23.9 percent; and Northern (ward 4), 56.6

Table 5.10: Areal Distributions of Voters and All Inhabitants:
Norwich (1784) and Northampton (1796)

Wards	NORWICH Population Population	Percentage Electorate
Conisford	19.4	18.0
Mancroft	15.3	21.4
Wymer	30.3	24.8
Northern	35.0	30.8

Parishes	NORTHAMPTON Percentage Population	Percentage Electorate
All Saints	55.7	57.2
St. Sepulchre	21.0	19.0
St. Giles	18.3	18.5
St. Peter	5.1	5.3

SOCIAL STRATIFICATION

The search for correlations between social, economic, and
political characteristics described in Chapter 7 employs the
economic and occupational measures adopted so far. However, the abundance of occupational data and the relative
scarcity of economic data for much of the electorate as a
result of inadequate and/or incomplete economic records
necessitated another set of occupational categories. The
seven occupational groups encompassing the electorate in
Table 5.1 are hierarchical to a limited degree since function
and status were inexorably linked in the later eighteenth
century, but an analysis of behavioral patterns demanded
another system more closely related to what might be called

percent. The Northern ward's concentration of Nonconformists had no
measureable impact on its proportional contribution to the Norwich electorate. Nonparochial Records, 1753, 1260, 653: (Old Meeting House);
1963, 3132: (Tabernacle); 1965, 1966: (Octagon Chapel); 361: (St. Mary's
Baptist); 1785: (St. Margaret's Baptist), PROP. Also see, John Foster, "A
Class Dimension," in The Study of Urban History, ed. H. J. Dyos, New York,
1968, pp. 288-91.

social stratification, implying both social status and economic rank. Recently, R. S. Neale proposed a five-tier model describing "class" conflict in the nineteenth century. Though perhaps not as applicable in the late eighteenth century, Neale's model is a marked improvement over many traditional discussions of social conflict, or the lack of it, in the unreformed political system (or the reformed system for that matter). Neale's five categories incorporate Dahrendorf's insistence on measuring conflict through a fluid model stressing process rather than through static, cross-sectional models.[34] The social and physical mobility evident in the lives of these voters over an extended period graphically underscores the importance of movement and change within any realistic model of social interaction. Unfortunately, as interesting and heuristically useful as it seems, Neale's scheme cannot be implemented with existing data for most of the nineteenth century, much less the eighteenth. The detailed census returns available for the period following 1841 might allow the model to be tested; before 1841, it cannot be applied quantitatively.[35]

Hence a traditional three-tier model is employed once again in this assessment of social stratification in the electorate. In Table 5.11, the electorates of all four boroughs are grouped into three strata roughly denoting socio-economic rank, with the elite, consisting of landed and commercial groups, separated from laboring men (skilled and unskilled) by a cluster of relatively "respectable" if somewhat lackluster occupations. Smaller retailers, assorted nonmanual workers engaged in a variety of trades, farmers, members of the drink trade, and extraordinarily skilled and therefore highly regarded and well-compensated craftsmen comprise this middling category. Certainly some

[34] Neale, *Class and Ideology*, pp. 15-40.

[35] The census-takers became more and more precise in their terminology and careful in their delineation of English workers in each successive census until the excellent census of 1841 that describes individuals and families reasonably well. See Wrigley, ed., *Nineteenth-Century Society*.

of the classifications stretch a point, and others tend to blend distinctly dissimilar kinds of work, but all in all, the classification scheme resolves more difficult questions than it raises. Of the many questions encountered by such an effort, the most critical involves the ability of occupational categories to reflect economic reality. Given the economic heterogeneity of most occupations, can it be assumed that these occupational groups convey genuine economic distinctions as well as less tangible, but more easily defended gradations of social rank? Or is the three-tier model, or any other occupationally based scheme too severely damaged by the incidence of economic disparities of considerable magnitude between occupations and within occupations? For instance, Gardiner Haywood, Gentleman, of Norwich, paid a tax in 1796 of 16s. 6d. on an annual rental of £3 and stock amounting to £50, while William Decaux, a Norwich cabinetmaker, paid £23 tax for his house assessed at a rather steep £111 and stock of £150.[36] In the proposed occupationally-based, three-tier model, Haywood counts among the elite and Decaux falls among the middling sort though their relative financial standing calls for a reversal of their ranks. Ezekial Garrett, on the other hand, seems well placed in the laboring category for 1790 since a greater congruence marked his occupation (worsted weaver) and his relative poverty evinced by a total tax of twelve shillings. Yet his neighbor and fellow weaver, John Playford of St. Stephen's parish, rented a house for £44 a year and paid taxes totalling £8.16s.0d.[37] The examples of Haywood and Decaux cast doubts on the economic accuracy of the three occupational groups, and the relative po-

[36] Norwich Poor Rate Assessments, PD17; Land Tax Assessments, C23/B/R18, NNRO. In this example and the one that follows, both poor rates and land tax assessments could be found for the individuals cited. Ordinarily, this was not the case, and the Norwich land tax registers were used exclusively in measuring mean rentals.

[37] Norwich Poor Rate Assessments, PD136; Land Tax Assessments, C23/SA/R1/29, NNRO.

207

sitions of Playford and Garrett lend support to Francis Place's objection to the jumbling of the "most skilled and the most prudent workmen with the most ignorant and imprudent laborers and paupers" into the "lower orders" even though the differences "in many cases will scarce admit of comparison."[38] The question, then, is simply whether or not these examples are isolated and atypical or representative of economic diversity within and between occupations sufficient to invalidate occupationally based hierarchical divisions. Fortunately, even though eighteenth-century economic data will not allow widely based or even reasonably precise measurements of wealth, general accounts provide some indication of the validity of the three categories, and individual-level data allow the economic reality of the three-tier model to be tested for portions of the Maidstone and Norwich electorates.

Campbell's contemporary economic observations concerning all eighteenth-century trades lend some general, if qualified, support to a tripartite division of the electorate. Ten of the seventeen occupations listed in Campbell's *London Tradesman* (1747) with requirements of £50 for apprentices and in excess of £1,000 to establish a master fall among the elite in Table 5.11, six others rank among the

Table 5.11: Socio-Economic Stratification of Four Borough Electorates: 1761-1802
(Average of All Elections—Weighted Percentage)

Socio-Economic Category	Norwich	Maidstone	Northampton	Lewes
I. Gentlemen, Professions, and Commercial Elite	14.1	11.2	8.7	18.5
II. Middling Sort	24.3	26.1	25.6	30.0
III. Working Men—Craftsmen, Artisans, Skilled and Unskilled Laborers	61.6	62.7	65.7	51.5

[38] BL Add. MSS. 27834, f. 45, cited in Asa Briggs, *The Making of Modern England*, New York, 1959, p. 12.

middling sort, leaving only one severely misplaced. The single "lesser" occupation with such steep monetary prerequisites, soapboiler, occurred rarely in the electorates examined, and any master soapboiler appearing at the hustings probably would have claimed the title "soap dealer" and placed himself squarely among the elite where he belonged on the basis of his relative wealth. Just two of the twenty-two occupations demanding £20 for apprenticeships and £200 or so to be established as a master would be considered elite occupations in Table 5.11, and both of these, lawyer and surgeon, are exceptional cases. Both undoubtedly belong in the first category; Campbell himself treats "law, physic, and divinity" in a separate category quite apart from the merchants and tradesmen who make up the bulk of the £20/£200 occupations, despite his personal aversion to doctors. While recognizing the remunerative aspects of a medical career, Campbell characterized doctors as men possessing "a license to kill as many as entrust [them] with their health." Nevertheless, medicine would do well even "when other professions would starve," forcing Campbell to recommend it highly.[39]

---

[39] Campbell lists the following trades as those requiring £50 for an apprenticeship and/or £1,000 or more to be set up as a master: banker, brewer, coachmaker, conveyancer, coal factor, insurer, lace-man (gold or silver), timber merchant, merchant, mercer, money scrivener, notary public, painter (artist), wool stapler, woolen draper, soapboiler, and sugar baker. The following twenty-three trades required £30 for an apprenticeship and/or upwards of £500 to set up as a master: bookseller, pawnbroker, chemist, chinashopman, cloth worker, distiller, druggist, enginemaker, fellmonger, goldsmith, grocer, hosier's shop, ironmonger, leatherdresser, letter-founder, nurseryman, optical-instrument maker, oil-shop man, sailmaker, shipbuilder, gunsmith, starchmaker, and threadman. An additional group of twenty-two needed £20 and/or £200 respectively: apothecary, attorney, blockmaker, calico printer, cabinetmaker, cooper, jeweller, leather seller, mathematical-instrument maker, lighter builder, leather-cutter, packer, pewterer, saddler, silkman, ropemaker, silk throwster, stationer, surgeon, teashop owner, tobacconist, and upholdster. Among these trades, as well as virtually all others, journeymen collected wages ranging from £23 to £100 annually. Only twenty-one occupations allegedly

Testing the three occupational groups with a large but nonrandom sample of voters in both Norwich and Maidstone for whom economic and occupational information exists lends the scheme more specific and somewhat more persuasive support. The examples of Haywood, Decaux, Garrett, and Playford are, in fact, atypical; the social status of most of the individual voters examined corresponded closely with their economic status. A consistently strong correlation (γ = .47) between economic and social rank existed among Norwich voters at three different points before 1797, and a larger sample with better economic records in Maidstone resulted in an even higher correlation (γ = .61). Without the economic deviation of a few specific occupational groups such as hotpressers and carpenters, correlations in Norwich would have paralleled Maidstone figures. Clearly, an analysis based on three occupational categories *can* roughly delineate economic rank.[40]

Adopting the three new categories as a supplement to

---

were sufficiently remunerative *and* steady to guarantee an income of £50/annum to a journeyman. These were: drapery and herald painter, engraver, pattern-drawer, printer, jeweller, snuff-box maker, silver chaser, house carver, cabinetmaker, chair-maker, mirror framer, coach carver, instrument-maker, wine cooper, bolt-smith, sailmaker, enameller, fine-drawer, watch finisher, tapestry-weaver, and land surveyor. Statistical tests using Gamma were run on the economic breakdown suggested by Campbell's three categories with results less impressive than the occupational breakdown described in Appendix III that provides the basis of this discussion. Campbell's occupational categories yielded γ of .35 for identifiable Norwich voters and .56 for Maidstone's electorate.

[40] There are no hard and fast rules about the strength of a measure of association such as τ_b and γ, but William Buchanan has provided some useful indicators. "It can be said very roughly that a γ of .6 or above is high and one of below .2 is not worth attention unless the data falls in some particularly meaningful pattern." γ was used in this test because it does not assume linearity and there was no reason to assume linearity in these relationships. However, even using a measure that does require linearity such as τ_b yielded impressive results of .31 and .42 respectively. Values of τ_b over .15 are worthy of attention and values over .4 are quite high. William Buchanan, "Nominal and Ordinal Bivariate Statistics," *American Journal of Political Science* 18(1974):638.

the functional description of the electorate, the social stratification of the electorate evident in Table 5.11 reinforces
the general impression conveyed in Table 5.1. The borough electorates of the late eighteenth century were restricted; the lower orders were underrepresented, and the
very lowest may have been excluded by and large. Nevertheless, at least half the electorate in each of these boroughs
could not claim membership in the social elite, no matter
how defined. Contrary to Neale's contention, sufficient economic diversity existed within the unreformed electorate
to raise the serious possibility of social and/or economic
conflict.[41] The disparities among the electors lend credence
to the allusions to social conflict or socially based voting
made in the course of election contests in all four boroughs.
Before the full impact of the Industrial Revolution, England may not have been a society of "classes," but social
conflict was possible nonetheless. The question of its existence occupies the next chapter when, at long last, voting
behavior takes center stage.

[41] Rudé classified Englishmen into three economic classes comprised of
the substantial property owners (£50+), the middling sort (£10-49), and
the lesser sort (less than £10). Interestingly enough, the proportions of
Middlesex voters in these three groups corresponded closely to the percentages in Table 5.11. Rudé counted 13 percent in the substantial category, 28.8 percent in the middling class, and 58.2 percent in the lesser
orders. George Rudé, *Wilkes and Liberty*, London, 1962.

CHAPTER SIX

The Voter Decides: The Development of Partisan Behavior

MODERN ELECTORAL studies have focused much attention on, and given much credit to "partisan identification" in the electorate.[1] Political scientists have demonstrated the importance of partisan identification as a determinant of voter choice in recent American elections, and have shown that a voter's "identification" with a party remains more stable than his or her actual voting habits.[2] This modern emphasis has led some historians to search for partisan identification among past electorates in both the United States and England.[3] However, since opinion data are required to isolate partisan identification, the constraints of the exclusively behavioral data available for most historical research doom such searches to failure before they begin. Shively, Butler, and others have argued convincingly that the concept itself may be appropriate only for twentieth-century American voters, but appropriate or not, trying to infer partisan identification from behavioral data is tantamount to jousting with windmills.[4] Instead of

---

[1] Ian Budge, Ivor Crewe, Dennis Farlie, eds., *Party Identification and Beyond*, London, 1976.

[2] Contrary to David Butler and Donald Stokes, *Political Change in Britain*, New York, 1971, pp. 39-47, Richard Rose found "no distinction between party identification and voting choice" in Great Britain. Richard Rose, *Electoral Behavior*, London, 1975, p. 496.

[3] W. A. Speck et al., "Computer Analysis of Pollbooks: A Further Report," *BIHR* 48(1975):64-90.

[4] W. P. Shively, "Party Identification, Party Choice, and Voting Stability," *APSR* 66(1969):1203; P. E. Converse, "The Nature of Belief Systems in Mass Publics," in *Ideology and Discontent*, ed. D. Apter, London, 1964; Butler and Stokes, *Political Change in Britain*, pp. 41-44.

partisan identification, partisan behavior is the proper focus for this analysis of voting preferences. Partisan behavior is, quite simply, politically coherent behavior. And, at later eighteenth-century elections, politically coherent behavior was a voter's undivided support of a single political party. Undivided party support (voting for just one party), however, did not necessarily entail "full" support. An elector could cast only one of his two votes for a party's two candidates, thus according a party his undivided allegiance while not supporting it completely. The incidence of "unnecessary plumping" is important, and its implications will be considered separately; the following assessment does not equate full support alone with partisan behavior. An unnecessary plump, although clearly not full support, counts in the following analysis as a party vote. Thus, the wide variety of choices confronting voters in this electoral system which gave each participant *two* votes at parliamentary elections partially shapes the measurement of partisan behavior.

It may seem unduly inclusive to define partisan behavior as undivided party support, but given the existence of the double vote, even the relatively straightforward partisan choices facing the electors in Norwich and Maidstone by no means guaranteed that the two parties in either town could easily achieve undivided support from their adherents. And the frequency with which parties, particularly the "independents," proposed single candidates rather than full slates failed to create an atmosphere conducive to consistent double voting for one party. Plumping (casting only one vote) was demanded by partisanship too often for unnecessary plumping to seem very strange.[5] The complex

---

[5] The Norwich elections of 1761, 1780, and 1802 were contested by two candidates from each "party." However, only 1790 and 1796 were truly three-man campaigns because of the general acceptability of Sir Harbord Harbord. For example, at the 1768 election, both Edward Bacon (his former running mate) and Thomas Beevor (an ardent opponent of the Administration) attempted to tie themselves to Harbord. Harbord was

political frameworks of Lewes and Northampton made undivided support an even more ambitious goal. The voter's option of splitting votes between parties posed serious problems for postreform politicians and "had enormous consequences for the political system as a whole in arresting the development of party at a local level and tending to promote center politics."[6] And if the double vote erected such a barrier to the polarization of the mid-nineteenth-century English electorate, it should have posed an even greater impediment to the development of partisan ties in the less sophisticated political environment of the later eighteenth century. For this reason, the political behavior of the electors in the four boroughs that have formed the principal focus of this study could not be expected to exhibit levels of partisan loyalty comparable to those identified by T. J. Nossiter and D. G. Wright in English boroughs after the Reform Act. Yet surprisingly, straight-party voting and split-voting (the two best measures of partisanship) in each of these unreformed boroughs occasionally approximated, and sometimes even exceeded, the levels found among the voters of the later nineteenth century.

Except for the elections of 1790 and 1796, Norwich voters displayed the lowest levels of split-voting among the

---

truly an independent M.P. and could be seen as an "independent" candidate because of his opposition to the Administration on several issues, including general warrants. Thus the campaign involved three candidates, but it was not a typical three-man race. The only real question involved the second seat. A similar situation prevailed in 1784. Harbord was ill before the election and did not campaign. He had been a Blue-and-White candidate in 1780, yet he supported Pitt and was therefore acceptable to both the Orange-and-Purples and the Free Blues. The Maidstone election of 1784 also involved three candidates, but like the Norwich election that year, one of the candidates was acceptable to both sides. In this instance, Sir Horace Mann, an independent in the best sense of the word, was the overwhelming favorite of Ministerialists and independents alike. *Miscellaneous Pieces in Prose and Verse Relative to the Contested Election*, Norwich, 1768, *passim*; *The Election Magazine*, Norwich, 1784.

[6] T. J. Nossiter, "Elections and Political Behavior in County Durham and Newcastle, 1832-74," Ph.D. diss., Oxford University, 1968, p. 165.

four boroughs (Table 6.1). Except for the unusually large number of split-votes cast in these two elections, less than 13 percent of the Norwich electorate voted simultaneously for both parties at elections over the entire period. The figures for 1784 and 1802 are nothing short of remarkable; almost no one split his vote at either of these contests. In comparison, Nossiter found that an average of more than 20 percent of the voters split their votes between the parties at elections held in several northeastern boroughs between 1832 and 1868. An even greater proportion of the postreform Bradford electorate split their votes; splitters actually outnumbered straight-party voters in Bradford thirty years *after* the Great Reform Act.[7] Electors in Maidstone, Lewes, and Northampton never achieved levels of split-voting as low as Norwich's voters in 1784 or 1802, but during the 1790s, voters in all three towns proved capable of behaving in a manner comparable to the voters in the reformed boroughs examined by Nossiter and Wright. A pronounced downward trend in split-voting marked Maidstone elections after 1780 (until the election of 1802), and a correspondingly sharp drop in the number of electors splitting occurred in Lewes at the elections of the 1790s, albeit in a less clear pattern. Split-voting reached twin peaks in the Maidstone elections of 1774 and 1780, after which the practice of dividing one's support declined steadily among the Maidstone electorate to less than 25 percent at the hotly contested election of 1796. At the same time, Lewes split-voting dropped to less than 22 percent in 1790 following the formation of the "Coalition" of Thomas Kemp and Henry Pelham in 1780. The death of Henry Pelham in 1797, however, was followed by a surge in the number of Lewes electors splitting their votes.

[7] T. J. Nossiter, *Influence, Opinion, and Political Idioms in Reformed England*, Brighton, 1975, p. 178; D. G. Wright, "Politics and Opinion in Bradford, 1832-1868," Ph.D. diss., University of Leeds, 1966, pp. 491, 135, 184, 1030; D. G. Wright, "A Radical Borough: Parliamentary Politics: Bradford, 1832-1841," *Northern History* 4(1969):132-66.

Table 6.1: Split Voters at Parliamentary Elections (Percentage)

	1761	1768	1774	1780	1784	1790	1796	1802
Norwich	12.3	10.9	NC	12.6	1.7	24.6	18.7	3.1
Maidstone	52.1	42.4	78.7	77.4	52.6	36.7	23.4	59.1
Lewes	NC	NA	NA	43.2	NC	21.6	27.6	42.3
Northampton								
Parl. Parties	NC	2.6	24.1	NC	43.6	61.1	25.3	NC
Patron,								
Nonpatron	NC	NA	29.6	NC	55.0	29.7	47.7	NC

NA = not applicable
NC = no contest

Even Northampton experienced a notable decline in split-voting during the 1796 election and finally achieved levels more comparable to the boroughs contested by parties. In the absence of partisan activity, the measurement of straight-party and split-voting during the last three contested elections in Northampton (1784, 1790, 1796) relies on the strong links and positive associations between individual Northampton candidates and the parliamentary parties. However, the political framework supplied by the parliamentary parties competed with another framework at each of these elections within which an elector might reasonably have chosen to operate, or perhaps more accurately, within which he might have been forced to operate. Two aristocratic families, the Comptons (Earl Northampton) and the Spencers (Earl Spencer), invariably supplied a single candidate for these contests, and the political predilections of the Compton and Spencer candidates invariably fell at opposite ends of the political spectrum. Northampton voting patterns were therefore inextricably entangled in a complicated mesh involving these local families and the parliamentary parties. Split-voting by Northampton voters seems to indicate a vacillation between local and national concerns; each framework apparently accounted for a greater proportion of the voters at specific elections (Table 6.1). National political concerns achieved considerable salience

216

in 1784 and again in 1796, while the intervening elections may have owed more to local family loyalties. Nevertheless, whatever local considerations determined the votes of some Northampton electors, the need to assess partisan behavior in Northampton comparatively dictates a heavy reliance on the gauge provided by national political parties and national political concerns. This reliance is reflected in Figure 6.4.

These comparisons of split-voting at specific elections in each of the boroughs across the period are the most appropriate point of departure for this analysis of unreformed voting behavior; such comparisons directly address the hypotheses formulated in earlier chapters and, at the same time, highlight the difficulties encountered in any analysis of the unreformed electoral system. The complexities of the ballot itself, as well as the varying impact of local partisan strengths and varying political structures, dictate great caution in examining voting patterns. The summary statistics occasionally employed in this analysis can be interpreted only in light of the circumstances peculiar to individual elections. Summary statistics serve as useful indicators, but the variety so much in evidence both across the political system and across time demands considerable attention to particular, and sometimes unique, conditions and circumstances in seeking broader trends. Hanham explained the situation well, noting that "general elections were not general" before the second Reform Act, much less before the first.[8] The figures on split-voting in Table 6.1, for example, appear to lend themselves readily to a comparison of the changes in electoral behavior in each borough over the forty years after 1760, yet several entries conceal as much as they reveal. The 1768 Northampton

[8] H. J. Hanham, ed., *Dod's Electoral Facts*, Brighton, 1972, introduction. Also see, J. Dunbabin, "Parliamentary Elections in Great Britain, 1868-1900: A Psephological Note," *EHR* 71(1966):83; J. Cornford, "The Transformation of Conservatism in the Nineteenth Century," *Victorian Studies* 7(1963):35-66.

election, for example, illustrates the difficulty often encountered in interpreting summary statistics. The percentage of the votes split between the parties at this election seems impressively low, but patronage and corruption accounted for the scarcity of split-votes cast at the election. The parliamentary party attachments of two of the candidates at the infamous "election of the three earls" happened to coincide with the joint campaign of two of the earls. Hence, the alliance of the Earls of Halifax and of Northampton, each supporting Ministerialists, in opposition to the single anti-Ministerialist, sponsored by Earl Spencer, provided a basis for apparently partisan behavior that had precious little to do with the parliamentary parties.[9] Nor could this "partisan" behavior be ascribed to local party feeling. In the debaucheries of this election, nothing resembling "party" in any meaningful sense of the word affected Northampton's voters.

Fortunately for the intelligibility of Table 6.1, partisan considerations cannot be discounted so completely in any other election, although complications frequently obstruct the interpretation of other electoral proportions. For instance, a striking overall difference separates the levels of split-voting in Norwich from those in the three remaining boroughs, yet the difference is paradoxical. Overall, Norwich voters split their votes far less frequently than normal for electors in Maidstone, Northampton, and Lewes, but just as the electors in these other towns were achieving unprecedentedly low levels of split-voting, the number of Norwich electors splitting their votes increased dramatically to a peak of almost 25 percent in 1790, double previous levels even for elections in the 1760s. Widely divergent levels of split-voting at Norwich and Northampton elections might have been expected from the discussion in the two preceding chapters that indicated the existence of full-blown

[9] J. C. Cox, *Records of the Borough of Northampton*, 2 vols., Northampton, 1898.

party politics in Norwich by 1780 (and some partisan activity as early as the 1760s), in contrast to the complete absence of local party organizations in Northampton. However, differences in the levels of sophistication of local partisan organizations which help explain the disparity between Norwich and Northampton do not explain the noticeable divergence of the behavior of electors in Maidstone and Lewes. Political activity in Lewes never achieved the pronounced national orientation attained in Maidstone. In fact, Maidstone partisan fervor fell only slightly short of the partisanship exhibited by Norwich voters. Thus, the general decline in split-voting at Maidstone elections, which corresponds nicely to increasing rancor of local partisan disputes, stands in sharp contrast to the rise in the number of splitters at Norwich elections, and it exacerbates the paradox already posed by the behavior of the Norwich voters. Local partisan activity in Norwich either increased or remained stable at a remarkably high level over the decades following the formation of the two parties, and, theoretically, levels of split-voting should have declined in response to this relatively constant pressure from Norwich election managers despite the fact that the exceedingly small proportion of the Norwich electorate splitting votes between the parties at the elections of the 1760s and 1770s left little room for improvement.[10] Why then did the number of Norwich splitters rise dramatically in 1790 and continue at an unprecedentedly elevated rate in 1796? And why did Maidstone voters begin to exhibit signs of strongly partisan behavior at the same time?

A structural rather than a behavioral consideration resolves this complicated paradox. The number of candidates involved in each contest explains much, though not all, of

[10] As illustrated in Table 6.1, the percentage of the electorate splitting their ballots in Norwich was less in 1761 than the lowest level achieved in the other boroughs. The four-man contests in the 1760s, however, with clearly defined, if locally oriented, parties, account for the remarkably low percentages in Norwich early on.

219

the variation in split-voting in individual boroughs over time. It also helps explain the major discrepancies between Norwich and the other boroughs, and the divergent trends in split-voting at Norwich and Maidstone elections. Only Norwich commonly experienced contests involving four candidates, and it seems clear that four-man contests were indispensable in the elimination of split-voting. In four-man contests where each party sponsored two candidates, fewer impediments stood between electors and partisan ballots—either party could be supported with both of an elector's votes. Elections involving only three candidates, standard fare except in Norwich, inevitably required plumping to support one of the two parties, and electors were understandably loath to waste one of their votes. In the nineteen contests held in Maidstone, Northampton, and Lewes during these four decades, only the 1774 race in Lewes involved four candidates. To make matters worse, all four candidates in 1774 were virtually identical politically, and the formation of a completely locally-oriented party (the Coalition) at the subsequent Lewes election in 1780 obviated any potential effect this solitary four-man race might have had on the Lewes electorate. Three candidates contested the remaining eighteen contests in Lewes, Northampton, and Maidstone. All but the Maidstone contest of 1784 that really involved two candidates vying for a single seat pitted two candidates of one party against one candidate from the other.

Norwich also experienced several three-man races, but two of them (1768 and 1784) degenerated into two-man contests for Norwich's second parliamentary seat alone; in both instances, Sir Harbord Harbord was generally acceptable to both sides and took his seat virtually without opposition. The two Norwich contests which saw a genuine battle between *three* candidates over two seats occurred in 1790 and 1796. Not coincidentally, on both occasions the number of Norwich voters splitting their votes rose to levels twice as high as those of earlier Norwich elections and fell

220

into line with the normally high levels of split-voting in the other constituencies. The frenetic and highly sophisticated partisan activity in Norwich proved inadequate to the challenge posed by three-man races. Voters simply refused in large numbers to throw away their second vote, party or no party. Hence, the persistence of split-voting in the Maidstone, Northampton, and Lewes electorates is less impressive than the real declines in splitting at the elections of the 1790s in the face of three-man contests.[11]

Voting patterns of Maidstone voters at municipal elections underline the significance of the number of candidates contesting an election. At those Maidstone parliamentary elections in which undivided support for the Whig candidate meant throwing away one vote, split-voting fell noticeably after 1780.[12] Yet the corresponding drop in levels of split-voting at Maidstone municipal elections occurred much more rapidly, in a more pronounced fashion, and with greater durability than at the parliamentary elections because these municipal elections, invariably contested over the same issues and by the same individuals that fought parliamentary elections, allowed voters to cast partisan ballots without penalty (Table 6.2). The number of candidates for the Maidstone common council varied widely, but the variance always corresponded exactly to the num-

[11] The proportion of split votes in Maidstone in 1796 had dropped to just one-third of the 1774 proportion. Similarly, Lewes split-voting fell in 1790 to one-half the 1780 level, and even in Northampton, 1796 saw an unexpected decline to 25 percent. All of this occurred in the face of three-man contests that forced "plumping" for independent partisan ballots.

[12] Using the uncertainty coefficient to measure consistent straight-party voting at Maidstone's municipal elections, two things became apparent. First, a very strong relationship existed between straight-party voters across Maidstone municipal elections. Second, the relationship, already strong by 1784, increased in strength through 1796 and maintained its strength in 1802. The scores across these two decades were: 1780 = .30, 1784 = .32, 1790 = .43, 1796 = .49, and 1802 = .41. These scores are impressively high and particularly revealing when compared to the parliamentary pattern in Figures 6.5 and 6.6.

221

ber of vacant seats on the council, and the two slates of candidates were exactly matched. Two slates of three candidates each vied for the three open council seats in 1788. Two slates, each comprised of seven candidates, stood for the seven open council seats in 1791 and again in 1793. Thus, at each municipal contest, an elector could cast votes equal to the number of vacant seats and, with the proposed slates of candidates invariably equal to the number of vacancies, each elector could vote a straight ticket and use all of the votes allocated to him no matter which party he chose. Since neither party required "necessary" plumps from electors at municipal contests, each received far fewer "unnecessary" plumps. Predictably, the level of split-voting at Maidstone city elections fell precipitously following the municipal contest of 1774. Less than 20 percent of the Maidstone electorate split their votes between the sets of candidates at the 1786 common council election, and the city elections of the 1790s experienced a further decline. On average, 7 percent of the voters at Maidstone municipal elections split their ballots after 1786. Nine of every ten cast straight-party votes, besting by a considerable margin the proportion of the electorate willing to cast strictly partisan ballots at the unevenly contested parliamentary elections. At a second election held in 1793 a few weeks after the larger election reported in Table 6.2, every one of the forty-four citizens participating in the brief election cast a straight-party ballot.[13] Parliamentary elections in Maidstone never elicited partisan behavior of comparable strength. As indicated by the behavior of the Norwich electors at the three-man contests of the 1790s, local parties could not count on the undivided support of the voters even in the most "partisan" constituencies unless they provided candidates to contest both (or all) of the available seats.

[13] Maidstone Municipal Records, Election Papers VII, KRO. Following the 1793 election involving six candidates from each party, another election was held to fill the seats of John Brenchley, George Bishop, and T. B. Hammonds, all deceased.

Table 6.2: Split Voting at Maidstone Parliamentary and Municipal
Contests (Percentage)

Election Year	Parliamentary Elections	Municipal Elections
1761	52.1	
1764		44.1
1768	42.4	30.5
1774	78.7	50.4
1780	77.4	
1784	52.6	
1786		17.4
1790	36.7	4.3
1791		5.9
1793		8.8
1796	23.4	
1799		6.1
1801		10.7
1802	59.1	

The incidence of plumping at parliamentary elections
reinforces the impression created by the apparent difficulty
encountered by parties engaged in three-candidate campaigns. Electors were not obligated to cast both votes under
any circumstances, and a party could contest both seats in
a campaign without attracting an individual elector's full
support, even if the party managed to win his undivided
support. Though this kind of behavior was possible and
potentially dangerous to a party's chances of victory, instances of "unnecessary" plumping were comparatively rare
in all boroughs. Electors were unwilling to waste a vote for
no good reason. To the dismay of many candidates standing alone, they tended to be equally loath to waste votes
for excellent reasons. Even Northampton's voters, the least
politicized of the lot, seldom chose not to use both votes in
parliamentary elections. Unnecessary plumps accounted for
just 3 percent of Northampton's vote over the five elections
contested there after 1761, and none of the other consti-
uency averages exceeded 10 percent. Indeed, of the nearly

223

twenty contested elections in these four boroughs, large numbers of unnecessary plumps were cast in a solitary election. Hints of the change in William Windham's party allegiance that did not actually occur until 1794 apparently contributed to the uncertainty that resulted in plumper votes by 34 percent of Norwich's electors, an unprecedented total, in the 1790 election. These wholesale defections to plumping were spread evenly through the ranks of Free Blue voters, but most revealing was the behavior of the Free Blue candidates themselves. Windham, as was his habit, voted for his ostensible running mate, Thomas Beevor, and not for himself. Beevor, on the other hand, cast a single vote in his own behalf, as did most of the electors that supported his candidacy. This willingness to cast single votes for Beevor in the face of Windham's political ambiguity seems to indicate a widespread and remarkably sophisticated perception of political issues among Norwich's electorate. Virtually all of these Norwich electors reverted to normal patterns at the by-election of 1794 and the general election of 1796, however, when Windham's new political position squarely in the Government's camp became clear. Curiously, Windham cast his first vote for himself in 1796, and unlike those of most of his supporters in that election, his vote was a plumper. Perhaps he felt more comfortable in his role as champion of the Administration and director of the war with France, at least comfortable enough to vote for himself.[14]

Moreover, despite the unmistakable aversion of electors in every borough toward unnecessary plumping, the rise in the levels of straight-party voting after the elections of the 1760s and '70s was accompanied by a marked increase in the willingness of Maidstone and Lewes voters to plump when necessary to support a party (Table 6.3). Norwich electors were not unwilling to plump if required by partisan considerations; rather the opposite. Their strong predis-

---

[14] In previous years, Windham invariably had voted for his opponents.

position to plump for single party candidates as early as 1768 left little room for improvement. Voters in Maidstone and Lewes simply fell into line with Norwich electors in the 1790s and exhibited a greater willingness to cast partisan plumper votes than in previous elections. In 1790, Maidstone voters finally managed to plump for single party candidates as frequently as the Norwich voters had plumped as early as 1768, and Northampton voters joined the group in 1796.

The 1796 Northampton election was not fought over political issues, and it was not fought by rival political parties. Spencer Perceval and the other two candidates ran their own campaigns without regard to the partisan preferences of the other men in the race. Even so, more striking political differences could not have distinguished the two principal candidates, the incumbents. A quarter of the Northampton electorate, having voted for Edward Bouverie, a Foxite Whig, could not be convinced to cast their other vote for either of the Tory candidates. Overall, Northampton voters behaved in an impressively partisan manner at the 1796 election in spite of Northampton's adverse political structure and apolitical climate. These increases in the numbers of necessary plumps during the 1790s changed the ratio between necessary and unnecessary plumps in three of the boroughs. One-half (52 percent) of all plumpers cast during the election of 1784 could be

Table 6.3: "Necessary" Plumping in Parliamentary General Elections (Percentage)

	1761	1768	1774	1780	1784	1790	1796	1802
Norwich	*	30.5	*	*	*	33.7	27.8	*
Maidstone	9.7	1.6	4.8	7.9	9.7	28.2	24.0	7.3
Lewes	NC	NA	*	4.8	NC	18.5	18.1	12.5
Northampton	NC	NA	5.6	NC	4.0	5.8	26.1	NC

* Plumping not necessary—i.e., four-man race
NC = no contest
NA = not applicable

justified by partisan considerations. By the next general election, necessary plumps accounted for three-fifths (61 percent) of all single votes. In 1796, almost nine-tenths (89 percent) of the plumpers in all of these boroughs cast politically defensible single votes.[15]

At the election of 1802, Norwich voters regained their normal pattern of solid partisan voting, recovering nicely from the irregularities of 1790 and 1796, but in Maidstone and Lewes, the 1802 election reversed the pattern of the 1790s. The sharp decline in the proportions of necessary plumps and the corresponding rise in the levels of split-voting at the 1802 contests is puzzling.[16] Whether the 1802 election was atypical in these three towns, or whether the trends of the 1780s and 1790s failed to persist into the early nineteenth century cannot be established without comparable data. However, examinations of Colchester, several Buckinghamshire boroughs, and the major Norfolk boroughs in the years immediately preceding the Great Reform Act suggest an atypical election in 1802. Party development appears to have continued unabated or indeed with increased tempo in the first third of the new century if the work of Speight, Davis, Hays, and others, is any indication.[17] But until truly comparable figures on splitting, plumping, and straight-party voting are compiled, the question must remain moot.

Votes cast at specific elections generally support the idea

[15] For example, in plumping for Bartlett Gurney, the Norwich voters were casting politically rational votes since Gurney was the solitary Opposition candidate. The Maidstone voters choosing to cast single ballots for Christopher Hull also voted reasonably since Hull, too, was the single choice open to opponents of Pitt's ministry.

[16] The general election of 1802 does not seem to have been atypical, and the change in Norwich and Maidstone is therefore all the more puzzling. V. Griffiths, *Picture of Parliament*, London, 1803.

[17] M. E. Speight, "Politics in the Borough of Colchester, 1812-47," Ph.D. diss., University of London, 1969; R. W. Davis, *Political Change and Continuity*, London, 1972; B. D. Hayes, "Politics in Norfolk, 1750-1832," Ph.D. diss., Cambridge University, 1958.

that partisan behavior increased in the last twenty years of the eighteenth century, but behavior at single elections reveals less than the behavior of individual electors at successive elections. A partisan vote at one election may well indicate some political awareness on the part of an elector, and it may be an indication of partisan behavior. In fact, the increasing levels of straight-party voting illustrated in Tables 6.1, 6.2, and 6.3 make a strong case for enhanced political awareness and partisan behavior in the electorate. The real test of partisanship, however, was the behavior of electors over time. Successive partisan votes and especially increasing numbers of voters casting successive partisan votes are much more convincing evidence of meaningful partisan behavior. Given the complexities created by the double vote, partisan voting across several elections required a great deal from individual voters. In addition to the possibility of switching from the full support of one party to a straight-party vote for the other party, electors could (and sometimes did) split their votes after casting a straight-party ballot at one election. Or, having split their votes at one contest, voters could cast straight-party ballots at the next. And, of course, electors could consistently split their votes between parties election after election. Whatever personal reasons might have prompted the division of an elector's support at one election, or several elections, neither split-voting nor inconsistent party voting indicate partisan ties or political awareness.[18]

A high "floating" vote characterized several early eighteenth-century elections, and the proclivity of Augustan electors to switch from party to party has been pointed to as an indication of constant decision making in the electorate. Their willingness to switch parties allegedly dem-

---

[18] For a further discussion of the ramifications of the double vote, see Jeremy Mitchell, "Electoral Change and the Party System in England, 1832-1868," Ph.D. diss., Yale University, 1976, pp. 291-318; Jeremy Mitchell, "Electoral Strategy Under Open Voting: Evidence from England, 1832-1880," *Public Choice* 28(1976):17-36.

onstrated the political awareness and interest of the electorate during the reign of Queen Anne and revealed the "participatory" nature of the electoral system. This scenario has been vigorously challenged recently, and seems somewhat limited as an explanation of Augustan popular politics, but however appropriate or inappropriate for popular political behavior in the age of Anne, it must be stood on end for an explanation of the behavior of voters after the accession of George III.[19]

In the years following the Wilkes affair, divisive political issues began to lend ideological meaning to the increasingly well-defined parliamentary parties. These issues, like the India Bill and the question of the use of the royal prerogative were not invariably identified with specific parties, nor were all of the members of the nascent parliamentary parties invariably in agreement. Matthew Bloxham, for instance, was a Tory of the first rank, being returned for Maidstone in 1788 with Government assistance and the full support of the Maidstone Ministerialists under John Brenchley. Bloxham supported Pitt consistently but voted for the repeal of the Test Act in 1789 and favored its repeal in 1790. He changed his mind in 1791, though, and voted against repeal. Despite individual members like Bloxham who waffled on major issues and peculiarities like Lord North's alliance with the Opposition to the Government after 1784, the parliamentary parties frequently maintained stable postures. The Opposition party argued consistently for peace, condemning both the American and French Wars, and the Oppositionists were generally more tolerant of Nonconformity, particularly after the excesses of the French Revolution began to alter the attitudes of men like Bloxham. With the additional stability lent by the

[19] W. A. Speck et al., "Computer Analysis of Pollbooks: An Initial Report," *BIHR* 43(1970):105-12. The challenge has been posed by Norma Landau, "Independence, Deference, and Voter Participation: The Behaviour of the Electorate in Early-Eighteenth-Century Kent," *Historical Journal* 22(1979):561-83.

local parties, a definite if somewhat vaguely defined political choice began to confront the electors in these four boroughs. Increasingly, a Ministerial vote could be distinguished from an anti-Ministerial vote on several grounds. Hence the political system mandated consistency, not inconsistency, from the electorate, despite its idiosyncracies. The most politically rational choice open to an elector at contests in these boroughs, assuming relatively stable political preferences among the voting public, was a straight-party vote at one election followed by a straight-party vote for the same party at the subsequent election. Political awareness was demonstrated by a voter's loyal support of *one* of the parties, not by instability on the part of the electorate (floating voters). And, in light of the many studies of political socialization in several countries (including Butler's examination of modern Britain) which argue that attachments to political parties (as well as other social organizations) increase with the duration of the attachment, the increasing political awareness emerging out of the new political conditions of the 1780s and '90s should have led to higher levels of partisan "loyalty" over time.[20] Adam Przeworski has pointed to "stable patterns of behavior" as one of the most important hallmarks of "developed" political systems.[21] For the later eighteenth century, at least, Przeworski's contention holds true. Successive straight-party voters demonstrated political maturity. Therefore, the number of "straights" (straight-party voters) at each contest should have increased over these eight elections in Norwich and Maidstone certainly, and possibly elsewhere, while the number of "floaters" should have declined commensurately.

The basis of this partisan behavior, however, differs significantly from many other situations in one important respect. In looking for "partisan identification," some studies

[20] Butler and Stokes, *Political Change in Britain*, p. 42.

[21] Adam Przeworski, "Contextual Models of Political Behavior," *Political Methodology* 1(1974):44-50.

have tested the theory that "most voters identify with a party in their youth and stay loyal to it through their lives."[22] J. H. Plumb referred to such a conceptual framework in asking whether or not the early eighteenth-century electorate "was born to its political commitment."[23] But with the possible exception of those voters just entering the electorate at the turn of the nineteenth century, it seems unlikely that partisan allegiances were acquired by the members of the unreformed electorates examined here at an early stage in their lives. Partisan allegiances, where they existed, probably were not learned by these voters in their youth simply because the parties with which they might have identified did not exist during their childhoods, at least not in the shape that they existed subsequently. A middle-aged Norwich "Tory" of 1784 could hardly have learned his partisan affiliation at his father's knee. The more plausible alternative suggested herein explains the growth of partisan ties in response to the newly emerging importance of the parties and the increasing clarity of the issues at the relatively frequent elections held after 1761.

Norwich is the most suitable of the four boroughs in which to seek evidence of this posited rise in straight-party voting and corresponding decline in the "floating" vote. Split-voting at single elections was less common in Norwich than in the three other boroughs, somewhat simplifying the measurement of consistent and inconsistent party voting. However, the elevated levels of consistent straight-party voting common in Norwich as early as the elections of the 1760s limited any potential increase in party loyalty among Norwich's voters. The proportion of consistent straight-party voters rose slowly over the period, nonetheless, broken only by the plunge in 1796 caused primarily by some of Windham's former backers remaining loyal to him in spite of his shift of parties. Several of those who chose to

[22] Speck, "A Further Report," p. 86.

[23] J. H. Plumb, "The Growth of the Electorate in England from 1600-1715," *Past and Present* 45(1969):90-116.

remain in Windham's camp recorded excellent reasons for doing so, but surprisingly, Windham's supporters did not prove as loyal as might have been expected after such a long association.[24] An overwhelming majority of the voters formerly casting ballots for Windham remained "Blue-and-White" rather than following Windham to the "Orange-and-Purple" fold, demonstrating their political awareness quite effectively in the process. Thirty-six percent of Windham's 1790 supporters remained loyal to him in 1796, while almost 50 percent of those casting votes for Windham in 1790 cast straight-party ballots (plumpers no less!) for the single Free Blue candidate, Bartlett Gurney, in 1796. The loyalty of the minority of Windham's followers affected the level of consistent party voting reported in Figure 6.1, but does not alter the impression of increasing partisan loyalty conveyed by the steady upward trend at the other elections. Consistent straight-party voting reached its zenith in the ensuing "normal" election of 1802, continuing the general overall rise that can be summarized best with a least-squares regression line. Despite being depressed by the unusual results of the 1796 election, the slope for the straight-party voters is positive, albeit not pronounced ($+1.14$), and the steady advance over the period is unmistakable. More striking, though, is the degree to which Norwich electors fulfilled the second expectation. The number of voters who changed their partisan affiliation (floated) between elections declined substantially from a peak of over 30 percent in the elections before 1784 to just over 10 percent in 1802 (Figure 6.1). Again, the only break in the decline that had fallen below 10 percent by 1790 accompanied Windham's party switch in 1794, thus reinforcing instead of contradicting the general pattern of decline. The steep downward slope of a regression line plotted through these points (-4.62) emphasizes the de-

[24] Only 288 (41.4 percent) of the 695 voters who supported Windham in 1790 and also voted in 1796 gave him their votes again.

231

creasing tendency of Norwich voters to switch their allegiances from one party to another at successive elections; the temporary shift in 1796 was followed by another decline, and overall, ignoring the remarkably steep fall in 1790, the pattern pointed steadily downward.[25]

Voting patterns in the other party-contested boroughs

FIGURE 6.1   *Straight-Party and Floating Voters at Norwich Elections*

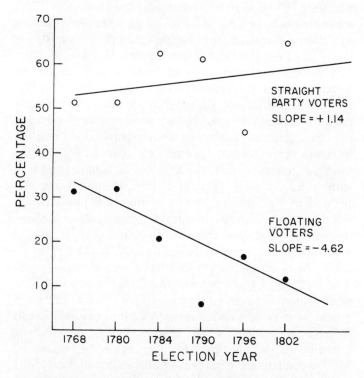

[25] A least-squares regression line may seem an odd choice of measure with so few data points in each of these figures, but a regression line possessed the one distinct advantage of summarizing easily and quickly the patterns in Norwich despite its internal complexity. Linear regression lines were less appropriate for summarizing the changes in the voting habits of electors in the other three boroughs.

also support the hypothesis, although the exaggerated changes in voting patterns at elections in both Lewes and Maidstone reversed the model set by the Norwich electorate. The early partisanship of Norwich voters left little room for improvement, and Figure 6.1 highlighted instead the decline in the number of "floating" voters. Conversely, the genuine "floating" vote was so negligible from the first elections in Maidstone and Lewes that very little downward movement was possible (Figures 6.2 and 6.3). Three-man elections reduced "floating" by drastically increasing the amount of split-voting common in both boroughs. In fact, though the number of floating voters declined slightly in Maidstone after 1780 and also declined marginally in Lewes, single instances of higher levels of floating in early elections would have resulted in negative slopes in both towns if regression lines had been statistically appropriate. The situation actually can be summarized more easily; there were almost no floating voters in either constituency in the first place, and their virtual absence is notable at each of the contested elections before and including 1802. Thus, the general trends fall exactly in line with expectations. On the other hand, a pronounced rise in party loyalty occurred suddenly in Maidstone with the 1784 election and even more drastically in Lewes by 1790. Regression lines, if plotted, would be strongly positive. Maidstone and Lewes voters responded in much the same manner to the changing political environment as their counterparts in Norwich. All three boroughs experienced a major upsurge in partisan behavior.

The measurement of the changes in the voting habits of each electorate reflected in the three figures examined so far, although accurate, is not complete. An accurate comparison of differences among these electorates must also take into account the number of voters in each borough behaving in either a consistently partisan or a consistently nonpartisan manner. Despite their increasing partisanship, voters in neither Maidstone nor Lewes behaved in as con-

233

FIGURE 6.2   *Straight-Party and Floating Voters at Maidstone Elections*

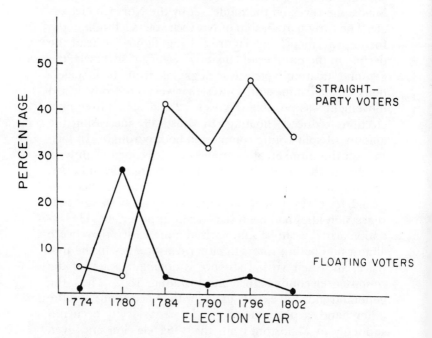

sistently partisan a fashion as electors in Norwich. The combined partisan vote (i.e., consistent or floating) left a very small proportion of the Norwich electorate unaccounted for, yet failed to account for as many as half of the voters in Maidstone and Lewes at specific elections. Table 6.4 reveals the continuation of split-voting, particularly consistent split-voting, among Maidstone and Lewes electors in contrast to the overwhelmingly partisan behavior of Norwich voters. These figures underscore the impact of three-man races in determining electoral behavior. Levels of consistent split-voting were most comparable among all three boroughs (excluding Northampton) at the elections of 1790 and 1796, and it is not a coincidence that these were the elections at which Norwich experienced genuine three-man

234

FIGURE 6.3   *Straight-Party and Floating Voters at Lewes Elections*

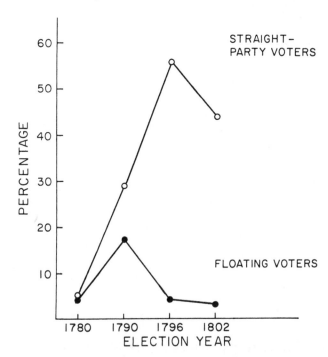

contests rather than the customary four-man campaigns. Nevertheless, the number of nonpartisan voters in Maidstone and Lewes during and after the 1784 elections strengthens the already persuasive patterns evident in Figures 6.1 through 6.3. A noticeably higher proportion of both electorates cast partisan ballots in 1784, 1790, and 1796 than in earlier elections. At the 1802 general election, nonpartisanship regained some of the ground it had lost, but the declines of the 1790s are no less convincing.

In the absence of political parties actively engaged in contesting elections, it is hardly surprising that Northampton failed to sustain an increase in consistent party voting in the elections after 1780. On the other hand, the number

235

Table 6.4: Nonpartisan Voting Patterns across General Elections
(Percentage Repeating Voters Only)

	1761-1768	1768-1774	1774-1780	1780-1784	1784-1790	1790-1796	1796-1802
Norwich							
Party to Split	2.4	NC	12.3	2.0	22.3	12.8	2.6
Split to Party	11.5	NC	2.3	11.5	2.8	17.8	19.4
Consistent Split	.1	NC	NC	1.2	1.2	6.7	.6
Maidstone							
Party to Split	30.4	42.9	1.9	45.5	11.9	14.6	39.9
Split to Party	33.7	18.6	58.4	2.1	29.0	24.2	3.4
Consistent Split	12.9	16.4	6.4	7.2	25.2	12.6	21.2
Lewes							
Party to Split	NC	NA	23.4	NC	17.2	18.2	27.9
Split to Party	NC	NA	33.0	NC	31.0	11.9	11.5
Consistent Split	NC	NA	34.0	NC	10.5	9.1	13.4
Northampton							
Party to Split	NC	24.1	NC	39.2	29.8	6.7	NC
Split to Party	NC	2.3	NC	14.1	9.6	36.9	NC
Consistent Split	NC	.2	NC	9.1	32.7	22.8	NC

NA = not applicable
NC = no contest

of electors who completely changed their party preferences dramatically and unexpectedly decreased over the period (Figure 6.4). By the 1790s, the proportion of "floaters" in Northampton had dwindled to levels comparable to those found in Maidstone and Lewes (Figures 6.2 and 6.3). Although a rise in the number of electors who consistently split their votes or who alternated between party voting and split-voting partially offset this decided fall in the number of "floating" voters at Northampton elections, the lack of a commensurate decline in the number of straight-party voters accompanying the decline in the ranks of the "floating" voters reinforces the possibility that the Northampton electorate was not entirely impervious to political events after the heated contest of 1784. Rather, the election of

1784 may have politicized some Northampton voters.[26] The 1784 Northampton contest was more blatantly political than any of its predecessors, and certainly the numbers of both "loyal" and "floating" voters differed radically in the two succeeding elections; the steep increase in the former at the 1790 election was coupled with a sharp decrease in the latter, and this pattern persisted in 1796. Hence, patterns of electoral behavior changed in all four boroughs over the decades following the accession of George III, and, most

FIGURE 6.4   *Straight-Party and Floating Voters at Northampton Elections*

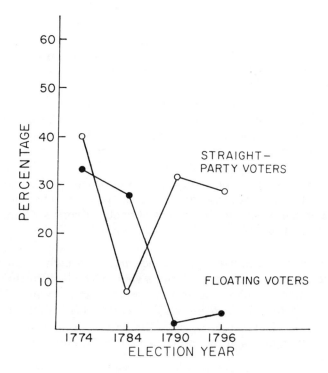

[26] Lewis Namier and J. Brooke, *The House of Commons, 1754-1790*, 3 vols., London, 1964, 1:13, 2:346.

importantly, these changes indicate electorates increasingly prone to politically "rational" behavior, even in Northampton.

COMPARATIVE PARTISAN BEHAVIOR

The preceding analysis does not provide an adequate basis for comparing the relative changes in each of the boroughs over these years because so frequently specific circumstances surrounding individual elections complicate or invalidate direct comparisons. A comparative assessment of behavior across all boroughs and across time rather than in a single borough across these elections requires a more inclusive measure of the consistency of electoral behavior from one election to the next. If, instead of measuring only partisan behavior as in Figure 6.4, the relationship between electoral decisions at successive elections is considered by including the full range of choices open to each voter, a useful basis is established for contrasting the changes in each borough electorate (Figure 6.5). The "uncertainty coefficient" which provides the comparison in Figure 6.5 measures the relationship between an elector's choices in two successive elections on a scale ranging from -1 to $+1$. Essentially, this coefficient indicates the "proportion by which 'uncertainty' in the dependent variable (a voter's second vote in this case) is reduced by knowledge of the independent variable (that voter's initial vote)." Reductions in the level of "uncertainty" and the correspondingly greater success in predicting an elector's vote on the basis his former choice result in higher positive (or negative) scores. If each elector's first vote invariably predicted his second vote, unity is achieved (either $+1$ if the parties were invariably the same, or -1 if they were invariably different).[27]

[27] The "uncertainty coefficient" seemed most appropriate for testing the relationships between these nominal-level variables. Since the second vote could hardly be other than the dependent variable, the figures in Figures 6.5 and 6.6 are the asymmetric values of the coefficient. Norman

FIGURE 6.5   *Consistent Straight, Split, and Floating Voters at Successive Parliamentary Elections*

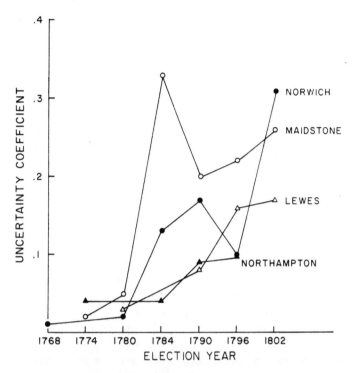

The relationships between the four borough electorates measured in this fashion by Figure 6.5 correspond almost exactly with the expectations raised by the discussion in Chapters 3 and 4 of the varying incentives for partisan development among the four constituencies. Politically coherent behavior of a different magnitude developed among voters in Maidstone and Norwich where impressively high and generally increasing scores in excess of .15 marked elections after 1780. The development of consistent par-

Nie et al., *Statistical Package for the Social Sciences*, New York, 1975, pp. 226-27.

tisan behavior among Lewes electors far outdistanced the almost negligible change in the Northampton electorate at the elections following 1784. The votes of Lewes electors at the election of 1790 predicted a significant portion of their behavior in 1796, and their 1796 votes predicted their behavior in 1802 even more successfully. The deviation resulting from the peculiar circumstances in Norwich in 1796 is still evident in Figure 6.5 as it was in Figure 6.1 and Table 6.1, but discounting this aberration, the shifts in Norwich and Maidstone occurred a decade earlier and were of a different magnitude than those in the less politically active and less politically sophisticated environments of Lewes and Northampton. However, the formation of the Coalition in Lewes in 1780 had a measurable impact on the Lewes electorate; there too, parties were "crucial in structuring the behavior of the electorate" beginning in 1784, albeit never as crucial as in Norwich and Maidstone where nationally oriented political parties fought electoral battles fiercely.

If all voters who consistently split their votes between parties at election after election are excluded from consideration, the already strong relationship linking partisan voting at successive elections with relative party development and local political structures is strengthened considerably. Using the uncertainty coefficient again, Figure 6.6 measures the partisan loyalty of those electors in each town who always cast partisan ballots (including occasional unnecessary plumps).[28] As much as Figure 6.5, this comparison of the boroughs points to the far higher degree of partisan loyalty among the voters in Maidstone by the election of 1784. The discrepancy between Norwich and Maidstone actually increased over the last three elections of the century. Voters in both boroughs showed a pronounced

[28] Thus in Figure 6.6, the "splitters to party," "party to split," and "consistently split" votes in Table 6.4 were excluded to allow an assessment of the behavior of strictly partisan voters, though not necessarily partisan in the same fashion at each election.

240

FIGURE 6.6 *Consistent Straight-Party Voting at Norwich, Maidstone, and Lewes Elections*

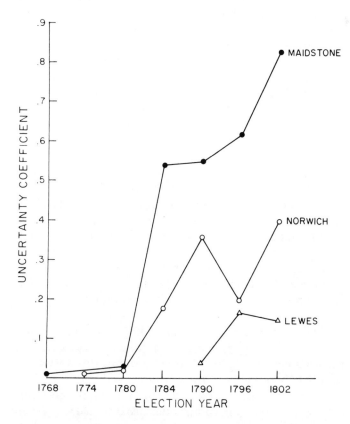

and growing tendency to support the same party at each election in which they voted, but while the votes of Norwich electors at one contest predicted their votes at subsequent elections with increasing accuracy, Maidstone partisan votes began to be almost infallible predictors of future behavior. While Norwich's partisan voters evinced an impressively strong tendency to vote for the same party at successive elections by 1802 (as shown by the uncertainty coefficient

241

of +.4), Maidstone's partisan voters attained a strikingly high level of partisan loyalty (+.83). As early as 1784, this index of partisanship in Maidstone reached a very impressive +.54. In the 1780s, Maidstone Ministerialists at one election were likely to vote for Ministerialist candidates at the next election, and vice versa. By the end of the century, Maidstone "independent" and Ministerialist voters were almost certain to remain within their respective party folds. In comparison, partisan voters in Norwich floated from one party to the other much more frequently, though they remained reasonably loyal to their original choice of parties. Conversely, Lewes voters floated more often than not and, while behaving more consistently after 1790 than before, were never willing to vote consistently in great numbers. The end of the original Lewes Coalition in 1796 may have hindered their progress toward partisanship, if the minor changes in the 1790s can be called progress. However, the apparently greater loyalty of the Maidstone electorate delineated in Figure 6.6 misrepresents the overall relationship linking individual voters to parties in Maidstone and Norwich. This deficiency is remedied by Table 6.5.

The measurement of partisan loyalty among partisan voters exclusively in Figure 6.6 considered proportions of the total electorates of all three boroughs that varied substantially both between the boroughs and over time in individual boroughs. These differences in the proportionate numbers of strictly partisan voters are essential to a general

Table 6.5: Percentages of the Electorate Included in Figure 6.6
(Partisan Voters)

	1761-1768	1768-1774	1774-1780	1780-1784	1784-1790	1790-1796	1796-1802
Norwich	86.0	NA	85.4	83.9	73.5	62.6	77.3
Maidstone	31.3	8.4	16.6	45.2	33.9	48.5	35.5
Lewes	NA	NA	NA	NA	41.3	60.8	47.2

NA = not applicable

measurement of partisan loyalties and partisan ties in Norwich and Maidstone. The persistence of three-man contests in Maidstone led to a continuation of split-voting by many Maidstone voters, and a majority of the Maidstone freemen never cast consistent straight-party ballots. Straight-party voters came closest to comprising a majority at the elections of 1784 and 1796. At the three other elections following 1774, only a third of the electorate cast successive straight-party ballots. In every instance split-voting dominated the voting patterns of electors returning to participate in their second (or more) election. Hence Table 6.5, which is nothing more than the reciprocal of Table 6.4, makes it clear that the major transformation altering voting patterns in both Maidstone and Norwich affected the electorates in the two boroughs quite differently.[29] Maidstone voters in toto did not necessarily surpass the partisanship demonstrated by Norwich voters as Figure 6.6 seems to indicate. Actually, while the Maidstone voters won over to partisan voting were more intensely and consistently loyal than electors in Norwich, relatively few Maidstone voters proved capable of sustained partisan behavior. The Maidstone voters who *were* sufficiently mobilized by the local parties to render their undivided support at successive elections evinced a greater polarization than their Norwich counterparts, but this polarization was offset by the far higher level of partisanship found in the Norwich electorate generally. The overwhelming majority of the Norwich electorate was sufficiently mobilized by the local parties to cast consistently partisan ballots; the proportion of returning Norwich electors included in Figure 6.6 never fell below 60 percent, and averaged almost 80 percent. Their partisan loyalty was weaker than the impressively loyal Maidstone voters, but it is difficult to determine which electorate was the more politicized. The

[29] Obviously, the figures in Tables 6.4 and 6.5 total 100 percent since all repeating voters are taken into account in one or the other. Equally obviously, these totals are unrelated to Table 6.1 that includes *all* voters instead of just repeating voters.

243

Norwich parties were more generally effective in mobilizing the electorate; the Maidstone parties, while less able to prevent split-voting, were amazingly successful in preventing the disaffection of their former supporters.

A party's electoral success did not depend upon its ability to mobilize and maintain the support of experienced voters alone. Effectiveness in recruiting voters just entering the electorate could be critical, as well as their relative success in "crystallizing" the support of those voters who had split their votes in previous contests.[30] The potentially significant, and quite possibly decisive, impact of "new" and previously nonpartisan voters is obvious from the proportionate numbers of new voters at each election (Table 3.1) and the large number of split-voters identified in Table 6.4, particularly in Maidstone and Lewes. Frequently as many as a third of the electors at any of these elections were voting in their first parliamentary contest. Experienced voters were critical to the development of partisan politics, but party leaders in Norwich and Maidstone must have realized the necessity of attracting as well as maintaining voters. Certainly the level of propaganda accompanying most campaigns implies a recognition of electioneering as a means of polling the apathetic and convincing waverers in addition to winning converts from the other party's ranks and continuing to attract the votes of former party adherents.[31]

Oddly, the electioneering process seems to have had a minimal impact on voters just entering the electorate (Table 6.6). Neither party in Maidstone or Norwich could chalk up a disproportionate gain among inexperienced voters. The similarity of the voting patterns of experienced and

[30] Jean Blondel, *Voters, Parties, and Leaders*, Harmondsworth, 1963, p. 70; Henry Degras, *How People Vote*, London, 1956; and the entire range of studies of American voting behavior, most notably Bernard Berelson et al., *Voting*, Chicago, 1954.

[31] As Speck notes, "it seemed inconceivable that these [the vast quantities of propaganda] represented so much wasted ink and paper." Speck, "A Further Report," p. 65.

Table 6.6: Recruitment of New Voters and Mobilization of
Experienced Voters: Norwich and Maidstone
(Percentage)

	All Voters	New Voters	Experienced Voters
Maidstone			
1784			
Taylor-Geary	25.4	25.5	27.9
Taylor-Edwards	27.9	22.3	24.8
Geary-Edwards	21.9	29.1	25.0
Taylor	9.7	7.3	8.9
Geary	3.8	3.6	3.4
Edwards	11.3	12.1	10.1
1802			
Bloxham-Major	18.7	19.3	19.6
Bloxham-Durrand	36.3	35.9	37.7
Major-Durrand	22.8	24.2	23.4
Bloxham	6.5	5.1	4.7
Major	8.2	8.3	7.5
Durrand	7.3	7.2	7.2
Norwich			
1784			
Hobart-Harbord	41.6	39.8	42.9
Hobart-Windham	1.7	1.6	2.0
Harbord-Windham	46.4	46.9	45.3
Hobart	5.2	5.1	5.2
Harbord	2.5	3.5	2.6
Windham	2.5	3.1	1.9
1802			
Windham-Frere	44.3	43.0	45.6
Smith-Fellowes	49.4	50.0	48.5
Smith-Windham	1.8	2.0	1.8
Frere-Fellowes	.2	.3	.2
Smith-Frere	.8	.6	1.1
Windham-Fellowes*	.3	.6	.1

* The Norwich vote in 1802 has been abbreviated in this table because
the single votes cast were also distributed equally by the three groups of
voters. The vote distributions for other elections have not been included
because the distributions were equally alike.

newly entering electors over the eight general elections implies one of two things. Either partisan efforts were equally successful in winning new partisans, or they were equally unsuccessful; new voters behaved very much like old voters, and not just in terms of partisan decisions. Across the entire spectrum of possible vote combinations resulting from the double vote, the voting patterns of inexperienced voters matched those of returning electors. Table 6.6 includes the votes of Maidstone and Norwich electors in 1784 and 1802. Expanding its focus to any other contested election in these two freeman boroughs would not alter substantially the similarity of the voting patterns. New voters were just as likely to split, plump unnecessarily, or cast fully partisan ballots as the voters returning to participate in their second (or more) election. It may be true that the "swing of the pendulum [in modern elections] is caused mainly by the new voters and nonvoters," but election outcomes in Norwich and Maidstone were impervious to the presence of new voters in the electorate. Nonvoting also apparently had very little impact since all indications are that very few qualified voters missed opportunities to exercise their franchises.[32]

Party gains from the ranks of former splitters also balanced almost exactly the previous party adherents who subsequently divided their loyalties. At the 1768 Norwich election, the Ministerialists gained *two* additional votes from the variations in split-voting, and the net gains by either party at the elections of 1780, 1784, and 1790 produced less than forty new supporters. The major Ministerialist coup in winning split-voters produced a net increase of 130 votes (5.7 percent of the total) in 1796 followed by a net loss to the Whigs in 1802 of 173 (6.1 percent). Maidstone parties gained and lost voters to split-voting at a somewhat more impressive rate. Net party bonuses ranged from the Whig edge of 5 votes in 1802 to the maximum of 126 votes

[32] William Ivor Jennings, *Party Politics*, 3 vols., Cambridge, 1961, 1:305.

(19.7 percent of all votes cast) captured by the Ministerialists in 1784, no doubt largely the result of the widespread antipathy evoked by Charles Fox and his India Bill.[33]
Hence, neither party succeeded generally in winning support at the expense of the other. Movements within the
electorate were often extensive, but the net result was stability in most instances. The number of straight-party voters lost to splitting offset the number of splitters won to
straight-party voting; Whig gains among ex-Tories generally offset Tory converts from the Whig camp.

But if electioneering had little measurable net affect in
the boroughs with two strong parties, where the parties
were unequally matched and also unable to benefit from
national issues or national support, relative partisan success
in winning and retaining support could be decidedly different. Variations in split-voting were of even less overall
importance in Lewes. Neither party ever made a respectable inroad into the numerous splitters. Net gains at Lewes
elections never exceeded 2 percent, yet the successes of the
Lewes parties in recruiting and mobilizing voters affected
election outcomes significantly. Unlike the constancy of
partisan endeavors in Norwich and Maidstone, the electoral
appeals of the Lewes "Coalition," though reasonably successful in winning adherents among new voters, fell on
relatively stony ground among experienced electors in the
very first Lewes election (1780) contested along these lines.
In succeeding elections, the Coalition continued to win new
electors while retaining most of their earlier partisans. The
organization of the Lewes "independents" never matched
the vigorous Coalition activity during contested elections
there. The "independents" were most successful among
new voters, but from the sparseness of the surviving evidence of "independent" activity, it seems highly unlikely
that the "independents" were capable of waging a viable

[33] J. Hartley, *A History of the Westminster Election*, London, 1784; John
Cannon, *The Fox-North Coalition*, London, 1969; M. D. George, "Fox's
Martyrs," *TRHS*, 4th ser., 21(1939):133-68.

campaign against the Coalition.[34] In addition to pointing
very clearly to the weakness inherent in single-candidate
campaigns, the partisan choices of Lewes voters confirm
the disparity in the sophistication and efficacy of the two
Lewes political organizations, just as the virtual standoff in
partisan recruitment at Norwich and Maidstone elections
documented the capable election efforts of both parties in
these two boroughs (Table 6.7). The Lewes Coalition proved
its ability to attract large numbers of voters while retaining
previous supporters time and again. The independents
managed at best to attract a quarter of the new voters in
the electorate at any election, and failed even more miser-
ably to maintain voters from election to election. With a
single exception, former party support lost to splitting, and
party voters won from earlier split-voters, proved far less
critical to Lewes election outcomes than the retention of
old voters and the winning of new recruits. Henry Shelley,
the independent candidate in 1802, unseated a Coalitionist

Table 6.7: Party Preferences of New Voters and Mobilization of
Experienced Voters: Lewes (Percentage)

	Coalition	Independent	Split
1780			
New Voters	58.2	9.1	32.7
Experienced Voters	48.4	2.1	49.5
1790			
New Voters	56.7	23.5	19.8
Experienced Voters	61.0	10.1	28.9
1796			
New Voters	50.8	24.6	24.6
Experienced Voters	58.0	14.7	27.3
1802			
New Voters	33.9	18.7	47.4
Experienced Voters	48.5	10.3	41.2

[34] There are no indications of any serious political activity on the part
of Lewes's "independent" candidates in the elections of the 1780s and
1790s in either newspapers or manuscript collections.

with a six-vote margin by winning a slightly larger share of the former split-vote.

The remarkable similarity of the voting patterns of returning and beginning electors in Norwich and Maidstone suggests that continued participation at elections had little effect on voters, and the behavior of electors who voted in at least three parliamentary elections corroborates this interpretation. Norwich voters with at least ten years in the electorate and two prior parliamentary elections to their credit cast votes much as the other electors, and were no more likely to be partisan, nonpartisan, or "floaters" than the rest (Table 6.8). Nor did long-term participants and inexperienced voters in Maidstone behave differently. Aggregate measurements of the voting choices of three-time voters, however, fail to address the potentially more inter-

Table 6.8: "Experienced" Norwich Voters
(Percentage of Those Participating in Their Third Parliamentary Election)

	Straight Party Votes	Complete Party Switch	Votes Split Between Parties
1780			
All Voters	51.4	34.0	12.6
Experienced Voters	50.6	35.4	13.4
1784			
All Voters	62.4	21.5	1.7
Experienced Voters	63.8	20.7	1.8
1790			
All Voters	61.4	12.1	24.6
Experienced Voters	60.5	12.4	24.0
1796			
All Voters	45.2	17.6	18.7
Experienced Voters	45.2	17.7	21.1
1802			
All Voters	65.3	12.0	3.1
Experienced Voters	66.0	11.3	2.9

esting question concerning the effects of repeated *partisan* behavior. Studies of electoral behavior in modern Britain also have pointed to the relative unimportance of the length of time an individual spends in the electorate.[35] Instead of merely the duration of electoral participation, the "duration of party support," plays a critical role in strengthening party loyalty among late twentieth-century English voters. Admittedly, these data do not permit a very sophisticated measure of the effects of long-term party support among late eighteenth-century voters, but the partisan choices of electors in Norwich and Maidstone who cast successive partisan ballots conform to the pattern of modern voters. Support for the same party at successive elections rose substantially among Norwich voters during the last elections of the century (Table 6.9), and longer partisan attachments

Table 6.9: Effects of Partisanship: Party Choices of Previous Party Voters; Norwich and Maidstone (Percentage)

	1780	*1790*	*1802*
Norwich			
Whig Voters in *One* Prior Election			
Anti-Ministerialist	64.2	85.8	93.3
Ministerialist	35.8	14.2	6.7
Whig Voters in *Two* Prior Elections			
Anti-Ministerialist	78.6	94.2	96.8
Ministerialist	21.4	5.8	3.2
Maidstone			
Administration Voters in *One* Prior Election			
Anti-Administration	42.9	18.7	20.2
Administration	57.1	81.4	79.8
Administration Voters in *Two* Prior Elections			
Anti-Administration	39.5	7.3	9.5
Administration	60.5	92.7	90.5

[35] Butler and Stokes, *Political Change in Britain*, p. 42.

improved the chances of subsequent partisan support. By 1802, a previous partisan vote from a Norwich "Whig" virtually assured a second Whig vote from that elector, and two party votes for either party in Norwich elections (or for the Ministerialists in Maidstone) almost guaranteed a third party vote as early as 1790. Long-term support for the Maidstone anti-Ministerialists and the Norwich Ministerialists, not included in Table 6.9, did not lead to continued support equally well. Yet an increase in the length of a voter's "partisan attachment" significantly enhanced the probability that the same party would be chosen again, although the 97 percent partisan loyalty of two-time "Whig" voters in the Norwich election of 1802 pales somewhat in comparison to the 93 percent loyalty rate of all returning "Whig" voters. Partisan behavior, not voting experience by itself, affected these electors.

The relationship between partisan loyalties and time among Lewes electors is less clear (Table 6.10). At the election of 1796, voters who had cast *one* vote previously for the Coalition were more likely to do so again than those who had voted for the Coalition twice before. So too, one-time independent voters in 1796 cast proportionately more independent votes than two-time independents. Yet during the preceding and succeeding elections, the normal pattern exhibited by Maidstone and Norwich electors emerged in strength; the likelihood of an elector's continued support for a party was directly related to the number of votes previously cast for that party. Discounting the 1796 Lewes election, partisan behavior increased directly with the duration of partisan attachment. However, the correlation between *one* previous vote for a party and continued support for that party was so strong, and growing, that long duration was in a sense unnecessary.

Isolating and identifying partisan behavior is one thing; explaining it is something else again. The growth of the parliamentary parties and the more coherent and cohesive local partisan organizations provided frameworks around

251

Table 6.10: Effects of Partisanship: Party Choices of Previous Party
Voters; Lewes (Percentage)

	1796	1802
Coalition Voters in		
One Prior Election		
Coalition	77.0	67.0
"Independent"	23.0	33.0
Coalition Voters in		
Two Prior Elections		
Coalition	71.4	76.1
"Independent"	28.6	23.9
"Independent" Voters in		
One Prior Election		
Coalition	28.6	22.1
"Independent"	71.4	77.9
"Independent" Voters in		
Two Prior Elections		
Coalition	44.4	11.1
"Independent"	55.6	88.9

which political conflicts could flourish in the last two decades of the eighteenth century. The question is, were the
bases of the conflicts more than, or even other than, political? The pursuit of this question requires another look at
the pollbooks and some additional information concerning
individual electors.

CHAPTER SEVEN

The Voter's Decision: The Social Foundations of the Vote

M ANY OF THE QUESTIONS which began this study of electoral behavior have been addressed, in spite of the complex and frequently idiosyncratic nature of the unreformed political system. The development of partisan behavior after 1780 within the framework created both by the parliamentary parties and local partisan organizations has been identified in two of the four boroughs examined. Partisan behavior on an impressive scale shaped elections in Norwich and Maidstone as competing political parties closely identified with national issues and the parliamentary parties began to dominate local as well as national elections. Even voters in Northampton and Lewes, while never achieving the political sophistication of electors in Norwich and Maidstone, occasionally proved susceptible to the influence of national political developments. Yet, so far the behavior of these electorates has been assessed in political terms almost exclusively, ignoring, by and large, the question posed indirectly by the initial discussion of voting procedure and directly by the subsequent description of the issues raised at specific elections. At the Norwich contest described in the first chapter, Thomas Ward, a common cordwainer, supported the Free Blues, while Robert Starkey, a self-ascribed gentleman, plumped for the solitary Orange-and-Purple candidate. Were the votes of these men a reflection of underlying social tensions in the often acute cleavages of later eighteenth-century English society? Can such tensions, if they existed, be identified from an analysis of the voting habits of men like Ward, Starkey, and their fellow voters who followed one of the myriad occupations found in urban settings? The pronounced partisan behavior of Norwich and Maidstone voters points to an increasingly categorical and rigidly defined political cleavage in the electorate, leaving the question of whether or not differences other than explicitly political ones provided the foundation for the heated—often violent—conflicts displayed so often in parliamentary elections, municipal elections, and in popular behavior such as petitioning and rioting.[1]

Frequently, historians have assumed that broad social concerns contributed to the political conflicts of the period, and contemporary evidence from several of the elections in these boroughs reinforces that assumption. Social concerns were articulated by participants or observers of contested elections as early as the 1761 Norwich election, in which Harbord Harbord felt that all of the *gentlemen* of the town could be found upon the poll in favor of the two Corporation candidates.[2] Implications of social or status distinctions behind voting decisions also occurred at the Norwich parliamentary elections of 1784, 1790, and 1802, the Northampton election of 1784, and the Lewes elections of 1790 and 1802.[3] References to the social or economic status of voters were not unique to these four boroughs. It seems unlikely that coincidence alone can account for the

[1] For a discussion of "prescriptive" and nonprescriptive" behavior, as well as the value of both for analyses of past public opinion, see Lee Benson, "An Approach to the Scientific Study of Past Public Opinion," *Public Opinion Quarterly* 31(1968):522-67. Quite clearly, *both* played important roles in the political reality of unreformed England. In addition to Benson's discussion, see: George Rudé, *The Crowd in History*, New York, 1964 and George Rudé and Eric Hobsbawm, *Captain Swing*, New York, 1968.

[2] Historical Manuscripts Commission, *Report of the Manuscripts of the Marquess of Lothian*, London, 1905, p. 243, and *Miscellaneous Pieces in Prose and Verse Relative to the Contested Election*, Norwich, 1768, pp. xi, 14, 29.

[3] Chapter 4 contains a brief account of the references to socio-economic considerations at the Norwich elections of 1761, 1768, 1784, 1790, and 1802 as well as those in Northampton in 1784, Maidstone in 1784 and 1790, and Lewes at the elections of 1790 and 1802.

254

social and economic references that appeared during elections in each of the towns considered. Reports in the *Annual Register* expressed concern that similar considerations motivated and exacerbated political conflicts in a number of other parliamentary boroughs during the 1790s.[4]

The partisan choices and respective social positions of Messrs. Ward and Starkey summarize rather nicely the prevailing interpretation in accounts of popular political activity during the years following the agitation aroused by John Wilkes and his less self-serving successors like Thomas Paine. Broadly speaking, this interpretation echoes in somewhat muted tones the argument voiced by students of modern British elections. In their view, "class is the basis of party politics; all else is embellishment and detail."[5] Similarly, at the end of the eighteenth century, the lower orders (to the extent that they possessed the franchise) allegedly contributed the preponderance of Whig party followers as well as the bulk of the support for radical candidates in later elections. The more "respectable" orders supposedly voted in overwhelming numbers for Administration candidates, or, to use the term loosely, "Tories." Objective evidence for such "class" interpretations of unreformed politics is scarce, and subjective evidence is equally rare, but historians wielding sometimes vague definitions of "class" and undaunted by the paucity and ambiguity of the surviving evidence, have made strong arguments attributing much, if not everything to "class," however defined. Many accounts proffer "class" explanations, or at least "class" terminology, either consciously or unconsciously.[6] R. B. Rose,

[4] The *Annual Register* observed that "the dangerous spirit of opposition between high and low, rich and poor, gentleman and mob, was extremely conspicuous." *Annual Register*, London, 1802, 44:184. Also, Christopher Wyvill, *Political Papers*, 6 vols., London, 1794-1802, 5:23-24, 51.

[5] P.G.P. Pulzer, *Political Representation and Elections: Parties and Voting in Great Britain*, London, 1967, p. 98.

[6] In addition to the works of Rudé, Hobsbawm, Rose, and others cited in Chapter 4, the traditional class interpretation was argued nicely by the Hammonds and to a lesser extent, the Webbs. The new interest in legal

for example, after noting that "it was not always clear whether rich dissenters were attacked because they were dissenters or because they were rich," dismissed religious fervor or Machiavellian manipulation by the Government as the source, or sources, of the 1791 Priestly riots in Birmingham. Rose argued instead that the demonstrations stemmed from "an explosion of latent class hatred."[7] Earl Fitzwilliam echoed similar sentiments in a 1793 letter to Portland that stated his determination never to "act in party with men who call 40,000 weavers to dictate political measures to the Government."[8]

George Rudé has presented perhaps the best evidence of measurable economic differences within popular political groupings. By examining the assessments of individual Middlesex voters who could be identified on land tax rolls in 1768 and 1769, Rudé discovered a marked disparity between the "annual average value of property" held by Wilkite and Proctorite voters in Westminster during the Middlesex elections of the late 1760s. Proctor's supporters owned property with an average value of thirty-eight pounds per annum while Wilkes's followers held property with an average annual value of only twenty-five pounds.[9] However, even if Rudé's evidence can be applied generally, both Wilkites and Proctorites in Rudé's sample were far too prosperous to allow much of an argument for significant economic cleavages in the electorate. A larger sample from parishes outside Westminster also revealed a slightly less well-to-do body of Wilkites, yet again substantial property

history has given these "class" interpretations a new twist. J. L. Hammond and B. Hammond, *The Village Laborer*, London, 1912; J. L. Hammond and B. Hammond, *The Town Laborer*, London, 1932; S. Webb and B. Webb, *English Poor Law History*, London, 1929; Douglas Hay, *Albion's Fatal Tree*, New York, 1975; E. P. Thompson, *Whigs and Hunters*, London, 1975; J. S. Cockburn, *Crime in England*, Princeton, 1977.

[7] R. B. Rose, "The Priestly Riots, 1791," *Past and Present* 18(1960):84.

[8] Fitzwilliam to Portland, September 22, 1793. Cited in Frank O'Gorman, *The Rise of Party in England*, London, 1975, p. 160.

[9] George Rudé, "The Middlesex Elections of 1768-89," *EHR* 75(1960):614.

holdings across the board prevent any argument that the political conflict grew out of a struggle between seriously disparate economic ranks. Though Proctorite assessments averaged £53.5 to the Wilkites £36, more than half of both groups owned property with an annual value of less than £10. The two groups of voters probably were separated by some genuine economic inequalities; a mere 8 percent of Wilkes's supporters were worth more than fifty pounds per year compared to 21 percent of the rated voters who cast ballots for Proctor. That these inequalities indicated the existence of "class" politics is another matter. Nevertheless, resounding phrases have been used to describe the political activity provoked by Wilkes that would not seem out of place in an account of the later nineteenth century.[10]

Contradicting "class" interpretations such as these, many social historians have contended that England was not "a class society divided into mutually hostile layers" before the middle of the nineteenth century at the earliest.[11] Substantial evidence buttresses such claims, and can be found even among the indicators of socially and/or economically based conflicts already noted. Rudé, for example, noted that regardless of the overall economic disparity between Wilkites and Proctorites, "the most substantial of all the substantial freeholders" in Middlesex backed John Wilkes at the elections of 1768 and 1769. Wilkes's appeal among the smaller property-holders failed to forestall his strong following among the wealthiest county residents.[12] By the same token, the observations and contentions produced during elections in Norwich and elsewhere can be made to argue against

[10] As in the tables contained in Chapter 4, these are decimalized pounds. For example, see Ian Christie, *Wilkes, Wyvill, and Reform*, London, 1962, pp. 30, 36, 38.

[11] Harold Perkin, *The Origins of Modern English Society, 1780-1880*, London, 1969, p. 26.

[12] The Whiggish sympathies of Middlesex's wealthiest voters do not tally well with Christie's view of the difference in "middle-class" and elite political opinions. Rudé, "Middlesex Elections," pp. 615-16.

257

a socio-economic undercurrent in political conflicts as easily as they can be shaped to suit a "class" model. After denouncing the artisans to be found calling for the election of "King-killer" William Smith before the Norwich election of 1802, William Windham expressed his dismay at the "men of property" helping to swell the ranks of the "Jacobinical" Free Blues. Similar examples discounting the impact of social and economic gradations in the electorate and elsewhere are as common as are incidents pointing to the effects of "class" in Georgian England.[13]

As currently stated, both sides of the question appear fairly plausible and each seems equally vulnerable. Every anecdote and specific example mustered to demonstrate the existence of "class" conflict can be countered with a contrary example illustrating the critical importance of deference, demagoguery, and the like; the argument can proceed interminably at an anecdotal level, with no satisfactory conclusion possible. Fortunately, claims concerning socioeconomic conflict, or the lack of it, only need suggest the possibility that social and economic cleavages existed in considerable strength in at least some portions of English society, possibly as early as the 1760s. The task then becomes one of employing admittedly deficient but nevertheless much more concrete data concerning these electors to evaluate the possible existence and potential impact of such a cleavage or cleavages on political conflict.

"Class" is an exceptionally complex and elusive subject.

---

[13] *The Poll for Members of Parliament*, Norwich, 1802, pp. xi, xii; *A Vindication of the Political Conduct of William Windham*, Norwich, 1802, p. 61; V. Griffiths, *The Picture of Parliament*, London, 1803, p. 104. Also see, D. C. Moore, *The Politics of Deference*, Hassocks, 1976; R. S. Neale, *Class and Ideology in the Nineteenth Century*, London, 1972, pp. 7-10, 62-64; Richard W. Davis, *Political Change and Continuity*, Newton Abbot, 1972, p. 52; Karl von den Steinen, "The Fabric of Interest in the County," *Albion* 4(1972):206-18. Moore's general emphasis on deferential behavior has been challenged recently by J. R. Fisher, "Issues and Influence: Two By-Elections in South Nottinghamshire in the Mid-Nineteenth Century," *The Historical Journal* 24(1981):155-65.

The hopelessly muddled, if very popular, "nondefinitions" of "class" are analytically useless, and such untestable positions, though often interesting heuristically, have no place in this search for measurable cleavages, socio-economic or otherwise, in English society.[14] Undoubtedly, "class" ascriptions presuppose some largely unmeasurable consciousness on the part of these individuals ascribed to a class, yet if "class" is to be examined seriously, it must be defined, however inadequately, in a manner that permits analysis. It is this sort of measurable "class" division within the electorate that voting records and tax rolls might reveal.

One initial caveat stands above the many that might be suggested before undertaking a search for more substantial evidence of an objectively measured "class" dimension to political behavior. Occupational strata, no matter how satisfactorily defined, are poor substitutes for some more realistically complex definition of groups in society that might constitute social classes. Social strata may, in fact, closely approximate social classes, but as Neale insists, equations of the two require additional, generally unavailable, supporting evidence. Supplementary evidence is so sorely lacking quantitatively as well as qualitatively for the eighteenth century that serious obstacles impede the definition of social strata, much less social classes in these towns. The composition of the electorate in each of the four boroughs has been described with two rather different classification schemes, the second of which, it was argued, resembled "class" to a certain degree by reflecting differences of status and economic condition in contrast to the initial scheme that distinguished occupations functionally. However, this three-tiered occupational scale was not meant, and is not meant, to imply the existence of social classes in eighteenth-century urban society. Rather, more distinct and defensible social "strata" are described by the occupationally defined

[14] E. P. Thompson, *The Making of the English Working Class*, London, 1963.

socio-economic groupings proposed in Table 5.11. In lieu of better social groupings, these strata will be used along within specific economic "ranks" (also organized in three tiers) to search for social and/or economic cleavages in the electorate. Although a more continuous measurement of economic gradations would have been preferable, neither the economic information nor the other evidence regarding the voters in these towns lent itself to standard analytical procedures.[15]

Whatever their deficiencies, occupational groupings clearly are the relevant categories for a behavioral analysis of the vote. Occasionally, straightforward functional categories such as the seven suggested early in the fifth chapter can prove useful, but generally, the three-tiered division of the electorate (that has been shown to convey economic inequalities in addition to differences of status) is most appropriate.

[15] The data available for these unreformed voters were overwhelmingly nominal (e.g., occupation, address, religious denomination). The one solid bit of interval data (rentals) was only available for about 15 percent of the Norwich electorate and half the Maidstone voters, while nominal data was almost always available for all voters. Therefore, an analysis of these data posed substantial obstacles to ordinary statistical analysis. In one effort to overcome the limitations of nominal data analysis, "dummy" regression was attempted by assigning ordinal values to occupations and votes, thus allowing an asymmetrical test of the relationship between social rank and Toryism (see note 23), but simple cross-tabulations were the most appropriate form of measurement given the limitations of the data. Since Table 5.11 indicated an imperfect but significant relationship between occupational strata and economic rank, it seemed defensible to assume that assessing occupational strata in three tiers reflected occupational and economic differences, albeit imperfectly, and to test the entire electorate accordingly.

One other promising method of nominal data analysis that was attempted deserves a brief note. Log-linear analysis is frequently effective in overcoming the problems of nominal data, and it was attempted briefly in the analysis of these data, but its results were exceedingly complicated and ultimately inconclusive. The results of these tests have not been reported because they did not contribute meaningfully to the discussion and certainly did not contradict the conclusions drawn from the crude comparisons of the various strata.

Save for Nossiter's use of larger occupational categories in
his examination of the reformed electorate in England's
northeast, specific occupations have served as the basic unit
of measurement in previous historical studies of English
electoral behavior. Thus the tendency of butchers to vote
Tory in some boroughs at several nineteenth-century elections has been documented with great effort, along with
the equally common tendency of grocers to champion radical or Whig candidates both before and after the Reform
Act, yet very little is known of more general (and more
meaningful) groups.[16] There are peculiar circumstances in
which an analysis of the partisan preferences of specific
occupations might be of interest, but specific occupations
have limited utility even for descriptive purposes, and their
value for an analysis of the voting patterns of an entire
community is even more marginal. Discovering patterns in
the voting habits of the lower orders and those voters of
middling and elite status may allow the formulation of
"fruitful" interpretations (to use Eric Allardt's terminology)
concerning the social foundations of political activity among
these electors; examining and trying to explain the Toryism
of butchers and the Whiggism of grocers most certainly
will not.[17]

At the same time that the number of occupations to be
investigated was limited by relying almost exclusively on
three social strata, two other considerations narrowed the

[16] T. J. Nossiter, *Influence, Opinion, and Political Idioms in Reformed England*, Brighton, 1975, pp. 166-69, 211-12. For an example of the use of
specific occupations, see: W. A. Speck and W. A. Gray, "Londoners at the
Polls under Anne and George I," *Guildhall Studies in London History*
1(1975):251-62; D. G. Wright, "A Radical Borough," *Northern History*
4(1969):132-66; J. R. Vincent, *Pollbooks: How Victorians Voted*, Cambridge,
1967. Oddly enough, a letter during the 1802 Norwich election arguing
that a Free Blue victory was necessary for prosperity was addressed to
Norwich's weavers exclusively and was signed, "A WEAVER."
[17] Eric Allardt, "Aggregate Analysis: The Problems of Its Informative
Value," in *Quantitative Ecological Analysis*, ed. M. Dogan and S. Rokkan,
Cambridge, 1969, pp. 42-47.

perspective further, one geographical and one longitudinal. First, Lewes voters are neglected entirely in this analysis since the political parties in Lewes were unusually disassociated from either the parliamentary parties or the major political debates of the day, at least until 1796. One of the "Coalition" candidates at Lewes elections between 1780 and 1796 invariably voted for and defended all Government measures except during the Fox-North ministry's short time in office. The other Coalitionist attacked the Government at every opportunity and vigorously promoted Foxite causes. Yet this "Coalition" won a consistent and overwhelming majority among the Lewes voters. Therefore, a socio-economic analysis of the votes of the Lewes electorate, though possibly of some general interest, cannot be interpreted within a meaningful political framework. Northampton politics may not have been well developed structurally, and most Northampton elections passed without any indication of serious debate over political issues. But at least the structure of Northampton politics did not actively suppress the development of a relationship between individual electors and political preferences related to national issues. Voting patterns in Northampton can be understood within the context of national political concerns, as can those found in the two well-developed and politically agitated boroughs, Maidstone and Norwich.

The second limitation is chronological. After excluding Lewes altogether, most of the early elections in the three remaining boroughs receive scant notice here even though they received equal attention during the data analysis that led to the creation of the following tables and figures. References to social differences appeared very early in Norwich and demand some attention, but after examining the overall voting patterns of electors in these three boroughs and finding completely random behavior in the early elections, it was clear that this discussion should concentrate on the social bases of the partisan behavior that began to emerge at the five post-1774 general elections. Reasonably

well defined political parties, parliamentary and local, were
essential to a generally applicable interpretation of the relationship, if any, between social and political cleavages.
This prerequisite was met after 1774. Parliamentary political alignments, factions, or whatever they might have been
called, took on a coherence and a substance in the 1780s
that lent definition to local political affairs. Nonrandom
voting patterns before 1774 would have been exceedingly
difficult to explain since the parties were neither well developed nor well defined, and the political issues before
the populace were often confused or even missing altogether. Nevertheless, had voters in one or more elections
behaved in anything other than a random fashion before
1774, the elections of 1761 and 1768 would have been
included for full consideration. Since voting behavior did
not fall into any pattern, explicable or otherwise, before
1780, the elimination of the first two elections from this
discussion simplifies matters considerably without sacrificing any pertinent detail.

Turning first to the distinctively dissimilar political environments of Maidstone and Northampton, one borough
where partisan feeling ran high and one where partisan
feeling may not have run at all, very little evidence from
either electorate points to any measurable relationship linking an elector's social status and his choice of parties. The
behavior of the electorate, divided into three social strata,
at the Maidstone elections beginning in 1780 (Table 7.1)
lends no support to the hypothesized link between the lower
orders and the anti-Ministerialists, nor do the voting patterns at the Northampton elections of 1784, 1790, and 1796
(Table 7.2). The proportionately greater support accorded
Administration candidates by the Northampton elite in 1796
and the relative lack of support for the anti-Ministerial
candidates among the Maidstone elite in 1780 are effectively discounted by contradictory patterns, or the absence
of patterns, at other elections. Elite voters cast the greatest
proportionate vote for anti-Administration candidates at

263

Table 7.1: Anti-Ministerial Voters as a Proportion of All Partisan
Voters in Maidstone by Occupational Strata
(Percentage)

	Occupational Strata		
Election Year	I (Elite)	II (Middling)	III (Working Men)
1780	39.5	47.3	54.2
1784	17.0	21.7	18.6
1790	46.9	44.4	46.2
1796	36.1	31.9	34.9
1802	20.7	25.3	13.4

Table 7.2: Administration Supporters as a Proportion of the Partisan
Voters in Northampton by Occupational Strata
(Percentage)

	Occupational Strata		
Election Year	I	II	III
1784	91.4	90.7	94.2
1790	82.1	89.4	83.4
1796	74.6	59.5	64.5

Maidstone elections in 1790 and again in 1796 when the radical, Christopher Hull, stood for election. Administration candidates captured the bulk of the votes of *each* social group in the Northampton elections of 1784 and 1790, and the party choices of Maidstone voters from *every* social stratum also favored Administration candidates at every election. As indicated in Table 7.1, some discrepancy marked the voting choices of the social strata at the Maidstone contest in 1802, but this election result argues against rather than for any special "Whig" appeal to voters of inferior social stature. More than a quarter of the "middling" stratum voted for the single Whig candidate, John Durrand, and more than 20 percent of the "elite" cast anti-Ministerial ballots; working men proved least supportive, casting a mere 13 percent of their votes for him alone.

The one major tendency persisting across the period in

Maidstone concerned partisanship itself rather than partisan support (Table 7.3). Social stratification among the Maidstone electorate may have had little to do with a voter's particular partisan choice, but it was strongly associated with the more general question of whether or not he cast a partisan ballot, whatever party he ultimately chose. In fact, each social stratum occupied the same relative position in every Maidstone election of the period. The voters from the ranks of the working men cast far fewer partisan ballots than their social "superiors" in Category II. In turn, the electors in Category II were less likely to be partisan than the elite. After 1780, between two-thirds and 84 percent of the elite cast partisan ballots at the elections in question. Their partisanship was followed by that of the middling ranks who cast between half and three-quarters of their ballots for one of the two parties after 1780. In contrast, less than 30 percent of the votes from the lowest occupational strata were partisan ballots in 1802. At each of the other elections, the lower orders cast the smallest proportion of partisan ballots even though they managed to vote in a strongly partisan fashion in 1790 and overwhelmingly so in 1796. Moreover, although the percentage of straight-party voters in each of Maidstone's social strata generally increased over the period, the increase among the elite was more pronounced on the one hand and able to withstand the challenge of the 1802 general election on the other. After the deviation of 1796 when two Ministerialists were returned to parliament, Maidstone reverted in 1802 to her long-standing practice of returning one member from each party. During this initial contest of the nineteenth century just over half of the middling sort cast party ballots, and the majority of straight-party voters that had been achieved in the 1790 and 1796 elections by the lower orders disappeared. The elite, though losing a few of its members to split-voting, maintained an overwhelmingly partisan stance, most of it in support of the two Tory candidates. The relatively large numbers of nonpartisan voters at Maidstone

265

Table 7.3: Proportion of Straight-Party Votes Cast by Each
Occupational Stratum in Maidstone (Percentage)

	Occupational Strata		
Election Year	I	II	III
1774	26.1	15.7	5.6
1780	23.5	20.4	11.4
1784	63.2	54.1	39.3
1790	77.1	72.1	60.9
1796	83.6	74.6	72.1
1802	68.0	50.3	29.6

parliamentary elections in comparison to Norwich, a difference that proved so critical to the relative development
of partisan behavior in Maidstone, consisted in large part
of men from the less prestigious occupations. Partisan mobilization in Maidstone was not confined to one social group,
yet the higher an individual voter's standing on the social
scale, the more likely he was to cast straight-party ballots.
The Maidstone elite resembled the broadly and heavily
politicized Norwich electorate in the post-1780 election, but
the similarity was restricted to those in the highest social
stratum. Maidstone voters outside of the gentle and professional "classes" continued to split their votes between the
parties election after election, though in noticeably fewer
numbers at the 1790 and 1796 elections.

In contrast to the similarities of the partisan choices of
each social stratum at various Northampton and Maidstone
elections, measurable partisan distinctions emerged among
Norwich's social strata in the election of 1761 and persisted
on a somewhat reduced and variable scale over most subsequent contests (Table 7.4). A much larger proportion of
the partisan voters among the lower occupational ranks
backed the two anti-Corporation candidates in 1761. There
was some basis in fact for Harbord Harbord's comments
about the absence of gentlemen on the poll for the two
challengers in 1761. The voting pattern at the 1761 election, however, is not directly comparable to the patterns at

266

the other elections. Rather than indicating a preference for parliamentary candidates favoring or opposing the national Administration, the 1761 vote denoted an individual voter's stance toward the Norwich Corporation. Norwich elections beginning in 1768 are of greater interest. The branding of Edward Bacon as a "foe to the poor" in 1768 must have struck a sensitive note among the Norwich electorate.[18] Voters in the middling and lower occupational ranks cast twice as many votes as the elite (proportionately) for the anti-Administration candidate, Thomas Beevor, and against Bacon.

After 1768, the votes of Norwich's social strata followed no definite pattern with the exception that the elite cast proportionately fewer votes for anti-Ministerial candidates at every election but one (1784), and usually cast far fewer than voters in either of the other strata. The striking dissimilarities of elite electors and voters in Category III were considerably diminished in 1780, and all but vanished at the 1784 contest. During these two elections, the middling sort persisted in their adamantly and distinctively anti-Administration attitude. Almost two-thirds of the partisan voters in Category II backed anti-Administration candidates in 1780, and these voters gave a majority to the Nor-

Table 7.4: Anti-Ministerialists among Norwich's Partisan Voters by Occupational Strata (Percentage)

Election Year	Occupational Strata		
	I	II	III
1761	7.4	19.6	28.9
1768	21.3	45.3	43.1
1780	44.1	63.3	50.6
1784	48.7	61.0	48.4
1790	50.4	57.1	55.6
1796	23.5	39.8	38.3
1802	42.1	57.5	58.4

[18] *Miscellaneous Pieces in Prose and Verse Relative to the Contested Election,* Norwich, 1768.

wich "Free Blues" in three of the following four elections. Partisan voters in the third stratum did not support anti-Administration candidates with any regularity although their behavior closely paralleled that of the middling voters at the elections after 1790. A second pattern began to take shape during the 1790 election and developed into a notable contrast at the 1796 and 1802 Norwich contests. The Norwich elite stood well apart from both the middling sort and the lesser sort; they cast far fewer votes for anti-Administration candidates and far more for Ministerialists. The middling and lesser sorts converged in casting similarly higher proportions of "Whig" votes than the elite at this and all subsequent elections.

In shifting from the voting choices of each social stratum to the social structure of partisan support, however, the never-pronounced political positions of Norwich's social strata fades into nothingness (Table 7.5). The social composition of the voters for one party duplicated the social makeup of the opposite party in all three boroughs with notable precision. Nothing distinguished the two groups of partisan voters in any of these elections except their failure to mirror the larger electorate. With the sole exception of the Norwich anti-Ministerialists, the elite in each town contributed a higher proportion to both partisan camps than their overall numbers warranted. Barely 11 percent of Maidstone's electorate ranked in the elite occupational category. Yet fully a quarter of Maidstone's partisan voters, either Ministerialist or anti-Ministerialist, were of gentle or professional status. The figures for Northampton were skewed just as seriously. Less than 9 percent of the voters in Northampton laid claim to one of the occupations in Category I, yet more than 22 percent of the partisan voters of *either* political persuasion came from that occupational category. The disparities in the contributions of the other occupational strata generally were not as pronounced, nor did they fall into a prescribed pattern. The middling ranks were slightly underrepresented in the Maidstone and Nor-

Table 7.5: Partisan and Nonpartisan Voters in Maidstone, Norwich, and
Northampton Elections After 1774
(Percentage All voters/All elections)

Occupational Strata	Overall	Ministerialists	Anti-Ministerialists	Nonpartisan (Splitters)
Maidstone				
I	11.2	24.5	26.0	8.2
II	26.1	22.2	20.3	14.4
III	62.7	53.3	53.7	77.4
Norwich				
I	14.1	18.3	15.3	12.2
II	24.3	19.5	26.1	18.9
III	61.6	62.2	58.6	68.9
Northampton				
I	8.7	22.3	22.4	4.3
II	25.6	31.4	33.3	12.6
III	65.7	46.3	44.3	83.1

wich parties and somewhat overrepresented among Northampton's partisan voters. Working men, artisans, and the
like in the last category contributed a little less than their
proportionate share to the Maidstone parties, considerably
less than their share in Northampton, and essentially contributed an appropriate number of voters to the Norwich
partisan vote. Thus, just as the partisan votes of Maidstone's
social strata indicated a social element in partisanship, the
social distribution of partisan voters in these towns again
suggests less social division between the parties than between partisan and nonpartisan voters. Most Norwich electors had been won to partisan behavior by the end of the
century, and the two Norwich parties reflected the larger
electorate much more accurately than in the other towns.
At elections in Northampton and Maidstone, on the other
hand, voters from the lesser occupations provided a larger
number of split votes; relatively few splitters came from
the elite and middle ranks. The political issues affecting
the behavior of voters in Maidstone had less impact on
Maidstone's working men, and the difficulty encountered

269

in assuming a political stance in the normally nonpartisan Northampton elections baffled a larger segment of the voters from the lowest occupational category than those from the elite and from the middling sort.

The substantial similarities in the social compositions of the partisan voters at Maidstone and Northampton elections when all elections are considered simultaneously (Table 7.5) recur if the elections are considered individually. An examination of specific Norwich elections beginning in 1780 (Table 7.6) also reinforces the impression of social equality among the parties conveyed by Table 7.5. Although the two groups of partisan voters in Norwich underwent alterations during the 1780s and '90s, these changes stemmed primarily from the gradual shift toward "elite" occupational titles in the entire electorate following the 1761 election. As demonstrated in Table 5.7, the proportion of the Norwich electorate describing itself with gentle, professional, or entrepreneurial titles rose from less than 12 percent in 1761 to just over 22 percent in 1802. Conversely, the number of self-ascribed craftsmen, artisans, and other laboring men declined slowly over the same period. Both the increase in the elite and the decrease in the lesser ranks contributed to the changing makeup of Norwich's partisan voters, and, critically, the composition of both Ministerialist and anti-Ministerialist parties followed the same general trend. Variations can be detected in the two camps, but on the whole the social composition of the Norwich partisan voters delineate social patterns underlying political choices no more successfully than the examinations of the voting patterns of social strata or the social parameters of each group of partisan voters over the entire period, which is to say not at all. The tendency of the middling ranks to be found voting for Free Blue candidates in Norwich, noted already in Table 7.4, is perhaps the only noteworthy feature in this comparison. The contributions of the other social strata conform almost exactly to the expectations raised by the general occupational shift in the Norwich electorate.

270

Though little distinguished the parties socially in these three boroughs and even less separated the social strata politically in Northampton, measurable, and occasionally substantial economic disparities between voters with conflicting political stances add to the implications of socially based voting among Norwich's social strata (Table 7.4). As shown in Chapter 5, the three-tiered occupational structure adopted in the analysis so far measures economic as well as social inequality, yet economic diversity within specific occupations could be, and often was, extreme. These occupational strata were even less economically homogenous.[19] Hence, however well the three occupationally defined strata denote differences of rank, status, and relative wealth, they obscure important differences within the electorate. Unfortunately, measuring the economic positions of these voters more precisely and accurately is usually impossible; those voters in Category III who actually were quite comfortable financially, as well as those among the "elite" with sorely deficient incomes, can be isolated only

Table 7.6: Occupational Stratification of the Norwich Partisan Voters at Each Election Following 1768 (Percentage)

Election Year	Anti-Ministerialists Occupational Strata			Ministerialists Occupational Strata		
	I	II	III	I	II	III
1780	11.6	25.2	63.2	16.3	16.2	67.5
1784	13.5	25.2	61.7	14.9	16.8	68.3
1790	14.8	26.1	59.1	15.8	21.8	62.4
1796	17.0	29.8	53.2	22.5	21.2	56.3
1802	19.9	24.5	55.6	22.1	21.3	56.6

[19] Several occupations presented particular problems. Almost two-thirds of Norwich's woolcombers, innkeepers, and hotpressers fell into the top economic third of the electorate, and carpenters fell entirely in the top two-thirds. Nevertheless, the section considering Table 5.11 demonstrated the relative success of these occupational categories in identifying economic disparities between occupational groups.

occasionally, and then imperfectly. Thus, the problems ordinarily encountered in multivariate analysis when the dependent variable (voting in this instance) happens to be nominal are magnified, and a socio-economic analysis of the electorate that attempts to go beyond straightforward comparisons of voters in several occupational categories must be conducted in a disjointed, unwieldy, and regrettably imprecise fashion.

Economic data of adequate quality for individual Northampton electors have not survived in sufficient quantity for an examination of economic variations related to the voting choices of the Northampton electorate.[20] Economic data for Maidstone and Norwich voters also suffer from a number of deficiencies, but nonrandom samples from each electorate can be identified on surviving tax rolls, and these assessments, though of limited scope and occasionally questionable meaning and accuracy, allow several informative comparisons of partisan voters in these two boroughs.[21] Grouping these samples of voters economically rather than occupationally yields a pattern unlike the occupationally based analyses in the first six tables in this chapter. The mean annual rentals of partisan voters for whom economic data can be found in both Maidstone and Norwich reveal economic variations among the supporters of each party (Table 7.7). Moreover, while the occupational differences

[20] Economic records from Northampton were less complete and less useful than those from Norwich and Maidstone.

[21] See Chapter 5, note 28 for a fuller discussion of the sources of the economic data used and a comparison of the electorate and the total taxpaying populace. Individual land tax assessments were employed for the Norwich electorate. Records were found for approximately 10 percent of the Norwich electorate. In Maidstone, the poor rate was more complete, and economic records for about half of the resident Maidstone electorate were identified. The range in both boroughs was broad; total rentals varied from more than one pound to more than a hundred pounds. The taxpayers in both towns were a somewhat more occupationally elite group than the electorate, but the differences were not pronounced, nor were there any noticeable variations in their political behavior.

of Norwich occupational strata alone lend credibility to the oft-maintained association of the social elite and the Ministerial party, these mean rentals apparently tie the wealthier voters in the electorates of both Maidstone and Norwich to the Ministerialist cause. However, the disparities in the mean rentals of Maidstone's partisan voters disappear when the more representative median rentals are compared. The Maidstone anti-Ministerialists, for example, seem to have attracted voters of higher economic standing at the 1796 election than the Ministerialists despite the radical candidate (Christopher Hull) proposed by the anti-Ministerialists.

The disparities among the Norwich electors, though present in both comparisons of mean and median rentals, appeared very late. Distinctly lower mean rentals for anti-Ministerialist partisans did not emerge until after 1790 if the slight discrepancies in the rentals of 1784 and 1790 are discounted. The median rentals of Norwich voters repeat the pattern, yet again substantial differences separated the Ministerialist and anti-Ministerialist voters only *after* 1790. Variations at the other elections were small, and given the

Table 7.7: Mean and Median Annual Rentals of Partisan Voters in Maidstone and Norwich (In Decimalized Pounds Sterling)

	Anti-Ministerialists		Ministerialists	
Election Year	Mean	Median	Mean	Median
Maidstone				
1780	15.5	9.5	20.7	10.8
1784	17.9	7.1	25.1	11.6
1790	14.4	11.5	28.7	11.8
1796	15.1	12.6	21.7	10.3
Norwich				
1780	26.5	20.8	27.3	19.6
1784	25.7	19.9	29.9	23.1
1790	25.5	20.1	27.8	22.3
1796	22.2	16.7	28.5	22.5

problems and limitations of the Norwich samples, probably inconsequential. The Norwich tax rolls yielded comparatively few records and resulted in a considerably smaller proportion of the electorate available for comparisons than in Maidstone.[22] With such a small data base, even the relatively large differences in the mean and median annual rentals of the Norwich voters in 1796 and 1802 at best simply raise the possibility that economic status played a role in determining the partisan choices of Norwich electors in certain social strata. Conversely, the samples of the Maidstone electorate for whom economic data could be obtained accounted for a substantial proportion of the total electorate and posed fewer interpretational problems. Hence, it seems unlikely that economic differences separated Maidstone's partisan voters. The very wealthiest electors in Maidstone tended to vote for Ministerialist candidates, skewing the mean rentals, but little can be inferred from the behavior of this tiny cluster of exceedingly wealthy men in the Maidstone electorate.

Necessarily crude measurements of the combined effects of economic and occupational variables in Maidstone and Norwich generated interesting, if mixed, results. Regression analysis (using "dummy" variables to test nominal data) completely failed to identify socio-economic variations among the electors with partisan preferences, never achieving an r^2 or regression coefficient worthy of mention. Whether examining all voters or partisan voters exclusively, socio-economic variations were not statistically related to partisan choice.[23] The type and quality of the data, in addition to

[22] The percentage of the electorate in Norwich for whom economic records could be found ranged from 9.7 percent to 14.8 percent. The overall total was reduced by the complete lack of economic data for 1802. For the Maidstone electorate, the total with economic data ranged from 43.9 percent in 1796 to 59.1 percent in 1774.

[23] Regression was attempted with negligible results. A combination of measures, including "dummy" regression to take occupation into account, yielded r^2's never greater than .06. At any rate, multiple regression was not completely justifiable since the variables used were not selected a priori

the nature of the measurements attempted, reduced the utility and reliability of most standard statistical manipulations, but the apparent total absence of any meaningful relationship with the possible exception of Norwich voters in 1796 and 1802 confirmed rather convincingly the equally impressive absence of occupational patterns among the partisan electors. The Norwich elite may have been unlike their fellow electors as much politically as they were socially and economically, but the behavior of the two other groups was indistinguishable for the most part. Nevertheless, dividing the members of each occupational strata in Maidstone and Norwich economically according to their annual rentals and the taxes assessed on their property achieves interesting, if mixed, results. On the whole, subdividing each occupational group into three economic categories yielded little more than regression; the relative economic positions of members of the Norwich and Maidstone elite had no measurable effect on their votes, and the same was true with the middling sort in Maidstone. However, the poorer element of the middling sort in Norwich were more likely to cast anti-Ministerialist votes than their better-off counterparts. An economic threshold separated the voters of the middling occupational ranks who were on the bottom of the economic scale from *all* those higher on the economic scale.[24] After leaving the poorest group, an increase in wealth

with the intention of explaining the total voting variations. In order to run a dummy regression, the dependent variable (vote) was altered to + 1 and − 1 for 'Tory and Whig respectively. R. S. Schofield recently provided an interesting discussion of the dilemma faced by historians wishing to explain "the distribution of one characteristic of a group of people in terms of other characteristics of the group" when the available data are extremely limited, as is almost always the case in historical research. E. Hanushek et al., "Model Specification: The Use of Aggregate Data, and the Ecological Correlation Fallacy," *Political Methodology* (1974):90; R. S. Schofield, "Quantitative Analysis of the Long Parliament," *Past and Present* 68(1975):124-29.

[24] Paul R. Abrahamson, "Intergenerational Social Mobility and Partisan Choice," *APSR* 66(1972):1291-94 and Richard Rose, *Electoral Behavior*, London, 1975, p. 504. Both contain useful descriptions of "thresholds."

produced no measurable decrease in Whig support (Table 7.8). Apparently, once the members of this stratum achieved a measure of economic security, most voted for Orange-and-Purple candidates regardless of their relative wealth.

Unlike the elite in both towns, economic differences within occupational strata seemed to have some impact on the voters in the lowest occupational groups in Maidstone as well as in Norwich, at least at particular elections (Table 7.9). Beginning with the Norwich election of 1784 and the 1790 contest in Maidstone, the higher the economic rank of individuals within the lowest occupational strata, the less likely they were to cast anti-Administration ballots. Three times as many of Maidstone's poorest voters in the lowest strata supported anti-Administration candidates as their wealthier occupational counterparts. In the heavily partisan Maidstone election of 1796, twice as many (proportionately) of the poorest members of Category III voted for the "Whig" candidate, Christopher Hull, as the wealthiest members of that occupational category. The wealthiest Norwich working men were affected earlier and even more drastically, though the effect was not felt as systematically across the economic strata, yet the complex pattern of their votes after 1784 indicates another economic threshold. Rather than the poorer voters in an occupational strata behaving differently as was the case among Norwich voters from the middling occupational ranks, the wealthiest voters

Table 7.8: Support for Anti-Administration Candidates from Economic Ranks within Middling Occupational Stratum in Norwich (Percentage)

| | | Economic Ranks | |
Election Year	Lowest Third	Middle Third	Highest Third
1780	85.7	68.4	65.1
1784	58.3	46.1	42.3
1790	58.4	44.4	53.8
1796	66.7	40.9	41.7
1802	80.2	33.2	40.9

in the lowest occupational group deviated from the norm. Only 12 percent of the votes of these prosperous laboring men went to anti-Ministerial candidates in 1796 and a mere 10 percent of their votes were cast for the Free Blues at the election of 1802. In sharp contrast, almost 40 percent of the poorer laboring men voted for the anti-Ministerialists in 1796 and more than half of the less well-to-do voters supported the Free Blues in 1802.

One point stands above the rest in this complex picture of the relationships between socio-economic status and partisan choice in the three boroughs where parliamentary general elections were fought within the context of parliamentary political parties (if they were fought at all). Although occupational stratification and relative wealth were related to partisan choice in Norwich under certain circumstances, and were clearly related to partisan behavior (though unrelated to nonpartisan behavior in Maidstone, Northampton, and possibly Norwich), the total political impact of these socio-economic variables tended to be negligible. Even in Norwich where some measurable differences emerged in the 1790s, the influence of both economic and occupational status should have been more pronounced if

Table 7.9: Support for Anti-Administration Candidates from Economic Ranks within Lowest Occupational Stratum in Norwich and Maidstone (Percentage)

Election Year	Lowest Third	Middle Third	Highest Third
Norwich			
1780	53.5	33.2	66.9
1784	58.3	48.3	46.2
1790	58.1	53.8	41.1
1796	36.6	40.6	11.8
1802	64.9	51.8	10.9
Maidstone			
1780	53.7	42.3	61.1
1784	20.0	11.2	20.9
1790	62.5	41.2	20.5
1796	42.9	35.7	18.2

serious socio-economic cleavages underlay the political disputes of Norwich's voters. Though Norwich contained consistently partisan voters and experienced the most potentially divisive contests, more than 60 percent of the Administration vote came from the lowest occupational stratum (Table 7.5), and on average, almost as many electors within the lowest social stratum voted for Administration as anti-Administration candidates (Table 7.4).

The failure of these economic and social variables to explain partisan choice adequately is underlined by a comparison of the partisan preferences of the voters in the two lower occupational strata (Categories II and III) in each of the larger areal political units into which Norwich was divided. The thirty-six parishes within Norwich's walls were grouped into twelve lesser wards and four "great" wards. After 1790, the disparities of the voting patterns *within* each of the two occupational strata across the four great wards exceeded the disparities found *among* the three occupational strata over Norwich as a whole (Table 7.10). Political variations among the wards tended to be small, with a few notable exceptions, before the election of 1790. A remarkably strong areal pattern then emerged and persisted in 1796 and 1802, overshadowing the measurable, if somewhat unimpressive diversity of the partisan choices of the Norwich elite at those contests and the equally minor variations in the voting patterns of economic gradations within particular occupational strata in Norwich and Maidstone. The proportionate differences between the number of anti-Ministerial voters in the highest occupational stratum (I) and remaining strata (II and III) in Norwich were dwarfed by the conspicuous political disagreements exhibited by the lesser and middling sorts in Norwich's four "great" wards. Particularly striking were the voting disparities of identical occupational strata in the Conisford and Northern wards. The anti-Ministerialists won a majority of the votes of the electors in the lowest occupational category in the Northern ward at every election beginning in 1790, and their vote

Table 7.10: "Free Blue" Support among Occupational Strata in
Norwich's Four Wards (Percentage)

Election Year	Conisford	Mancroft	Wymer	Northern
Occupational Category III				
1780	49.1	66.7	51.9	54.9
1784	52.2	47.8	44.6	51.2
1790	37.3	60.0	51.7	56.5
1796	29.2	32.1	48.8	63.0
1802	36.6	59.4	60.0	74.7
Occupational Category II				
1780	61.5	72.7	50.0	62.5
1784	90.1	65.2	43.8	72.7
1790	40.3	55.3	58.2	63.6
1796	25.0	23.5	18.2	57.1
1802	40.2	50.0	54.5	88.9

totals attained new heights at each contest. By 1802, the
Norwich Free Blues secured almost 75 percent of the working man's vote in the Northern ward. Conversely, the Free
Blues were unable to secure the votes of even 40 percent
of the electors from the same occupational stratum living
in Conisford ward. Put another way, the contest of 1802
saw twice as many laboring men in the Northern ward
casting Free Blue votes as their occupational equals across
the Wensum River in Conisford ward. Norwich's working
men were not distributed equitably across Norwich's parishes and wards, and the Northern ward's increasingly
disproportionate share of the lesser orders was the most
notable change in Norwich's spatial organization over the
forty-year period ending in 1802 (see Map 7.1). Norwich's
middling sort and elite were distributed much more uniformly throughout the town. This concentration of the lesser
sort in the Northern ward may have been an element in
the exaggerated Whiggery of its working men, but the explanation behind this notable areal pattern in the Norwich
vote seems to have been less related to occupational distributions, or occupations for that matter, than it was to

279

MAP 7.1   *Proportional Density of the "Lesser Sort," Norwich, 1802*

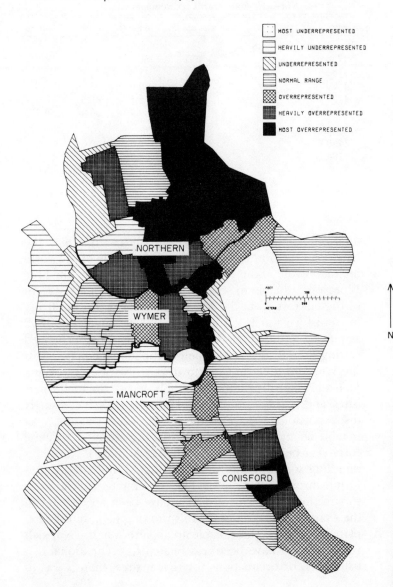

MOST UNDERREPRESENTED
HEAVILY UNDERREPRESENTED
UNDERREPRESENTED
NORMAL RANGE
OVERREPRESENTED
HEAVILY OVERREPRESENTED
MOST OVERREPRESENTED

NORTHERN

WYMER

MANCROFT

CONISFORD

FEET
METERS

N

another aspect of the lives of these voters, their religious affiliations.[25]

The partisan preferences of the middling sort (II) living in Conisford parishes and the equally "respectable" voters residing in the parishes of the Northern ward achieved a comparable degree of dissimilarity; again more than twice as many Northern ward voters from this occupational stratum cast anti-Ministerial ballots in 1802 as their Conisford counterparts (Table 7.10). The Free Blue candidates were approaching unanimity among the middling voters of the Northern ward while failing to achieve a simple majority in Conisford. The voting patterns of particular social strata in the two other wards were less distinctive, but normally the proportion of Free Blue voters from both lower and middling occupational groups in Mancroft and Wymer fell between the extremes set by the Conisford and Northern voters.

As residents of a single parish community, Maidstone voters could not be subjected to a similar test, but, surprisingly, a strong parish bias divided the Northampton electorate (Table 7.11). While the boundaries of the Northampton wards were defined too inadequately to allow a similar comparison of voting across wards, the boundaries of Northampton's four parishes were stable and clearly defined, making it possible to divide the borough roughly into two halves, with St. Giles and St. Sepulchre constituting the northern half and St. Peter and All Saints the southern

[25] An extensive spatial analysis of Norwich's social structure was conducted using both electoral data and information from the Norwich directories of 1783 and 1801. From these comparisons of the distribution of Norwich's various social strata at seven points in time, it was clear that the increasingly disproportionate share of the lower orders in the Northern ward was the most striking feature of Norwich's changing occupational makeup from 1761 to 1802. Using a simple index that divided a parish's proportion of the social strata in question by its proportionate share of the total population at that point, it was possible to assess the changing distribution of Norwich's voters and respectable citizens. The poor were omitted since they appeared neither in the pollbooks nor in the directories.

THE VOTER'S DECISION

half.[26] Focusing on the elections of 1784, 1790, and 1796 (at which each of the parliamentary candidates could be placed within the fold of one of the parliamentary parties despite the lack of partisan activity in Northampton itself), variations within occupational categories stand in striking contrast to the similarities of the partisan preferences among *all* occupational strata in these three Northampton elections (Table 7.2). Voters with laboring and artisanal occupations who lived in the two southern parishes cast ballots for anti-Ministerial candidates with greater frequency than similarly employed voters in the two northern parishes. Areal disparities in the voting patterns of electors from Northampton's middling occupations were less pronounced in 1784 and 1790, but middling voters from the southern parishes joined their socially inferior fellow electors at the election of 1796. They cast twice as many ballots (proportionately) for the Whig incumbent, Edward Bouverie, as the shopkeepers and small tradesmen in the northern sector of the town.

The elite in both Norwich and Northampton were not visibly affected by their place of residence and are not included in Tables 7.10 or 7.11, but the occasionally extreme areal differences within the two larger social strata were sufficient to insure that locational variations persisted even when all voters were considered (Table 7.12). In Norwich,

Table 7.11: Support for Anti-Administration Candidates among Occupational Strata in Aggregated Northampton Parishes (Percentage)

	Occupational Category III		Occupational Category II	
Election Year	Northern	Southern	Northern	Southern
1784	.9	10.8	7.5	10.7
1790	5.3	28.0	8.1	13.3
1796	21.6	44.7	21.4	49.1

[26] County Land Tax Returns, Northampton, E184, PRO.

the Northern ward as a whole after 1784 was less favorably disposed toward "Ministerial" candidates than the voters in other parts of the city. The contrast was especially glaring in Conisford and Mancroft. An equally noticeable anti-Ministerial bias is evident among all Northampton voters in the two southernmost parishes.

Isolating these sometimes acute areal differences in partisan preferences suggests much about the social bases of voting preferences. Although the behavior of social strata varied widely from ward to ward (or parish to parish), hidden occupational or economic variations among the areal units of these towns might have accounted for the perceived variations. The behavior of voters from the lowest social stratum in a particular ward could have been affected by the ward's overall social composition. The response of a tiny minority (whether occupational, economic, or otherwise) can be quite different from the response of the same individuals when they comprise the majority. Such an hypothesis is even suggested by the inequitable distribution of wealth and voters in the Norwich wards and Northampton parishes.[27] Economic dissimilarities among the

Table 7.12: Proportion of Partisan Voters Supporting Administration Candidates in Norwich and Northampton (Percentage)

Election Year	Norwich Wards				Northampton Parishes	
	Conisford	Mancroft	Wymer	Northern	Northern	Southern
1780	51.1	42.1	48.5	43.8		
1784	50.1	44.3	57.6	47.8	66.4	43.6
1790	50.5	42.1	50.6	37.3	41.7	28.3
1796	69.5	73.5	60.1	48.2	60.1	41.7
1802	51.3	52.4	41.2	27.8		

[27] Interestingly, Nossiter found some evidence of the contextual effect in several northern boroughs after the Reform Bill. He concluded "the lower down the scale a voter's occupation, the more likely he was to incline to the politics of the district in which he lived." Nossiter, *Influence, Opinion, and Political Idioms*, p. 173. Also see T. Falkonen, "Individual and Structural Effects in Ecological Research," in *Quantitative Ecological Analysis*. In

Norwich wards occasionally reached extreme proportions, and occupational groups were not dispersed evenly across Norwich (Table 7.13). Mancroft ward, for example, contained a higher proportion of "elite" electors, and paid the highest per capita land tax of the four wards. Conisford voters differed radically both occupationally and economically. Conisford's voters whose occupations placed them in the first category contributed just over 7 percent of the ward's electorate, while voters with similarly elite occupations made up almost 30 percent of the Mancroft vote. Conisford residents also paid a land tax approximately half as large per capita as Mancroft's inhabitants.

However, the economic and occupational variations among the Norwich wards did *not* correspond to the partisan differences demonstrated in Tables 7.10 and 7.12. The electorates of both Conisford and Northern wards who proved to be political polar opposites were dominated by a markedly inferior occupational stratum. Voters in these two wards also were poorer than voters in the other two wards, though Conisford voters were poor even in comparison to the inferior economic positions of electors in the Northern ward. If political choices were related to aggregate and/or individual poverty and social inferiority, it seems unlikely that Conisford voters would have turned in majorities for Administration candidates at each election while Northern voters turned out as consistently and stood as adamantly for the Free Blues. In fact, the votes of the economically and socially deficient residents of Conisford ward closely resembled those of the electors in the wealthiest and occupationally most exclusive ward, Mancroft. Electoral support of the Orange-and-Purple party in 1796 and 1802 in the two wards was virtually indistinguishable. By the same token, only minor occupational differences separated the Northampton parishes (Table 7.13), nor were they unlike

addition, D. Price, "Micro- and Macro-Politics," in *Political Research and Political Theory*, ed. O. Garceau, Cambridge, 1968.

economically. In neither borough, then, did social or economic differences coincide with the radically divergent areal voting patterns at the elections of the 1790s and after.[28]

[28] One obvious area of "corruption" that has apparently been ignored in this discussion is landlord influence. However, because land tax rolls identified occupiers *and* owners in many parishes, and because the Norwich pollbooks distinguished freeholders from freemen, it was possible to at least try to assess the influence of landlords. These efforts to identify the extent of landlord control yielded the following conclusions:

(1) In most Norwich parishes, there were far too many landlords to believe that landlord influence, if it existed, could have had a measurable impact on elections, and too many, really, to believe that tenants would have been much under the influence of a particular landlord. Unfortunately, most landlords were identified too sketchily to allow a systematic test of the relationship between their votes and those of their tenants.

(2) Though the proportions varied widely from parish to parish and from year to year, many Norwich voters and residents were owner/occupiers. Of the voters identified on the tax rolls, approximately 57 percent were owner/occupiers, and approximately 51 percent of the entire town listed on the land tax were also owner/occupiers. The variance was just about as broad as it could be, ranging from 0 percent in St. Benedict's parish in 1796 to 89 percent in St. Michael Coslany in 1790. This level of private ownership should have contributed to Norwich's independence.

(3) Lewes voters, who were more likely to be renters than Norwich residents (39 percent owner/occupiers), only succumbed to landlord influence in very limited numbers. Using the local census of 1790 that identified landlords much more effectively than most other records, Lewes residents were divided into owner/occupiers and tenants of five major landlords. Using Fisher's Exact Test to compensate for small cell sizes, the votes of the tenants were not significantly different from other Lewes voters overall, and those landlords who did seem to exert pressure successfully were not able to command total allegiance. For example, the most striking discrepancy between tenants and other voters was exhibited by the voters renting from Lord Pelham, yet even he failed to sway all of his tenants.

Vote	Overall Vote, 1790	Lord Pelham's Tenants
Pelham-Kemp	54.1%	62.1%
Pelham-Shelley	11.7	14.3
Kemp-Shelley		8.6
Pelham (plump)	3.2	5.7
Kemp	2.7	1.5
Shelley	18.5	7.8

285

Table 7.13: Areal Economic and Occupational Differences in Norwich
(Percentage)

Occupational Strata	Conisford	Mancroft	Wymer	Northern
I	7.3	27.1	21.2	14.2
II	16.2	27.2	14.7	9.5
III	76.5	45.7	64.1	76.3
Economic Status				
X̄ per capita land tax*	.14	.35	.23	.20
X̄ per capita tax assessment*	2.31	4.19	3.92	3.52

* In decimalized pounds sterling.

Instead, another variable was closely tied to areal and individual partisan preferences—religion.

According to Herbert Butterfield, religious differences among Englishmen had produced by the reign of George III "remarkably different types of mentality and outlook" among Nonconformists and members of the Church of England. He also felt "the significance of the breach . . . was clearest of all when these people turned to the question of politics."[29] Butterfield's contention is one of the clearer statements of the orthodox position voiced by so many observers of unreformed politics. In their view, Nonconformity supported the Whig party both in the eighteenth and nineteenth centuries. In turn, the Church was one of the mainstays of the Administration party.[30] George III's ac-

---

(4) Maidstone and Northampton voters defied the analysis possible in Norwich and Lewes, principally because the records available for voters in both towns failed to identify landlords or failed to identify them well enough and systematically enough to place any confidence in the results of an examination.

[29] Herbert Butterfield, *George III, Lord North, and the People*, London, 1949, p. 183.

[30] V. A. Hatley, "Some Aspects of Northampton History," *Northamptonshire Past and Present* 3(1966):247. One of the few arguments that Dissenters should *not* interfere in politics is in the Gurney MSS., 2/403, Friend's Library, London. Also, Norman Sykes, *Church and State in Eighteenth Century England*, London, 1934, p. 77; *Gentleman's Magazine*, January 11, 1790,

tivities against the Nonconformists alone might have justified widespread opposition to the successive "Tory" ministries of North and Pitt, just as Charles Fox's actions on behalf of the Dissenters during the fated efforts to repeal the Test and Corporation Acts, on the other hand, should have strengthened the bond for which so many have argued. Statements like the Bishop of Bristol's dismissal of Nonconformist principles as "worse than Hottentots" and the steady pressure of the Anglican clergy in favor of Ministerial candidates also should have helped determine the behavior of Churchmen and Dissenters alike.[31]

The attitudes about which Butterfield wrote could have developed quite easily under these conditions; Nonconformists and members of the Church of England may indeed have seen the world through different eyes, and, as importantly, identified themselves accordingly. Thomas Lacqueur has argued recently that the Established Church underwent a critical shift in the late eighteenth century. Primarily a local concern in the early years of the century, churches increasingly became and were seen as becoming part of the larger, impersonal national institution.[32] As the Church began to be perceived in this larger context, the new national focus reinforced the essential differences of the two religious communities. Socio-economic differences did not serve to distinguish and define feelings of "us" and

p. 1138; E. A. Smith, "The Election Agent in English Politics," *EHR* 84(1969):13; John Dixon MSS. 92, T131A, Book of Political Extracts, p. 51, NNRO.

[31] Nathaniel W. Wraxall, *Historical Memoirs of My Own Time*, 5 vols., London, 1884, 2:226-27; T. W. Copeland, *The Correspondence of Edmund Burke*, 10 vols., Chicago, 1938-1978, 6:15; Keith Feiling, *The Second Tory Party*, London, 1938, pp. 138, 204. Also, William Smith MSS., 12/58:2-4, Dr. Williams's Library, London.

[32] According to Money, no "continuous predisposing condition" existed in Birmingham politics "until the bitterness of Churchmen and Dissenters . . . provided a polarizing issue within Birmingham itself." John Money, "Taverns, Coffee Houses, and Clubs," *Historical Journal* 14,1(1971):23-24; Thomas Lacqueur, "What Was Popular Religion in the Eighteenth Century," paper delivered at the Annual Meeting of the American Historical Association, San Francisco, December 29, 1978.

"them" in these localities, but religion may have done so with growing effectiveness as the focus of the Church was transformed. James Obelkevich has pointed to the existence of religious communities in nineteenth-century Lincoln and argued that religious dogma was ultimately less critical than the sense of community definition that sprang from religious differences.[33] Such seems to have been the case nearer the turn of the nineteenth century. Doctrinal disputes aside, religion in these towns took on political significance in exactly this sense. Religion was a social phenomenon, and as such should have been reflected in the voting behavior of these electors. Many contemporary observers clearly expected such behavior.

However, some historians have voiced suspicions about the existence of any meaningful relationship between religious and political affiliations. R. A. Smith's denial of "any particular religious coloring" to national politics under George III corroborates John Brooke's assertion that "eighteenth-century politics had dropped its concern for religion" by the later decades of the century.[34] One of the most recent looks at unreformed politics, after examining the evidence on which many of the allegations of church-party connections are based, concurred that the most often cited claims of Nonconformist ties to the anti-Administration party may well have been political rhetoric at best and the product of "Whig" history at worst.[35] Pointing to the lack of solid evidence linking Nonconformists and Whig politics, James Bradley argued that no reasonably supported conclusions can be drawn from the existing evidence, particularly for ordinary Nonconformists.

[33] James Obelkevich, *Religion and Rural Society: South Lindsey, 1825-1875*, Oxford, 1976, pp. 313-31.

[34] R. A. Smith, *Eighteenth Century English Politics*, New York, 1972, p. 69; John Brooke, "Party in the Eighteenth Century," in *Silver Renaissance*, ed. Alex Natan, London, 1961, p. 22.

[35] James E. Bradley, "Whigs and Nonconformists," *Eighteenth Century Studies* 9(1975):1-27.

Contemporaries were, on the whole, equally uncertain about Nonconformist political sympathies. Despite Fox's attention "to the Cause of Dissent" that prompted him at one point to profess his willingness to "take any part they [the Dissenters] desire of me," Edmund Burke was unsure of the side Nonconformists would choose even in late 1789. Writing to Fox in September of that year, Burke felt the Dissenters were "inclined to come over to" Fox's camp, but stressed the need for additional encouragements to insure their backing. Dissenters were, he contended, "a set of men powerful enough in many things, but most of all in Elections," and their "good or ill humor" was going to be "sensibly felt at the General Election."[36] Burke, Christopher Wyvill, Richard Price, and many of their fellows, though possibly uncertain or in disagreement over the particular political predispositions of the Dissenters at any given time, tended to agree, however, that Nonconformists exhibited a united front, and no small number believed with Burke that their numbers were potentially significant in the course of political disputes. Comments about the strength of Dissent were commonplace.[37] Even George III acknowledged their political weight, advising Lord North in 1772 not to press for votes against the repeal of the Test and Corporation Acts from those M.P.'s returned on the "Dissenting interest."[38]

Accepting, then, the considerable potential influence of Nonconformist electors, the question becomes whether or not their allegiance was a durable mainstay of the anti-Administration party with the possible exception of the

[36] Copeland, *Correspondence of Edmund Burke*, 6:15.

[37] In 1772, Walpole noted that the "Ministers, afraid of disobliging the Dissenters before the General Election, suffered the bill to pass the House of Commons." Horace Walpole, *Last Journals*, ed. A. F. Steuart, 2 vols., London, 1910, 2:89. Also, Davis, *Dissent in Politics*, p. 36; G. M. Trevelyan, *History of England*, London, 1937, p. 561; Frank O'Gorman, *The Whig Party and the French Revolution*, London, 1967, p. 49.

[38] W. B. Donne, ed., *The Correspondence of George III with Lord North*, 2 vols., London, 1967, 1:101; Walpole, *Last Journals*, 1:89.

general election of 1784 when the Fox-North alliance rendered partisan ties less distinct. More specifically, were the religious preferences of electors in Norwich, Maidstone, and Northampton related to partisan choices? Unfortunately, Maidstone Dissenting voters proved almost impossible to isolate. Rowse estimated Maidstone's Nonconformist population as nearly half the total population by the early nineteenth century, yet no more than a handful of Maidstone's voters could be identified positively as Nonconformists through Dissenting church rolls, baptismal or death records.[39] Even though a substantial Nonconformist population made up a large share of Maidstone's several thousand inhabitants and certainly found its way into the electorate in sizeable numbers, most of the Nonconformist voters in Maidstone defied identification. The small cluster of Maidstone electors who could be tied to Dissent behaved much as their fellow Nonconformists in Norwich and Northampton, since anti-Ministerialist candidates won the preponderant share of their votes at each election after 1780, but too few could be identified for a strong inference.

Data survival and record-linkage requirements kept the number of definite Nonconformists available for analysis fairly low in Norwich and Northampton as well, but in both boroughs, reasonably large, albeit nonrandom samples were created by linking voting data and church records.[40] These positively identified Nonconformists in the electorates of Norwich and Northampton provide the basis for the first quantitative assessment of Dissenting politics in the late eighteenth century. Rather than isolating and treating sep-

[39] The methods employed to identify Dissenting voters are described in Appendix I. Records of Nonconformist baptisms, marriages, and deaths, along with church membership rolls, were combined to form comprehensive lists of the identifiable Dissenters in each borough, and these lists were linked to the lists of voters.

[40] Nonconformist Registers, PROP. These registers were gathered in 1837. J. D. Chambers, *Population, Economy, and Society in Pre-Industrial England*, London, 1972.

arately the Baptists, Independents, and the other disparate and clearly distinctive elements within the framework of English Nonconformity, this analysis imposes an ecumenicism partly justified by the assumptions of George III, Edmund Burke, and others that Dissenters could be discussed collectively, and partly prescribed by the difficulty encountered in positively identifying Nonconformists. Even as a group, the numbers of Nonconformist electors definitely identified in the Norwich and Northampton electorates were barely large enough to allow meaningful analysis. Moreover, the singularly uniform political behavior of these Nonconformists, of whatever description, substantially reduced the need to separate Dissenting voters into their various denominations. In short, comprehension was mandatory for a voting analysis. Religious convictions are not at issue, nor could they be considered since neither ideas nor the intensity with which ideas were held can be measured with the available data. At issue is the existence of a community of like minds enforced by the decidedly inferior position of all Nonconformist denominations in English society.

The behavior of these two fairly large groups of Dissenters in Norwich and Northampton reveals the development of an unmistakable and growing relationship between Dissenters and the Whig party at the elections following the general election of 1774, not just among the Dissenting elite but within the rank and file as well. The association of religious and political preferences were of a different magnitude than the few weak links between socio-economic status and partisan preference. Religion may have been *the* determinant of many votes. The bond of religion apparently overcame even the normally nonpartisan tendencies of Northampton voters. Moreover, though inference from ecological correlations must be made with considerable caution and skepticism, particularly when the relationships are complicated, the areal religious distributions in these boroughs corresponded closely to the as yet unexplained and

291

often exaggerated variations in the partisan choices of the Norwich wards and reinforce the evidence of individual Nonconformist voting patterns.

Turning first to the individual partisan choices of Norwich Dissenters, the Nonconformist movement toward anti-Administration candidates over the first two decades of George III's reign could hardly have been more definite. A majority of the positively identified Dissenters voted for Administration candidates in the Norwich contests of 1761 and 1768, as did most of the entire Norwich electorate. At the 1780 election, though, the Norwich Dissenters diverged from the overall pattern and left the Administration camp; the anti-Administration candidate, William Windham, captured 60 percent of the identifiable Dissenting vote (Figure 7.1). At the hotly contested election of 1802, the Free Blues in Norwich won an impressive 90 percent of the Nonconformist vote. The entire Norwich electorate cast a proportionately heavier vote for Free Blue candidates in the elections after 1790, but the anti-Administration victories among the Dissenters apparently developed more rapidly and with greater impact than among the voting populace as a whole. Initially, the Norwich Nonconformists behaved essentially like the other electors, and their degree of partisanship paralleled the larger electorate for the entire period. No partisan bias appeared among the Nonconformists until the radical shift to the anti-Ministerialists at the 1780 election. The Norwich electorate split their votes evenly between the two parties in 1780; the Free Blues attracted 45 percent of the vote to the Orange-and-Purple's 42 percent and Norwich returned one government supporter and one government opponent. In contrast, the identifiable Nonconformists cast 63 percent of their ballots for the Free Blues and only 21 percent for the Orange-and-Purple candidates. The discrepancy between the overall voting pattern and the votes of the Nonconformist sample widened in 1784 and continued to be drastically unlike the general vote at each of the remaining general elections examined.

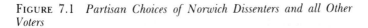

FIGURE 7.1   *Partisan Choices of Norwich Dissenters and all Other Voters*

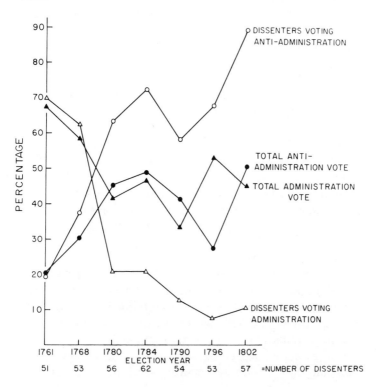

Without a larger and more randomly collected sample of the Norwich Dissenting electorate, and in the absence of some indication of the religious preferences of the voters in the "unidentified" category, acceptably rigorous statistical inferences concerning the impact of Dissent on partisan choice cannot be drawn; this sample of Norwich Dissenters might not be a representative sample although there are no indications that its nonrandomness skewed the results. Nevertheless, the commanding strength of the anti-Administration stance taken by these Nonconformists makes

293

an exceptionally strong argument that the Norwich Dissenters as a group voted overwhelmingly and consistently "Whig" in the elections of the last two decades of the century.

The votes of the Norwich clergy reinforce this image of religiously based voting choices. The number of clerics in the Norwich electorate ranged from a low of 58 at the 1790 election to a high of 108 participating in the 1802 election. With the single exception of the 1790 election, the Norwich clergy voted overwhelmingly for the Administration party. The 1790 deviation, when the clergy split most of their votes, possibly resulted from the ambivalence of William Windham's political position. Though still nominally a Free Blue in 1790, Windham rejected many of the demands of the Free Blues, he appealed to the principles of many of the Ministerialists in opposing issues like the reform of parliament, and he joined their ranks officially before the next general election in 1796.[41]

Voting patterns among identifiable Dissenting voters in Northampton suggest the same relationship between religious and partisan affiliations, though the lack of local parties and the occasional exertions of the politically opposed leading families (the Spencers and Northamptons) produced a higher degree of nonpartisan voting among the Northampton electorate generally (including the identifiable Nonconformists) than among the voters of Norwich. Figure 7.2 illustrates the radical divergence of Northampton's Nonconformists at the general elections of 1784, 1790, and 1796. As in Norwich, identifiable Nonconformists in the electorate cast more anti-Administration and fewer Administration votes than the overall electorate. Because of the possibility of split voting, these trends did not have to occur simultaneously, and each underscores in a differ-

---

[41] Windham "turned coat" in 1794, joining Pitt's ministry as Minister of War. For an ex-opponent of war and an ex-Foxite, a more striking change could hardly have been accomplished.

ent way the image of Nonconformist political behavior. The relative paucity of partisan votes by Nonconformists and others alike, however, reduces the comparability of the Norwich and Northampton voting patterns. Because of the generally high level of partisan voting across the Norwich electorate, the affinity of the Norwich Nonconformists for anti-Administration candidates stands out clearly in Figure 7.1; Norwich Dissenters gave "Whig" candidates over- whelming majorities at each election following 1768. Northampton voters cast fewer partisan ballots as a rule, and in the three Northampton elections that can be taken seriously (1784, 1790, and 1796), the Nonconformists gave anti-Administration candidates a majority but once. Even so, the Northampton voting patterns clearly point to an interweaving of Dissenting and anti-Administration sym- pathies. The overall anti-Administration vote in North- ampton remained exceedingly small at the elections of 1784 and 1790 as a result of both the necessity of plumping for the single anti-Administration candidate and the relatively strong support mustered by Administration forces. At both contests, the Nonconformists cast twice as many partisan ballots for the anti-Administration candidate. Their will- ingness to vote for the Administration fell precipitously at the same time. Administration candidates won almost 40 percent of the overall vote in 1790 yet attracted less than 14 percent of the Nonconformist vote. This trend contin- ued in the subsequent election. Administration candidates easily won the 1796 election with approximately 50 percent of the total vote; less than 8 percent of the Nonconformist vote went to the Ministerialists. A majority of the identifi- able Dissenters plumped for the single government op- ponent, Edward Bouverie. Though it meant throwing away one of their ballots, they refused to back either of the sup- porters of the Administration.

Possibly the best comparison of the voting patterns of Norwich and Northampton Dissenting electors is accom- plished by comparing the proportionate differences of

FIGURE 7.2 *Partisan Choices of Northampton Dissenters and All Other Voters*

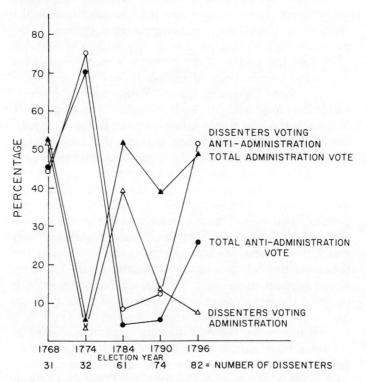

Administration and anti-Administration votes among positively identified Dissenters to the partisan stances of the other voters in each community (Figures 7.3 and 7.4).[42] By

---

[42] Figures 7.3 and 7.4 are simply a visual demonstration of the difference between the voting choices of the identifiable Dissenters in Norwich and Northampton and the other electors in both towns. The percentage of the total anti-Administration vote at the Norwich election of 1796 was only 27 percent, while the Dissenting "Whig" vote at that same election was 68 percent. Thus the Norwich Dissenting vote for the Free Blue candidate was some 141 percent higher than the overall anti-Administration vote and is plotted accordingly in Figure 7.3. Similarly, in 1796,

296

graphing the results of such comparisons, the predilection of Norwich voters for partisan ballots and the corresponding scarcity of straight-party ballots in Northampton are ignored in favor of a measure of *relative* anti-Administration support and Administration support by the Dissenting electorate. Nonconformists in Norwich and Northampton deviated from the norm beginning with the 1774 Northampton and 1780 Norwich contests, and a sharp and steady trend away from the ranks of the Administration permeated both groups of Nonconformist voters. The movement toward anti-Administration candidates was equally striking in both towns, with the single noticeable deviation in Norwich at the election of 1790 when Norwich voters were confused by William Windham's variable and sometimes paradoxical political views. The effects of the confusion are reflected in the fall in the proportionate strength of the anti-Administration party among Norwich Dissenters, just as the confusion affected the level of straight-party voting and consistent party voting of the entire Norwich electorate (see Figure 6.6 and Table 6.1). Precise inferences are possible in neither Northampton nor Norwich, but in both boroughs the apparent relationship is sufficiently strong to point convincingly to religion as a significant determinant of partisan choice. Even when a borough like Northampton lacked the local partisan framework that played such a critical role in the development of widespread and consistent partisan behavior, religion helped shape political behavior. The lack of a partisan framework impeded the development of partisan ties among the Nonconformists somewhat more than among the Northampton electorate as a whole in 1784 and 1790, and their partisan behavior

51.5 percent of the Northampton Dissenters voted for the Whig candidate, Edward Bouverie, as opposed to the overall straight-Whig vote of 26.1 percent at that election. Thus the Northampton anti-Administration vote plotted in Figure 7.4 was approximately 98 percent higher than the ordinary vote, just as the Dissenting votes for the Administration candidates at that election were almost 80 percent lower than the norm.

297

FIGURE 7.3 *Partisan Votes of Norwich Dissenters Compared to Overall Vote*

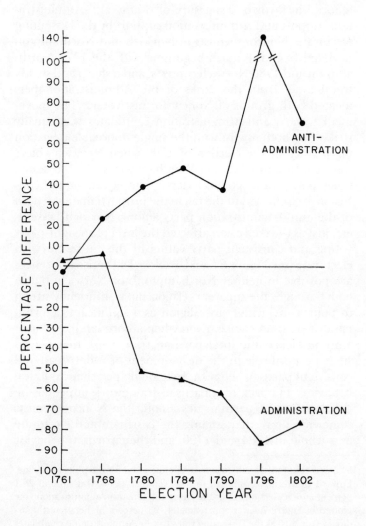

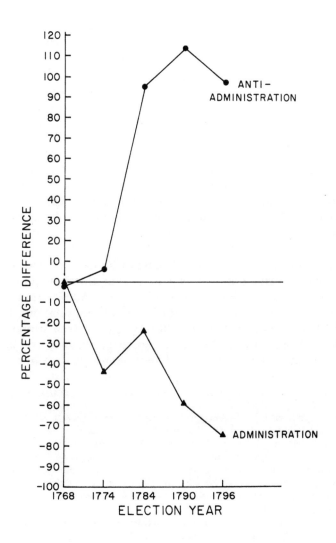

FIGURE 7.4 *Partisan Votes of Northampton Dissenters Compared to Overall Vote*

left much to be desired. Nevertheless, those Northampton Nonconformists who *were* won to partisanship almost invariably aligned themselves against the Administration by 1796.

The partisan predilections of the identifiable Dissenters in Norwich and Northampton were not hidden correlates of occupational and/or economic differences. Nonconformity has often been linked to social inferiority; allegedly, one had only to "scratch a cordwainer to find a Dissenter."[43] The Norwich Ministerialists voiced the opinion in 1802 that "religious mysticism" (Nonconformity generally) drew its strength from artisans and other citizens with equally inferior occupations and economic standings. These assessments, if accurate, raise the possibility that the anti-Administration votes cast by Dissenters might have reflected their socio-economic status instead of their membership in a particular religious community, or that at best religious differences might have been one of a larger set of politically significant socio-economic variables. Instead of confirming the suspicions of Everitt and others who have argued for social distinctions among religious groups, the occupational distributions of the overwhelmingly anti-Administration Dissenters in Norwich and Northampton lend substance to E. A. Payne's comment that "the Whigs . . . drew support from Nonconformity in all its social gradations."[44] The Norwich Dissenters were well represented in each of the occupational categories employed in this analysis (Table 7.14). Actually, if these figures indicate the occupational

[43] Alan Everitt, *The Pattern of Rural Dissent*, Leicester, 1972, p. 37; Smith, *English Politics*, p. 65; R. G. Cowherd, *The Politics of English Dissent*, New York, 1956, p. 15. Cowherd argued that "at the beginning of the nineteenth century, the Dissenters were primarily middle class." John Man divided Reading Nonconformists into distinct social categories. He found the Calvinists of the "best" quality, the Methodists of "middling quality" and the Baptists of "the lower class." John Man, *Stranger in Reading*, London, 1810, pp. 138-46.

[44] E. A. Payne, "Toleration and Establishment," in *From Uniformity to Unity*, ed. G. Nuttall and O. Chadwick, London, 1962, p. 257.

distribution of all enfranchised Norwich Nonconformists, their ranks were biased toward the "middling and lesser merchants and tradesmen" rather than the occupations of laboring men, craftsmen, and artisans. The Northampton Dissenters mirrored even more precisely the occupational parameters of the Northampton electorate (Table 7.14). Northampton Nonconformists tended to be found among the more respectable of Northampton's artisans, but on the average, each occupational gradation managed a reasonably proportionate representation.

A move from the behavior of individual Dissenters to an explanation of the disparate partisan stands of the various Norwich wards and Northampton parishes ventures into much less certain territory, particularly in Northampton. Yet again religious differences emerge as the single variable corresponding to voting patterns; the aggregate figures for Norwich are as impressive as the behavior of individual Nonconformists in both boroughs. The economic and social ranks of the Norwich wards were completely unrelated to their political characteristics (Table 7.13), but major religious differences distinguished the four wards (Table 7.15). The residents of the Northern and Conisford wards were as unlike in their choices of religion as they were in their choices of parliamentary candidates. Voters in the Conisford and Northern wards had achieved an impressive political polarity by the contest of 1802; 65 percent of Conisford's resident voters cast "Tory" ballots and 75 percent of the electors in the Northern ward voted "Whig." In

Table 7.14: Areal Economic and Occupational Differences in Northampton (Percentage)

Occupational Strata	St. Giles	St. Sepulchre	St. Peter	All Saints
I	9.2	9.3	9.0	8.5
II	24.3	24.9	22.6	26.1
III	66.5	65.8	68.4	65.4

contrast to their political dissimilarities, these two wards were the poorest of the four by a considerable margin and contained the largest proportions of voters claiming occupations in the lowest occupational category, again by a comfortable margin over the other wards. A radical discrepancy in their shares of the Nonconformist populace, however, offset their occupational and economic parity. Norwich's Dissenting electors seem to have been heavily concentrated in the Northern ward. Conisford ward appears to have held few indeed. Less than 5 percent of the homes of Norwich's identifiable Dissenters at each of the seven parliamentary elections of the period fell within the boundaries of Conisford ward; well over 50 percent were located across the Wensum in the "Great" Northern ward. The Northern ward also held a larger proportion of all Norwich's citizens, but taking population differentials into account by constructing a simple index of Nonconformity (Table 7.15), the relative positions of the Conisford and Northern wards persist.[45] Dissenting voters tended to live outside Conisford, and the Northern ward contained many more Dissenters than a random distribution would have produced. By the same token, partisan preferences rarely marked the voters of Norwich's two other wards (Mancroft and Wymer) where the proportion of the Dissenting population tended to be unremarkable. The same case for the impact of religious differences on areal voting patterns cannot be made for the Northampton electorate since the Nonconformists seem to have been distributed residentially almost exactly in proportion to the distribution of the electorate, but the concentration of Nonconformist chapels in All Saints parish suggests that the southern parishes, where anti-Administration voting proved so popular, might

[45] Nonconformist registers (on deposit at the Public Record Office) for all of the Norwich Dissenting chapels were used to identify Norwich's Nonconformist electors. Therefore, the spatially skewed distribution of Norwich's Dissenters as illustrated in Table 7.15 is not an artifact caused by varying survival rates of Nonconformist records. See note 33, Chapter 5.

have been a stronghold of Dissent. Certainly the anti-Ministerialist bias of the voters in the southern parishes was unrelated to aggregate occupational or economic differences, just as anti-Ministerialist votes in Northampton were unrelated to individual socio-economic variations (Table 7.15).

In order to be applied more generally, the political impact of Dissent must be examined in more than just these two boroughs for which such impressive evidence exists, and the third (Maidstone) for which insufficient data implies that "the names Whig and Tory were mere labels for local, religious parties."[46] Yet such unambiguous behavior by Norwich and Northampton Dissenters suggests that religious differences may have stimulated and embittered political disputes wherever electorates contained a large Nonconformist element. More than forty English borough constituencies experienced contested elections regularly, often consecutively, in the years following 1761.[47] Another

Table 7.15: Occupational Compositions of Norwich and Northampton Nonconformists and Other Voters (Percentage)

Functional Occupational Categories	Norwich		Northampton	
	Nonconformists	Electorate	Nonconformists	Electorate
I. Gentlemen, Professions	8.4	11.6	6.5	6.3
II. Merchants, Entrepreneurs	10.1	5.1	3.1	4.6
III. Retailers	19.1	16.3	21.1	19.5
IV. Agriculturalists	—	3.3	—	.7
V. Craftsmen, Artisans, Skilled Workmen	59.7	60.6	56.0	54.9
VI. Laborers	1.7	1.2	11.0	12.2
VII. Other	1.0	1.9	2.3	1.8

[46] W. T. Selley, *Eighteenth Century England*, London, 1939, p. 345.

[47] The frequently contested borough constituencies were: Abingdon, Bedford, Barnstaple, Boston, Bridgewater, Bristol, Beverley, Colchester, Cirencester, Canterbury, Coventry, Crickdale, Dorchester, Dover, Down-

group of twenty-two boroughs have been identified as places where "Nonconformity wielded a considerable amount of political power."[48] Twelve of the twenty-two strongly "Nonconformist" boroughs were also contained among those forty boroughs with frequently contested elections, and another five experienced contests in more than four of the eight general elections between 1761 and 1802. Thus, all together, three-quarters of the boroughs with strong Dissenting interests went to the polls more often than not over these four decades. In comparison, a completely random sample of England's borough constituencies would contain no more than 30 percent in which contests occurred more than half the time. In such a random sample, another 30 percent would have remained completely uncontested over these eight parliamentary elections, yet not one of the twenty-two "Nonconformist" boroughs completely avoided contested elections.[49]

This assay of the connections tying political dissent to religious Nonconformity has yielded ore of exceptionally high quality. A clear-cut, intense, and strengthening relationship between Opposition politics and Nonconformity dominated popular political behavior in the boroughs where the relationship could be measured. It would push the argument too far to take a leaf from the standard "class"

---

ton, Evesham, Great Grimsby, Great Marlow, Honiton, Hertford, Hindon, Hull, Hythe, Ilchester, Ipswich, Leominster, Liverpool, Leicester, London, Lewes, Maidstone, Northampton, Norwich, Nottingham, Okehampton, Penryn, Plymouth, Pontefract, Poole, Reading, Rochester, Seaford, Shaftesbury, Sudbury, Southwark, Westminster, and Worcester.

[48] The following boroughs seem to have been "strongholds" of Nonconformity, based on the accounts of James Bradley, Namier and Brooke, Sedgwick, and others: Cirencester, Taunton, Preston, Exeter, Leicester, Liverpool, Norwich, Nottingham, Coventry, Worcester, Portsmouth, Hertford, Maldon, Ipswich, Cambridge, Bridport, Bristol, Maidstone, Great Yarmouth, Lewes, Tiverton, and Harwich.

[49] The number of boroughs involved is too small for a normal test of significance, but using Fisher's Exact Test (a derivative of x^2), this pattern is statistically significant.

Table 7.16: Areal Distribution of Norwich and Northampton
Nonconformists
(Percentage)

	Proportion of All Nonconformist Voters Identified	Proportion of Entire Population	Index of Nonconformity*
Norwich Wards			
Conisford	3.3	19.7	.17
Mancroft	17.2	20.9	.82
Wymer	23.0	29.2	.79
Northern	56.5	30.2	1.87
Northampton Aggregated Parishes			
Northern	38.3	38.7	1.0
Southern	61.7	61.3	1.0

* PINV
  PEP

interpretation of modern British politics, and assert that
religion was the basis of partisan politics and that all else
was "embellishment and detail." But these figures argue
persuasively the significance of religion in popular politics.
There is little evidence that the political turmoil of the later
eighteenth century "was possibly as much social as religious
in its origin."[50] Social conflicts may have led to some political
conflict, particularly nonprescriptive conflicts, such as the
Birmingham riots, yet even rioting often displayed religious undertones, or overtones. Religion appears to have
been a central element, and perhaps the critical element in
the political and social perceptions of Nonconformist voters
in Norwich and Northampton. Their Anglican counterparts should have been affected as well, if somewhat less
dramatically. Their fellow Nonconformists in other English
parliamentary constituencies may well have shared their
views, if the few identifiable Maidstone dissenters are any
indication.

[50] Lewis B. Namier and John Brooke, *The House of Commons, 1754-1790*,
3 vols., London, 1964, 1:20.

CHAPTER EIGHT

Interpretations and Speculations

I T WOULD BE inappropriate to end this discussion of popular politics with a set of conclusions since, if nothing
else, these four boroughs graphically illustrate the extraordinary variety of unreformed politics and unreformed political behavior. Even so, this analysis of the actions of more
than 14,000 voters at elections scattered across four boroughs and four decades does provide a substantive basis
for interpretive statements concerning the behavior of the
unreformed electorate. Moreover, since the issues examined in the preceding chapters have not been limited to
the four principal boroughs exclusively, the results of these
analyses are broadly suggestive.

The eighteenth century undoubtedly enjoyed political
corruption of every variety, yet neither the incidence nor
the effects of corruption seem to have been as pervasive as
they are often alleged to have been. Nor did patrons suc-
ceed in eliminating the popular element in English politics.
Frequently, county electorates were prevented from participating actively in politics and they were almost always
denied a chance to use their franchises in parliamentary
elections. It is equally true that the eighteenth century wit-
nessed a general increase in the number of influenced borough seats in the Commons. Nevertheless, the number of
contested elections in boroughs with broader franchises
rose substantially following the general election of 1761.
Fundamental changes seem to have affected large sections
of England's electorate in the late 1770s and radically altered the behavior patterns of many English borough voters in the ensuing two decades. These changes occurred
simultaneously with, and may have been directly related

to, the increasing opportunities for electoral participation in many boroughs. There were, to be sure, extreme differences in the behavior of the voters in the four electorates examined; the electors of Norwich and Maidstone were affected both more drastically and much earlier than those in Lewes and Northampton. By the 1790s, though, a substantial proportion of the voters in all four constituencies had begun to behave in a remarkably partisan manner. Even in the absence of local partisan organizations, the Northampton electorate proved capable of decidedly partisan behavior at the election of 1796.

Participation at specific parliamentary elections was uniformly high in each of these boroughs, as was consistent participation over two or more elections. And in Norwich and Maidstone, where the opportunities for popular political participation were much greater as a result of recurring municipal elections, the frequency with which electors cast votes for a single party (if it was possible to do so without discarding a vote) rose precipitously. Moreover, it was increasingly the case that partisan votes were cast even when it was necessary for an elector to waste a vote in order to do so. Borough electors also supported the same parties with greater consistency at the general elections following 1780; by 1802 it was highly unlikely in Maidstone and not very likely in Norwich that an elector would switch his support from one party to the other between elections. The voting data suggest that given the opportunity to vote freely, as the borough voters often were, the unreformed electorate behaved in a characteristically and remarkably modern manner. Their partisan behavior frequently resembled, and sometimes surpassed, that of electors in eras more clearly dominated by party politics.

The difficulties encountered in the analyses of each borough have underlined the importance of a relatively detailed knowledge of the logistics and specific circumstances of particular borough elections. The data from these four boroughs, however, point to at least fifty-six other fre-

307

quently contested boroughs containing well over 40 percent of the entire borough electorate, which may have been undergoing similar experiences. With the addition of these four boroughs, a total of sixty borough constituencies encompassing more than half of England's borough electors provided settings with tremendous potential for the development of partisan behavior. The realization of that potential seems to have depended largely upon (1) the number and frequency of opportunities for electoral participation, which were, in turn, determined largely by municipal governmental structures; (2) the level of sophistication of local party organizations; and (3) the proportionate local strength of Nonconformity. Frequent parliamentary contests may have been a necessary condition for the development of partisan behavior, but they were not sufficient; other political and social characteristics were equally important. And, since relatively high levels of partisan behavior should have developed in those boroughs that met these three requirements, it seems highly probable that by the late 1780s, party politics generally and partisan considerations specifically had become crucial in structuring the behavior of a substantial proportion of the English borough electorate.

The development of this partisan behavior does not seem to have been a reflection of measurable social and/or economic inequalities within the electorate. A noticeable, albeit marginal, disparity marked the socio-economic status of the two groups of partisan voters in Norwich in the 1790s, and in Maidstone at the election of 1796. The poorer and socially inferior Norwich and Maidstone voters tended to support anti-Ministerialist candidates late in the century while a slightly greater proportion of the wealthier and more respectable electors voted for Ministerialists. These minor and unusual socio-economic distinctions lend little support to the argument that the French Revolution introduced an element of "class" consciousness and class conflict into English popular politics. If class conflict was being introduced into English popular politics, its impact was severely limited. Instead, the transformation of political behavior appears to have preceded the development of economic and social cleavages among partisan electors.

On the other hand, the relationship between partisan choice and religion in its broadest sense was exceptionally pronounced. In addition to the high correlation between the partisan choices and religious preferences of *individual* voters, partisan political battles seem to have been most common in those boroughs with strong Dissenting contingents. It was more than coincidental that the rapid increase in partisan behavior at Norwich elections corresponded exactly with the beginnings of a tight bond linking the Norwich Dissenters and the Blue-and-White Party. It also may have been more than coincidence that the general rise in partisan behavior took place along with the tremendous surge in the number of Dissenters in England.[1] Religion may not have been a divisive issue in the 1760s, but with the introduction of "fundamental and profound" issues at the general election of 1768, religious divisions took on new meaning and helped stimulate the development of partisan alignments in the 1780s.[2]

Men are generally assumed to act less upon "convictions" and "beliefs" than upon social and economic concerns, yet these data argue strongly for the impact of ideology on the electorate. The "ideology" underlying these later eighteenth-century conflicts, however, was not ideology in the usual sense of the word; these electors were not at odds over intangibles, abstractions, or vague political principles. Their ideological concerns were well-grounded in harsh reality. For example, four of the five elections in which partisan behavior was evident were held during the course of two unpopular wars, and in both instances, the Whigs were the vociferous advocates of peace. The "Whig" stand

---

[1] J. T. Krause, "The Changing Adequacy of English Registration, 1690-1837," in *Population in History*, ed. D. V. Glass, Chicago, 1965, p. 387.

[2] John Cannon, *Parliamentary Reform*, Cambridge, 1972, p. 61.

on other major issues such as parliamentary reform and the relative power of the Crown and parliament were not as clear-cut, but on a number of fronts, imprecise and far from unanimous stands were sufficient for voters to make "partisan" choices accordingly. For example, the Whigs were the champions of the movement to repeal the Test and Corporation Acts that Dissenters found so onerous, and they emerged as the recognized leaders of the struggle for Nonconformist rights. In a constituency like Norwich, specific elections like that of 1802 when William Smith led the Blue-and-White ticket reinforced the association that had begun to take shape nationally. It is hardly surprising that Nonconformists voted for the Whigs in such large numbers. As Richard Davis has pointed out, Dissenters were left with little choice—"they almost had to be Whigs."[3] This is not to argue that there was a nascent "democratic consciousness" among England's common people or even among ordinary electors in the late eighteenth century.[4] Rather, the behavior of these voters connotes simple, clearly defined, well-articulated struggles fought over issues of vital importance to the electorate, particularly those within the electorate with religious ties (or convictions) that placed them on the fringe of the body politic. Thus the issues at these elections often were neither difficult nor abstract; no recondite reasoning was required of the average voter. The evidence of votes, petitions, and other overt popular political activity suggests convincingly "that a considerable proportion of electors were perfectly aware of the issues at stake."[5]

Thus, the political, religious, and social cleavages that were to become so obvious in later nineteenth-century England were already evident among portions of the populace by the end of the eighteenth century. The demonstration

[3] Richard W. Davis, *Dissent in Politics*, London, 1971, p. 68.
[4] As is argued in E. P. Thompson, *The Making of the English Working Class*, London, 1963, pp. 74, 102.
[5] George Rudé, "The Middlesex Electors of 1768-69," *EHR* 75(1960):606.

of the existence of these elements in the 1790s raises as
many questions as it answers since the nature of the Victorian political system seems to have been quite different
from its Hanoverian predecessor despite the existence of
similar concerns in both. Social and economic considerations, not religious persuasions, have been identified as the
primary determinants of partisan choice in the mid-nineteenth century. Therefore, several questions loom large.
How, why, and when did the shift from religiously-colored
to class-dominated politics take place? The answers undoubtedly will be complex since developments across the
country were virtually never uniform.[6] However, by tracing
the spread of partisan political behavior, and by then examining the changing social bases of that behavior, it may
be possible to document the transition and explain the
emergence of what Alford and others have called "pure
class politics" in modern Britain.[7] The electors of Norwich,
Maidstone, Northampton, and Lewes under George III
have revealed a great deal of the eighteenth-century political system. A comparative analysis of their successors will
expand our knowledge of both centuries and improve our
understanding of the relationship between social and political change in a developing democracy.

[6] See Michael Hechter, *Internal Colonialism*, Berkeley, 1975.
[7] Robert Alford, *Party and Society: The Anglo-American Democracies*, Chicago, 1963.

APPENDIX I

Nominal Record Linkage

B EHAVIORAL ANALYSES often require both aggregate and individual-level data, but the latter often are not available, particularly for historical research. Even when such records have survived, the information necessary for an adequate identification of specific individuals usually is dispersed too widely to be useful. Fortunately, through a process known as nominal record linkage,[1] it is possible for clearly related but physically distinct bits of information concerning individuals to be accumulated into single inclusive records in accordance with explicitly stated and uniformly applied linkage rules. The nominal record linkage programs that will be described in this appendix, while devised for this analysis of English electoral behavior in the late eighteenth century, are far more broadly applicable. Even though the linkage programs will be discussed exclusively in terms of the English electorate, they could be employed by any other research project for which the linkage algorithm is appropriate.[2]

In the general elections held in England between 1761 and 1802, usually more than sixty borough constituencies were contested to the point of an actual poll, thus giving more than 50,000 borough electors the opportunity of voting to decide who was to represent them in the House of

[1] E. A. Wrigley, ed., *Identifying People in the Past*, London, 1973. The bibliography included in this general discussion of the problems is complete except for the following: Michael Katz and John Tiller, "Record Linkage for Everyman: A Semi-Automated Process," *Historical Methods Newsletter* 5(1972); Gloria Guth, "Surname Spellings and Computerized Record Linkage," *Historical Methods Newsletter* 10(1976).

[2] An algorithm is a set of operational rules specifying the steps through which a problem can be solved, or a goal achieved.

Commons. As described in Chapter 1, each elector cast his votes (or vote) in public, and they were recorded in poll-books, often accompanied by additional information such as the voter's occupation and address. Many of these polling lists have survived, and fortunately, a considerable amount of supplementary information concerning individual voters also can be found in poor rate assessments, rolls of Dissenting congregations, and petitions to the throne. It is therefore at least theoretically possible to identify each elector in some detail, but the theory is difficult to realize in practice since the information necessary to identify each individual adequately can be found only in several unrelated and physically distinct sets of records. It is difficult to collect all of the data concerning an individual at one election (or at any one point in time), and it is even more difficult to trace an individual across several elections, but both efforts were imperative to this research. Thus the information contained in the lists of voters at each election had to be linked to the supplementary evidence from tax rolls, directories, and the like, and the resulting lists for specific elections had to be compared to allow all of the information concerning each individual to be connected. If Thomas Ward, for example, voted in the elections of 1780, 1784, and 1790, it was necessary to combine the three sets of data concerning Ward into an extended record that would allow an analysis of his behavior over the several elections. Overcoming the first linkage problem allowed cross-sectional analysis, but accomplishing the second task made it possible to conduct the longitudinal analysis that was necessary to test the hypotheses most important to this study.

The same basic linkage problems were involved in dealing with both obstacles. Whether looking at voting records for a single election or combining records from eight successive elections, the problems involved were those of selection according to a limited number of "identifiers" or "sorting keys." Each bit of information concerning an in-

313

dividual is a potential identifier or sorting key, but if it is to be useful in linking two records, it must have appeared in each. Occupation and address were common identifiers in later eighteenth-century pollbooks, but if one list contained only occupations and another only addresses, then of course neither would be useful in an attempt to link the two. If, on the other hand, each list contained both addresses and occupations, then both could be used as sorting keys. Before discussing the general problems inherent in the use of keys, the identifiers common to *all* of the lists noted above must be considered separately: surnames and given names.

For the purposes of record linkage, names are simply strings of characters, and as such they are different from other identifiers only in the sense that the size of the string and differences in spellings result in more variations than are normal in other character strings. For example, the John Smith, cordwainer of St. Swithen's parish found on list A might very well be the same person who is found on list B as John Smythe, cordwainer of St. Swithen's, but even if the other conditions specified in the program are met and would allow linkage, the names must be recognized as identical by the program before they can be linked. This problem of variant spelling has been addressed frequently by those interested in nominal linkage and a number of possible solutions have been suggested, such as SOUNDEX and other coding schemes, but to eliminate the problems of variant name-spelling encountered in these records, a unique coding system was used that proved to be very effective.[3] Each surname was coded in a string of up to seven characters not ending in "e," "s," "es," or a double consonant. If the surname was longer than seven letters, it was reduced by the systematic deletion of first vowels and then

[3] In addition to the discussions contained in the works cited in note 1, that found in Ian Winchester, "The Linkage of Historical Records by Man and Computer: Techniques and Problems," *JIH* 1(1970) is useful, particularly for its test of SOUNDEX.

consonants proceeding from right to left. Thus Boling-broke or any of its various spellings became Blngbrk. Virtually all surname problems were eliminated by this simple procedure, but it was aided by the uniform spelling of a handful of other names. Smith, for example, was always coded with an "i" rather than a "y," and if double consonants were normal in a name, it was spelled accordingly. Cannon was never coded as Canon. Given names also were reduced to a two-character string, with a unique string for each, such a P- for Paul, PE for Peter, and PA for Patrick.

Unfortunately, names are seldom unique, and all too often, several identical names were encountered in a single list. If names were the only keys at our disposal, then often linkage would not be worthwhile since both the lack of certainty over the links that could be made (i.e., matching identical names that were unique to each list), and the numbers of cases where links were not possible (i.e., two or more identical names on each list) could invalidate any subsequent attempts to analyze the results. However, the additional sorting keys available, such as occupation and address, reduced the problem substantially. The probability of finding two entries of John Smith, cordwainer, of St. Swithen's on list B is much less than the probability of finding two otherwise unidentified John Smiths on each list. Fortunately, in the case of the electors with whom this analysis was concerned, five or six keys were almost always available. Even so, identical entries occasionally were found on specific lists. In those cases, all of the identical entries were deleted. Some account must be taken of these individuals even if only a few were affected. Unless an entry was distinguishable from the other entires on a single list, no linkage program could make the necessary discriminations in subsequent comparisons of several lists. Only a minuscule proportion of the electors was deleted in processing the initial lists for this study (less than .5 percent), but in comparing lists, considerably more entries were involved because of the difference in the number of identi-

315

fiers that were useful in linking two or more lists. Those
individuals who were list-unique, but not unique across lists
were excluded from consideration by that specific linkage
program, but they were not deleted from the data set. Consider, for example these two fictitious lists:

List A	List B
John Smith, cordwainer, St. Swithen, Whig	John Smith, cordwainer, Whig
John Smith, cordwainer, St. Peter Mancroft, Tory	John Smith, carpenter, Whig
John Smith, carpenter, All Saints, Whig	John Smith, plumber, Tory
John Smith, plumber, St. Margaret, Tory	John Smith, mason, Whig
John Smith, mason, St. James, Tory	

In both cases, all of the entries are list-unique, but the fact
that only names and occupation can be used as keys in
linking the two creates a problem with the two John Smiths
entered as cordwainers on list A. With no addresses for list
B, it is impossible to determine which John Smith, cordwainer, from list A should be linked to the single John
Smith, cordwainer, on list B. It has been argued that in
such a situation, one could use an individual's vote as an
additional key, thus linking the St. Swithen Smith from list
A to the one from list B since they both voted Whig.[4] Yet

[4] W. A. Speck and W. A. Gray, "Londoners at the Polls Under Anne
and George I," *Guildhall Studies in London History*, 1(1975):251-62; W. A.
Speck et al., "Computer Analysis of Pollbooks: An Initial Report," *BIHR*
43(1970):105-12; W. A. Speck et al., "Computer Analysis of Pollbooks: A
Further Report," *BIHR* 48(1975):64-90; Gloria Guth, "Some Problems of
Computerized Record Linkage," paper delivered at the Pacific Coast Con-
ference on British Studies, March, Claremont, Ca., 1974. There are situations in which vote could be used, in an effort to link records, but those
instances rarely occur if there are several sorting keys available. Speck,
Guth, and others using early eighteenth-century voting records might
occasionally find records such as the following:

such a procedure is completely unjustified and would negate the very purpose behind the linkage process. In this research, to prevent similar situations, before any two lists were linked they were presorted, using all of the keys available for the specific linkage step involved, and those that were not list-unique for that particular run were temporarily excluded from consideration, and included again only after the linkage was complete. Obviously this decreased the number of links that were made, but there was no alternative in these circumstances; no other legitimate links could be made.

As seen in the previous examples, sorting keys in addition to surnames and given names were critical in the linkage process, but they also presented problems of their own. Finding two list-unique John Smiths, cordwainers, of St. Swithen's leaves little doubt that a link should be made, but all too often (especially when tracing an individual over time) rather than being identical on all keys, the two entries varied slightly. Finding a John Smith, cordwainer, of St. Swithen's on list A and a John Smith, leather-dresser, of St. Swithen's, on list B raised a difficult question. If the John Smiths were still list-unique then the entries probably referred to the same person since the addresses were identical and the occupations were analogous. The problem was more difficult, however, if on list B in addition to John Smith, leather-dresser, of St. Swithen's, one also found John Smith, cordwainer, St. Margaret's. Could a link be justified

---

List A	*List B*
William Smith, Whig	William Smith, Whig
William Smith, Whig	William Smith, Whig

In linking records such as these, the fact that party choice was consistent in both cases would make it possible to link the four entries and to use the information for certain kinds of analysis. However, when occupation and address are added to the records, such situations rarely occur, and are made less useful by the need to look at behavior across an extended period. The appearance of a single William Smith on another list for example, would raise the problem of how this information could be linked to one of the other records.

in this instance? Obviously the assumptions that were made in order to link or not to link such entries had to be clearly stated and uniformly applied. Basically links were made only if reasonable certainty could be achieved, with reasonable certainty operationally defined as list-unique entries that agreed on all but one major point (such as address or occupation), or on two minor points (e.g., variant name spelling and analogous occupational titles).

Both the capabilities and the goals of these programs varied considerably, but there were three principal areas in which they were all similar. The first was the common requirement of list-unique entries. The inclusion of identical entries prevented the successful completion of any run that contained duplicates. The second commonly shared attribute was a reliance on the SORT/MERGE package program that is available on the Control Data Corporation's 6400, 6600, and 7200 model computers.[5] By relying on a packaged program for simple data sorting, it was possible to shorten the necessary programming time considerably without sacrificing any power or reliability. Only the programs that were concerned simply with data manipulation did not incorporate the SORT/MERGE package at some point. Finally, all of the linkage programs were based on the model of increasingly less perfect matches being linked from a continuously diminishing data base. Therefore, the programs were designed to run successively rather than simultaneously to allow linkage of perfectly matching records first, followed by the linkage of less perfectly matched records. This procedure greatly decreased the likelihood of improper links interfering with proper ones. Virtually every linkage decision required agreement on at least four keys (surname, given name, junior or senior, and one other), but the number of variations that were possible even with

[5] Every computer company has a similar package available for its users, but it might well be difficult to alter these programs to work with another SORT/MERGE package. Theoretically it should be a relatively simple matter, but in practice it can be extremely difficult, if not impossible.

318

relatively few sorting keys made the order of the linkage important. A complete description of the fifteen separate programs required to accomplish these goals has been published.[6]

While these programs provided a more "automated" linkage system than many of the suggestions that have been made heretofore, the researcher also was allowed a great deal of manual control over situations that required decisions far beyond the capabilities of all but the most elaborate computer programs. When massive files are being examined, as was the case in this research, it is certainly beneficial to use a system that will resolve automatically as many problems as possible, but it is nevertheless the case that a point of diminishing returns can be reached, even in programming. It is not necessary, and perhaps not even desirable, to rely on the machine for every decision. In this instance, after the computerized linkage had progressed as far as possible, computer-assisted manual linkage was employed to accomplish a few remaining links that proved beyond the capabilities of the automated linkage for a variety of unusual, and often unique reasons. Through these procedures, odd spelling errors and mispunches that may have been overlooked could be corrected, but more importantly, clearly identical but nonunique sets of records could be linked using essentially the same assumptions found in the earlier programs. Therefore, by the end of the last program, this combination of automated linkage and computer-assisted manual linkage had resulted in the amalgamation of all of the information available for each individual in the file.

In the study which these programs made possible, almost 30,000 individual voting records and over 50,000 card images of data were considered at some point in the linkage process, and this mass of information was reduced to ex-

[6] John Phillips, "Nominal Record Linkage and the Study of Individual-level Voting Behavior," *Laboratory for Political Research*, University of Iowa (1976):1-17.

tended records for 14,250 individual electors. With additional sorting keys, it would have been possible to reduce this final total, but only slightly. The file that was the end product of these programs is as accurate and as complete as the surviving data allowed. Happily, the data allowed a sufficiently high degree of both.

OCCUPATIONAL CLASSIFICATIONS

I. Gentry and Professions	Attorney Clergyman	Doctor/Surgeon Esquire Gentleman
II. Merchants and Entrepreneurs	Banker Broker Conveyancer Factor	Manufacturer Mercer Woolstapler Warfinger
III. Retailers	Apothecary Druggist Baker Barber Butcher Chandler Confectioner Draper Fruiterer Grocer Innkeeper/ Publican	Haberdasher Misc. Man (Chinaman, Glassman) Monger Salesman Shopkeeper Stationer Silversmith Goldsmith/ Jeweller Upholdster Watchmaker
IV. Agriculture	Farmer Husbandman	Miller Yeoman
V. Craft Trades/Artisans/ Skilled Workmen	Bookbinder Brazier Bricklayer Carver Carpenter Cordwainer Cooper Corkcutter Currier Cutler Dyer Gardener Glazier Glover Hatter Hosier Hotpresser	Hoyman Joiner Mason Misc. Maker (e.g., Lace, Comb, Stay) Painter Plasterer Saddler Sawyer Tailor Tallow Chandler Throwsterer Turner Weaver Woolcomber Woolsorter Wright

OCCUPATIONAL CLASSIFICATIONS

VI. Laboring Men	Carter	Porter
	Coachman	Servant
	Laborer	Waiter
VII. Other	City Employee	Musician
	Clerk (lay)	Soldier/Sailor
	Dancing/Music/	Surveyor
	Schoolmaster	Writer

OCCUPATIONAL RANKINGS

I. Elite

All of Category I
All of Category II
Surveyor

II. Middling Sort

All of Category III
Remainder of Category VII
   except soldier/sailor
All of Category IV except husbandman
cabinetmaker
dyer
enameller
engraver
instrument-maker
tanner
tapestry-weaver
watch-finisher
wine cooper

III. Lesser Sort

All of Category V (with above
   exceptions)
All of Category VI
articled clerk
soldier/sailor

APPENDIX III

GENERAL ELECTION RESULTS: 1761-1802

Election Year	Total Votes	Total Electorate
Norwich		
1761 Edward Bacon (S)	1,507	2,245
Harbord Harbord (I)	1,729	
Nockold Thompson (O)	718	
Robert Harvey (O)	499	
1768 Harbord Harbord (I)	1,802	2,726
Edward Bacon (S)	1,596	
Thomas Beevor (O)	1,136	
1774 NO CONTEST		
Sir Harbord Harbord (I)*		
Edward Bacon (S)		
1780 Sir Harbord Harbord (I-O)	1,382	2,367
Edward Bacon (S)	1,199	
John Thurlow (S)	1,103	
William Windham (O)	1,069	
1784 Sir Harbord Harbord (I-O)	2,305	2,529
William Windham (O)	1,297	
Henry Hobart (S)	1,233	
1790 Henry Hobart (S)	1,442	2,444
William Windham (O)	1,361	
Sir Thomas Beevor (O)	656	
1796 Henry Hobart (S)	1,622	2,299
William Windham (S)	1,159	
Bartlett Gurney (O)	1,076	
1802 Robert Fellowes (O)	1,532	2,862
William Smith (O)	1,439	
William Windham (S)	1,356	
John Frere (S)	1,328	
Norwich By-Election Results		
1786 Henry Hobart (S)	1,450	2,833
Sir Thomas Beevor (O)	1,383	
1787 Henry Hobart (S)	1,393	2,706
Sir Thomas Beevor (O)	1,313	

Election Year		Total Votes	Total Electorate
1794	William Windham (S)	1,236	2,006
	James Mingay (O)	770	
1799	John Frere (S)	1,345	2,531
	Robert Fellowes (O)	1,186	

Maidstone

1761	William Northey (O)	452	782
	Rose Fuller (O)	483	
	Gabriel Hanger (O)	440	
1768	Charles Marsham (O)	697	749
	Robert Gregory (O)	433	
	Arthur Annesley (S)	331	
1774	Sir Horace Mann (I)	541	692
	Heneage Finch (S)	456	
	Robert Gregory (O)	225	
1780	Sir Horace Mann (I)	550	707
	Clement Taylor (O)	399	
	Charles Finch (S)	362	
1784	Clement Taylor (O)	406	642
	William Geary (I)	393	
	Gerard Edwards (I)	324	
1790	Clement Taylor (O)	419	643
	Matthew Bloxham (S)	419	
	Robert Parker (S)	158	
1796	General Oliver Delancey (S)	415	583
	Matthew Bloxham (S)	328	
	Christopher Hull (O)	281	
1802	John H. Durrand (O)	415	619
	Matthew Bloxham (S)	381	
	John Henniker Major (S)	310	

Maidstone By-Election Results

1777	Charles Finch	235	436
	Charles Stanhope (Lord Mahon)	201	
1788	Matthew Bloxham (S)	328	635
	George Byng (O)	307	

324

Election Year	Total Votes	Total Electorate

Northampton

1761 NO CONTEST
Spencer Compton (S)
Frederick Montague (O)

1768 Sir George B. Rodney (S)	611	1,140
Sir George Osborne (S)	611	
Thomas Howe (O)	538	
1774 Wilbraham Tollemache (O)	786	904
Sir George Robinson (O)	692	
Sir James Langham (S)	266	

1780 NO CONTEST
George Spencer, Viscount Althorpe (O)
George Rodney (S)

1784 Charles Compton, Lord Compton (S)	823	893
Fiennes Trotman (S)	500	
Charles Bingham, Lord Lucan (O)	433	
1790 Charles Compton, Lord Compton (S)	822	893
Edward Bouverie (O)	599	
Colonel Manners (S)	265	
1796 Spencer Perceval (S)	720	991
Edward Bouverie (O)	512	
William Walcot, Jr. (S)	474	

1802 NO CONTEST
Spencer Perceval (S)
Edward Bouverie (O)

Lewes

1761 NO CONTEST
Sir Francis Poole (O)
Thomas Sergison (O)

1768 Thomas Hampden (O)	115	184
Thomas Hay (O)	110	
Thomas Miller (O)	92	
1774 Thomas Miller (O)	120	192
Thomas Hay (O)	102	
John T. Hampden (O)	82	
William Kemp (O)	40	

GENERAL ELECTION RESULTS, 1761-1802

Election Year	*Total Votes*	*Total Electorate*
1780 Henry Pelham (S)	96	153
Thomas Kemp (O)	91	
Thomas Hay (O)	76	
1784 Henry Pelham (O)	38	Contest
Thomas Kemp (S)	32	Conceded
Sir Henry Blackman (S)	7	
1790 Henry Pelham (O)	154	226
Thomas Kemp (S)	149	
Henry Shelley, Jr. (I)	88	
1796 Thomas Kemp (S)	215	279
John C. Pelham (S)	156	
William Green (O)	127	
1802 Francis Osborne, Lord Osborne (S)	214	334
Henry Shelley, Jr. (I)	179	
Thomas Kemp (S)	173	

NOTES:

(S) = Administration supporter; (O) = Administration opponent; (I) = independent

The figures for the polls occasionally differed in various sources; the vote totals in this appendix are from the pollbooks. For example, the *Kentish Chronicle* reported the number of electors in the 1796 Maidstone election as 589, yet only 583 voters actually cast ballots. The *Kentish Gazette* was closer in 1802, reporting 622 voters instead of the actual 619. Also, these figures are those recorded at the end of the poll and before any "scrutiny" such as the ones at Lewes in 1802, Norwich in 1786, and Northampton in 1768.

*Upon the death of his father in 1770, Harbord Harbord succeeded as second baronet.

BIBLIOGRAPHY

PRIMARY SOURCES

Manuscript Materials

BRISTOL. CENTRAL LIBRARY.
The Bristol Pollbook, 1774
CAMBRIDGE. CAMBRIDGE UNIVERSITY LIBRARY.
William Smith MSS.
LEWES. EAST SUSSEX RECORD OFFICE.
Glynde Palace MSS.
Shiffner MSS.
Hook MSS.
Woolgar MSS.
LONDON. BRITISH LIBRARY.
Fox Papers: BL Add. MSS. 47559, 47580, 47579
Liverpool Papers: BL Add. MSS. 38203, 38212, 38213, 38307
Newcastle Papers: BL Add. MSS. 32864, 32912, 32915-930, 32987, 32989
Perceval Papers: BL Add. MSS. 49179-214
Wilkes Papers: BL Add. MSS. 30868, 30870
Windham Papers: BL Add. MSS. 37846, 37885, 37906-908
LONDON. DR. WILLIAMS'S LIBRARY.
Harmer MSS.
Northampton MSS.
Odgers MSS.
Old Meeting, Norwich MSS.
William Smith MSS.
LONDON. LIBRARY OF THE SOCIETY OF FRIENDS.
Gurney MSS. 13291-293
Register of the Kent Monthly Meetings
Register of the Norfolk Monthly Meetings
Register of the Northamptonshire Monthly Meetings
LONDON. PUBLIC RECORD OFFICE, CHANCERY LANE.
County Land Tax Returns: E181-84
Home Office: H.O.55
Register of Bankrupts: B6

BIBLIOGRAPHY

Rodney Papers
Stationery Office: S.O.94
LONDON. PUBLIC RECORD OFFICE, PORTUGAL STREET.
Nonparochial records:
Maidstone:
Earl Street Presbyterian, 936
Week Street Chapel, 1010, 3575
Northampton:
Castle Hill Meeting, 1276, 1277, 1142
College Street Baptist, 902
King's Head Lane, 1275
Norwich:
Octagon Chapel, 1965, 1966
Old Meeting House, 1753, 1260, 653
St. Mary's Baptist, 361
St. Margaret's Baptist, 1785
Tabernacle, 1963, 3132
MAIDSTONE. KENT RECORD OFFICE.
Manuscript Poll Books:
Parliamentary: 1790
Municipal: 1764, 1768, 1771, 1772, 1774, 1775, 1782, 1786,
1788, 1791, 1793, 1794, 1795, 1799, 1801
Municipal Records:
Election Papers VII
Polhill MSS.
Rodney MSS.
Parish Poor Rate Assessments, Vols. 8-12
NORTHAMPTON. CITY RECORDER'S OFFICE.
Northampton Register of Freemen, 1730-1835
NORTHAMPTON. NORTHAMPTONSHIRE RECORD OFFICE.
All Saint's Poor Rate, 1779
Brooke MSS.
Fitzwilliam MSS.
Papers on Parliamentary Representation, 1732-1835
Spencer MSS.
St. Giles' Churchwarden's Account Books, 111, 112, 247
St. Peter's Churchwarden's Account Book, 23
St. Sepulchre Rate Books, 210-12
NORWICH. COLMAN AND RYE LOCAL HISTORY LIBRARY.
Copy of the Poll for Alderman, 1781
Miscellaneous Pieces in Prose and Verse Relative to the

Contested Election, 1768
Miscellaneous Verses and Squibs on the Norwich Election
NORWICH. NORWICH AND NORFOLK RECORD OFFICE.
Castle Corporation Minute Book
Dixon MSS. 92
Folkes MSS. 4338
Frasham MSS. 87
Molyneaux Letter Book
Norwich Corporation Assembly Books (Common Council) CS16, Vols. 10-11
Norwich Court of Mayoralty Books
Norwich Guardians of the Poor Minute Books
Norwich Freeman Admissions Book, 1761-1802
Norwich Parish Land Tax Assessments, 1761-1802, C23/S: A, B, and C/R16-291
Norwich Parish Poor Rate Assessments, 1761-1802, PD1-PD165
Norwich Register of Freemen, 1752-1816
Walsingham MSS. 154

Printed Primary Sources and Contemporary Printed Works

Amyot, Thomas. *Speeches in Parliament of W. Windham.* London, 1812.
An Alphabetical List of the Freemen Who Polled. Chester, 1784.
Annual Register. Vol. 33 (1793). London, 1824.
Aspinall, A. and Smith, E. A., eds. *English Historical Documents.* Vol. 11. London, 1959.
Bailey's British Directory. London, 1798.
Baring, Cecilia A., ed. *The Diary of William Windham.* London, 1866.
Barrow, J. H., ed. *Mirror of Parliament.* 2 vols. London, 1835.
Belsham, William. *Memoirs of the Reign of George III.* London, 1805.
Bogue, D., and Bennett, J. *History of Dissenters.* London, 1808.
Burke, Edmund. *Works.* 6 vols. London, 1848.
Chambers, John, *General History of Norfolk.* 2 vols. Norwich, 1829.
Chase, W. *The Norwich Directory.* Norwich, 1783.
Cobbett, W., ed. *The Parliamentary History of England.* 36 vols. London, 1806-1820.
The Contest: or A Collection of Papers Published during the Contest in Norfolk in 1767 and 1768. Norwich, 1768.
Complete Collection of the Papers Which Appeared . . . Northumberland, 1774. Alnwick, 1826.

Copeland, T. W., ed. *The Correspondence of Edmund Burke*. 10 vols. Chicago, 1958-1978.

A Correct Copy of the Evidence on the Norwich Petition by Which the Election of Henry Hobart (1786) Was Declared Void. Norwich, 1787.

Cox, J. C., ed. *The Records of the Borough of Northampton*. 2 vols. Northampton, 1898.

Crosby, George. *Crosby's Parliamentary Record*. Leeds, 1849.

Crouse, J. *Observations on the Present Controversy about the Mode of Assessment for the Poor's Rate in Norwich*. Norwich, 1795.

——. *The Norwich Directory*. Norwich, 1783.

Cursory Observations on a Speech of Mr. Windham's Addressed to the Electors of Norwich—Particularly Quakers, by a Child of Peace. Norwich, 1794.

Cutbush, Henry. *Handbook of Parliamentary Elections*. London, 1841.

Dinmore, Richard. *An Exposition on the Principles of the English Jacobins with Strictures on the Political Conduct of C.J.F., W. P., and E. B*. London, 1794.

The Election Budget. Norwich, 1818.

The Election Budget for 1799. Norwich, 1799.

The Election Magazine. Norwich, 1784.

Exact List of the Burgesses and Freeholders Who Polled. Nottingham, 1774.

Firth, William. *An Address to the Electors of Norwich*. Norwich, 1794.

Freeman, J. *History of the Town of Northampton*. Northampton, 1817.

Griffiths, V. *Picture of Parliament or A History of the General Election of 1802*. London, 1803.

Godwin, William. *Enquiry Concerning Political Justice*. London, 1796.

Gunn, J.A.W., ed. *Factions No More*. London, 1971.

Hanham, H. J., ed. *Dod's Electoral Facts*. Brighton, 1972.

Hansard, T. C. *The Parliamentary Debates*. London, 1806-1820.

Hatley, V. A. *Northamptonshire Militia Lists*. Northants, 1973.

Historical Manuscripts Commission. *Report on the Manuscripts of the Earl of Dartmouth*. 3 vols. London, 1887-1896.

——. *Report on the Manuscripts of the Marquess of Lothian*. London, 1905.

——. *Report on the Manuscripts of the Earl of Rutland*. 4 vols. London, 1888-1905.

Horsfield, T. W. *History of Lewes*. Lewes, 1824-1827.

House of Commons Sessional Papers, *Report of the Commission on Municipal Corporations*. Vols. 23-26. London, 1835.

Howlett, J. *Observations on the Increased Population, Healthiness, and Care in the Town of Maidstone*. Maidstone, 1782.

Hudson, W., and Tingey, J. C., eds. *Records of the City of Norwich*. 2 vols. Norwich, 1910.

James, William Roberts. *The Charters and Other Documents of Maidstone*. London, 1825.

Jones, John Gale. *A Sketch of a Political Tour Through Rockingham, Chatham, Maidstone, and Gravesend*. London, 1796.

Journals of the House of Commons.

Laprade, W. T., ed. *Parliamentary Papers of John Robinson 1774-1784*. Camden Miscellany, Third Series, Vol. 33. London, 1922.

Lee, William. *Ancient and Modern History of Lewes*. London, 1795.

A Letter to a Country Gentleman. Norwich, 1780.

Man, John. *Stranger in Reading*. London, 1810.

March, J. *Proceedings and Speeches at Meeting to petition Parliament against Lord Grenville's and Mr. Pitt's Treason and Sedition Bills*. Norwich, 1795.

Miscellaneous Pieces of Prose and Verse Relative to the Contested Election. Norwich, 1768.

Moens, W.J.W. *The Walloons and Their Church at Norwich*. London, 1887.

A Narrative of the Contested Election. Norwich, 1780.

A Narrative of the Contested Election. Norwich, 1785.

A New Election Budget in Five Numbers. Norwich, 1802.

Oldfield, T.H.B. *Representative History of Great Britain and Ireland*. 6 vols. London, 1816.

————. *The History of the Boroughs of Great Britain*. 2 vols. London, 1794.

Papers and Squibs Relating to the Chester Election of 1784. Chester, 1784.

Payne, T. *The Norwich Directory*. Norwich, 1802.

Piggott, Charles. *A Political Dictionary*. London, 1795.

Proceedings and Speeches of Meeting at St. Andrew's Hall, 11 Nov., 1795 to Petition Parliament against the Treason and Sedition Bills. Norwich, 1795.

Rowles, W. *A General History of Maidstone*. London, 1809.

A Short Treatise on the Institution of the Corporation by a Freeman. Maidstone, 1786.

Smith, Verena, ed. *The Town Book of Lewes, 1702-1837.* Lewes, 1972.

Stacy, John. *Topographical and Historical Account of Norwich.* London, 1819.

Stooks-Smith, Henry. *Register of Parliamentary Contested Elections.* London, 1842.

Thelwall, John. *An Appeal to Popular Opinion.* Norwich, 1796.

———. *The Rights of Nature.* London, 1796.

———. *The Peripatetic.* London, 1793.

Town and Country Magazine. London, 1774.

The Universal British Directory. London, 1794.

Vindication of Mr. Windham's Opponents. London, 1794.

Vindication of the Political Conduct of William Windham. London, 1802.

Walpole, Horace. *Correspondence.* Edited by W. S. Lewis. 42 vols. New Haven, 1967.

———. *Last Journals.* Edited by A. F. Steuart. 2 vols. London, 1910.

Willis, R. Legge. *A Glimpse Through the Gloom.* London, 1794.

Windham, William. *The Windham Papers.* Edited by Lord Rosebery. 2 vols. London, 1895.

Wraxall, Nathaniel. *Historical Memoirs of My Own Time.* 5 vols. London, 1884.

———. *A Short Review of the Political State of Great Britain.* London, 1787.

Wyvill, Christopher. *Political Papers.* 6 vols. London, 1794-1802.

Periodicals and Newspapers

Annual Register
The Cabinet (Norwich)
Canterbury Newsletter
Gentleman's Magazine
Kentish Chronicle or Canterbury Journal
Kentish Gazette
London Gazette
Maidstone Journal
Monthly Magazine
Norfolk Chronicle and Norwich Gazette

North Briton
Northampton Mercury
Norwich Mercury
Robin Snap (Norwich)
Lewes Journal

SECONDARY SOURCES

Articles

Abrahamson, Paul R. "Intergenerational Social Mobility and Partisan Choice." *American Political Science Review* 46(1972):1291-94.

Armstrong, W. A. "The Use of Information about Occupations." In *Nineteenth-Century Society*, edited by E. A. Wrigley. Cambridge, 1972.

Aspinall, A. "English Party Organization in the Nineteenth Century." *English Historical Review* 41(1926):389-411.

Atherton, Herbert. "The Mob in Caricature." *Eighteenth Century Studies* 12(1978):47-58.

Benson, Lee. "An Approach to the Scientific Study of Past Public Opinion." *Public Opinion Quarterly* 31(1968):522-67.

Bochel, J. M., and Denver, P. T. "Canvassing, Turnout and Party Support: An Experiment." *British Journal of Political Science* 1(1971):257-69.

Bradley, James E. "Whigs and Nonconformists." *Eighteenth Century Studies* 9(1975):1-27.

Buchanan, William. "Nominal and Ordinal Bivariate Statistics: The Practitioner's View." *American Journal of Political Science* 18(1974):625-46.

Burn, W. L. "Electoral Corruption in the Nineteenth Century." *Parliamentary Affairs* 4(1951):437-42.

Cameron, D. R. "Patterns of French Partisanship." *Public Opinion Quarterly* 36(1972):19-30.

Christie, I. R. "The Yorkshire Association, 1780-84: A Study in Political Organization." *The Historical Journal* 3(1960):144-61.

Clarke, P. F. "Electoral Sociology of Modern Britain." *History* 57(1972):31-55.

Colley, Linda J. "The Mitchell Election Division." *Bulletin of the Institute of Historical Research* 49(1976):80-107.

333

Colley, Linda J. "The Loyal Brotherhood and the Cocoa Tree." *The Historical Journal* 20(1977):77-95.

———. "The Principles and Practice of Eighteenth Century Party." *The Historical Journal* 22(1979):239-46.

Converse, P. E. "The Nature of Belief Systems in Mass Publics." In *Ideology and Discontent*, edited by D. Apter. New York, 1964.

Crittenden, John. "Aging and Party Affiliation." *Public Opinion Quarterly* 26(1962):648-57.

Crotty, W. J. "Party Effort and Its Impact on the Vote." *American Political Science Review* 65(1971):439-50.

Davis, Richard W. "The Whigs and the Idea of Electoral Deference." *Durham University Journal* 67(1974):79-91.

———. "Deference and Aristocracy in the Time of the Great Reform Act." *American Historical Review* 81(1976):532-39.

Ditchfield, G. M. "The Parliamentary Struggle over the Repeal of the Test and Corporation Acts, 1787-90." *English Historical Review* 352(1974):551-77.

Drake, Michael. "The Mid-Victorian Voter." *Journal of Interdisciplinary History* 1(1971):473-90.

Eulau, H. "Latent Partisanship in Nonpartisan Elections." In *The Electoral Process*, edited by M. Jennings. Englewood Cliffs, N.J., 1966.

Formisano, R. P. "Deferential-Participant Politics." *American Political Science Review* 68(1974):473-87.

Fryer, C. E. "Historical Revision: The General Election of 1784." *History* 9(1924):221-23.

George, M. D. "Pictorial Propaganda 1793-1815." *History* n.s. 31(1946):9-25.

———. "Fox's Martyrs." *Transactions of the Royal Historical Society*, 4th ser. 21(1939):133-68.

Ginter, Donald. "Financing of the Whig Party Organization." *American Historical Review* 71(1966):421-40.

———. "The Loyalist Association Movement of 1792-3 and British Public Opinion." *Historical Journal* 9(1966):179-90.

Guth, Gloria. "Surname Spellings and Computerized Record Linkage." *Historical Methods* 10(1976):10-19.

Hamilton, Howard. "The Municipal Voter: Voting and Non-Voting in City Elections." *American Political Science Review* 65(1971):1135-40.

Hanham, H. J. "The First Constituency Party?" *Political Studies* 9(1961):188-89.

Hanushek, E.; Jackson, J.; and Kain, J. "Model Specification: The Use of Aggregate Data and the Ecological Correlation Fallacy." *Political Methodology* 1(1974):87-106.

Hatley, V. A. "Literacy at Northampton." *Northamptonshire Past and Present* 15(1976):19-27.

―――. "Some Aspects of Northampton History." *Northamptonshire Past and Present* 3(1966):240-49.

Hawke, E. G. "William Pitt and Some Deluded Historians." *The Nineteenth Century and After* 94(1924):531-37.

Hill, B. W. "Executive Monarchy and the Challenge of the Parties, 1689-1832." *Historical Journal* 13(1970):379-401.

―――. "Fox and Burke: The Whig Party and the Question of Principle." *English Historical Review* 89(1974):1-24.

Holmes, Geoffrey. *The Electorate and the National Will in the First Age of Party*. (Pamphlet.) Kendall, 1976.

Horwitz, Henry. "The General Election of 1690." *Journal of British Studies* 11(1971):77-91.

Katz, Michael. "Occupational Classification in History." *Journal of Interdisciplinary History* 3(1972):63-88.

―――. "Social Structure in Hamilton, Ontario." In *Nineteenth-Century Cities*, edited by S. Thernstrom and R. Sennett. New Haven, 1969.

Kelley, Paul. "Radicalism and Public Opinion in the General Election of 1784." *Bulletin of the Institute of Historical Research* 45(1972):73-88.

―――. "British Parliamentary Politics, 1784-6." *Historical Journal* 17(1974):733-53.

Kraut, R. E. and McConahay, J. B. "How Being Interviewed Affects Voting: An Experiment." *Public Opinion Quarterly* 37(1973):398-406.

Landau, Norma. "Independence, Deference, and Voter Participation: The Behavior of the Electorate in Early-Eighteenth-Century Kent." *Historical Journal*, 22(1979):561-83.

Langford, Paul. "William Pitt and Public Opinion, 1757." *English Historical Review* 88(1973):54-80.

Laprade, W. T. "Public Opinion and the Election of 1784." *English Historical Review* 31(1916):224-37.

Laslett, Peter. "Le Brassage de la Population en France et en

Angleterre." *Annales de Démographie Historique* [Paris] (1968):99-109.

LeVine, Robert. "Political Socialization and Culture Change." In *Old Societies and New States*, edited by Clifford Geertz. New York, 1963.

Lucas, Perceval. "The Verrall Family of Lewes." *Sussex Archeological Collections* 58(1920):91-131.

McAdams, Donald R. "Electioneering Techniques in Populous Constituencies, 1784-96." *Studies in Burke and His Time* 14(1972):23-54.

Menzies, E. M. "The Freeman Voter in Liverpool, 1802-35." *Historical Society of Lancashire and Cheshire Transactions* 124(1973):83-107.

Mitchell, Austin. "The Association Movement, 1792-3." *The Historical Journal* 4(1961):56-77.

Mitchell, Jeremy C. "Electoral Strategy Under Open Voting." *Public Choice* 28(1976):17-35.

———, and Cornford, James. "The Political Demography of Cambridge, 1832-1868." *Albion* 9(1977):242-72.

Money, John. "Birmingham and the West Midlands, 1760-93: Politics and Regional Identity in the English Provinces in the Later 18th Century." *Midland History* 1(1971):1-19.

———. "Taverns, Coffee Houses, and Clubs." *Historical Journal* 14(1971):15-48.

Moore, D. C. "The Matter of the Missing Contests: Towards a Theory of Nineteenth Century English Politics." *Albion* 6(1974):93-119.

Nossiter, T. J. "Aspects of Electoral Behavior in English Constituencies." In *Mass Politics*, edited by E. Allardt and S. Rokkan. New York, 1970.

———. "Voting Behavior, 1832-1872." *Political Studies* 18(1968):380-89.

Phillips, John. "Nominal Record Linkage and the Study of Individual-level Voting Behavior." *Laboratory for Political Research*, University of Iowa (1976):1-77.

———. "Achieving a Critical Mass While Avoiding an Explosion." *Journal of Interdisciplinary History* 9(1979):493-508.

———. "The Structure of the Unreformed Electorate." *Journal of British Studies* 19(1979):76-100.

————. "Popular Politics in Unreformed England." *Journal of Modern History* 52(1980):599-625.

Plumb, J. H. "The Growth of the Electorate in England from 1600-1715." *Past and Present* 45(1969):90-116.

Pocock, J.G.A. "The Classical Theory of Deference." *American Historical Review* 81(1976):516-23.

Przeworski, Adam. "Contextual Models of Political Behavior." *Political Methodology* 1(1974):27-60.

Ransome, Mary. "Parliamentary History, 1689-1832." In *Victoria County History of Wiltshire*, edited by R. Pugh, 10 vols., 5:195-230. London, 1954.

Rector, W. K. "Lewes Quakers in the Seventeenth and Eighteenth Centuries." *Sussex Archeological Collections* 116(1978):31-40.

Reynolds, David. "A Spatial Model for Analyzing Voting Behavior." *Acta Sociologica* 12(1969):122-31.

Rogers, Nicholas. "Aristocratic Clientage, Trade, and Independency." *Past and Present* 61(1973):70-106.

Rose, J. H. "The Route of Coalition, 1784." *The Nineteenth Century and After* 95(1924):451-58.

Rose, R. B. "The Priestley Riots, 1791." *Past and Present* 18(1960):68-88.

Rudé, George. "The Middlesex Electors of 1768-89." *English Historical Review* 75(1960):601-17.

Schofield, R. S. "Age Specific Mobility in an Eighteenth Century Rural English Parish." *Annales de Démographie Historique* [Paris] (1971):261-74.

Shively, W. P. "Party Identification, Party Choice, and Voting Stability." *American Political Science Review* 66(1972):1203-25.

Smith, Daniel Scott. "The Estimates of Early American Historical Geographers." *Historical Methods* 12(1979):24-38.

Smith, E. A. "The Election Agent in English Politics 1734-1782." *English Historical Review* 84(1969):12-35.

Smith, Robert W. "Political Organization and Canvassing: Yorkshire Elections Before the Reform Bill." *American Historical Review* 74(1969):1538-60.

Speck, W. A., and Gray, W. A. "Computer Analysis of Pollbooks: A Further Report." *Bulletin of the Institute of Historical Research* 48(1975):64-90.

————. "A Computer Analysis of Poll Books: An Initial Report." *Bulletin of the Institute of Historical Research* 43(1970):105-12.

Speck, W. A., and Gray, W. A. "Londoners at the Polls Under Anne and George I." *Guildhall Studies in London History* 1(1975):251-62.

Spring, David. "Walter Bagelot and Deference." *American Historical Review* 81(1976):524-31.

Thomas, P.D.G. "The Beginnings of Parliamentary Reporting in Newspapers, 1768-1774." *English Historical Review* 74 (1959): 623-36.

Tratner, N. L. "Population and Social Structure in a Bedfordshire Parish: The Cardington List of 1782." *Population Studies* 21(1967):261-82.

———. "The Social Structure of a Bedford Parish in the Mid-Nineteenth Century." *International Review of Social History* 18(1973):90-106.

Von den Steinen, Karl. "The Fabric of Interest in the County: The Bucks Election of 1784." *Albion* 4(1972):206-18.

Ward, W. R. "The Administration of the Window and Assessed Taxes, 1696-1798." *English Historical Review* 67(1952):522-42.

Winkler, H. R. "Sir Lewes Namier." *Journal of Modern History* 25(1963):1-19.

Wright, D. G. "A Radical Borough in Parliamentary Politics: Bradford 1832-1841." *Northern History* 4(1969):132-66.

Books and Dissertations

Amyot, Thomas. *Some Account of the Life of William Windham.* London, 1812.

Armstrong, Alan. *Stability and Change in an English Country Town.* Cambridge, 1974.

Balls, F. A. "Parliamentary Elections in Norwich 1784-1832." Bachelor's thesis, University of East Anglia, 1954.

Barlow, R. B. *Citizenship and Conscience.* Philadelphia, 1962.

Baynes, A. D. *A Complete History of Norwich.* London, 1869.

Berelson, Bernard; Lazarsfeld, Paul; and McPhee, William. *Voting.* Chicago, 1954.

Birdsall, N. *History of Northampshire and Vicinity.* Northampton, 1821.

Black, E. C. *The Association: British Extra-Parliamentary Political Organization.* Cambridge, Mass., 1963.

Blondel, Jean. *Voters, Parties and Leaders.* Harmondsworth, 1963.

338

Bonsall, Brian. *Sir James Lowther and the Cumberland and Westmorland Elections of 1754-1775.* Manchester, 1960.

Bonwick, Colin. *English Radicals and the American Revolution.* Chapel Hill, 1977.

Brewer, John. *Party Ideology and Popular Politics at the Accession of George III.* Cambridge, 1976.

Brooke, John. *The Chatham Administration.* London, 1956.

Bulmer-Thomas, Ivor. *The Growth of the British Party System.* 2 vols. London, 1953.

Butler, David, and Stokes, Donald. *Political Change in Britain.* 2nd ed. New York, 1971.

Butler, J.R.M. *The Passing of the Great Reform Bill.* New York, 1914.

Butterfield, Herbert. *George III, Lord North and the People.* London, 1949.

———. *George III and the Historians.* London, 1957.

Campbell, Angus; Converse, Philip; Miller, Warren; and Stokes, Donald. *The American Voter.* New York, 1964.

Cannon, John. *The Fox-North Coalition.* London, 1969.

———. *Parliamentary Reform 1640-1832.* Cambridge, 1973.

Cestre, Charles. *John Thelwall.* Paris, 1906.

Christie, I. R. *The End of North's Ministry.* New York, 1958.

———. *Myth and Reality in Late Eighteenth Century English Politics.* Berkeley, 1970.

———. *Wilkes, Wyvill and Reform.* London, 1962.

———, and Labaree, B. *Empire or Independence.* London, 1976.

Clark, D. M. *British Opinion and the American Revolution.* New Haven, 1930.

Clark, H. W. *History of English Nonconformity.* 2 vols. New York, 1965.

Clifford, J. L. *Man Versus Society in the 18th Century.* New York, 1968.

Conacher, J. B. *The Emergence of British Parliamentary Democracy in the Nineteenth Century.* New York, 1971.

Connell, J. M. *Lewes: Its Religious History.* London, 1931.

Corfield, Penelope. "The Social and Economic History of Norwich, 1650-1850." Ph.D. dissertation, University of London, 1976.

Cowherd, R. G. *The Politics of English Dissent.* New York, 1956.

Cozens-Hardy, Basil, and Kent, E. A. *Mayors of Norwich, 1403-1835.* Norwich, 1938.

Davis, Richard W. *Dissent in Politics, 1780-1832: The Political Life of William Smith, M.P.* London, 1971.

————. *Political Change and Continuity.* London, 1972.

Degras, Henry. *How People Vote.* London, 1956.

Dyos, H. J., ed. *The Study of Urban History.* London, 1968.

Evans, John T. "The Political Elite of Norwich, 1620-1690." Ph.D. dissertation, Stanford, 1971.

————. *Seventeenth Century Norwich: Politics, Religion, and Government, 1620-1690.* Oxford, 1980.

Everitt, Alan. *The Pattern of Rural Dissent.* Leicester, 1972.

————, ed. *Perspectives in English Urban History.* London, 1973.

Eversley, D. *An Introduction to English Historical Demography.* London, 1966.

Feiling, Keith. *The Second Tory Party.* London, 1938.

Fritz, Paul, ed. *Triumph of Culture.* Toronto, 1972.

Forrester, E. G. *Northamptonshire County Electioneering, 1695-1832.* London, 1941.

Garceau, Oliver, ed. *Political Research and Political Theory.* Cambridge, Mass., 1968.

Gash, Norman. *Politics in the Age of Peel.* London, 1953.

George, M. D. *Catalogue of Personal and Political Satires.* London, 1938.

————. *English Political Caricature to 1792.* Oxford, 1959.

Ginter, D. E. *Whig Organization in the General Election of 1790.* Berkeley, 1967.

Glass, D. V. *Population in History.* Chicago, 1965.

Glass, D. V., and Revelle, Roger, eds. *Population and Social Change.* London, 1972.

Goodwyn, E. A. *Selections from Norwich Newspapers.* Ipswich, 1972.

Grego, Joseph. *A History of Parliamentary Elections and Electioneering.* London, 1892.

Hammond, J. L., and Hammond, B. *The Village Laborer.* London, 1912.

Hanham, H. J. *Elections and Party Management in the Time of Disraeli and Gladstone.* London, 1959.

Hayes, B. D. "Politics in Norfolk, 1750-1832." Ph.D. dissertation, Cambridge, 1958.

Hill, B. W. *The Growth of Parliamentary Parties 1689-1742.* London, 1975.

Hills, Wallace H. *The Parliamentary History of Lewes.* Lewes, 1908.

Hirst, Derek. *The Representative of the People?: Voters and Voting in England Under the Early Stuarts.* London, 1975.

Hoffman, R.J.S. *The Marquis, A Study of Lord Rockingham.* New York, 1973.

Holman, George. *Some Lewes Men of Note.* London, 1927.

Holmes, Geoffrey and Speck, W. A. *The Divided Society.* London, 1967.

Hopkinson, Robert. "Elections in Cumberland and Westmorland, 1695-1723." Ph.D. dissertation, University of Newcastle-Upon-Tyne, 1973.

Hoskins, W., ed. *The Victoria County History of the County of Leicestershire.* 5 vols. London, 1954.

Hudson, William. *Leet Jurisdiction of the City of Norwich.* Norwich, 1891.

―――. *Wards of Norwich.* Norwich, 1891.

Jarrett, Derek. *Britain, 1688-1815.* London, 1965.

Jennings, W. Ivor. *Parliament.* Cambridge, 1961.

―――. *Party Politics.* 3 vols. Cambridge, 1960-1962.

Jewson, C. B. *Jacobin City.* Glasgow, 1975.

Jupp, Peter. *English and Irish Elections.* London, 1973.

Katz, Michael. *The People of Hamilton, Canada West.* Cambridge, 1975.

Keech, William. *The Impact of Negro Voting.* Chicago, 1968.

Kennedy, William. *English Taxation.* London, 1913.

Ketton-Cremer, R. W. *Early Life and Diaries of William Windham.* London, 1930.

Lambert, Sheila. *Bills and Acts.* Cambridge, 1971.

Langford, Paul. *The Excise Crisis.* Oxford, 1975.

Lapalombara, Joseph, and Weiner, M., eds. *Political Parties and Political Development.* Princeton, 1966.

Laprade, T. W., ed. *Parliamentary Papers of John Robinson 1774-1784.* Camden Society. 3rd ser. 33. London, 1922.

McKenzie, R. T., and Silver, A. *Angels in Marble.* London, 1968.

McPhee, W. N., and Glass, W. A. *Public Opinion and Congressional Elections.* New York, 1962.

―――, and Ferguson, J. *Political Immunization.* New York, 1962.

Mitchell, B. R. and Deane, P. *Abstract of British Historical Statistics.* Cambridge, 1971.

Mitchell, Jeremy. "Electoral Change and the Party System in England, 1832-1868." Ph.D. dissertation, Yale, 1976.

341

Mitchison, R., ed. *Essays in Eighteenth Century History*. New York, 1966.

Money, John. *Experience and Identity: Birmingham and the West Midlands, 1760-1800*. Montreal, 1977.

Moore, D. C. *The Politics of Deference*. Hassocks, 1976.

Moses, J. H. "Elections and Electioneering in Nottinghamshire Constituencies, 1702-1832." Ph.D. dissertation, Nottingham University, 1965.

Munby, L. N. *East Anglia Studies*. Cambridge, 1968.

Namier, L. B. *England in the Age of the American Revolution*. London, 1930.

———. *The Structure of Politics at the Accession of George III*. 2nd ed. London, 1957.

———, and Brooke, John. *The House of Commons, 1754-1790*. 3 vols. London, 1964.

Natan, Alex. *Silver Renaissance*. New York, 1961.

Neale, R. S. *Class and Ideology in the Nineteenth Century*. London, 1972.

Nordlinger, E. A. *The Working Class Tories*. London, 1967.

Nossiter, T. J. "Elections and Political Behavior in County Durham and Westmorland, 1832-74." Ph.D. dissertation, Oxford, 1968.

———. *Influence, Opinion and Political Idioms in Reformed England*. Brighton, 1975.

Obelkevich, James. *Religion and Rural Society: South Lindsey 1825-1875*. Oxford, 1976.

O'Gorman, Frank. *The Rise of Party in England*. London, 1975.

———. *The Whig Party and the French Revolution*. London, 1967.

O'Sullivan, D. S. "Eighteenth Century Norwich Politics." Master's thesis, University of East Anglia, 1958.

Olney, R. J. *Lincolnshire Politics 1832-1885*. Oxford, 1973.

Owen, John B. *The Eighteenth Century*. New York, 1975.

Page, William, ed. *The Victoria County History of Northamptonshire*. London, 1902.

Patten, J.H.C. "The Urban Structure of East Anglia in the Sixteenth and Seventeenth Centuries." Ph.D. dissertation, Cambridge, 1972.

Pelling, Henry. *The Social Geography of British Elections*. New York, 1967.

Perkin, Harold. *The Origins of Modern English Society, 1780-1880.* London, 1969.

Perry, T. W. *Public Opinion, Propaganda, and Politics in 18th Century England.* Harvard, 1962.

Philbin, J. H. *Parliamentary Representation, 1832.* New Haven, 1965.

Phillips, N. C. *Yorkshire and English National Politics.* Christchurch, 1961.

Plumb, J. H. "Elections to the House of Commons in the Reign of William III." Ph.D. dissertation, Cambridge, 1936.

———. *England in the Eighteenth Century.* Baltimore, 1966.

Pole, J. R. *Political Representation in England and the Origins of the American Republic.* London, 1966.

Porritt, Edward, and Porritt, A. G. *The Unreformed House of Commons.* 2 vols. Cambridge, 1909.

Prest, John. *Politics in the Age of Cobden.* London, 1979.

Pugh, R., ed. *The Victoria County History of Wiltshire.* 10 vols. London, 1954.

Pulzer, P.G.P. *Political Representation and Elections: Parties and Voting in Great Britain.* London, 1967.

Read, Donald. *The English Provinces.* London, 1964.

Robertson, C. G. *England under the Hanoverians.* London, 1930.

Robson, R. J. *The Oxfordshire Election of 1754.* Oxford, 1949.

Rooke, M., ed. *Essays in Kentish History.* London, 1973.

Rose, Richard. *Electoral Behavior: A Comparative Handbook.* London, 1975.

Russell, J. M. *History of Maidstone.* London, 1881.

Salzman, L. F., ed. *The Victoria County History of the County of Sussex.* 9 vols. London, 1940.

Sedgwick, Romney. *The House of Commons, 1715-1754.* 2 vols. London, 1970.

Shorter, A. H. *Paper Mills and Paper Makers in England, 1495-1800.* London, 1955.

Shriver, David P. "The Problem of Corruption in British Parliamentary Elections, 1750-1860." Ph.D. dissertation, Case Western Reserve, 1974.

Silbey, Joel. *Political Ideology and Voting Behavior in the Age of Jackson.* Englewood-Cliffs, N.J., 1973.

———, and McSeveney, S. *Voters, Parties and Elections.* Lexington, Mass., 1972.

343

Smith, Ernest A. *Whig Principles and Party Politics.* Manchester, 1975.

Smith, R. A. *Eighteenth Century English Politics.* New York, 1972.

Speck, W. A. *Tory and Whig.* London, 1969.

Speight, M. E. "Politics in the Borough of Colchester, 1812-47." Ph.D. dissertation, London, 1969.

Thomas, P.D.G. *The House of Commons in the Eighteenth Century.* Oxford, 1971.

Thompson, E. P. *The Making of the English Working Class.* London, 1963.

Trevelyan, G. M. *British History in the Nineteenth Century.* London, 1922.

Townsend, James. *The Oxfordshire Dashwoods.* Oxford, 1922.

Turberville, A. S. *The House of Lords in the Eighteenth Century.* London, 1927.

———. *The House of Lords in the Age of Reform, 1784-1837.* London, 1958.

———. *The House of Lords in the Reign of William III.* London, 1913.

Veitch, G. S. *The Genesis of Parliamentary Reform.* London, 1913.

Vincent, J. R. *Pollbooks: How Victorians Voted.* Cambridge, 1967.

Walcott, Robert. *English Politics in the Early Eighteenth Century.* Cambridge, Mass., 1956.

Walker, Thomas. *A Review of Some of the Political Events in Manchester.* London, 1794.

Wallace, Graham. *Human Nature in Politics.* London, 1908.

Watson, J. Steven. *The Reign of George III.* Oxford, 1960.

Webb, R. K. *Modern England.* New York, 1969.

Wright, D. G. "Politics and Opinion in Bradford, 1832-1860." Ph.D. dissertation, University of Leeds, 1966.

Wrigley, E. A. *Nineteenth Century Society.* Cambridge, 1972.

———, ed. *Identifying People in the Past.* London, 1973.

INDEX

Abingdon, 66n, 303n
Adam, William, 14-15
Aldborough, 47-48, 61n
All Saints parish, Northampton,
 204, 281, 301, 302
Althorp, Viscount, *see* Spencer,
 George John
America, 9, 16-17, 21, 25n, 28-30,
 143-50, 154
American war, 28-29, 119-20,
 124, 126, 138, 145, 228
Anne, Queen, 15, 21-22, 61n, 95,
 173, 188n, 228
Annesley, Arthur, 142, 324
Ashford, 96-97
Astley, Edward, 139
Aylesford, Earl of, *see* Finch,
 Heneage

Bacon, Edward, 8, 79, 93n, 103,
 126, 128, 141-43, 145-46, 148,
 164-65, 169, 213n, 267, 323
Baggs, Charles, 150
Banbury, 66n
Baptists, 160n, 164, 291, 300n.
 Also see Nonconformity
Barnard family, 167
Barnard, William, 126n, 130
Barnstaple, 303n
Bedford, 66n, 303n
Bedfordshire, 58n
Beevor, Sir Thomas, 50, 79, 103,
 141-42, 151, 169, 213n, 224,
 267, 323
Ber Street ward, Norwich, 102n
Bere Alston, 175
Berkshire, 37n, 58n
Beverley, 303n

Bewdley, 66n
Bingham, Charles, Lord Lucan,
 32, 147, 325
Birmingham, 17, 37, 256, 287n,
 305
Bishop of Bristol, 287
Bishop, George, 128, 130, 222n
Blackman, Sir Henry, 93, 124n,
 325
Bloxham, Matthew, 128, 149,
 152, 155, 163n, 228, 245, 324
Blue-and-White party, 6, 21, 78,
 118-20, 126-31, 144-46, 149-50,
 153-55, 157-58, 164-68, 170,
 214n, 224, 230, 253, 258, 261n,
 268, 270, 277, 279, 281, 284,
 292, 294, 296n, 309-10
Bootle, Richard, 87
Boroughbridge, 47
Boscawen, Hugh, 2nd Viscount
 Falmouth, 55
Boston, 66n, 303n
Bouverie, Edward, 156, 225, 282,
 295, 297n, 325
Bradford, 215
Brenchley, John, 128-29, 222n,
 228
bribery, *see* electoral corruption
Brickdale, Matthew, 28-29
Bridgewater, 66n, 303n
Bridport, 304n
Bristol, 28-30, 39, 75, 122, 148,
 303n, 304n
Buckingham, 175
Buckingham, Marquis of, *see*
 Grenville, George
Buckinghamshire, 58n, 226
Buckinghamshire, Earl of, *see* Ho-
 bart, John

345

Library of Congress Cataloging in Publication Data

Phillips, John A., 1949-
   Electoral behavior in unreformed England.

   Bibliography: p.
   Includes index.
   1. Elections—England—History.   2. Voting—
England—History.   3. Great Britain—Politics
and government—18th century.   I. Title.
JN951.P48   324.942   82-47608
ISBN 0-691-05365-0   AACR2

John A. Phillips is Assistant Professor of History at the University
of California at Riverside. He has published articles in the *Journal
of British Studies*, the *Journal of Interdisciplinary History*, the *Journal
of Modern History*, and *Laboratory for Political Research*.